JEWISH FOOD

The Ultimate Cookbook

Jewish Food

13-Digit ISBN: 978-1-64643-172-4
10-Digit ISBN: 1-64643-172-3

This book may be ordered by mail from the publisher. Please include $5.99 for postage and handling.
Please support your local bookseller first!

Books published by Cider Mill Press Book Publishers are available at special discounts for bulk purchases in the United States by corporations, institutions, and other organizations. For more information, please contact the publisher.

Cider Mill Press Book Publishers
"Where good books are ready for press"
PO Box 454
12 Spring Street
Kennebunkport, Maine 04046
Visit us online
cidermillpress.com

Typography: Adobe Garamond, Brandon Grotesque, Lastra, Sackers English Script
Front cover image: Rosemary Rack of Lamb with Roasted Potatoes & Carrots, page 368
Back cover image: Chef's Special Matzo Ball Soup, page 41
Front endpaper image: Roasted Brussels Sprouts with Warm Honey Glaze, page 135
Back endpaper image: Fesenjan, page 132

Printed in China

1 2 3 4 5 6 7 8 9 0

First Edition

JEWISH FOOD

The Ultimate Cookbook

JOSHUA KORN & SCOTT GILDEN

With **KIMBERLY ZERKEL**

Photographs by
JIM SULLIVAN

CIDER MILL
PRESS

BOOK
PUBLISHERS
KENNEBUNKPORT, MAINE

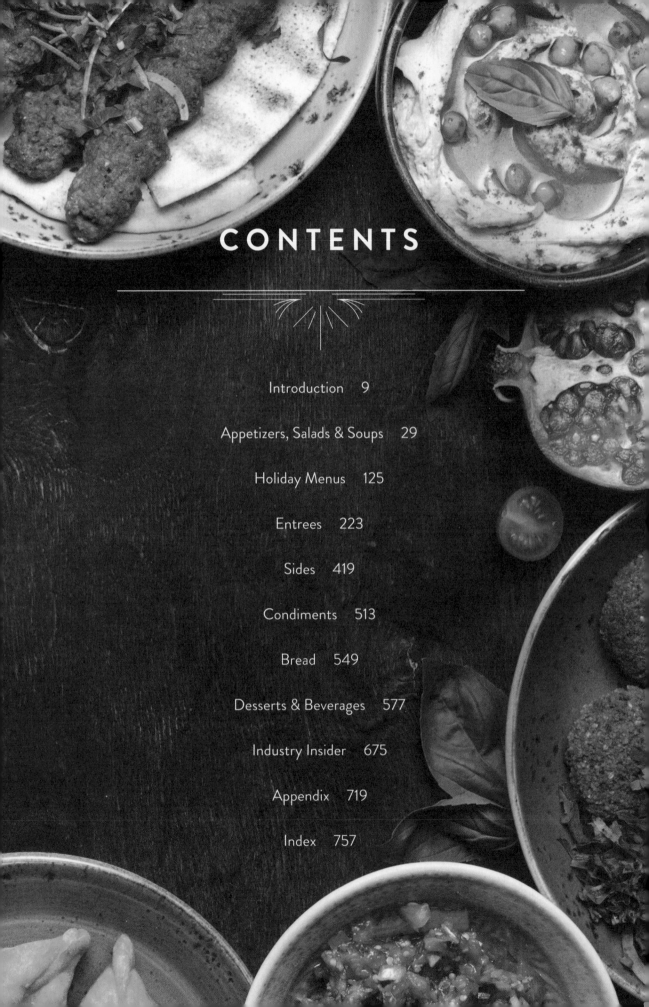

CONTENTS

Introduction   9

Appetizers, Salads & Soups   29

Holiday Menus   125

Entrees   223

Sides   419

Condiments   513

Bread   549

Desserts & Beverages   577

Industry Insider   675

Appendix   719

Index   757

INTRODUCTION

A collection of Jewish recipes is as vast, diverse, and rich in customs and traditions as the people who originally brought these dishes to life. But perhaps it is this very diversity that makes assembling traditional Jewish recipes into one cookbook so very difficult. For Jewish food is not one thing.

Try placing the many components together on one table—set the gefilte fish next to this plate of spaghetti al tonno, this matzo ball soup next to Persian ghormeh sabzi. Sprinkle everything with Ethiopian dukkah, and add a healthy dollop of labneh, a Mizrahi staple. Pile up Eastern European rugelach next to New York's beloved black-and-white cookies, but don't forget buñuelos from Mexico and sfenj from Morocco. What is the common thread?

It's certainly not one particular flavor profile or method of cooking. It's not even an adher-ence to dietary law or religious belief—the recipes in this book were not written to be strictly kosher, although almost all of them can be adapted as such. It is arguably not even about a shared Jewish experience. How could it be when you consider latkes to be a quintessential Hanukkah bite but your Israeli cousin argues that it's sufganiyot? When your family breaks a Yom Kippur fast with mouthfuls of quince jam and honey-drenched pastries while another does so with bagels and lox?

I'd like to think that the tie that binds these different elements together is family. My romanticized reverie was confirmed when speaking with Chef Scott Gilden, who waxes poetic about his mother's matzo ball soup. "Words can't explain how important this soup is to me," he emphasizes. "It brings me right back to sitting around the dinner table with

my Grandmother Honey, Auntie Beth, my two older brothers, and, of course, my mother." With care and deep emotion, he reiterates how honored he is to pass on this recipe from his home to others, knowing that each family will have their own personal spin and memories linked with the meal. "Every Jewish household that I have ever been to makes a slight variation of this soup. Some are more refined, and some have simply passed down from generation to generation. In the end, there are very few rules to a good matzo ball soup. I just know in my house, it was always done with care and love."

His narrative may contrast in tone with that of Chef Joshua Korn, who developed this beautiful collection of recipes alongside Chef Gilden. But family is still central. When recalling his mother's cooking, he lets out a hearty "Oy, gevalt," stating that she was the reason he became a chef. "I just knew growing up that humans weren't supposed to eat this way. Everything always burnt, brown, and dry, without salt in an effort not to affect dad's heart condition. Lord knows, burnt, dry, saltless potato kugel is only good for one thing—repairing the potholes on the Brooklyn Bridge." He laughs, yes, but also recalls lovingly that, "Food was important, not because we were starving, or ultimately poor, or anything. It was just always there. In times of joy and happiness, we ate food. In times of sadness, we ate food. In times of indifference, plague, or pestilence: eat food."

Somewhere in the middle of these stories are my own. I, who was not raised Jewish, but have childhood memories of my Aunt Helen preparing matzo brei for my Uncle Al in their Atlanta kitchen, recollections of dipping apples in honey at my dear friend Flora's Rosh Hashanah dinner in Berkeley, remembrances of after-

noons spent eating falafel on Rue des Rosiers in Paris, and a thousand likes for all of the Passover pictures loved ones posted online while sheltering in place. I write these words during a time in American history when we have witnessed Kamala Harris elected as the first female Vice President of the United States, making her husband, Doug Emhoff, not only the first "Second Gentleman," but also the first Jewish spouse to live at the White House. Do my stories tie in with the common thread? Do theirs? Do yours?

Chef Gilden reaches back out with another memory from a family member, Shari Kuritsky Gilden. She remembers watching her mother and grandmother prepare gefilte fish and fuss over classic Ashkenazi recipes and spreads, an experience she refers to as "tradition overload." While recalling large family gatherings, she remembers that "the house was overflowing with Jewish smells, family, and friends. There was always room, and the table just got bigger and bigger each year."

It is not the flavors, smells, methods, ingredients, traditions, or even storytelling that necessarily link this vast collection of Jewish recipes. The common thread is not the various dishes we nestle up one against another like an all-encompassing seder plate. The common thread is the table. In a culture and religion that always makes sure there's an extra chair on hand for a surprise guest, how could it not be?

Behind the many recipes we have collected for you is the desire to see you assemble around your very own table with those you cherish the most, and to either revisit the traditional recipes you have grown up loving, or be introduced to them for the very first time.

B'teyavon!

ORIGINS

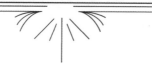

The recipes included in this book come from Jewish families all over the world. It was of utmost importance to honor the many traditions, histories, and ethnic backgrounds that make up Jewish cuisine. Many of the dishes you will discover are of Ashkenazic, Sephardic, and Mizrahi origin; but an ultimate collection of Jewish cooking would not be complete without Ethiopian, Jewish Chilanga, and Jewish Italian traditions as well. There are also the Jewish people of India, the first group to intro-duce a religion outside of India's native faiths. They have lived peacefully in this part of the world for thousands of years, their numbers only dwindling after many emigrated to Israel in the 1950s. Their cuisine has blended with the recipes from their adoptive home, as so much Jewish cooking has done over time. An exhaustive chronicle of all dietary customs and recipes would not fit on these pages; but here is a brief look at the origins and hallmarks of the kinds of cuisine you will find.

ASHKENAZIM

The Ashkenazi Jewish population originated centuries ago in Eastern Germany and Northern France before migrating and settling in Eastern Europe. Most Ashkenazim are originally from Poland, Belarus, Estonia, Latvia, Lithuania, Moldova, Russia, Slovakia, and the Ukraine; any references to life in the schtetl, or small village, are linked to the Ashkenazi people, as is

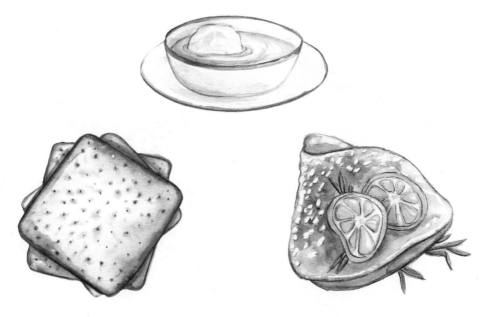

the Yiddish language. Today, the majority of the world's Ashkenazim live in the United States, followed by Israel, then Russia. Their displacement is, of course, related to centuries upon centuries of persecution. So the traditions—and recipes—that are still alive after all of these years are precious, having made their way to us after the most perilous of journeys.

When it comes to Ashkenazi cuisine, the list of renowned favorites is long. But it all starts with Schmaltz, the rendered chicken or goose fat that gives so many a dish its delicious, rich flavor. There's matzo, an unleavened bread to be eaten at Passover, and its famous offspring, matzo ball soup. For a Shabbat meal, one can expect to find roasted chicken, brisket, and plenty of carrots, beets, and cabbage, as well as dishes like kugel, kreplach, and chicken livers. The world over has come to know and love the Ashkenazic staple that is bagels and schmear, as well as fish-heavy items like gefilte fish, lox, and pickled herring. And baked goods like challah and rugelach are beloved.

A certain corner of Ashkenazi cuisine is pure New York City. Deli favorites like pastrami, corned beef, rye, knish, and even kosher pick-

les (which aren't even really kosher!) are much sought-after across the five boroughs and considered iconic for any New Yorker, even though their origins remain Eastern European. But then there are the very specific traditions, like Chinese takeout on December 25, that are an invention of American Ashkenazim.

SEPHARDIM

The Sephardic Jewish population originated from the Iberian Peninsula, modern-day Spain and Portugal. Some modern scholars refer to them as Hispanic Jews, but they have dispersed across the Mediterranean since the 15th century, living in Turkey, Greece, and the Balkans, as well as the Middle East and North Africa. North African Jews in particular can be referred to as Maghrebi, and Middle Eastern Sephardim are often confused with Mizrahim, but their origins and traditions are not the same. The largest concentration of Sephardic Jews lives today in Israel, followed by France.

Sephardi cuisine revolves in part around the fresh produce of the Mediterranean regions. These vegetables are cooked, stuffed, or baked and served alongside dishes with beans, chickpeas, bulgur wheat, and lentils. Many dishes feature rice and either braised or ground meat; ropa vieja, now Cuba's national dish, is originally a Sephardic meal, for instance. And some of North Africa's delicacies, such as pickled lemons in Tunisia and Morocco, are also Sephardic traditions.

When it comes to something sweet, Sephardic desserts are rich with rose water or orange blossom, as well as cinnamon, nuts, dates, coconut, and raisins. Baklava or other honey-soaked treats are common, often served with small, powerful cups of Turkish coffee, spiced with cardamom. Flan-like puddings can also be found on many a Sephardic table, particularly

sahlab, which was originally made from orchid powder, but now is mainly cornstarch and artificial flavorings.

On a Shabbat morning, expect to find bourekas, a pastry made with phyllo or brik pastry dough, as well as pastelas, a savory pastry chock-full of pine nuts, meat, and onions and sprinkled with sesame seed. And for holidays, Sephardim dip their apples in honey for Rosh Hashanah as well, but go on to have a full seder for the new year that includes dates, pomegranates, black-eyed peas, pumpkin, leeks, beets, and the head of a fish (so as to be the head, not the tail, that coming year). And, no, there aren't generally latkes at a Sephardic Hanukkah celebration, but oily, rich, fried foods are found

nonetheless, such as cheesy cassola, orange-glazed buñuelos, and spinach and leek keftes, which are fried patties.

Although Sephardic traditions are slightly lesser known than their Ashkenazic counterparts in the United States, it should be noted that America's oldest Jewish congregation—Congregation Shearith Israel—is Sephardic. The congregation was established in 1654 by a small group of Jews who fled Brazil after the Spanish defeated the Dutch; they settled in a town then called New Amsterdam. The culinary traditions of Sephardim, particularly those centered around cornstarch-based puddings, have influenced American cuisine ever since.

MIZRAHIM

Mizrahi Jews, sometimes referred to as Eastern or Oriental Jews, are the descendants of the Jewish people who have existed in North Africa and the Middle East since biblical times. Far too often, their identity is confused with the Sephardic Jewish population. When Sephardim fled the Iberian Peninsula in the 1400s, many of them settled in countries where the Mizrahi population was already centered. Mizrahim then adopted many Sephardic traditions, particularly when it came to religious liturgy. So, in many ways, Mizrahi and Sephardi are incredibly similar, but their origins are different.

Today, the vast majority of Mizrahi Jews live in Israel, where, alongside Separim, they make up half of the country's population. Subdivisions of the Mizrahi population include Babylonian Jews from modern-day Iraq and Kurdistan, Persian Jews from Iran, and Lebanese, Syrian, and Yemenite Jews. Some Mizrahim are also descendants of Maghrebi Jews from Egypt,

Libya, Tunisia, Algeria, and Morocco. Their populations in many of these countries are nearly non-existent today; known Jewish families in Egypt, Yemen, and Iraq are sometimes recorded in the single digits.

Mizrahi culinary tradition aligns with their countries of origin, however, most of these communities adopted the cooking methods and flavor profiles of their countries of choice while respecting Jewish dietary laws. One example of a well-known Mizrahi staple that results from this is the falafel. Apologies in advance for bursting anyone's bubble, but the falafel is not originally a Jewish food, rather an adopted dish from the community (likely Egyptian) that surrounded the Mizrahi people. Couscous and flatbreads from throughout the Middle East are also a staple of Mizrahi cuisine; look for pita, malawah, and lavosh on any Mizrahi table.

The center of a Shabbat or celebratory meal in the Mizrahi world is meat. Roasted lamb or

ground meat is common, usually served in an herb-dense sauce with stewed vegetables. The method of slow cooking is common in these kitchens, as well. Hearty stews that can cook overnight—particularly for Shabbat, when cooking and other work is forbidden—likely originated with the Mizrahi population. Other favorites include tebit, a chicken-and-rice dish, ingriyi, a meat dish with eggplant, and jeweled rice, a celebratory side dish "jeweled" with dried fruits and nuts.

Although quite a bit of Mizrahi food com-

bines sweet, savory, and sour flavors, their desserts are unmistakably sweet due to the use of dates. Take, for instance, kadaif, a pastry consisting of shredded dough, crushed nuts and dates, and loads of syrup (this is a common treat found at celebrations). Mizrahim also have their own variation of charoset, which is not exactly like the Ashkenazi mixture of apples, nuts, and wine. Mizrahi charoset features, you guessed it, dates, which make the mortar-like mixture thicker and undeniably sweeter.

HOLIDAYS

SHABBAT

Whether you say Shabbat, Shabbos, or the Sabbath, this seventh day of the week—Saturday—is all about rest. Shabbat translates to "He rested," and honors the seventh day that God rested while creating the heavens and the earth. Traditionally, all forms of work should be refrained from on Shabbat. For some, this means not even making a phone call; for others, it might mean simply refraining from answering emails or doing homework, and prioritizing time with family or loved ones.

Shabbat can be broken into three different phases—and, for our sake, meals. There is Friday evening when candles are lit and dinner is served, perhaps the most popular and regularly-guarded tradition for non-Orthodox Jews. The Shabbat dinner features both challah and wine, which are blessed before the meal begins. Meat or poultry is usually center-stage at this dinner, which is meant to stand out and feel more elevated than weekday meals. A beautiful roasted chicken is perfectly welcome at the Shabbat dinner table, as is a brisket, roast, or another luxurious main course. For Ashkenazi Jews, chicken soup, brisket, or gefilte fish can be a part of the experience as well; Sephardic Jews might enjoy chicken and rice alongside roasted vegetables.

For Saturday lunch, it is traditional to have a stew prepared the night before (so as to avoid the work of cooking on the Sabbath). The Ashkenazic version of this stew is called cholent, a hearty concoction filled with meat, potatoes, and beans (vegetarian or vegan-friendly recipes now exist as well). Sephardim will eat chreime (fish cooked in tomato sauce), or chamin, which is their version of cholent, as well as bourekas—phyllo dough pastries filled to the brim that vaguely resemble empanadas—on Saturday morning.

The end of Saturday is marked with the havdalah ceremony, which marks the separation between the Shabbat and the rest of the week. Work is resumed for the coming days and all look forward to another coming moment of rest, delicious food, and time with loved ones. Many of the recipes featured in this book are a perfect addition to a Shabbat table, as well as an update on some traditional favorites.

any whitefish would give its all for **LEVY'S**
real Jewish rye

ROSH HASHANAH

The biblical name for Rosh Hashanah is Yom Teruah, which translates to "the day of shouting or blasting" or "Feast of Trumpets." With a name as festive as that, you can be sure that there's going to be some delicious food.

Rosh Hashanah is the Jewish New Year. Traditionally, it is also the anniversary of the creation of Adam and Eve. For those practicing Judaism, it is a two-day celebration where services at the synagogue can be attended and a shofar is sounded. For almost everyone, including non-practicing Jews, it is a day to gather together with friends and family for festive and symbolic meals.

The key to a Rosh Hashanah menu is sweetness. A celebration wouldn't be complete without dipping apples in honey while wishing for a sweet new year. But variations on this sweet theme are seen throughout the meal. For Ashkenazic celebrations, fluffy and always slightly-sweet challah is a must, and the beautiful and beloved bread (sometimes preferred to be served in a round shape, to represent the cyclical nature of a year) can be used to soak up the sweet-and-sticky sauce from a perfectly-cooked brisket. For dessert, nothing says Rosh Hashanah more than an ultra-moist apple cake. Side dishes featuring beets, carrots, sweet potatoes, and squash are also common as the celebration coincides with the fall season in the Northern Hemisphere. And then, there are certain classics that just can't be overlooked. Matzo ball soup, gefilte fish, kugel, and latkes—essentially, it's the perfect occasion to celebrate old, cherished traditions alongside new beginnings.

For a Sephardic or Mizrahi Rosh Hashanah, it is more traditional to hold a seder, meaning the menu features food that is highly symbolic. Everything eaten should represent prosperity and be aligned with a specific blessing. The meanings assigned to each food vary, but often derive from their name in Hebrew. Leeks, beets, green beans, and dates play an important role, as do pumpkins, other squash, and pomegranates, which represent fertility. Apples are once again included for sweetness. Historically, a head of lamb or fish could be served, but a head of lettuce can also be used to symbolize leadership, followed by a blessing where it is asked that partakers "be the head, not the tail." The menu can also include plenty of couscous, lamb, and a bounty of fruits and vegetables.

If you are looking for traditional recipes or updated versions of Rosh Hashanah classics, there is a plethora of dishes that can add that much-desired sweetness to your new year table.

YOM KIPPUR

The irony of talking about Yom Kippur in a cookbook is that the holiest day of the year in the Jewish calendar is more closely associated with fasting, not feasting. It is the Day of Atonement, after all. The center of focus on this holy day is prayer, meditation, or even just quiet reflection, meaning it contrasts sharply with the more lively Rosh Hashanah celebration ten days before. Yom Kippur is one of the most highly observed holidays in Jewish tradition; even many non-practicing Jews will attend synagogue, fast, ask friends and family for forgiveness for any wrongs from the previous year, and work toward self-improvement.

But, even for a day centered on fasting, there's food. Of course there's food.

There are two Yom Kippur meals separated by a 25-hour fast in between. The pre-fast meal is called seudah hamafseket, which translates to "meal of separation" or "concluding meal." Traditionally, one would eat bread, water, and a hard-boiled egg dipped in ashes to commemorate the destruction of the Second Temple and the many other tragedies that have befallen the Jewish people. Over time, however, the meal has expanded to include rice, chicken, or fish. Ashkenazic Jews might eat kreplach or dip challah in honey (a nod back to the Rosh Hashanah celebrations before). For Sephardim, the meal can be festive, but meat and wine are to be avoided. The most important thing to take into consideration when preparing the pre-fast meal is salt; too much sodium can lead to dehydration the next day.

In America and Israel, Ashkenazic traditions call for breaking your fast brunch-style. This is what bagels, lox, and all their delicious accoutrements were made for. Greet your family and loved ones, get your tuchus over to the buffet-style table, and fill up on carbs and dairy in the form of schmear, kugel, quiches, and more. Sephardic tradition is more sweet than savory. One might break their fast with a spoonful of quince preserves or a small, sweet cake, and then finish a savory meal with a honey-soaked pastry or cake. A more traditional meal with soups, stews, or briskets might also be served.

The most important thing is to fill back up while looking forward to a sweet new year and an improved you.

PASSOVER

Passover is the major Jewish spring festival that lasts seven or eight days, starting on the 15th day of Nisan, or mid-March to April on the Gregorian calendar. This incredibly important holiday commemorates the liberation of the Israelites from Egyptian slavery. Perhaps more than any other festivity on the Jewish calendar, Passover is about history, tradition, and community. These elements are tied in to nearly every holiday, but Passover in particular is a reminder of the hardships that the Jewish people have faced from the time of Pharoah onward. Celebration is in order, of course, but at the heart of Passover is a remembrance of the bitterness of oppression—and gratitude for deliverance, fortitude, and resilience.

Yom Kippur is considered the holiest of holidays, but it is almost without question that Passover is the most culturally defining.

Memory and emotion are evoked at the seder. Much of the food eaten is deeply symbolic. Not only is this when matzo is served to represent the unleavened bread that Jews ate while fleeing Egypt, but all leavened bread (and desserts) should be abstained from throughout. Horseradish is eaten as a reminder of the bitterness of slavery, while haroset—a mixture of apples, nuts, and wine—symbolizes the mortar

כשר לפסח

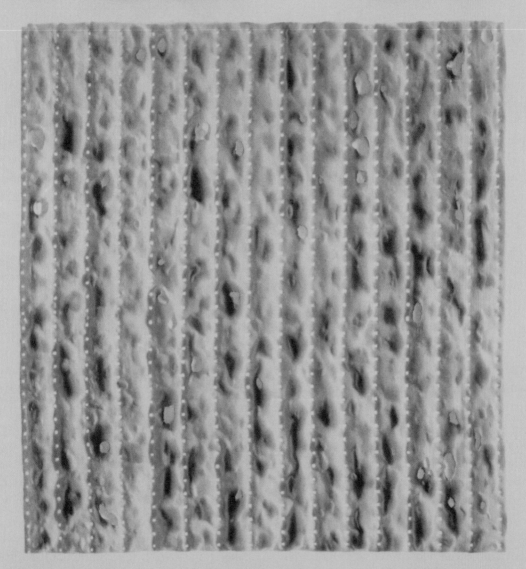

in the best Passover tradition!

the Jewish people used to construct pyramids, temples, and other buildings in Egypt.

For Sephardim and Ashkenazim, the Passover meal can feature lamb at the center. Not only is lamb in keeping with spring—the "lambing" season—but this meat in particular is symbolic of the paschal sacrifice. The main course can also be brisket. Sephardic Passover will then have a plethora of colorful side dishes, such as jeweled rice, crunchy salads, and other savory-sweet vegetables.

Ashkenazi Jews celebrate eating matzo in a variety of ways. Machine-made matzo wasn't common until the 19th century; before that, people would buy matzo from their bakeries and use the crumbs for matzo balls. So matzo ball soup is always welcome at a Passover meal, as well as matzo lasagna or even matzo icebox cake. Other desserts, such as macaroons and flourless chocolate cake are ideal treats for a leaven-free celebration.

HANUKKAH

In late fall and early winter, when the days have become their shortest and sunshine is scarce, along comes Hanukkah, the Festival of Lights. Winter celebrations in many cultures and religions commemorate the returning of light on or around winter solstice, but Hanukkah, like most Jewish holidays, is historical before being seasonal. The Hanukkah story begins with a second-century BCE fight between the Jewish people and their oppressors that led to the Maccabees' revolt, Jerusalem being recovered by the Jewish people, and the rededication of the Second Temple.

But you can't talk about Hanukkah without discussing oil. Because the holiday itself honors the miracle of the oil; when the Second Temple was back under Jewish control, it was discovered that much of what remained inside

had been ruined or desecrated. This included ritual oil that was used to keep the Temple's menorah lit. There was only enough oil to light the menorah for one day, yet it burned for a miraculous eight days, enough time to have a new oil press made. Thus, an eight-night celebration that includes lighting the candles of a nine-branch menorah called a hanukkiah was born.

Now, let's talk food. The miracle of the oil is taken quite literally here, and foods deep-fried in oil are on the menu. No Hanukkah celebration would be complete without latkes, the crispy, fried potato pancakes that are a beloved staple of Ashkenazi cuisine. The debate on whether or not to eat with applesauce or sour cream can be, in some families, as hot as the oil they're fried in.

In Israel, a Hanukkah favorite is the sufganiyot, the original jelly doughnut. Sufganiyot is fried dough filled with jelly or custard and then sprinkled with powdered sugar. Although wildly popular amongst Israelis around the Festival of Lights, this treat originated in Europe around the 1500s and became known as the Berliner. For history buffs, yes, this is *the* famous jelly doughnut JFK accidentally referenced during his "Ich bin ein Berliner" speech—little did he know, his grammatical faux pas was linked to Hannukah!

Sephardic tradition has its own version of the sufganiyot, the bimuelos or buñuelos. These decadent treats can be a dough fried up in a ball, or served flat and extra crispy. They can be served with sprinkled sugar, honey, cinnamon, or lightly perfumed with orange blossom water.

Other Hanukkah staples might include braided challah, brisket, couscous, or a variety of fried dishes (fritto misto, anyone?). And many an Ashkenazi celebration will also feature chocolate coins for children. The shiny gold and silver paper shimmers in such a way to tie into the theme of lights, of course. But the coins themselves harken back to Eastern European shtetls, where it was customary to tip workers around this time of the year with Hanukkah gelt.

A Hanukkah fact of note: in Western popular culture at least, Hanukkah seems to be the most well-known and celebrated Jewish holiday of the year. But for Jews, Hanukkah is a minor, yet beloved, festival. Non-Jewish familiarity with the eight-day celebration likely stems from it falling around the same time of the year as Christmas. But with the many lights, fried foods, and boisterous celebrating, it has little-to-nothing in common with Christmas. It's Jewish Independence Day!

RECIPES

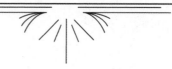

If bringing together the many dishes that make up Jewish cuisine wasn't already difficult enough, organizing them into one collection is a completely different task. Many of these recipes are meant to be prepared together for Shabbat or holiday meals. And though many Jewish chefs appreciate the flavors of Sephardic, Mizrahi, and Ashkenazi traditions, they aren't likely to blend those traditions together into one meal.

So instead of dividing up recipes along more traditional lines, we have decided to present these items to you in the most straightforward of terms: from salads and appetizers, to main courses, condiments, breads, sweets, and beverages, our collection invites you to explore options of all origins and decide one which ones speak to you.

Don't let tradition frighten you away from experimenting. All of these recipes, regardless of their background, can work in tandem should you so choose.

APPETIZERS, SALADS & SOUPS

From the small, colorful dishes that make up a mezze spread to borscht, blintzes, and beloved matzo ball soup, there's something to please everyone in this collection of starters. These appetizers, salads, and soups can be enjoyed at the beginning of a meal or eaten on their own for a lighter alternative.

ALBONDIGAS WITH PINE NUTS & CURRANTS

YIELD: 24 (2 OZ.) MEATBALLS / **ACTIVE TIME:** 35 MINUTES / **TOTAL TIME:** 1 HOUR AND 10 MINUTES

A mainstay of Sephardic cuisine, albondigas, or meatballs, come in various sizes and can be round or flattened. Chopped onions, garlic, roasted eggplant, fresh spinach, chopped leek, and grated carrots have been added to the meat or poultry of choice for centuries, with moistened bread binding the ingredients together. It is simmered or fried to perfection in a variety of sauces.

MEATBALL INSTRUCTIONS

1. Add 2 tablespoons of avocado oil to a large skillet over medium-low heat and sauté the garlic, onion, and celery until they become translucent and soft. Once softened allow the mixture to cool in a large bowl.

2. Add the remainder of the ingredients, except the currants and pine nuts, to the cooled onion mixture and mix until thoroughly incorporated, making sure not to overmix as overmixing causes tough meatballs.

3. Gently fold in the currants and pine nuts to the meat mixture and combine.

4. Shape mixture into 1-1½" meatballs, (about the size of a golf ball) by hand or using a spoon or ice cream scoop.

5. In the same skillet used to cook the onions and celery, add the remainder of the avocado oil and warm over medium heat until shimmering, but not smoking. Working in batches to avoid overcrowding, add the meatballs to the pan in a single layer. Sear meatballs, and continue to turn until they are nicely browned on all sides and remove from the pan, about 5 to 8 minutes in total cooking time.

6. Add the browned meatballs to the simmering sauce and cook for an additional 15 minutes, stirring occasionally to coat the meatballs and avoid burning.

7. Serve with saffron-infused rice, garnished with pine nuts and fresh mint.

SAUCE

1. In a medium pot on low heat, warm 2 tablespoons of olive oil. Add the garlic and onion and sauté until the vegetables have softened but not browned. Add the remainder of the ingredients and bring to a low simmer for 20 minutes, until thickened slightly.

INGREDIENTS:

½	CUP AVOCADO OIL, FOR FRYING
5	GARLIC CLOVES, MINCED
1	MEDIUM ONION, GRATED
2	CELERY RIBS, FINELY CHOPPED
1½	LBS. LEAN GROUND BEEF
½	LB. GROUND VEAL
2	EGGS, BEATEN
1	CUP PLAIN BREAD CRUMBS
3	TABLESPOONS CHOPPED ITALIAN FLAT LEAF PARSLEY
3	TABLESPOONS CHOPPED MINT LEAVES
1	TEASPOON CUMIN
1	TEASPOON PAPRIKA
1	TEASPOON TURMERIC
1	TEASPOON SUMAC, GROUND DRY
1	TABLESPOON SEA SALT
	BLACK PEPPER, TO TASTE
¼	CUP CURRANTS
¼	CUP TOASTED PINE NUTS, CHOPPED

SAUCE

2	TABLESPOONS OLIVE OIL
5	GARLIC CLOVES, MINCED
1	CUP DICED ONION
1	CUP WARM WATER OR CHICKEN STOCK (SEE PAGE 722)
1½	CUPS TOMATO PUREE
1	TABLESPOON HONEY
1	TABLESPOON FRESH LEMON JUICE
½	TEASPOON CUMIN
½	TEASPOON GROUND CORIANDER
½	TEASPOON TURMERIC
¼	TEASPOON SAFFRON (BLOOMED IN TOMATO PUREE, OPTIONAL)
2	TEASPOONS SEA SALT
2	TEASPOONS BLACK PEPPER, OR TO TASTE

BLINTZES WITH BERRY COMPOTE

YIELD: 8 / **ACTIVE TIME:** 1 HOUR / **TOTAL TIME:** 1 HOUR AND 35 MINUTES

Everything yummy rolled up in a flat pancake. The Jewish version of blintzes can be filled with anything from chocolate to mushrooms, meat, rice, or mashed potatoes and cheese. Although they're not part of any specific religious event, blintzes stuffed with a cheese filling and fried in oil are served on holidays such as Hanukkah as a symbolic and historic gesture.

1. In a bowl, beat together eggs, water, milk, salt, and flour until well-mixed. Let the mixture rest at room temperature for at least 30 minutes.

2. Heat a sauté pan and add a pat of butter.

3. Mix the batter again until smooth. Pour about ¼ cup batter into the pan and swirl it around. Make sure not to let it brown. Flip and cook the other side for a few seconds before turning it out of the pan and setting aside.

4. Repeat with remaining batter, placing pats of butter in the pan between each blintz.

5. After all of the blintzes have been made, place one on a work surface and spread 1½ tablespoons of filling in a line close to the edge nearest to you.

6. Fold blintz like an envelope, then roll up, and continue with remaining blintzes and filling.

7. Add butter to a skillet and fry the filled blintzes until golden brown.

8. Serve topped with the compote and sour cream, if desired.

FILLING

1. In a bowl, combine cheese, butter, egg yolk, vanilla, and sugar and mix until the batter achieves a smooth texture.

BERRY COMPOTE

1. Place all of the ingredients in a small saucepan over medium heat. Once the mixture begins to bubble, reduce heat slightly and use a wooden spoon to muddle and mash the fruit. Continue cooking over medium-low heat for 12 minutes, occasionally mashing fruit to combine. Remove from heat and let cool.

INGREDIENTS:

BLINTZES

4	LARGE EGGS
½	CUP WATER
½	CUP MILK
½	TEASPOON SEA SALT
1	CUP ALL-PURPOSE FLOUR
1	CUP UNSALTED BUTTER

FILLING

1	LB. FARMERS CHEESE, AT ROOM TEMPERATURE
1	TABLESPOON UNSALTED BUTTER, MELTED
1	LARGE EGG YOLK, AT ROOM TEMPERATURE
2	TEASPOONS VANILLA EXTRACT
¼	CUP SUGAR

BERRY COMPOTE

¼	CUP BLACK BERRIES
¼	CUP BLUEBERRIES
¼	CUP STRAWBERRIES
1	TABLESPOON WATER
1	TABLESPOON SUGAR
	SOUR CREAM (OPTIONAL)

BEEF, BEET & CABBAGE BORSCHT

YIELD: 8 SERVINGS / **ACTIVE TIME:** 45 MINUTES / **TOTAL TIME:** 3 HOURS

Although variants of this pleasantly sour-tasting soup exist without beets, most have come to know this Eastern European staple by the deep-red root vegetable that imparts such a distinctive color.

1. Prepare the short ribs by heating oil in a large, thick-bottomed pot over medium high heat. Add the short ribs or stew beef and brown lightly on one side, then turn over.

2. Add the onions and cook for about 5 minutes. Add the wine and stock and bring to a boil. Cover and simmer, stirring occasionally, until the meat is very tender, about 2 hours. Skim off excess fat from the liquid in the pot. Remove the meat to a baking sheet, let cool, and dice. Strain the broth and reserve; discard the bones and other solids.

3. Preheat the oven to 400°F.

4. Toss the beets, potatoes, celery, rutabaga, and carrots with olive oil and spread them out in a single layer on a foil-lined roasting pan. Roast for 15 minutes.

5. Wrap the peppercorns, coriander seeds, dill, oregano, and parsley sprigs in cheesecloth and tie into a bundle.

6. In a large pot, heat the avocado oil. Add the beets, rutabaga, leek, onion, carrots, celery, cabbage and the herb-spice bundle. Cook, stirring occasionally, until the cabbage is wilted, about 15 minutes. Add the tomatoes and wine and simmer for about 5 minutes.

7. Stir in the strained beef broth and simmer for about 30 minutes. Stir in the vinegar and the meat and simmer for 15 minutes. Season with salt and pepper.

8. Serve the borscht with chopped dill and horseradish.

TIP: The beauty of this soup is the shapes of the beets, carrots and other root vegetables that shine in the bowl. This is a great way to practice knife skills, try your best to make square dice and other varieties of shapes with the root vegetables. As an alternative cooking methodology; try roasting beets whole on a bed of kosher salt, then peel and cut after they've cooled. This cooking method will enhance the flavors of beet and draw out moisture.

INGREDIENTS:

SHORT RIBS

2	TABLESPOONS AVOCADO OIL
3	LBS. ENGLISH-CUT BEEF SHORT RIBS (OR 2 LBS. STEW BEEF)
1	LARGE ONION, CHOPPED
½	CUP DRY RED WINE
8	CUPS BEEF STOCK (SEE PAGE 721)

BORSCHT

4	LARGE BEETS, PEELED AND DICED
1	LARGE RUSSET POTATO, PEELED AND CUT INTO ½" CUBES
2	CELERY RIBS, DICED
1	SMALL RUTABAGA, PEELED AND DICED
1	LB. CARROTS, DICED
3	TEASPOONS OLIVE OIL
½	TABLESPOON WHOLE BLACK PEPPERCORNS
½	TABLESPOON WHOLE CORIANDER SEEDS
2	SPRIGS FRESH DILL
2	SPRIGS FRESH OREGANO
2	SPRIGS FRESH ITALIAN FLAT LEAF PARSLEY
2	TABLESPOONS AVOCADO OIL
1	LEEK, DICED
1	LARGE ONION, DICED
2	CUPS THINLY SLICED CABBAGE
7	OZ. CAN CHOPPED TOMATOES AND THEIR JUICES
½	CUP DRY RED WINE
2	TABLESPOONS RED WINE VINEGAR
	SEA SALT, TO TASTE
	FRESHLY GROUND PEPPER, TO TASTE
	DILL, FOR SERVING
	GRATED HORSERADISH, FOR SERVING

BONE MARROW MATZO BALL SOUP

YIELD: 8 SERVINGS / **ACTIVE TIME:** 35 MINUTES / **TOTAL TIME:** 24 HOURS

These fluffy dumpling-like balls are served in a chicken or vegetable broth, often with added vegetables for maximum flavor. A recipe that childhood memories are made of, it is often what we turn to when sick or aching from a bad day. The Real Jewish Penicillin . . . and the answer to all of life's hard times.

1. Soak marrow bones overnight in salted water to release impurities.

2. Preheat the oven to 400°F.

3. Pat dry the bones, arrange them on a baking sheet, and roast them for 20 to 30 minutes; cool slightly.

4. Using a spoon or a table knife, push the marrow out of the bones and transfer to a small bowl. You want 8 tablespoons of marrow.

5. Reserve 4 tablespoons of the marrow to add to your stock to intensify the flavor.

6. In a large bowl, cream the marrow with a fork until perfectly smooth, then add 2 egg yolks, parsley, salt, and nutmeg. Add matzo to make a soft dough.

7. Cover the bowl with plastic wrap and refrigerate for 2 hours.

8. After 2 hours, whip the remaining egg whites until they hold peaks and then gently fold into the bone marrow mixture.

9. In a large pot, bring the chicken stock to a simmer.

10. Using your hands, form small matzo balls and drop them into the simmering stock 5 at a time.

11. Cook for 10 to 15 minutes per batch, then transfer with a slotted spoon to a serving bowl.

12. Ladle chicken stock over matzo balls and serve.

INGREDIENTS:

4	LBS. MARROW BONES
2	EGGS, SEPARATED
2	TABLESPOONS CHOPPED CURLY PARSLEY
2	TEASPOONS SEA SALT
1	TEASPOON FRESHLY GROUND BLACK PEPPER
1	CUP MATZO MEAL
1	GARLIC CLOVE
2	QUARTS RICH BROWN CHICKEN STOCK (SEE PAGE 722)
1	DASH NUTMEG

BROCCOLINI SALAD

YIELD: 10 SERVINGS / **ACTIVE TIME:** 15 MINUTES / **TOTAL TIME:** 15 MINUTES

Blanching is a cooking process in which a food, usually a vegetable or fruit, is scalded in boiling water and salt, removed after a brief, timed interval, and finally plunged into iced water or placed under cold running water to halt the cooking process. Blanching the broccolini for this salad makes it the perfect al dente consistency.

1. In a large bowl combine all of the ingredients, except the oil and garlic.

2. In a sauté pan, warm ¼ cup of olive oil and toast the garlic until golden brown. While the mixture is still hot, pour it over the salad and mix well. Season to taste.

INGREDIENTS:

1	CUP DRIED CRANBERRIES
1	CUP SLICED ALMONDS, TOASTED
2	LBS. BROCCOLINI, BLANCHED AND COARSELY CHOPPED
½	CUP CRUMBLED FETA OR GOAT CHEESE
1	CUP BLUEBERRIES
½	CUP CHAMPAGNE VINAIGRETTE (SEE PAGE 516)
2	CUPS SLICED RED GRAPES
2	TABLESPOONS SEA SALT, PLUS MORE TO TASTE
1	TABLESPOON PEPPER, PLUS MORE TO TASTE
4	TABLESPOONS CHOPPED FLAT LEAF PARSLEY, MINT, BASIL, AND OREGANO
½	CUP EXTRA VIRGIN OLIVE OIL
½	CUP MINCED GARLIC

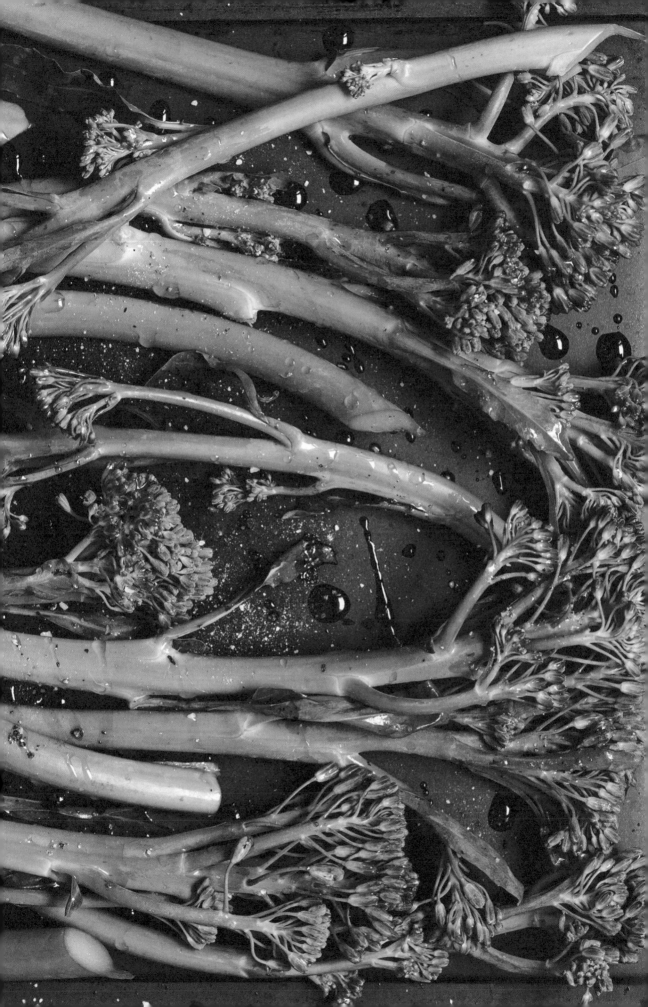

CHEF'S SPECIAL MATZO BALL SOUP

YIELD: 6 SERVINGS / **ACTIVE TIME:** 35 MINUTES / **TOTAL TIME:** 4 HOURS

May the Schmaltz be with you in this particularly decadent version of a classic.

1. In a large stockpot, place all of the soup ingredients and bring to a slow simmer with a cover on the pot. Simmer with a lazy bubble for 2 hours, until chicken is falling off the bone.

2. In a bowl, combine the eggs, Schmaltz, and sesame oil and whisk until emulsified.

3. Add the remainder of the ingredients, mix well, and refrigerate for 1 hour.

4. After 1 hour, using wet hands, make golf ball-size balls of the matzo meal.

5. Bring a large pot of salted water to a boil and cook the matzo balls for 30 minutes, covered; do not open the lid to check on the balls for any reason, just be patient and confident in your cooking.

6. When the matzo balls are fully cooked remove them with a slotted spoon and place them in a chicken soup pot to absorb additional flavor.

7. To serve, ladle a big portion of soup, vegetables, and shredded chicken with 1 of the giant Schmaltz balls and garnish with a few sprigs of dill.

INGREDIENTS:

SOUP

1	(4 LB.) WHOLE CHICKEN, GIBLETS REMOVED
8	QUARTS CHICKEN STOCK (SEE PAGE 722)
1¾	TEASPOONS SEA SALT
½	CUP SCHMALTZ (SEE PAGE 528)
2	LARGE SWEET WHITE ONIONS, SLICED
3	MEDIUM CARROTS, SLICED IN ¼"-THICK ROUNDS
2	MEDIUM PARSNIPS, SLICED IN ¼"-THICK ROUNDS
3	CELERY RIBS, DICED
1	SMALL WHITE TURNIP, PEELED AND DICED
1	SMALL YELLOW RUTABAGA, PEELED AND DICED
2	HEADS GARLIC, HALVED
½	TEASPOON BLACK PEPPERCORN CRACKED IN HALF
1	BUNCH FLAT LEAF PARSLEY
1	BUNCH DILL
3	BAY LEAVES
1	SMALL BUNCH THYME
¼	TEASPOON GROUND TURMERIC

SCHMALTZ BALLS

2	LARGE EGGS, BEATEN
3	TABLESPOONS SCHMALTZ (SEE PAGE 528)
1	TEASPOON SESAME OIL
½	CUP MATZO MEAL
½	TEASPOON BAKING POWDER
1	PINCH CINNAMON
1	TEASPOON CHOPPED FRESH DILL
½	TEASPOON BERBERE SPICE MIX (SEE PAGE 323)
½	TEASPOON DEHYDRATED GARLIC SPICE
¼	TEASPOON SEA SALT

CHICKEN SALAD

YIELD: 6 SERVINGS / **ACTIVE TIME:** 10 MINUTES / **TOTAL TIME:** 1 HOUR

A staple of any deli, the first chicken salads often used meat leftover from birds cooked for chicken soup. Don't feel that you have to skimp on the mayonnaise, you look skinny.

1. Combine all of the ingredients in a bowl and mix well.

2. Refrigerate before serving.

INGREDIENTS:

2½ CUPS COOKED CHICKEN, DICED AND CHILLED

1 CUP CHOPPED CELERY

1 CUP HALVED SEEDLESS GRAPES

¼ CUP DRIED CHERRIES

⅛ CUP CHOPPED PECANS

⅛ CUP SLIVERED ALMONDS OR WALNUTS

2 TABLESPOONS CHOPPED PARSLEY

2 TABLESPOONS CHOPPED MINT

2 TABLESPOONS CHOPPED CILANTRO

½ TEASPOON SEA SALT

¼ TEASPOON FRESH CRACKED BLACK PEPPER

½ TEASPOON GROUND SUMAC

1 CUP MAYONNAISE

Chopped Liver, page 46

CHOPPED LIVER

YIELD: 20 SERVINGS / **ACTIVE TIME:** 25 MINUTES / **TOTAL TIME:** 1 HOUR AND 10 MINUTES

We know, we know, chopped liver often gets a bad rap. But try this recipe shared by Beth Krieger, aka Aunite Beth, and realize why this mainstay has withstood the test of time and deserves a lot more love.

1. Prepare the livers by cutting off any tough or stringy pieces.

2. Add 2 teaspoons Schmaltz to a large skillet over medium heat. Put half of the chicken livers into the skillet and fry them for 4 minutes on each side. Season the livers generously with salt and pepper as they are cooking. The livers should be cooked to medium, meaning firm and browned on the outside while slightly pink on the inside. Do not overcook the livers!

3. When the livers are done, pour them into a medium-size bowl along with the leftover Schmaltz from the pan.

4. Add another 2 teaspoons Schmaltz to the skillet, and repeat the process until all of the livers are cooked.

5. Add the onions to the skillet and reduce heat to medium-low. Cover the skillet and cook for about 10 minutes. Uncover the skillet, stir the onions, and continue to sauté them for another 30 minutes.

6. Add the cooked onions to the mixing bowl along with 4 of the diced hard-boiled eggs and the Gribenes. Season with salt and pepper.

7. Place all of the ingredients in a food processor and pulse in 20-second intervals until a roughly textured paste forms. Season to taste with salt and pepper.

8. Refrigerate the chopped liver until ready to serve. Garnish with the remaining egg, Gribenes, and parsley.

INGREDIENTS:

1½	LBS. CHICKEN LIVERS
¼	CUP SCHMALTZ (SEE PAGE 528), DIVIDED
	SEA SALT, TO TASTE
	FRESHLY GROUND BLACK PEPPER, TO TASTE
4	LARGE SWEET ONIONS, SLICED
5	HARD-BOILED EGGS, DICED
½	CUP GRIBENES (SEE PAGE 528), PLUS MORE TO GARNISH
2	TABLESPOONS MINCED PARSLEY, TO GARNISH

CHUSHKI BUREK

YIELD: 12 SERVINGS / **ACTIVE TIME:** 1 HOUR / **TOTAL TIME:** 1 HOUR AND 45 MINUTES

This traditional Bulgarian meal combines the sweet smokiness of roasted peppers with the rich creaminess of a cow or sheep's milk cheese. The peppers are breaded and fried for an extra layer of indulgence.

1. Set the broiler to high.

2. Arrange the whole peppers on a baking sheet and place in the oven under the broiler (with 2 to 3" of space between the peppers and the flame) until peppers are wrinkled and charred, turning them several times during roasting. Smaller more delicate peppers will take about 15 minutes total; larger bell peppers could take up to 40 minutes.

3. Remove the peppers from the oven, place them in a bowl, and cover with tin foil or plastic wrap while they cool.

4. When completely cooled, peel as delicately as possible, discarding the seeds and keeping the shape of the pepper for filling (smaller peppers should stay whole with one cut lengthwise, bell peppers can be halved).

5. Add all of the cheeses to a medium bowl and mix well.

6. Beat the eggs with the salt and pepper in a shallow bowl, and prepare a small pile of the flour on a plate or a clean work surface.

7. Gently take each pepper and coat it in flour on all sides, shaking off any excess (this should prevent the cheese from 'escaping' mid-frying).

8. Place a heaping teaspoon of the cheese filling in the middle of the pepper and very gently wrap the pepper around to close. Generously flour the outside of the pepper again. Repeat with the remaining peppers.

9. Fill a large pan with a ¼" of oil and warm over high heat. Add the butter and garlic clove.

10. When sizzling, take one of the stuffed peppers and dip it in the egg wash, gently turning to coat all sides, then carefully place it in the hot oil. Repeat with the remaining stuffed peppers, being careful not to overcrowd the pan.

11. Turn the heat down to medium, the peppers should sizzle and form small bubbles around them. Turn the peppers gently after 2 minutes, then again after 2 more minutes. After another 2 minutes (fried on 3 sides for a total of 6 minutes), carefully remove them from the pan and place on a plate lined with paper towels. Serve immediately.

INGREDIENTS:

- 12 SMALL SWEET RED PEPPERS, OR 6 RED BELL PEPPERS
- 1 CUP BULGARIAN CHEESE, PREFERABLY SHEEP'S MILK 20% FAT
- ⅓ CUP FARMER'S CHEESE
- ½ CUP GRATED KASHKAVAL CHEESE
- 2 TABLESPOONS RICOTTA CHEESE
- ¼ CUP GRATED PARMESAN CHEESE (OPTIONAL)
- 2 EGGS
- 1 PINCH SEA SALT
- 1 PINCH BLACK PEPPER
- ALL-PURPOSE FLOUR, FOR DUSTING
- AVOCADO OIL, FOR FRYING
- 1 TABLESPOON UNSALTED BUTTER
- 1 GARLIC CLOVE

CITRUS SALAD

YIELD: 6 SERVINGS / **ACTIVE TIME:** 20 MINUTES / **TOTAL TIME:** 4 HOURS

The bright mixture of citrus is what makes this side dish so very special. The color is appealing, but it especially acts as a palate cleanser after eating heavier bites of this or that.

1. In a large bowl, combine all of the ingredients, except the lettuce, mix well, cover, and refrigerate for several hours.

2. If desired, serve in a lettuce-lined bowl or on individual lettuce-lined plates.

INGREDIENTS:

1   CUP CUBED FRESH PINEAPPLE

1   CUP FRESH ORANGE PIECES

1   CUP FRESH TANGERINE PIECES

1   CUP SOUR CREAM

½   CUP MINIATURE MARSHMALLOWS

½   CUP SWEETENED SHREDDED COCONUT

     LETTUCE LEAVES, TO SERVE (OPTIONAL)

CONCIA

YIELD: 4 SERVINGS / **ACTIVE TIME:** 1 HOUR / **TOTAL TIME:** 24 HOURS

A traditional zucchini salad that pairs sautéed or fried zucchini with bright mint and vinegar. Both earthy and refreshing, concia is a perfect starter, or accompaniment to a heavier meal.

1. Salt the zucchini slices on all sides and let rest on a paper towel-lined tray for 10 minutes. Pat dry the salted zucchini.

2. Pour enough oil into a large saucepan to be ½" deep in the pan. Place over medium heat.

3. Gently place about 6 pieces of zucchini into the pan, making sure that the pieces all lay flat and do not overlap. Fry the zucchini on each side for about 5 minutes, or until golden brown. Transfer to a baking rack or a paper towel-lined tray to drain any excess oil. Continue frying the rest of the zucchini in batches.

4. Place the fried zucchini in a mixing bowl. Add salt, pepper, garlic, basil, and vinegar and gently mix until each piece of zucchini is evenly coated. Transfer to an airtight container and refrigerate for at least 5 hours, and up to 24 hours.

5. Serve at room temperature.

INGREDIENTS:

3	ZUCCHINIS, SLICED LENGTHWISE INTO ¼" THICK PIECES
	AVOCADO OIL, FOR FRYING
	SEA SALT, TO TASTE
	BLACK PEPPER, TO TASTE
6	GARLIC CLOVES, FINELY CHOPPED
½	BUNCH BASIL LEAVES, FINELY CHOPPED
4	TABLESPOONS WHITE WINE VINEGAR

CRUNCHY POMEGRANATE SALAD

YIELD: 16 SERVINGS / **ACTIVE TIME:** 30 MINUTES / **TOTAL TIME:** 30 MINUTES

Symbolism aside, the pomegranate is an incredible ingredient to incorporate into your meal. The pop of each seed when bitten into followed by mouth-puckering tartness simply can't be recreated by any other fruit.

1. In a large bowl, beat the cream until it begins to thicken.

2. Add sugar and vanilla; beat until stiff peaks form.

3. Fold in pomegranate seeds and apples. Sprinkle with pecans and serve immediately.

INGREDIENTS:

2	CUPS HEAVY WHIPPING CREAM
¼	CUP SUGAR
2	TEASPOONS VANILLA EXTRACT
2½	CUPS POMEGRANATE SEEDS
2	MEDIUM APPLES, PEELED AND CUBED
1	CUP CHOPPED PECANS, TOASTED

CRUSHED AVOCADO

YIELD: 6 SERVINGS / **ACTIVE TIME:** 10 MINUTES / **TOTAL TIME:** 10 MINUTES

The zip of za'atar guarantees that no one will confuse this for guacamole.

1. In a bowl, combine all of the ingredients and gently incorporate. It should be chunky, as the texture is lovely in the mouth with chips or breads.

INGREDIENTS:

2	CUPS RIPE AVOCADO
½	CUP FRESH LEMON JUICE
1	TABLESPOON FINE SEA SALT
1	TEASPOON BLACK PEPPER
2	TABLESPOONS ZA'ATAR (SEE PAGE 545)
½	CUP CHOPPED CILANTRO
¼	CUP EXTRA VIRGIN OLIVE OIL

CUCUMBER TOMATO MANGO RELISH

YIELD: 10 SERVINGS / **ACTIVE TIME:** 10 MINUTES / **TOTAL TIME:** 10 MINUTES

Sweet with mango, crunchy from dried chickpeas, and spiced with za'atar, this cuts through fatty meats and heavy starches.

1. Add all of the ingredients, except the chickpeas, to a large mixing bowl and mix well. Season to taste.

2. Garnish with crushed crispy chickpeas.

INGREDIENTS:

6	CUPS HALVED HEIRLOOM CHERRY TOMATOES
4	CUPS DESEEDED AND DICED PERSIAN CUCUMBERS
2	SMALL MANGOS, DICED
1	CUP DICED RED ONION
2	TABLESPOONS RED WINE VINEGAR
4	TABLESPOONS FRESH LEMON JUICE
2	TABLESPOONS ZA'ATAR (SEE PAGE 545)
1	TABLESPOON SUMAC
4	TABLESPOONS SEA SALT, PLUS MORE TO TASTE
2	TABLESPOONS BLACK PEPPER
4	TABLESPOONS CHOPPED DILL
½	CUP EXTRA VIRGIN OLIVE OIL
4	TABLESPOONS CRUSHED CRISPY CHICKPEAS, TO GARNISH

CUCUMBER, MINT & SUMAC SALAD

YIELD: 4 SERVINGS / **ACTIVE TIME:** 15 MINUTES / **TOTAL TIME:** 15 MINUTES

Cucumber and mint combine for the perfect mixture of refreshing flavor, sure to lighten any warm-weather meal. Sumac adds an extra layer of brightness and acidity.

1. Place the cucumbers, 1 tablespoon of sumac, olive oil, lemon juice, and kosher salt in a large bowl and mix well to coat evenly. Season to taste.

2. Transfer the salad to a serving bowl and sprinkle the remaining sumac and mint on top. Serve immediately.

INGREDIENTS:

- 12 PERSIAN CUCUMBERS, CUT INTO QUARTERS LENGTHWISE ON THE BIAS
- 1½ TABLESPOONS GROUND SUMAC, DIVIDED
- ¼ CUP EXTRA VIRGIN OLIVE OIL
- ¼ CUP FRESH LEMON JUICE
- 1 TEASPOON KOSHER SALT, PLUS MORE TO TASTE
- ¼ CUP MINT LEAVES, FOR GARNISH

FALAFEL

YIELD: 9 SERVINGS / ACTIVE TIME: 1 HOUR / TOTAL TIME: 24 HOURS

Now known as Israel's national dish, these fried chickpea balls likely originated in Egypt. Mizrahi Jews have been eating falafel for centuries, and you can now nosh on them in countries around the world.

1. Place the chickpeas in a large bowl and cover them by about 3" of cold water. Add baking soda and stir; this will help soften the chickpeas. Cover the bowl and let them soak overnight in a cool, dark place, or in the refrigerator. The chickpeas should soak at least 12 hours and up to 24 hours.

2. The next day, drain the chickpeas and rinse well. In a food processor combine all of the remaining ingredients, except the oil. Pulse until a rough, coarse meal forms. Scrape the sides of the processor periodically and push the mixture down the sides. Process until the mixture is somewhere between the texture of couscous and a paste. Don't over-process, you don't want it turning into hummus!

3. Cover the bowl with plastic wrap and refrigerate for 1 to 2 hours.

4. In a large deep skillet heat avocado oil for shallow frying. The ideal temperature to fry falafel is between 300°F and 325°F; the best way to monitor the temperature is to use a deep fry or candy thermometer.

5. Form the falafel mixture into round balls or patties using a 1½ oz. ice cream scoop.

6. When the oil is at the right temperature, fry the falafels in batches of 5 or 6 at a time, until golden brown on both sides. Once the falafels are fried, remove them from the oil using a slotted spoon and let them drain on a paper towel-lined plate.

7. Serve the falafels fresh and hot; they go best with a plate of hummus and topped with creamy tahini sauce. You can also stuff them into a pita with lettuce, tomatoes, pickles, and Yogurt Sauce.

YOGURT SAUCE

1. Add all of the ingredients to a bowl, mix well, and refrigerate. Serve chilled.

INGREDIENTS:

FALAFEL
- 1 LB. DRY CHICKPEAS
- ½ TEASPOON BAKING SODA
- ¼ CUP TAHINI
- 1 SMALL ONION, ROUGHLY CHOPPED
- ¼ CUP CHOPPED PARSLEY
- 5 GARLIC CLOVES
- 1½ TABLESPOONS CHICKPEA FLOUR
- 2 TEASPOONS SALT
- 2 TEASPOONS TOASTED SESAME SEEDS
- 1 TEASPOON TURMERIC
- 1 TEASPOON SUMAC
- 2 TABLESPOONS ZA'ATAR (SEE PAGE 545)
- 2 TEASPOONS CUMIN
- 1 TEASPOON GROUND CORIANDER
- 1 TEASPOON BLACK PEPPER
- ½ TEASPOON CAYENNE PEPPER
- 1 PINCH GROUND CARDAMOM
- 1 TEASPOON BAKING POWDER (OPTIONAL; MAKES THE FALAFEL MORE FLUFFY)
- AVOCADO OIL, FOR FRYING

YOGURT SAUCE
- 2 CUPS PLAIN YOGURT
- 1 GREEN ONION, MINCED
- 2 CUCUMBERS, GRATED WITH JUICE
- ¼ RED ONION, GRATED
- 1 TABLESPOON DILL
- 1 GARLIC CLOVE, MINCED OR SMASHED INTO A PASTE

Falafel, page 59

FAVA BEANS WITH POMEGRANATES

YIELD: 4 SERVINGS / **ACTIVE TIME:** 20 MINUTES / **TOTAL TIME:** 30 MINUTES

Spring in a dish with these young fava beans and plenty of fresh herbs.

1. In a bowl, combine the onions with sumac and red wine vinegar and a pinch of sea salt. Allow to sit for 10 minutes. The onions will turn bright red and become slightly pickled.

2. Add avocado oil to a large saucepan over medium-low heat and sauté the garlic and fava beans until the beans become bright green in color. Season with sea salt, pepper, za'atar, and lemon juice.

3. Remove from heat and add fresh herbs and pomegranates and garnish with onions, pomegranate molasses, extra virgin olive oil, and Labneh.

INGREDIENTS:

½ RED ONION, THINLY SLICED

1 TEASPOON SUMAC

1 TEASPOON RED WINE VINEGAR

½ TEASPOON SEA SALT, PLUS MORE TO TASTE

2 TABLESPOONS AVOCADO OIL

2 GARLIC CLOVES, CHOPPED

1½ LBS. FRESH YOUNG FAVA BEANS, POD AND INNER SHELL REMOVED

¼ TEASPOON BLACK PEPPER

1 TEASPOON ZA'ATAR (SEE PAGE 545)

JUICE OF ½ LEMON

½ CUP FRESH PARSLEY

¼ CUP FRESH DILL

¼ CUP FRESH MINT

¼ CUP POMEGRANATE SEEDS

1 TEASPOON POMEGRANATE MOLASSES

2 TABLESPOONS EXTRA VIRGIN OLIVE OIL

2 TABLESPOONS LABNEH (SEE PAGE 530)

Fried Eggplant with Garlic & Cumin, page 66

FRIED EGGPLANT WITH GARLIC & CUMIN

YIELD: 4 SERVINGS / **ACTIVE TIME:** 30 MINUTES / **TOTAL TIME:** 1 HOUR

A perfect example of decadent simplicity. Fried eggplant is enhanced with pungent garlic and earthy cumin to create this favorite.

1. Sprinkle both sides of the eggplant with salt, place the slices onto a tray in a single layer, and set aside for 30 minutes. Pat dry the eggplant slices.

2. Fill a large, heavy-bottomed pan with 1" of oil and set over high heat. Once the oil is sizzling, gently place about 5 eggplant slices into the pan in one layer and fry on both sides, about 3 to 5 minutes per side. Transfer the fried eggplant slices onto a paper towel-lined tray and continue frying the remaining slices in batches.

3. Plate the eggplant slices in one layer on a platter. Sprinkle the garlic and cumin over the eggplant slices and drizzle with Chimichurri. Serve warm.

TIP: Try this same recipe using a grill instead of frying for a deeper smoky flavor.

INGREDIENTS:

1   MEDIUM EGGPLANT, CUT IN ROUND DISCS ABOUT ½" THICK

½   TEASPOON SEA SALT AVOCADO OIL, FOR FRYING

4   GARLIC CLOVES, FINELY CHOPPED OR CRUSHED

1   TEASPOON GROUND RAS EL HANOUT

2   TABLESPOONS CHIMICHURRI (SEE PAGE 521)

FRIED EGGPLANT WITH MINT VINAIGRETTE

YIELD: 4 SERVINGS / **ACTIVE TIME:** 15 MINUTES / **TOTAL TIME:** 45 MINUTES

Any heaviness from the rich fried eggplant in this appetizer is offset by the light and refreshing mint vinaigrette.

1. Sprinkle both sides of the eggplant with salt, place the slices onto a tray in a single layer, and set aside for 20 minutes. Pat dry the eggplant slices and wipe off any excess salt.

2. Heat avocado oil in a 12" skillet over medium heat. Once the oil is hot, place about 4 pieces of eggplant into the pot and fry on both sides until golden brown, about 3 to 5 minutes on each side. Transfer the fried eggplants onto a paper towel-lined plate. Continue frying the remaining pieces of eggplant in batches and add more oil to the pan if needed.

3. In a bowl, combine the pomegranate concentrate, olive oil, mint, ras el hanout, salt, and pepper and mix well.

4. Layer the fried eggplant on a serving plate, dress with the vinaigrette, and sprinkle the pomegranate seeds on top. Serve warm or cold.

TIP: Try this same recipe using a grill instead of frying for a deeper smoky flavor.

INGREDIENTS:

2	MEDIUM EGGPLANTS, SLICED CROSSWISE INTO ¼" PIECES
1	TABLESPOON COARSE SEA SALT
¼	CUP AVOCADO OIL, OIL FOR FRYING
2	TABLESPOONS POMEGRANATE CONCENTRATE
⅓	CUP OLIVE OIL
1	CUP CHOPPED MINT LEAVES
1	TEASPOON RAS EL HANOUT
1	TEASPOON KOSHER SALT
¼	TEASPOON GROUND BLACK PEPPER
1	TABLESPOON POMEGRANATE SEEDS, FOR GARNISH

Ful Medames, page 70

FUL MEDAMES

YIELD: 5 SERVINGS / **ACTIVE TIME:** 15 MINUTES / **TOTAL TIME:** 30 MINUTES

Hummus certainly deserves its worldwide popularity, but it sometimes means dishes like ful don't get the recognition they deserve. Think of it as hummus made with fava beans instead of chickpeas—it's usually chunkier, containing more cumin and topped with fresh herbs, onion and chilies. Originally Egyptian, it has made its way across the Arab world, to Israel. If you've hit your hummus limit, give this ful a try.

1. Add the oil to a large, non-stick skillet and sauté the onion and garlic for about 4 minutes. Add the tomatoes and cook for another 4 minutes. Stir in the fava beans, cumin, ras el hanout, and red pepper and cook on medium-low heat for about 10 minutes.

2. Remove from the heat and mash the fava beans lightly, right in the skillet, until most of the beans are mashed. Scoop into a serving bowl, and mix in the lemon juice and parsley. Serve with warm pita bread.

TIP: Look for canned fava beans in Middle Eastern grocery stores. Some common spellings are ful medames, foul moudammes, foul mudammes, and foul moudammas.

INGREDIENTS:

1	TABLESPOON AVOCADO OIL
1	MEDIUM ONION, CHOPPED
3	GARLIC CLOVES, MINCED
2	MEDIUM TOMATOES, CHOPPED
2	(15 OZ.) CANS FAVA BEANS, RINSED AND DRAINED, OR 3 CUPS COOKED AND SHELLED FAVA BEANS
1	TEASPOON GROUND CUMIN
1	TABLESPOON RAS EL HANOUT
¼	TEASPOON CAYENNE OR RED CHILI PEPPER
3	TABLESPOONS FRESH LEMON JUICE
¼	CUP PARSLEY
	SEA SALT, TO TASTE

HEART-BEET SALAD

YIELD: 1 SERVING / **ACTIVE TIME:** 20 MINUTES / **TOTAL TIME:** 20 MINUTES

Beets and goat cheese are a classic combination, but the truffle flavor and hazelnuts elevate this salad to be something special.

1. In a medium bowl combine arugula, kale, hazelnuts, beets, hemp, orange, and dressing and gently mix to coat the salad.

2. To serve, place a scoop of goat cheese on a chilled plate and spread it into a swoop, using the back of a spoon. Add the mixed salad and top with pomegranate seeds, hazelnuts, and hemp hearts.

INGREDIENTS:

1	OZ. ARUGULA
1	OZ. KALE, TORN
4	OZ. ROASTED BEETS, DICED
4	ORANGE SEGMENTS
1	OZ. POMEGRANATE VINAIGRETTE (SEE PAGE 532)
3	TABLESPOONS TRUFFLE GOAT CHEESE SPREAD, TO SERVE
1	TEASPOON MIX OF CHOPPED FRESH TARRAGON, PARSLEY, CHIVES, AND CILANTRO, TO SERVE
½	TEASPOON POMEGRANATE SEEDS, TO SERVE
¼	TEASPOON CRUSHED TOASTED HAZELNUTS, TO SERVE
¼	TEASPOON HEMP HEARTS, TO SERVE

ISRAELI SALAD

YIELD: 4 SERVINGS / **ACTIVE TIME:** 15 MINUTES / **TOTAL TIME:** 15 MINUTES

The origins of the name are, like most things, a bit murky. This salad can be either Israeli or Palestinian. We like to think of it as simply delicious, all names and complications aside.

1. In a large bowl, toss together the tomatoes, cucumbers, pepper, and scallions.

2. Immediately before serving, season with olive oil, lemon juice, salt, and pepper and mix well. Taste and adjust seasoning, if desired. Leftover salad will keep, covered in the refrigerator, for 2 to 3 days.

INGREDIENTS:

3   MEDIUM TOMATOES, DESEEDED AND DICED

3   PERSIAN CUCUMBERS, DICED

1   RED BELL PEPPER, DICED

3   SCALLIONS, WHITE AND LIGHT GREEN PARTS THINLY SLICED

2   TABLESPOONS EXTRA VIRGIN OLIVE OIL

2   TABLESPOONS FRESH LEMON JUICE

    SEA SALT, TO TASTE

    FRESHLY GROUND BLACK PEPPER, TO TASTE

ISRAELI SPICY CHICKPEA SOUP
WITH CRÈME FRAÎCHE

YIELD: 12 SERVINGS / **ACTIVE TIME:** 15 MINUTES / **TOTAL TIME:** 45 MINUTES

This hearty and warming pureed soup is great on a winter day. Chef Korn used to serve this soup at the iconic Tribeca Grill in New York City. When no one was looking, a little butter-poached lobster tail and claw with black malossol caviar might have been garnished on top. Don't tell the rabbi

1. Combine all of the ingredients, except the stock, tomato concasse, lime juice, and berbere, in a large pot and sauté for 10 minutes, adding the salt and pepper in stages to layer the flavor.

2. Add the stock and bring to a simmer and cook for 20 minutes, seasoning again with salt and pepper.

3. Using a slotted spoon, reserve 2 cups of the cooked vegetables from the soup for garnish and mix them with the tomato concasse.

4. Place the rest of the ingredients in a blender and blend until thick and smooth. Adjust seasoning with lime juice and berbere.

5. Pass through a fine mesh sieve to get rid of any chunky vegetables. The soup should have a velvety smooth and silky texture with a beautiful golden color.

6. To serve, garnish with reserved ingredients and a dollop of crème fraîche, and if desired dill and caviar.

INGREDIENTS:

24	OZ. CHICKPEAS
1	YELLOW BELL PEPPER, DESEEDED
6	GARLIC CLOVES, SLICED
2	ONIONS, DICED
2	CELERY STALKS, DICED
2	CARROTS, DICED
2	BAY LEAVES
4	TABLESPOONS RICE WINE VINEGAR
2	TABLESPOONS AJI-MIRIN
1	CUP MIX OF CHOPPED FRESH TARRAGON, PARSLEY, CHIVES, AND CILANTRO
3	TABLESPOONS SESAME OIL
3	TABLESPOONS EXTRA VIRGIN OLIVE OIL
2	TABLESPOONS SRIRACHA
2	TEASPOONS TURMERIC
4	TABLESPOONS SALT, DIVIDED
4	TABLESPOONS BLACK PEPPER, DIVIDED
2	GALLONS CORN STOCK OR VEGETABLE STOCK (SEE PAGE 533 OR PAGE 729)
1	CUP TOMATO CONCASSE, SPIKED WITH CILANTRO
¼	FRESH LIME JUICE
1	TABLESPOON BERBERE SPICE MIX (SEE PAGE 323)
1	DOLLOP CRÈME FRAÎCHE, FOR GARNISH
1	SPRIG DILL, FOR GARNISH (OPTIONAL)
	CAVIAR, FOR GARNISH (OPTIONAL)

JEWISH-STYLE FRIED ARTICHOKES

YIELD: 8 SERVINGS / **ACTIVE TIME:** 1 HOUR AND 15 MINUTES / **TOTAL TIME:** 2 HOURS

Carciofi alla giudìa, or Jewish-style artichokes, originated in the Jewish-Roman ghetto of Rome and are still popular in Jewish-Roman restaurants during the spring when artichokes are in season. The artichokes are seasoned with lemon juice, salt, and pepper, and then deep fried in olive oil. The finishing touch is the sprinkling of a little cold water on the artichokes for added crispness, resulting in a golden sunflower, its leaves crunching with every bite.

1. Prepare a large bowl of ice water. Squeeze two lemons into the bowl of water, stir, then throw in the squeezed lemon halves. This lemon water will keep the artichokes fresh and green until you're ready to fry them. Keep a couple of fresh lemon halves on hand as you prep.

2. Rinse the artichokes under cold water. Pat them dry with a clean kitchen towel or paper towel. With kitchen shears or sharp scissors, remove the thorny tips from the leaves. For each artichoke, remove the bitter, fibrous end of the stem with a knife, leaving about 1½" of stem attached to the artichoke (see page 743).

3. Use a serrated knife to peel the outer skin from the remaining stem. The stem has a more bitter taste than the rest of the artichoke; removing the skin helps to take away some of the bitterness. Rub the peeled stem with fresh lemon to keep it from browning.

4. Peel off 5 to 6 layers of external leaves from the artichoke, snapping off the leaves and setting them aside, until you reach inner leaves that are fresh looking and white at the base.

5. With a serrated knife or sharp chef's knife, slice the artichoke horizontally, about ¾" above the base (heart), to remove the pointy top of the artichoke, leaving a flat crown of leaves on the base of the artichoke while exposing the inner purple leaves.

6. Slice the artichoke in half lengthwise, splitting the stem and heart in half vertically to reveal the inner fuzzy choke.

7. Scoop out the fuzzy white spines and purple leaves from each artichoke half with a melon baller, leaving behind two hollowed out halves of heart, each with a small crown of flat leaves.

8. Rub the heart with lemon, then place it in the bowl of lemon water. Repeat the process with the remaining artichokes.

INGREDIENTS:

5   LEMONS

4   LARGE ARTICHOKES

      AVOCADO OIL, FOR FRYING

      SALT AND PEPPER, TO TASTE

Continued . . .

9. When ready to cook, remove the artichoke halves from the lemon water. Pour the lemon water and juiced lemon halves into a large pot; you will need about 1½" of water, so if you don't have enough, add more water to top it off. Place a steamer basket inside the pot and bring water to a boil. Place the cleaned artichoke halves in the steamer basket and cover the pot with a lid. Reduce heat to medium.

10. Let the artichokes steam for 15 to 20 minutes, until a knife or fork can be inserted easily into the thickest part of the stem. You want the artichokes to be lightly steamed and a bit tender, but still firm—they should only be partially cooked.

11. Place the steamed artichoke halves onto a layer of paper towels and let them drain and dry completely before frying.

12. Heat 1" of oil to 325°F, hot enough for frying but not so hot that it smokes. While the oil is heating, sprinkle the artichoke halves with salt and pepper, making sure to sprinkle inside the layers of leaves as well.

13. Gently place the artichokes into the heated oil and let them fry for about 15 minutes, using a pair of tongs to turn them once halfway through cooking, until the artichokes are golden brown and the leaves are crisp.

14. Remove from the oil and let them drain on paper towels or a wire rack.

15. Serve warm with fresh sliced lemon wedges.

TIP: Use a serrated bread knife to peel and cut the outer leaves and stems of the artichokes as the knife's teeth will cut easier. These artichokes are great with Chermoula (see page 517).

KISHKA

YIELD: 8 SERVINGS / **ACTIVE TIME:** 20 MINUTES / **TOTAL TIME:** 2 HOURS

Search your favorite deli's menu and you'll find kishka, we promise. Not everybody kvells over this sausage-like specialty, but those who know *know.*

1. Preheat the oven to 425°F degrees. Line a baking sheet with a double layer of foil 12" long, topped with a sheet of parchment paper the same size.

2. Add 4 tablespoons fat to a skillet over medium-low heat and sauté onion and garlic until soft and golden. Cool slightly and pour everything, including fat, into a food processor.

3. Add remaining 2 tablespoons of fat, celery, carrot, matzo meal, salt, pepper, and paprika to the food processor and pulse until vegetables and fat are incorporated into a paste. Transfer the mixture to parchment paper and shape into a sausage-like cylinder about 9" long and 2" in diameter. Enclose parchment and foil firmly around the cylinder, folding ends under.

4. Bake for 30 minutes, then reduce heat to 350°F and cook until the kishka is solid, 45 to 60 minutes more. Unroll kishke to expose surface; return to oven just until top is lightly browned and slightly crisped, 10 to 15 minutes.

5. Let cool slightly before cutting into rounds. If desired, serve as a side dish with pot roast or roast chicken.

INGREDIENTS:

6	TABLESPOONS SCHMALTZ (SEE PAGE 528)
1	MEDIUM TO LARGE ONION, DICED
1	GARLIC CLOVE, CHOPPED
1	STALK CELERY, CUT INTO CHUNKS
1	LARGE CARROT, PEELED AND CUT INTO CHUNKS
1	CUP MATZO MEAL
1	TEASPOON SEA SALT, OR TO TASTE
⅛	TEASPOON FRESHLY GROUND BLACK PEPPER, OR TO TASTE
⅛	TEASPOON HOT PAPRIKA

KACHORI

Pillowy and delectable fried dumplings filled with peas and a combination of spices, these are a favorite amongst the Indian-Baghdadi Jewish community. This recipe is also linked with Jewish Chilanga traditions.

1. In a large bowl, add the flour, salt, oil or ghee, juice of ½ lemon, and semolina and mix well. Gradually add ⅓ cup of water, stirring the mixture together with a wooden spoon until a dough forms. Knead the dough until it is smooth, about 3 to 5 minutes. If the dough feels dry, continue adding water 1 tablespoon at a time until the dough is semi-stiff and not too sticky. Cover with a towel and set aside.

2. Add the olive oil to a large skillet over medium heat. Add the asafoetida and once it sizzles, about 2-4 minutes, add the peas. Add 4 tablespoons of water to the peas, cover, and let cook for 5 to 6 minutes, or until the peas are tender and the water has evaporated. Add the jalapeño, ginger, garam masala, fennel seeds, salt, sugar, and remaining lemon juice and stir. Cook the mixture until the jalapeño has softened and the mixture is evenly coated with the seasonings, approximately 10 to 15 minutes. Remove the pan from heat, coarsely mash the mixture with a potato masher, and set aside to cool for about 15 minutes.

3. Pour oil into a medium-sized pot over medium-high heat. Heat the oil until a thermometer inserted into the oil reads 350°F.

4. Transfer the dough onto a lightly floured surface. Using a rolling pin, roll out the dough into a very thin circle, about ¹⁄₁₆" in thickness. Cut out 2¼" circles from the dough, using a cookie cutter or the edge of a glass cup. Take a circle of dough and roll it out to about 4" in diameter. Place 1 tablespoon of the cooled filling into the center of the dough. Using your fingers, bring up the edges of the dough toward the center, over the filling, and form a little basket shape by crimping the edges together to seal the dumpling. Continue with the remaining dough and filling.

5. Using a slotted spoon, gently place about 4 or 5 dumplings into the oil once it is hot. Fry the dumplings for about 5 minutes until they are golden brown, flipping them occasionally in the oil. Transfer the cooked dumplings onto a paper towel-lined plate and continue frying the rest of the kachoris.

6. Serve hot with a side of mint raita.

INGREDIENTS:

1	CUP ALL-PURPOSE FLOUR
½	TEASPOON KOSHER SALT
1	TABLESPOON AVOCADO OIL OR GHEE
	JUICE OF 1 LEMON, DIVIDED
2	TABLESPOONS SEMOLINA FLOUR
⅓-½	CUP WATER
1	TABLESPOON OLIVE OIL
½	TEASPOON ASAFETIDA (GARLIC PASTE KNOWN AS HING IN INDIAN MARKETS)
2	CUPS FRESH GREEN PEAS OR DEFROSTED FROZEN PEAS
1	LARGE JALAPEÑO, FINELY CHOPPED
2	TABLESPOONS GRATED GINGER
1	TABLESPOON GARAM MASALA
1	TABLESPOON COARSELY GROUND FENNEL SEEDS
1	TEASPOON SEA SALT
½	TEASPOON SUGAR
6	CUPS AVOCADO OIL, FOR FRYING

Kemia de Zanahorias, page 85

KEMIA DE ZANAHORIAS

YIELD: 6 SERVINGS / **ACTIVE TIME:** 10 MINUTES / **TOTAL TIME:** 20 MINUTES

Whether served warm or at room temperature, the spicy harissa pulls together this salad of cooked carrots and sautéed garlic. Caraway seeds add an extra layer of flavor and texture.

1. Bring a large pot of water to a boil with 1 tablespoon of salt. Add the carrots into the boiling water and cook for about 5 minutes, or until fork-tender.

2. Add the oil to a skillet over medium-high heat. Once the oil is hot add the garlic and sauté until golden. Add the cooked carrots, harissa, and paprika and sauté for 3 minutes until the carrots are coated.

3. Transfer to a mixing bowl and add the caraway seeds, vinegar and remaining 1 teaspoon of salt. Mix well.

4. Serve warm or at room temperature.

INGREDIENTS:

1	TABLESPOON PLUS 1 TEASPOON SEA SALT, DIVIDED
6	CARROTS, CUT INTO ¼" ROUNDS
5	GARLIC CLOVES, THINLY SLICED
3	TEASPOONS OLIVE OIL
1	TEASPOON HARISSA
1	TEASPOON GROUND PAPRIKA
1	TEASPOON CARAWAY SEEDS
1	TABLESPOON WHITE WINE VINEGAR

KEMIA DE REMOLACHAS

YIELD: 6 SERVINGS / **ACTIVE TIME:** 15 MINUTES / **TOTAL TIME:** 45 MINUTES

This cold beet salad is often served alongside its cucumber and carrot counterparts. The beets are lightly seasoned with salt and pepper before being fully dressed with olive oil and cumin.

1. Place the beets and 1 tablespoon salt in a pot and submerge completely in cold water. Bring to a boil and cook for about 30 minutes, or until the beets are fork-tender.

2. Add the olive oil to a skillet over medium heat. Add the beets, cumin, remaining 2 teaspoons of salt, and pepper and sauté until coated, about 3 minutes.

3. Transfer to a bowl and serve warm or at room temperature.

INGREDIENTS:

3	BEETS
1	TABLESPOON PLUS 2 TEASPOONS SEA SALT, DIVIDED
1	TABLESPOON OLIVE OIL
2	TEASPOONS GROUND CUMIN
2	TEASPOONS SEA SALT
¼	TEASPOON GROUND BLACK PEPPER

Kreplach, page 88

KREPLACH

YIELD: 90 DUMPLINGS / **ACTIVE TIME:** 20 MINUTES / **TOTAL TIME:** 2 HOURS

Salty, warm, comforting goodness in a bowl. The dumpling is filled with a combination of breast meat and chicken livers and can be served fried with onions or in broth as a soup.

1. Heat 4 tablespoons of the Schmaltz in a medium pan over medium-high heat. Season the chicken and liver pieces lightly with salt. Add to the pan and sear, turning occasionally, until browned on all sides and cooked through, 5 to 7 minutes. Transfer the pieces to a plate and set aside to cool slightly.

2. Add the remaining oil to the pan along with the onions and sauté, stirring occasionally, until the onions are golden brown and beginning to caramelize, about 10 minutes. Season lightly with salt and remove from the heat. Set aside to cool slightly.

3. Transfer the chicken and liver to a food processor, along with the onions, 1½ tablespoons of the beaten egg, the ½ teaspoon of the salt, and all of the pepper. Pulse the mixture until it is finely ground and season to taste. Transfer to a small bowl and cover loosely with plastic wrap. Set aside to cool completely.

4. Meanwhile, make the dough: Combine the flour and salt in a medium bowl and make a well in the center. Whisk the egg with 1 cup water and the remaining egg from the filling. Pour the egg mixture into the well in the dry ingredients and mix with a fork until the dough forms.

5. Turn the dough onto a lightly floured surface and knead until soft and smooth, 1 to 2 minutes. Return the dough to the bowl, cover with a towel or plastic wrap, and let rest for 20 minutes.

6. Line a baking sheet with wax or parchment paper and drizzle evenly with oil. Divide the dough into thirds with a dough cutter or chef's knife. Transfer one-third of the dough to a heavily floured surface, keeping the other two-thirds covered. Using a rolling pin, roll out the dough as thinly as possible into a 20" x 14" rectangle.

7. Using a pizza cutter or chef's knife, cut the rolled dough into 2" squares. Place ½ teaspoon of filling in the middle of each square. Lightly brush the edges with water and fold each square in half over the filling to form a triangle, pressing the edges gently together to create a tight seal. Fold the two longer corners inward to connect and clasp along the longest edge of each dumpling, pressing to seal tortellini-style. Place on the prepared baking sheet, cover

INGREDIENTS:

FILLING

6	TABLESPOONS SCHMALTZ (SEE PAGE 528), OR AVOCADO OIL
5	OZ. CHICKEN BREAST, CUT INTO ½" PIECES
3	OZ. CHICKEN LIVERS, CUT INTO ½" PIECES
½	TEASPOON KOSHER SALT, PLUS MORE TO TASTE
3	MEDIUM ONIONS, ROUGHLY CHOPPED
1	EGG, LIGHTLY BEATEN, DIVIDED
½	TEASPOON FRESHLY GROUND BLACK PEPPER

DOUGH

3½	CUPS ALL-PURPOSE FLOUR, SIFTED
1	TABLESPOON SEA SALT
1	EGG, LIGHTLY BEATEN
1	CUP LUKEWARM WATER
	AVOCADO OIL, FOR DRIZZLING

loosely with plastic wrap, and continue with the remainder of the dough and filling.

8. While forming the dumplings, bring a large pot of generously salted water to a boil. Working in two batches, gently slide the dumplings into the water. Simmer for 3 to 4 minutes, or until the dumplings float to the surface. Remove the dumplings with a slotted spoon to a wax or parchment paper-lined tray.

9. To serve, add the cooked dumplings to hot chicken soup or fry them in a pan with onions.

TIP: The filling can be made in advance and refrigerated in an airtight container for 1 to 2 days. The dumplings can be made ahead and placed on a wax or parchment paper-lined tray in the freezer until firm, then transferred to a resealable airtight bag and stored in the freezer for 1 to 2 weeks. Add the frozen dumplings directly to boiling water and continue to cook 2 to 3 minutes after they float to the surface.

MUSHROOM BARLEY SOUP

YIELD: 10 SERVINGS / **ACTIVE TIME:** 15 MINUTES / **TOTAL TIME:** 1 HOUR AND 15 MINUTES

Healthy and hearty, this is an essential recipe to have on hand for cold winter nights.

1. Heat the avocado oil over medium heat in a large stockpot and sauté the onion, carrots, celery, mushrooms, parsley, garlic, thyme, and bay leaf until soft, about 5 minutes.

2. Lower the heat and add the flour, stirring every 45 seconds for about 5 minutes until thick. Add the stock in 3 stages, starting by slowly stirring in 1 quart to avoid lumps.

3. Turn the heat to medium high, and add barley.

4. Stir well and add salt.

5. Simmer, covered, for about an hour or until the barley is tender and the soup is thickened, stirring often.

6. Add additional chopped parsley, mix thoroughly, and serve.

INGREDIENTS:

¼	CUP AVOCADO OIL
1	CUP CHOPPED ONION
1	CUP DICED CARROTS
1	CUP CHOPPED CELERY
1	LB. CREMINI OR BUTTON MUSHROOMS, SLICED
¾	CUP CHOPPED PARSLEY, PLUS MORE TO SERVE
3	GARLIC CLOVES, MINCED
1	TEASPOON THYME
1	BAY LEAF
2	TABLESPOONS ALL-PURPOSE FLOUR
4	QUARTS BEEF STOCK OR CHICKEN STOCK (SEE PAGE 721 OR PAGE 722)
1	CUP WHOLE BARLEY
3	TEASPOONS SEA SALT
1	TEASPOON FRESHLY GROUND BLACK PEPPER

Liverwurst, page 94

LIVERWURST

YIELD: 10 SERVINGS / **ACTIVE TIME:** 1 HOUR / **TOTAL TIME:** 3 HOURS

You could call it pâté, but what would Bubbe say? This spread made from offal—the internal organs of an animal—is best on crackers or toast.

1. Remove all membranes from the liver and soak in water for one hour. Drain well.

2. Using a meat grinder, grind the liver and onion together 3 times until very fine textured. Add all of the other ingredients and grind together.

3. Preheat the oven to 300°F.

4. Press the raw liver into a terrine mold, or empty and clean metal coffee cans lined with parchment paper; any size can may be used but slices will be smaller and more liverwurst-like if the can is smaller, roughly 3" to 4" in diameter.

5. Set cans in a shallow pan of water and bake for 1 to 1½ hours. Use the lesser time for smaller cans.

6. Let cool in cans until rolls slide out without breaking. Slice thin or thick and place on your favorite rye bread or bagel. Store in the refrigerator for up to 1 week.

INGREDIENTS:

2	LBS. BEEF LIVER
1	SMALL ONION
¾	LB. SCHMALTZ (SEE PAGE 528)
½	CUP ALL-PURPOSE FLOUR
½	PINT MILK
1	TEASPOON SEA SALT
1	TEASPOON PEPPER
½	TEASPOON CLOVES
½	TEASPOON ALLSPICE
1	TEASPOON SUGAR
2	EGGS

MEZZE'D UP SALAD

YIELD: 1 SERVING / **ACTIVE TIME:** 10 MINUTES / **TOTAL TIME:** 1 HOUR AND 10 MINUTES

This salad is a multi-component salad, basically an homage to traditional mezze but on one dish instead of many. We have four salims or mezze plated on a single dish, so it may seem a little messed up but it's not, it's Mezze'd Up.

1. In a bowl, combine the quinoa, baby kale, cucumber, grapes, onions, strawberries, and mint and mix well. Cover and refrigerate for at least an hour.

2. In a medium mixing bowl, toss the baby lettuce with the vinaigrette. Then distribute the dressed lettuce on a platter to act as a bed for all the other mezze.

3. This salad is meant to be very colorful and visually appealing, so try to plate the 3 mezze in alternating diagonal rows, placing the relish, then the kale and quinoa, and then the salim in alternating rows.

4. Finally garnish with radish and a sprinkling of the crushed salty root vegetable chips.

INGREDIENTS:

4   OZ. COOKED RED QUINOA

½   OZ. BABY KALE, CHOPPED, MARINATED WITH A SQUEEZE OF FRESH LEMON JUICE

½   OZ. PERSIAN CUCUMBER, DICED

½   OZ. RED GRAPES, HALVED

½   OZ. RED ONIONS, BRUNOISE

¼   OZ. PICKLED RED ONIONS

½   OZ SLICED STRAWBERRIES

¼   OZ. MINT, CHOPPED

3   OZ. MIXED BABY LETTUCE

1½   OZ. CILANTRO LIME VINAIGRETTE (SEE PAGE 522)

3   OZ. CUCUMBER TOMATO MANGO RELISH (SEE PAGE 57)

3   OZ. ROASTED CORN AND BLACK BEAN SALAD (SEE PAGE 107)

6   SLICES FRENCH RADISH, FOR GARNISH

1   OZ. ROOT VEGETABLE CHIPS, CRUSHED

ORANGE & POMEGRANATE SALAD WITH HONEY

YIELD: 6 SERVINGS / **ACTIVE TIME:** 20 MINUTES / **TOTAL TIME:** 20 MINUTES

The pomegranate has long been a symbol of fertility, and thus of the unlimited possibilities for the Jewish New Year. Its pop of color and tartness is only enhanced by the orange.

1. Supreme the oranges by cutting a thin slice from the top and bottom of each orange and then standing the orange upright on a cutting board. With a knife, remove the peel and outer membrane from the oranges. Cut crosswise into ½" slices.

2. Arrange orange slices on a serving platter and sprinkle with pomegranate seeds.

3. In a small bowl, combine honey and orange flower water, mix well, and drizzle over fruit.

INGREDIENTS:

5	MEDIUM ORANGES OR 10 CLEMENTINES
½	CUP POMEGRANATE SEEDS
2	TABLESPOONS HONEY
1-2	TEASPOONS ORANGE FLOWER WATER OR ORANGE JUICE

POMEGRANATE GLAZED FIGS & CHEESE

YIELD: 4 SERVINGS / **ACTIVE TIME:** 35 MINUTES / **TOTAL TIME:** 1 HOUR

A combination of simple, mouthwatering ingredients. This dish balances the rich creaminess of the cheese and the candy sweetness of figs with a tart pomegranate glaze.

1. Prepare the glaze by adding pomegranate juice, anise seeds, peppercorns, bay leaf, and kosher salt in a small pot and cooking over medium-high heat until the mixture reduces to ⅓ cup. Strain, cool, and reserve in the refrigerator, covered. Bring to room temperature before using.

2. In a bowl, combine the cheeses and mix until smooth. Add 1 tablespoon of the prepared glaze and the sea salt and pepper. Place in a pastry bag that has been fitted with a ½" tube and refrigerate until ready to put figs under the broiler.

3. When ready to serve, heat the broiler. Cut figs in half from tip to stem and place in a heatproof dish cut-side up. Brush each cut side with some of the glaze and dust evenly with a thin layer of the superfine sugar.

4. Prepare 4 plates by piping a ½- to ¾"-wide by about 6- to 7"-long strip of cheese mixture on each plate.

5. Place figs under broiler until just heated through and glazed, about 5 minutes.

6. To serve, shingle 6 fig halves on top of each cheese strip and garnish with pomegranate seeds, if desired, and drizzle remaining pomegranate glaze around and over.

INGREDIENTS:

16	OZ. POMEGRANATE JUICE
1	TEASPOON ANISE SEEDS
1	TEASPOON BLACK PEPPERCORNS
1	BAY LEAF
1	PINCH KOSHER SALT
½	CUP RICOTTA CHEESE
½	CUP MASCARPONE CHEESE
1	PINCH SEA SALT
⅛	TEASPOON FRESHLY GROUND BLACK PEPPER
12	JUST-RIPE (NOT OVERRIPE) FRESH FIGS
1	TEASPOON SUPERFINE SUGAR
	FRESH POMEGRANATE SEEDS (OPTIONAL)

POBLANO MATZO BALL SOUP

YIELD: 8 SERVINGS / **ACTIVE TIME:** 30 MINUTES / **TOTAL TIME:** 3 HOURS

When you're ready to experiment with new flavor combinations in your matzo ball soup, the poblano gives this traditional soup a surprising kick.

MATZO BALLS

1. In a blender, purée the poblano pepper and cilantro with enough of the seltzer to make it smooth.

2. In a large bowl, beat the eggs until well combined.

3. Gradually mix in the purée, Schmaltz, and remaining seltzer, followed by the matzo meal, sea salt, and pepper and mix until fully incorporated.

4. Cover and refrigerate for 2 hours.

5. Bring a large pot of chicken stock to a rolling boil.

6. Form the matzo mixture into balls of your preferred size.

7. Drop into boiling stock and simmer for 30 minutes.

SOUP

1. Place the chicken in a large stock ot, cover with stock and water, and bring to a boil over medium heat. Reduce to a simmer and cook for 20 minutes, skimming any foam or fat that rises to the surface.

2. Remove the chicken from the pot and set aside to cool.

3. Add the carrots, celery, onion and bay leaf to the pot, bring back to a simmer, and cook until the vegetables are about half cooked, about 12 minutes.

4. Add the rice and cook, stirring every few minutes, until the grains are just al dente, about 12 minutes.

5. When the chicken is cool enough to handle, pick off the meat, and shred it.

6. When the rice is done, add the meat to the broth and simmer until warmed through, about 1 minute.

7. Stir in the parsley, and season to taste.

8. To serve, ladle broth and vegetables into bowls and add matzo balls.

INGREDIENTS:

MATZO BALLS

½	POBLANO PEPPER
¼	BUNCH CILANTRO
½	CUP SELTZER WATER
4	EGGS
6	TABLESPOONS SCHMALTZ (SEE PAGE 528)
1	CUP MATZO MEAL
	SEA SALT, TO TASTE
	BLACK PEPPER, TO TASTE
2	QUARTS CHICKEN STOCK (SEE PAGE 722)

SOUP

1	(5 LB.) WHOLE CHICKEN
4	CUPS CHICKEN STOCK (SEE PAGE 722)
2	CARROTS, SLICED THIN
2	CELERY STALKS, SLICED THIN
1	MEDIUM ONION, CHOPPED
1	BAY LEAF
½	CUP BLACK RICE
2	TABLESPOONS CHOPPED PARSLEY
	SEA SALT, TO TASTE

RED GEFILTE FISH VERACRUZANA

YIELD: 10 SERVINGS / **ACTIVE TIME:** 30 MINUTES / **TOTAL TIME:** 2 HOURS

I f you're thinking of the white-fish spread, think again. This patty of white fish, vegetables, and matzo meal is cooked in a rich tomato sauce—the perfect bite for a Jewish Chilanga Passover.

1. Place all of the broth ingredients in an 8- to 10-quart stockpot, bring to a boil, lower heat, cover, and simmer for 15 minutes.

2. Remove from heat and then remove the bones from the broth, keeping the broth hot on low heat, while you make the fish mixture.

3. Place all of the ground fish, grated carrots, and onions in a large bowl and mix. Add matzo meal, eggs, salt, and pepper and with hand mix gently but thoroughly, until fish is light in texture and holds its shape.

4. Using damp hands, take about ⅓-½ cup quantities of the fish mixture, shape into oval patties, and gently drop into the fish broth, which is hot but not boiling. When you have dropped the last fish patty into the broth, raise the heat and simmer for 1 hour.

5. As the gefilte fish cooks, start the sauce by adding oil to a large saucepan over medium-high heat. Add the 4 garlic cloves and sauté for a few minutes, removing them from the oil when they begin to turn golden. Add the onions and shallots and stir until translucent then add back the roasted garlic cloves and fry the capers and the green olives, mix for 2 minutes, and then add the diced tomatoes. Stir and then allow to simmer for 5 minutes. Add the parsley, bay leaves, oregano, cinnamon, and fish stock with carrots and onions. Season with salt and pepper to taste, and simmer for 10 more minutes.

INGREDIENTS:

FISH BROTH

1	TEASPOON CARAWAY SEEDS
1	TEASPOON FENNEL SEEDS
1	TEASPOON CUMIN SEEDS
1	TEASPOON CORIANDER SEEDS
1	STAR ANISE
1	CINNAMON STICK
5	BAY LEAVES
1	BUNCH PARSLEY STEMS
3	MEDIUM CARROTS, SLICED INTO ROUNDS
3	CELERY RIBS
3	WHITE SWEET ONIONS, SLICED THIN
	FISH BONES AND HEADS FROM SNAPPER AND PIKE
1	GALLON WATER
1	CUP WHITE WINE
1	CUP RED WINE
1	ORANGE PEEL
1	LEMON, HALVED

FISH MIXTURE

4	LBS. GROUND PIKE
2	LBS. GROUND RED SNAPPER
2	LARGE CARROTS, PEELED AND GRATED
½	LARGE ONION, PEELED AND GRATED
4	LARGE EGGS
¾	CUP MATZO MEAL
1½	TABLESPOONS FINE SEA SALT
1½	TEASPOONS WHITE PEPPER

Continued . . .

6. After the fish has simmered for 1 hour in the broth, transfer the fish loaves to the pan containing the sauce. Simmer the fish in the sauce for 10 minutes and then remove from heat. Arrange the fish on a serving platter and cover with the sauce from the pan. Garnish with all the vegetables from the sauce and serve warm or hot.

VERACRUZANA SAUCE

2	TABLESPOONS OLIVE OIL
4	WHOLE GARLIC CLOVES, PEELED
1	CUP TEXAS ONIONS, SLICED THIN ON BIAS
¼	CUP SLICED SHALLOTS
2	GARLIC CLOVES FINELY MINCED
6-8	OZ. JAR CAPERS
8-10	OZ. CAN GREEN OLIVES, CUT IN HALF
4	CUPS TOMATOES DICED
⅓	CUP PARSLEY
2	BAY LEAVES
⅛	TEASPOON CINNAMON
¼	TEASPOON DRIED OREGANO
2	CUPS FISH STOCK FROM ABOVE, WITH SLICED CARROTS AND THINLY SLICED ONIONS
	SALT AND PEPPER, TO TASTE

ROASTED BEET & LEEK RISOTTO

YIELD: 4 SERVINGS / **ACTIVE TIME:** 45 MINUTES / **TOTAL TIME:** 1 HOUR

Beets, leeks, and rice are humble ingredients that are elevated to new heights in this recipe. This is a beautiful vegetarian side dish for Rosh Hashanah.

1. Add oil to a heavy skillet and sauté the onions and leeks until soft and translucent. Add the beets and continue to stir.

2. Over low heat, add the rice and coat evenly with the oil and vegetable mixture and begin to toast the rice.

3. Deglaze with the wine, stirring constantly and allowing the wine to fully absorb into the rice mixture.

4. Repeat with the stock, adding the liquid in at least 3 parts, constantly stirring. Add the beet juice, stirring vigorously.

5. Remove from heat and stir in the tofu cream cheese and margarine, if using, and add the herbs de Provence.

INGREDIENTS:

- 2 TABLESPOONS AVOCADO OIL
- ½ LARGE SPANISH ONION, MINCED
- WHITE BOTTOMS OF 2 LEEKS, MINCED
- 1 MEDIUM RED BEET, PEELED AND DICED
- 1 CUP ARBORIO RICE
- ½ CUP DRY WHITE WINE
- 2 CUPS WARM CHICKEN OR VEGETABLE STOCK (SEE PAGE 722 OR 729)
- ½ CUP BEET JUICE
- ¼ CUP PAREVE TOFU CREAM CHEESE (OPTIONAL)
- 1 TABLESPOON MARGARINE (OPTIONAL)
- 1 TEASPOON HERBS DE PROVENCE

ROASTED BEETS WITH CILANTRO-BASIL PESTO

YIELD: 2 SERVINGS / **ACTIVE TIME:** 20 MINUTES / **TOTAL TIME:** 1 HOUR

Beets are an essential part of Eastern European diets. But with this cilantro-basil pesto, the humble beetroot gets an Italian twist in what's sure to become a new family favorite.

1. Preheat the oven to 400°F.

2. Wrap individual beets in foil and use a fork to pierce a few holes into each foil-wrapped beet. Place beets on a baking sheet and roast until a knife easily pierces through the beets, about 40 minutes. Let cool.

3. Place the remaining ingredients, except the olive oil, in a food processor and blend until a thick paste forms. Then, with the food processor running, slowly drizzle in the olive oil, blending until smooth. Set aside.

4. Once the beets have cooled, unwrap them and use a paper towel to rub off the skin.

5. Slice beets into ¼" circles and arrange in a bowl or on a platter. Drizzle with the pesto. Refrigerate any extra pesto in an airtight container for up to a week.

INGREDIENTS:

- 2   BUNCHES MEDIUM-SIZED BEETS, SCRUBBED AND ENDS AND TOPS REMOVED
- 1   PACKED CUP CILANTRO LEAVES, WASHED AND DRIED
- 2   PACKED CUPS BASIL LEAVES, WASHED AND DRIED
- ¼   CUP PARMESAN CHEESE (OR NUTRITIONAL YEAST, IF MAKING PAREVE)
- ¼   CUP PINE NUTS (OPTIONAL)
- 2   GARLIC CLOVES
- ½   TEASPOON SALT
- ½   CUP OLIVE OIL

ROASTED CORN & BLACK BEAN SALAD

YIELD: 10 SERVINGS / **ACTIVE TIME:** 30 MINUTES / **TOTAL TIME:** 1 HOUR

The grilled corn adds a pleasant smokiness to this hearty salad.

1. In a large bowl combine all of the ingredients, mix well, and season to taste.

INGREDIENTS:

10	CORN COBBS, BLACKENED OVER OPEN FLAME THEN SHUCKED
2	RED ONIONS, BRUNOISE
2	RED PEPPERS, DESEEDED AND BRUNOISE
2	YELLOW PEPPERS, DESEEDED AND BRUNOISE
1	JALAPEÑO, DESEEDED AND BRUNOISE
4	OZ. BROWN BEECH MUSHROOMS OR WHITE BEECH MUSHROOMS, LIGHTLY SAUTÉED.
1	CUP FRESH FAVA BEANS OR ANOTHER BEAN OF THE SEASON, BLANCHED AND SHOCKED
2	CANS OF BLACK BEANS, DRAINED AND RINSED
1	CUP MIX OF CHOPPED FRESH TARRAGON, PARSLEY, CHIVES, AND CILANTRO
1	TABLESPOON FINE SEA SALT
1	TABLESPOON BLACK PEPPER
2	TABLESPOONS FRESH LIME JUICE
1	TABLESPOON RED WINE VINEGAR OR SHERRY WINE VINEGAR
2	TABLESPOONS EXTRA VIRGIN OLIVE OIL
1	TABLESPOON TABASCO

ROMANIAN EGGPLANT SALAD

YIELD: 6 SERVINGS / *ACTIVE TIME:* 30 MINUTES / *TOTAL TIME:* 1 HOUR AND 30 MINUTES

The eggplant's richness is enhanced by oil and lemon. Many families choose to garnish with onion and serve alongside fresh challah.

1. Sprinkle the eggplant slices with salt and let stand on a roasting rack for 30 minutes.

2. In a large non-stick or ceramic skillet, heat oil over medium high heat. When oil is shimmering but not smoking, add the eggplant in a single layer and cook slowly until almost black on the first side, about 10 minutes. Turn and repeat on the other side and add more oil if needed. Remove the cooked eggplant to a plate.

3. Add 2 tablespoons olive oil, the red pepper, tomatoes, onion, coriander, and paprika to the skillet. Cook for about 12 minutes, stirring occasionally until the vegetables are very soft but not brown. Add the eggplant and the vinegar to the pan, breaking up the eggplant and mashing it coarsely with a wooden spoon until well combined.

4. Remove the pan from heat and stir in the parsley and lemon juice. Serve at room temperature.

INGREDIENTS:

3-4	MEDIUM-SIZED EGGPLANTS, CUT INTO THICK ROUNDS
2	TABLESPOONS SEA SALT
6	TABLESPOONS EXTRA VIRGIN OLIVE OIL
1	CUP CHOPPED RED BELL PEPPER
½	CUP CHOPPED SKINLESS, SEEDLESS ROMA TOMATOES
1	CUP CHOPPED WHITE ONION
1	TABLESPOON GROUND CORIANDER
1	TEASPOON SWEET PAPRIKA
¼	CUP SHERRY WINE VINEGAR
½	CUP CHOPPED FRESH PARSLEY
1	TABLESPOON LEMON JUICE

SALATA MECHOUIA

YIELD: 6 SERVINGS / **ACTIVE TIME:** 1 HOUR AND 15 MINUTES / **TOTAL TIME:** 3 HOURS AND 15 MINUTES

The smokey char of the grilled vegetables pairs perfectly with a burst of garlicky flavor. Enjoy alongside good bread.

1. Preheat the oven to 375°F.

2. Use a knife to poke a small slit in the jalapeño.

3. Place the tomatoes, green peppers, jalapeño, and garlic onto an aluminum foil-lined baking sheet. Transfer into the oven and roast for about 1 hour, or until the vegetables are browned and just tender.

4. Transfer all of the vegetables from the oven. Place the garlic cloves onto a small plate and set aside. Place the vegetables in a large bowl and cover with plastic wrap. Set aside for about 15 minutes.

5. Discard the plastic wrap and once the vegetables are cool enough to handle, peel the green bell peppers, jalapeño peppers, and tomatoes. Place the peeled tomatoes and peppers into a large colander set over a bowl. Let the vegetables drain.

6. Use a fork to smash the garlic that was set aside.

7. Transfer the drained vegetables onto a cutting board. Remove the seeds from the bell peppers. Finely chop all the vegetables and place them into a mixing bowl. Add the smashed garlic, salt, pepper, lemon juice, and olive oil and mix well until combined.

8. Serve immediately with pita bread.

INGREDIENTS:

1	JALAPEÑO PEPPER
6	LARGE PLUM TOMATOES
3	GREEN BELL PEPPERS
2	GARLIC CLOVES, PEELED
1	TEASPOON SEA SALT
¼	TEASPOON GROUND BLACK PEPPER
¼	CUP OF LEMON JUICE
3	TABLESPOONS OLIVE OIL, OR MORE TO TASTE

SPLIT PEA SOUP

YIELD: 10 SERVINGS / **ACTIVE TIME:** 30 MINUTES / **TOTAL TIME:** 2 HOURS

This is a love-it-or-hate-it kind of dish; some claim that it's their favorite soup, while others shy away from even trying it. Not to brag, but we think this recipe will settle the score.

1. In a large pot, heat the olive oil over medium heat and then sauté the onions until softened and beginning to brown, about 5 minutes.

2. Add the garlic, carrots, and celery and cook for 3 minutes, then add the bay leaves and thyme and season with sea salt and pepper.

3. Add the split peas, lemon zest, and vegetable stock to the pot, stir, bring to a boil, and then simmer, uncovered, for 1½ hours.

4. Remove soup and let cool for about 15 minutes.

5. Using an immersion blender, purée the soup until mostly smooth and silky.

INGREDIENTS:

2	TABLESPOONS AVOCADO OIL
1	LARGE ONION, CHOPPED
1	GARLIC CLOVE, MINCED
2	MEDIUM CARROTS, DICED
2	CELERY STALKS WITH LEAVES, DICED
2	BAY LEAVES
1	TEASPOON THYME
1	TEASPOON SEA SALT
	FRESHLY GROUND BLACK PEPPER, TO TASTE
1	LB. DRIED GREEN SPLIT PEAS
½	TEASPOON LEMON ZEST
1	CUPS VEGETABLE STOCK (SEE PAGE 729)

STRAWBERRY FIELDS SALAD

YIELD: 1 SERVING / **ACTIVE TIME:** 15 MINUTES / **TOTAL TIME:** 15 MINUTES

Do yourself a favor and hold on on making this salad until strawberries are in season.

1. In a medium bowl, combine all of the ingredients, except the herbs and pomegranate reduction, and toss to coat.

2. Garnish with herbs and pomegranate reduction.

INGREDIENTS:

3	OZ. ARUGULA
½	OZ. TUSCAN KALE, TORN
½	OZ. CHERRY TOMATOES, HALVED
½	OZ. FENNEL, SHAVED
1	OZ. STRAWBERRIES, SLICED
½	OZ. GOAT CHEESE, CRUMBLED
3	KALAMATA OLIVES, PITTED AND HALVED LENGTHWISE
1½	OZ. CHAMPAGNE VINAIGRETTE (SEE PAGE 516)
1	TEASPOON MIX OF CHOPPED FRESH TARRAGON, PARSLEY, CHIVES, AND CILANTRO
	POMEGRANATE MOLASSES, TO TASTE

TAHINI CHICKEN SALAD

YIELD: 6 SERVINGS / **ACTIVE TIME:** 1 HOUR / **TOTAL TIME:** 3 HOURS

Using tahini to make mayonnaise adds a nutty zip to this chicken salad.

TO PREPARE THE CHICKEN

1. Remove the skins from the chickens (see page 402).

2. In a large stockpot, combine the chicken, ¼ cup salt, herbs, and garlic. Add the water, topping it off with more if necessary, until the chicken is completely submerged. Squeeze in the lemon and drop it in.

3. With the heat on medium-low, bring the pot just up to a slow simmer, then turn the heat down to low, and let the chicken gently cook with the broth bubbling around it. When you glance into the pot, bubbles should be slowly floating to the top, less than an active simmer—this will keep the meat moist.

4. Check the chicken by cutting into the thickest part of the leg; it's ready when it's no longer pink at the center, about 1½ hours. When it's ready, pull the chicken out to cool; strain the broth, and save it for another use.

5. Once the chicken is cool enough to handle, pull all the meat off the bones, being mindful not to bring along the tendons or excess fat. Give it an even chop, then combine it in a bowl with the Tahini Mayonnaise, scallions, remaining ½ teaspoon salt, and lemon zest. Stir in the Dukkah shortly before serving.

TAHINI MAYONNAISE

1. Combine the egg yolks, tahini, lemon juice, water, and salt—preferably in a food processor, otherwise with a good whisk.

2. Slowly drizzle in the olive oil with the processor still going—or while you whisk vigorously—and continue to blend until the mixture is extremely thick and velvety. Be thorough in this step: a tight emulsion is the difference between having all those flavors hit you in equal measure or having them fall.

3. Once the mayonnaise is nice and smooth, use immediately or refrigerate for a couple of days.

INGREDIENTS:

- 2 (4-5 LB.) WHOLE CHICKENS, SKINS REMOVED
- 1¼ CUP SEA SALT, DIVIDED
- 2 SPRIGS FRESH OREGANO
- 2 SPRIGS FRESH THYME
- 4 FRESH BAY LEAVES
- 2 GARLIC CLOVES CRUSHED
- 1 GALLON WATER, PLUS MORE AS NEEDED
- 1 LEMON, HALVED
- ½ CUP TAHINI MAYONNAISE
- 1 BUNCH SCALLIONS, THINLY SLICED
- GRATED ZEST OF ½ LEMON
- ¼ CUP DUKKAH

TAHINI MAYONNAISE

- 2 EGG YOLKS
- ¼ CUP RAW TAHINI
- 3 TABLESPOONS LEMON JUICE
- 1 TABLESPOON WATER
- 1 TEASPOON SEA SALT
- ½ CUP EXTRA-VIRGIN OLIVE OIL

DUKKAH

1. Preheat the oven to 325°F.

2. Leaving the cloves intact, peel the garlic, trim the ends of each clove, and slice them as thinly and evenly as you can. Trim both ends of the shallot, halve it lengthwise, and thinly slice it, too. Place both in a cold pan with the olive oil, and set it over low heat until they're deep, even golden, about 30 to 40 minutes; stir occasionally, to make sure the heat circulates evenly. This is how they build flavor without any bitterness, so don't try to speed it up with a higher flame.

3. While the garlic and shallots cook spread out the pistachios on a baking sheet and roast them in the oven. Remove them from the oven when they're fragrant, after 6 or 7 minutes.

4. Line a plate with paper towels. Strain the garlic and shallots over a clean bowl, and spread them on the plate in an even layer to drain. Wipe out the pan, and fill it with the oil from the bowl along with the coriander seeds, black sesame seeds, and white sesame seeds. Toast, still over low heat, until they're crunchy and aromatic, another 8 minutes. Drain on the same plate as the shallots and garlic.

5. Add the shallots, garlic, and seeds to a large sealable plastic bag with the nuts, pink peppercorns, salt, sumac, and Aleppo pepper. Pound the mixture with a rolling pin or mallet, just until everything is roughly crushed.

DUKKAH

1	HEAD GARLIC
1	LARGE SHALLOT
¾	CUP EXTRA VIRGIN OLIVE OIL
1	CUP RAW PISTACHIOS
2	TABLESPOONS WHOLE CORIANDER SEEDS
2	TABLESPOONS BLACK SESAME SEEDS
2	TABLESPOONS WHITE SESAME SEEDS
1½	TABLESPOONS WHOLE PINK PEPPERCORNS
1	TABLESPOON MALDON OR OTHER FLAKY SEA SALT
2	TEASPOONS GROUND SUMAC
2	TEASPOONS ALEPPO PEPPER

TOMATO SALAD

YIELD: 4 SERVINGS / **ACTIVE TIME:** 20 MINUTES / **TOTAL TIME:** 20 MINUTES

Some people celebrate summer, but we celebrate tomato season. Is there anything more delicious and refreshing than plump, bright, perfectly-ripe tomatoes? This recipe is one of our favorite ways to enjoy them.

1. In a medium bowl, combine all of the ingredients and mix well. Taste and adjust seasoning, if necessary.

INGREDIENTS:

4   LARGE TOMATOES, PEELED, DESEEDED, AND CHOPPED

1   MEDIUM GREEN PEPPER, DICED

3   TABLESPOONS DRAINED CAPERS

4-5   SCALLIONS, WHITES ONLY, FINELY SLICED

¼   CUP EXTRA VIRGIN OLIVE OIL

2   TABLESPOONS FRESH LEMON JUICE

2   TEASPOONS SALT

½   TEASPOON BLACK PEPPER

TUNISIAN SPICED BUTTERNUT SQUASH SOUP

YIELD: 12 SERVINGS / **ACTIVE TIME:** 30 MINUTES / **TOTAL TIME:** 2 HOURS

This Tunisian-inspired soup layers its flavors. But harissa packs a punch that will make the squash in particular stand out from the rest.

1. Preheat the oven to 400°F.

2. Cut the butternut squash in half, the long way; place on a foil-lined baking sheet, skin-side down.

3. In a small bowl, mix together harissa, sea salt, pepper, lemon juice, lemon and lime zest, and olive oil.

4. Spread spice mixture onto the squash, evenly covering the entire inside; reserve some of the mixture to cover the parsnips and then add them to the baking sheet, along with the garlic cloves.

5. Put the baking sheet in the oven and cook for 1 hour, or until squash is fork tender.

6. While squash is roasting, heat avocado oil in a saucepan and sauté shallots until translucent; add garlic and sauté for another 3 to 4 minutes.

7. When squash is finished roasting, remove and let cool for about 30 minutes.

8. Using a large metal spoon, scoop out the flesh and place it into a food processor along with the parsnips, sautéed shallots, and some stock.

9. Pulse in batches until the mixture is smooth.

10. Put the pureed mixture back into the saucepan, and heat through with stock.

11. Allow to simmer on low for 25 minutes.

12. Season to taste before serving.

INGREDIENTS:

1	LARGE BUTTERNUT SQUASH
1	TEASPOON HARISSA
1	TEASPOON SEA SALT
½	TEASPOON FRESHLY GROUND PEPPER
¼	CUP FRESH LEMON JUICE
1	TABLESPOON LEMON ZEST
½	TABLESPOON LIME ZEST
2	TABLESPOONS EXTRA VIRGIN OLIVE OIL
2	PARSNIPS, PEELED AND CUBED
2	TABLESPOONS AVOCADO OIL
3	SMALL SHALLOTS, DICED
3	GARLIC CLOVES, SLICED
2	QUARTS CHICKEN STOCK (SEE PAGE 722)

VEGETABLE SOUP

YIELD: 12 SERVINGS / **ACTIVE TIME:** 30 MINUTES / **TOTAL TIME:** 2 HOURS

For when you need to eat your vegetables but a salad simply won't do. This warming recipe will leave you feeling full and glowing with good health.

1. In a large stockpot, heat oil and sauté onions for about 5 minutes over medium heat, then add carrots, celery, parsnip, leek, and garlic and sauté for another 5 minutes, until fragrant.

2. Add stock and bay leaves and bring to a boil. Reduce heat and let simmer for about 1 hour, uncovered.

3. After 1 hour, add lemongrass, parsley, and salt and simmer for another 30 minutes.

4. Remove bay leaf and serve.

INGREDIENTS:

2   TABLESPOONS AVOCADO OIL

1   LARGE ONION, ROUGHLY CHOPPED

2   LARGE CARROTS, PEELED AND ROUGHLY CHOPPED

2   LARGE CELERY STALKS WITH LEAVES, ROUGHLY CHOPPED

1   PARSNIP, PEELED AND ROUGHLY CHOPPED

1   LEEK, CLEANED WELL AND ROUGHLY CHOPPED

5   GARLIC CLOVES, SMASHED

9   CUPS VEGETABLE STOCK (SEE PAGE 729)

2   BAY LEAVES

1   STALK LEMONGRASS, SPLIT INTO FOUR SMALL PIECES

1   HANDFUL OF CURLY LEAF PARSLEY, ROUGHLY CHOPPED

2   TABLESPOONS SEA SALT

VEGETARIAN YEMENITE SOUP

YIELD: 12 SERVINGS / **ACTIVE TIME:** 20 MINUTES / **TOTAL TIME:** 1 HOUR AND 15 MINUTES

This is a comforting, healthful, and easy recipe to always have on hand. The blend of spices differentiates it from your repertoire of vegetable soups.

1. Combine half the celery root, carrots, onions, and the garlic in a food processor and pulse until chopped very small.

2. Add the olive oil to a large pot over medium-high heat and add the pureed vegetables and cook for 10 minutes, stirring frequently until onions are translucent.

3. Add tomato paste, sea salt, turmeric, cumin, coriander, and pepper and continue cooking for 4 minutes, stirring frequently.

4. Add stock, bring to a boil, and add the remaining celery root, carrots, and onions, along with the butternut squash and potatoes. Reduce heat and simmer, covered, for 40 minutes.

5. Remove from heat, add the mushrooms, and let stand, covered, for 10 minutes before serving.

INGREDIENTS:

3 CUPS CUBED CELERY ROOT, DIVIDED

2 CUPS SLICED CARROTS, DIVIDED

1½ CUPS CUBED BUTTERNUT SQUASH

1 CUP CHOPPED ONION, DIVIDED

3 GARLIC CLOVES

2 TABLESPOONS EXTRA VIRGIN OLIVE OIL

1 CUP SLICED PARSNIP

1 CUP CUBED RED BLISS POTATOES

4 TABLESPOONS TOMATO PASTE

2 TEASPOONS SEA SALT

2 TEASPOONS TURMERIC

1 TEASPOON CUMIN

1 TEASPOON CORIANDER

½ TEASPOON FRESHLY GROUND BLACK PEPPER

8 CUPS VEGETABLE STOCK (SEE PAGE 729)

10 OZ. ENOKI MUSHROOMS

HOLIDAY MENUS

When it comes to holiday celebrations, the menu is often one of the most important elements to consider. But holiday meals can vary widely based on Sephardic to Ashkenazic to Mizrahic traditions, meaning for Jewish people, there's no one right way to celebrate. These are merely suggestions for possible ways to feed those with whom you are celebrating.

EVE OF YOM KIPPUR

CHALLAH

YIELD: 2 LOAVES / **ACTIVE TIME:** 1 HOUR / **TOTAL TIME:** 5 HOURS

Challah is a special Jewish bread that's usually braided and eaten on occasions such as Shabbat and other major holidays. Beloved by young and old, challah is more than bread, it is a deeply meaningful symbol of cherished family traditions.

1. Add the bread flour, sugar, salt, and yeast in the bowl of a stand mixer fitted with a dough hook. Add the pâte fermentée, egg yolks, honey, water, and oil and mix on low speed until the dry ingredients are completely incorporated and the yeast has disappeared into the dough. Add a little extra water if this hasn't happened in 3 minutes. Increase the speed to medium to medium-high and mix until the dough is smooth, pulls away from the sides of the bowl (and leaves the sides clean), has a bit of shine, and makes a slapping noise against the sides of the bowl, about 5 minutes. Do the windowpane test to check to see if the gluten is fully developed. The dough will look smooth and feel slightly tacky.

2. Coat the inside of a large bowl with oil and transfer the dough to it. Lightly dust the top of the dough with flour and cover the bowl with plastic wrap or put the whole bowl in a large plastic bag. Let stand at room temperature until the dough is puffy and supple, about 1 hour and 30 minutes.

3. Turn the dough out onto a lightly floured surface. Flatten slightly and divide it into 4 equal pieces (each weighing about 7½ oz.). Working with one piece at a time (keep the rest covered with plastic), form a tight log roll. Then, with two hands, give the piece a few rolls on the floured surface so that it forms a thick rope about 18" long. Repeat to make 4 ropes.

4. Leave 2 ropes loosely covered with plastic. Take the first 2 ropes and form a two-strand braid. Form an "X" in front of you with one rope going from the upper right to the lower left on the bottom, and the other on top, going from the upper left to the lower right on top. Fold the top right arm of the X down over the center so it's now facing down toward you. Fold the bottom left arm of the X up over the center so it's now where the top right arm used to be. Do the same with the top left arm and the bottom right arm. Keep building your braid in this fashion until you have no dough left to cross. Turn the braid on its side so that what was the base is now one end of the loaf and squeeze the small end pieces of dough firmly together and tuck them under the braid. Set the braided loaf on a parchment-lined rimmed baking sheet and repeat the process

Continued . . .

INGREDIENTS:

2½	CUPS BREAD FLOUR, PLUS MORE FOR SHAPING
1	TABLESPOON, PLUS 2 TEASPOONS SUGAR
3¼	TEASPOONS KOSHER SALT
1¼	TEASPOONS ACTIVE DRY YEAST
1¼	CUPS PÂTE FERMENTÉE (SEE PAGE 131), CUT INTO WALNUT-SIZE PIECES
3	LARGE EGG YOLKS, BEATEN
2	TABLESPOONS HONEY
3	TABLESPOONS WATER, PLUS MORE IF NEEDED
3	TABLESPOONS CANOLA OIL, PLUS MORE FOR COATING THE BOWL
2	LARGE EGGS, BEATEN

with the remaining 2 ropes of dough to form a second loaf. Evenly space the loaves apart on the baking sheet.

5. Carefully brush the challahs with the beaten eggs, reserving whatever egg is left over for a second egg wash. Put the entire baking sheet in a large plastic bag, or cover the challahs loosely with plastic wrap, and let them stand at room temperature until they have risen, are supple, and hold indentations when pressed lightly, about 1 hour.

6. Preheat the oven to 350°F.

7. Uncover the challahs and gently brush them again with the remaining egg wash. Bake the loaves until they're mahogany colored and sound hollow when you tap them on the bottom, 45 minutes to 1 hour. Insert a thin knife in between the strands to make sure that the dough is firm—it should have the density of a well-baked cake.

8. Transfer the loaves to a wire rack to cool completely, at least 1 hour.

PÂTE FERMENTÉE

French for "fermented dough," this starter needs to be made 8 to 24 hours before preparing this challah recipe.

½ cup, plus 1 teaspoon lukewarm water
⅔ teaspoon active dry yeast
1⅓ cups, plus 1 tablespoon bread flour
1 teaspoon kosher salt

1. Put the water and yeast in the bowl of a stand mixer fitted with a dough hook, then add the flour and salt. Mix on low speed for 2 minutes until combined into a shaggy dough. Cover the bowl with plastic wrap and let stand at room temperature for 30 minutes.

2. Refrigerate the mixture for a minimum of 8 hours and a maximum of 24; there is no need to return it to room temperature before using.

3. If you're measuring the pâte fermentée rather than weighing it, be sure to deflate it with a wooden spoon or with floured fingertips before measuring.

FESENJAN

YIELD: 4 SERVINGS / **ACTIVE TIME:** 50 MINUTES / **TOTAL TIME:** 1 HOUR AND 30 MINUTES

An Iranian stew that is often flavored with pomegranate paste and ground walnuts and spices like turmeric, cinnamon, orange peel, cardamom, and rosebud. This gorgeous dish traditionally features chicken, but variations with ground meat or lamb also exist.

1. Preheat the oven to 350°F.

2. Spread the walnuts evenly on a rimmed baking sheet and bake until fragrant and toasted, 8 to 10 minutes. Set aside.

3. Place a Dutch oven over medium-high heat for 5 minutes. While the pot is heating, combine the salt, pepper, cumin, and turmeric in a small bowl and mix well. Pat the chicken pieces dry and season with the spice mixture, coating evenly.

4. Add the oil to the pot and swirl to coat. Working in 2 or 3 batches, brown the chicken on all sides, being careful not to overcrowd the pot, about 10 minutes per batch. Transfer the seared chicken to a bowl and repeat with the remaining chicken pieces.

5. Remove the pot from heat and let the oil cool slightly before discarding it. Wipe out any remaining burnt spices and return the pot to the stove.

6. Place the chicken in the pan along with the toasted walnuts, Pomegranate Confiture, and saffron, if using, and stir. Bring to a boil over medium-high heat, then reduce the heat to medium-low, cover with a lid, and simmer for 45 minutes, until the chicken is tender and the walnuts are caramelized.

7. Remove the lid and continue to simmer until the sauce has thickened and the chicken is evenly glazed, 15 to 20 minutes. Remove from the heat and serve immediately.

POMEGRANATE CONFITURE

1. Place the pomegranate seeds, sugar, and water in a medium saucepan over medium-high heat and bring to a boil. Lower the heat to a simmer and cook until the mixture is thick and syrupy, about 35 minutes. Stir the mixture occasionally to prevent the bottom from burning. Remove from heat and let cool completely before using.

INGREDIENTS:

2	CUPS SHELLED WALNUT HALVES AND PIECES
1	TABLESPOON, PLUS 1 TEASPOON SEA SALT
2	TEASPOONS FRESHLY GROUND BLACK PEPPER
2	TEASPOONS CUMIN
2	TEASPOONS TURMERIC
2	LBS. CHICKEN THIGHS AND DRUMSTICKS
3	TABLESPOONS AVOCADO OIL
1¼	CUPS POMEGRANATE CONFITURE (SEE RECIPE)
1	PINCH SAFFRON THREADS (OPTIONAL)

POMEGRANATE CONFITURE

6	CUPS POMEGRANATE SEEDS
3	CUPS SUGAR
¼	CUP WATER

ROASTED BRUSSELS SPROUTS
WITH WARM HONEY GLAZE

YIELD: 4 SERVINGS / **ACTIVE TIME:** 30 MINUTES / **TOTAL TIME:** 1 HOUR

By preheating the baking sheet, you'll ensure that every sprout in this goes-with-anything side has that irresistible crispy edge. The warm honey glaze adds a sticky sweetness that always seems to pair beautifully with brussels sprouts.

1. Place a rack in the bottom third of the oven and set a rimmed baking sheet on top; preheat the oven to 450°F. In a large bowl, combine the brussels sprouts and oil, toss well, and season with salt and pepper, to taste.

2. Carefully remove baking sheet from oven. Using tongs, arrange brussels sprouts, cut-side down, on the hot baking sheet. Roast on the bottom rack until tender and deeply browned, 20 to 25 minutes.

3. Meanwhile, bring honey to a simmer in a small saucepan over medium-high heat. Reduce heat to medium-low and cook, stirring often, until honey is a deep amber color but not burnt (it will be foamy), about 3 minutes. Remove from heat; add vinegar and red pepper flakes, if using, and whisk until sauce is smooth (it will bubble quite aggressively when you first add the vinegar).

4. Set the saucepan over medium heat, add butter and ½ teaspoon salt, and cook, whisking constantly, until glaze is glossy, bubbling, and slightly thickened, about 4 minutes.

5. Transfer brussels sprouts to a large bowl. Add glaze and toss to coat. Transfer to a serving platter and top with scallions and lemon zest.

INGREDIENTS:

- 1½ LBS. BRUSSELS SPROUTS, TRIMMED AND HALVED
- ¼ CUP AVOCADO OIL
- ½ TEASPOON SEA SALT, PLUS MORE TO TASTE

  FRESHLY GROUND BLACK PEPPER, TO TASTE
- ¼ CUP HONEY
- ⅓ CUP SHERRY VINEGAR OR RED WINE VINEGAR
- ¾ TEASPOON CRUSHED RED PEPPER FLAKES (OPTIONAL)
- 3 TABLESPOONS UNSALTED BUTTER
- 3 SCALLIONS, THINLY SLICED ON A BIAS
- 1 TEASPOON FINELY GRATED LEMON ZEST

ROASTED GARLIC POTATO KNISH

YIELD: 20 SERVINGS / **ACTIVE TIME:** 1 HOUR AND 25 MINUTES / **TOTAL TIME:** 2 HOURS AND 25 MINUTES

So some people serve these as hors d'oeuvres at dinner parties, some still want theirs from a street vendor. Who are we to judge? We're talking about potatoes, garlic, and Schmaltz, baked or fried to perfection here, so you do you.

1. Beat egg and Schmaltz, and then add in sifted flour, baking powder, and salt and knead until you have a dough that is not sticky. Add water as needed. Cover and refrigerate for at least an hour.

2. Preheat the oven to 400°F.

3. To start the filling, use a small sheet of tinfoil to roast the garlic by making a packet with garlic cloves and a drizzle of Schmaltz or olive oil. Roast until the garlic is soft, about 40 minutes. Then lower the oven to 375°F.

4. In a skillet, heat 1 tablespoon Schmaltz and caramelize the onions.

5. In a large stockpot, add water, salt, and whole potatoes and bring to a boil; cook until you can stick a knife into the potatoes and it comes out without resistance. Strain water and let potatoes cool enough to handle before peeling and crushing with a fork.

6. In a bowl, mix crushed potatoes with ¼ cup Schmaltz, scallions, roasted garlic, caramelized onions, eggs, 1 teaspoon salt, and ½ teaspoon black pepper.

7. There are many ways to form knishes but we like individual round ones. Roll out your dough until it is as thin as you can get it. Then using a paring knife cut out 6" round discs. Put a ½ cup of filling in each circle and fold in the sides to make a round knish.

8. Place the knishes on baking sheets, brush each one with egg wash, and bake until golden brown, about 25 minutes.

INGREDIENTS:

DOUGH

1	EGG, PLUS 1 FOR EGG WASH
½	CUP LIQUID SCHMALTZ (SEE PAGE 528), OR AVOCADO OIL
2	CUPS ALL-PURPOSE FLOUR, SIFTED
½	TEASPOON BAKING POWDER
½	TEASPOON SALT
	WATER AS NEEDED

FILLING

5	GARLIC CLOVES
¼	CUP LIQUID SCHMALTZ (SEE PAGE 528), PLUS 1 TABLESPOON AND MORE FOR DRIZZLING
1	LARGE WHITE ONION
½	TEASPOON SALT
1	LB. RUSSET POTATOES
1	BUNCH SCALLIONS, MINCED
2	EGGS
1	TEASPOON SEA SALT
½	TEASPOON BLACK PEPPER

KARTOFFEL KUGEL

YIELD: 6 SERVINGS / **ACTIVE TIME:** 30 MINUTES / **TOTAL TIME:** 1 HOUR AND 30 MINUTES

There are many variations of potato pudding. This one has a crisp crust and a moist, soft interior. Schmaltz and gribenes add richness and savory flavor, but you can also use vegetable oil and grated carrot if you're going meatless.

1. Preheat the oven to 375°F. Heat an 8" or 9" square baking dish in the oven.

2. Coat the bottom and sides of the baking dish with ¼ cup of the Schmaltz or oil and return to the oven until very hot, about 15 minutes.

3. Place the potatoes in a large bowl of lightly salted cold water; this keeps them from discoloring.

4. Place the onions into a large bowl and then grate the potatoes into the onions, stirring to mix.

5. Stir in the eggs, remaining ¼ cup schmaltz or oil, salt, pepper, and, if desired, Gribenes or carrot. Add enough matzo meal or flour to bind the batter.

6. Pour into the heated dish, top with crushed matzo, and bake until golden brown, about 1 hour. Although this is best when warm, the leftovers can be served at room temperature.

INGREDIENTS:

½ CUP SCHMALTZ (SEE PAGE 528) OR AVOCADO OIL

2 LBS. RUSSET POTATOES, PEELED

1 CUP CHOPPED YELLOW ONIONS

3 LARGE EGGS, LIGHTLY BEATEN

1 TEASPOON SEA SALT

FRESHLY GROUND BLACK PEPPER, TO TASTE

¼ CUP GRIBENES (SEE PAGE 528) OR GRATED CARROT, OPTIONAL

⅓ CUP MATZO MEAL OR ALL-PURPOSE FLOUR

CRUSHED MATZO, TO TOP

HONEY-GLAZED CARROTS
WITH CARROT TOP GREMOLATA

YIELD: 8 SERVINGS / **ACTIVE TIME:** 15 MINUTES / **TOTAL TIME:** 30 MINUTES

Dark honeys, like buckwheat, bring a touch of malty sweetness to these lightly glazed beauties. They're perfect for serving with a crispy-skinned roasted chicken. This recipe comes courtesy of Hannah Krieger, aka Honey and Grandma Honey.

1. Trim and peel the carrots; reserve the tops.

2. Rinse 1 bunch worth of carrot tops and pat dry. Coarsely chop the carrot tops to make ⅔ cup of carrot tops.

3. In a bowl, combine tops with garlic, lemon zest, oil, and remaining salt and mix well; let stand for at least 20 minutes before using.

4. Add carrots, butter, orange juice, honey, and 1 teaspoon salt to a pot over medium heat, cover, and cook until carrots are tender, about 10 minutes.

5. Uncover carrots and continue to cook, stirring occasionally, until sauce reduces enough to coat carrots, 10 minutes.

6. Remove from heat, stir in lemon juice and cayenne, and season to taste.

7. Transfer carrots to a platter and top with gremolata.

INGREDIENTS:

5	LBS. CARROTS, WITH TOPS
2	GARLIC CLOVES, FINELY CHOPPED
1	TABLESPOON LEMON ZEST
2	TEASPOONS EXTRA VIRGIN OLIVE OIL
4	TABLESPOONS UNSALTED BUTTER
⅓	CUP ORANGE JUICE
1	TABLESPOON AMBER HONEY
1¼	TEASPOONS SEA SALT
2	TABLESPOONS FRESH LEMON JUICE
⅛	TEASPOON CAYENNE PEPPER

TO BREAK THE FAST OF YOM KIPPUR

BAGELS

YIELD: 12 BAGELS / **ACTIVE TIME:** 1 HOUR / **TOTAL TIME:** 2 HOURS

It doesn't get much better than waking up on a Sunday morning or breaking a long Yom Kippur fast with lox piled high on a bagel. Traditionally, lox is served with cream cheese and garnished with tomato, red onion, cucumbers, and capers.

1. In a large bowl, dissolve the yeast in warm milk. Add the butter, sugar, salt, and egg yolk and mix well. Stir in enough flour to form a soft dough.

2. Turn the dough onto a floured surface and knead until smooth and elastic, 6 to 8 minutes. Place the dough in a greased bowl, turning once to grease the top. Cover and let rise in a warm place until doubled in size, about 1 hour.

3. Punch down the dough and divide into 12 balls. Push thumb through the centers to form a 1½" hole. Stretch and shape the dough to form an even ring. Place on a floured surface, cover, and let rest for 10 minutes, then flatten bagels slightly.

4. Preheat the oven to 400°F. Fill a Dutch oven two-thirds full with water and bring to a boil.

5. Drop the bagels, 2 at a time, into boiling water. Cook for 45 seconds; turn and cook 45 seconds longer. Remove with a slotted spoon drain well on a paper towel-lined plate.

6. Sprinkle with sesame or poppy seeds, if desired. Place the bagels 2" apart on greased baking sheets. Bake until golden brown, about 25 minutes. Let cool on wire racks.

INGREDIENTS:

1	TEASPOON ACTIVE DRY YEAST
1¼	CUPS WARM 2% MILK (110°F TO 115°F)
½	CUP UNSALTED BUTTER, SOFTENED
2	TABLESPOONS SUGAR
1	TEASPOON SALT
1	EGG YOLK
3¾-4¼	CUPS ALL-PURPOSE FLOUR
	VEGETABLE OIL, FOR GREASING
	SESAME OR POPPY SEEDS (OPTIONAL)

GRANDPA'S GRAVLOX

YIELD: 14 SERVINGS / **ACTIVE TIME:** 1 HOUR / **TOTAL TIME:** 72 HOURS

A tradition to preserve and a recipe to make your zeyde proud. This classic recipe is proof that with a little sugar, salt, and dill, already-delicious and fatty salmon can take on a flavor that you simply can't live without. Grandpa Phil Kramer shared this quintessential Brooklyn-style lox recipe. Make sure to use a very long and very sharp and thin slicing knife when cutting the lox. The thinner the better!

1. Carefully find any pin bones in the salmon by gently running your hand over the flesh; remove them using needle-nose pliers.

2. Score the skin, making 3 or 4 diagonal, 2 to 3" slashes. Center the fillet, skin-side down, on a large piece of cheesecloth or plastic wrap.

3. In a bowl, combine the remainder of the ingredients, mix well, and pack the mixture in an even layer over the flesh of the salmon; the layer of cure should be slightly thinner where the flesh of the fillet tapers and thins toward the tail.

4. Wrap the salmon loosely in the cheesecloth or plastic wrap and place it in a pan that is large enough to allow the fish to lay flat.

5. Refrigerate the fish for 3 days to allow it to cure. After the third day, gently unwrap the fillet and scrape off the cure. Slice the salmon and serve, or wrap and refrigerate for up to 1 week.

INGREDIENTS:

1	(3 LB.) SALMON FILLET, SCALES REMOVED, SKIN ON
2	CUPS PEELED AND GRATED RAW RED BEETS
1¾	CUPS PREPARED HORSERADISH
1	LARGE BUNCH DILL, ROUGHLY CHOPPED
¾	CUP SUGAR
½	CUP COARSE SEA SALT
2	TABLESPOONS CRACKED BLACK PEPPER

GRANDSON'S BEET & VODKA GRAVLOX

YIELD: 14 SERVINGS / **ACTIVE TIME:** 1 HOUR / **TOTAL TIME:** 72 HOURS

This is the quintessential New York Brooklyn style lox recipe from grandpa jazzed up because grandson was a big shot New York chef! Kids these days. Tradition or not, beet and vodka enhance this classic recipe, giving it a zing that even Bubbe can't argue with.

Still, make sure to use a very long and very sharp, thin slicing knife when cutting the lox. The thinner the better! And be sure to treat yourself to a shot of vodka and a taste of caviar as you prepare the salmon.

1. Carefully find any pin bones in the salmon by gently running your hand over the flesh; remove them using needle-nose pliers.

2. Score the skin, making 3 or 4 diagonal, 2 to 3" slashes. Center the fillet, skin-side down, on a large piece of cheesecloth or plastic wrap.

3. In a bowl, combine the cure ingredients, mix well, and pack the mixture in an even layer over the flesh of the salmon; the layer of cure should be slightly thinner where the flesh of the fillet tapers and thins toward the tail.

4. Wrap the salmon loosely in the cheesecloth or plastic wrap and place it in a pan that is large enough to allow the fish to lay flat.

5. Refrigerate the fish for 3 days to allow it to cure. After the third day, gently unwrap the fillet and scrape off the cure. Slice the salmon and serve, or wrap and refrigerate for up to 1 week.

6. Serve lox on toast points with caviar, crème fraîche, and dill sprigs.

INGREDIENTS:

1	(3 LB.) SALMON FILLET, SCALES REMOVED AND SKIN ON
2	CUPS PEELED AND GRATED RAW RED BEETS
¾	CUP PREPARED HORSERADISH
1	CUP VODKA
1	LARGE BUNCH DILL, ROUGHLY CHOPPED
1	LARGE BUNCH CILANTRO, STEMS AND LEAVES
¾	CUP SUGAR
½	CUP COARSE SEA SALT
2	TABLESPOONS CRACKED BLACK PEPPER
1	TABLESPOON SUMAC
	ZEST OF 1 LEMON
	TOAST POINTS, FOR SERVING
1	OZ. GOLDEN OSETRA CAVIAR, TO SERVE
	CRÈME FRAÎCHE, FOR SERVING
	FRESH DILL SPRIGS, FOR SERVING

MATJES HERRING
IN RED WINE SAUCE OR CREAM SAUCE

YIELD: 4 SERVINGS / **ACTIVE TIME:** 20 MINUTES / **TOTAL TIME:** 74 HOURS

This herring can be served raw in vinegar or baked in its marinade and then served cold. Never for the faint of heart, its strong, pungent flavor is only enhanced when served with cut onions.

1. In a pot, combine all of the ingredients, except the herring, bring to a boil, and then remove from heat and let cool.

2. As the stock is being prepared soak the herring in ice water for 3 hours.

3. Add the herring to the stock and refrigerate for 3 days; make sure to stir the marinating fish once per day.

4. Remove the herring from the marinade, slice into bite-sized pieces, and place in a serving bowl.

5. Sieve out and discard the bay leaves and most (but not all) of the pickling spices from the stock, keeping the onions and the marinade with the fish.

6. Finally, add Cream Sauce, combine well, and serve cold.

CREAM SAUCE

1. In a bowl, combine all of the ingredients and mix well.

INGREDIENTS:

½	CUP WHITE WINE VINEGAR
½	CUP RED WINE VINEGAR
1	CUP SUGAR
1½	CUPS WATER
1½	OZ. CARROTS, FINELY CHOPPED
4	WHITE SWEET ONIONS, THINLY SLICED
1½	OZ. CELERY ROOT, GRATED
2	TEASPOONS MASHED GARLIC CLOVES
3	TEASPOONS ALLSPICE
2	CINNAMON STICKS, CRUSHED
5	BAY LEAVES
5	WHITE PEPPERCORNS
5	BLACK PEPPERCORNS
15	CORIANDER SEEDS, TOASTED
2	TEASPOONS NIGELLA SEEDS
1	SMALL PIECE OF HORSERADISH, PEELED
5	SALTED HERRING FILLETS

CREAM SAUCE

3	CUPS FULL-FAT SOUR CREAM
1	CUP HEAVY CREAM
¼	CUP SUGAR
1	TEASPOON SUMAC
2	TEASPOONS GRATED HORSERADISH
1	TEASPOON FRESH CRACKED COARSE BLACK PEPPER
1	TEASPOON CHOPPED DILL
½	TEASPOON CUMIN
¼	TEASPOON SEA SALT

RED CABBAGE, DATE & BEET SALAD

YIELD: 6 SERVINGS / **ACTIVE TIME:** 30 MINUTES / **TOTAL TIME:** 1 HOUR AND 30 MINUTES

This salad is a beautiful burst of deep reds and savory-sweet ingredients.

1. Preheat the oven to 395°F. Line a baking sheet with parchment paper and cover with kosher salt.

2. Place the beets on the bed of kosher salt and bake for about 40 minutes, until fork-tender. Let the beets cool for 30 minutes and then peel them, discarding the peels and salt.

3. Julienne the beets, cutting them into 2" slices that are ⅛" thick or use a grater and grate the beets into a bowl.

4. Add all of the remaining ingredients to the beets, mix well, and season to taste. Serve immediately.

INGREDIENTS:

2	CUPS KOSHER SALT
6	LARGE RED BEETS
½	HEAD RED CABBAGE, CORED AND THINLY SLICED CROSSWISE
5	DRIED MEDJOOL DATES, PITTED AND THINLY SLICED LENGTHWISE
½	CUP TEHINA
⅓	CUP FINELY CHOPPED CILANTRO
⅓	CUP FINELY CHOPPED MINT
⅓	CUP FINELY CHOPPED SCALLIONS
1	TEASPOON SEA SALT
¼	CUP EXTRA VIRGIN OLIVE OIL
¼	CUP FRESH LEMON JUICE

PICKLED CUCUMBER SALAD

YIELD: 8 SERVINGS / **ACTIVE TIME:** 10 MINUTES / **TOTAL TIME:** 25 MINUTES

Pickles and other pickled veggies play a big part in Jewish cuisine. This salad in particular marries those traditional flavors in a dish with lots of squeaky bite.

1. In a large bowl, combine the sugar and vinegar and whisk until the sugar is dissolved.

2. Place the cucumber and onion slices in the marinade for at least 15 minutes.

3. Sprinkle with salt, pepper, and parsley and serve.

INGREDIENTS:

1   TEASPOON SUGAR

¼   CUP RICE VINEGAR

2   LARGE CUCUMBERS, PEELED AND THINLY SLICED CROSSWISE

½   MEDIUM RED ONION, THINLY SLICED

    SEA SALT, TO TASTE

    FRESHLY GROUND BLACK PEPPER

1   TABLESPOON CHOPPED CURLY-LEAF PARSLEY

PICKLED GREEN TOMATOES

YIELD: 2 PINTS / **ACTIVE TIME:** 15 MINUTES / **TOTAL TIME:** 1 WEEK

We're not saying you can't eat a pastrami sandwich without these, but why would you want to? Squeaky, soft, sweet, and acidic, each bite of pickled green tomatoes is a burst of different sensations.

1. Combine vinegar, water, sugar, spices, and salt in a saucepan. Bring to a boil, stirring until sugar is dissolved.

2. Fill clean containers tightly with tomatoes and onion.

3. Add boiling brine to cover completely. Let cool completely.

4. Cover, label, and refrigerate at least 1 week before serving, or up to 3 months.

INGREDIENTS:

1½	CUPS DISTILLED WHITE VINEGAR OR APPLE-CIDER VINEGAR
¾	CUP WATER
2	TEASPOONS SUGAR
½	TEASPOON WHOLE BLACK PEPPERCORNS
½	TEASPOON CORIANDER SEEDS
½	TEASPOON CARAWAY SEEDS
½	TEASPOON CUMIN SEEDS
3	WHOLE ALLSPICE BERRIES
2	DRIED BAY LEAVES
2	TABLESPOONS COARSE SEA SALT
1	LB. SMALL GREEN TOMATOES, CUT INTO ¼" SLICES
6	THIN SLICES WHITE ONION

ROSH HASHANAH

Modern Hummus, page 160

MODERN HUMMUS

YIELD: 20 SERVINGS / **ACTIVE TIME:** 1 HOUR / **TOTAL TIME:** 12 HOURS

While stories of origin might differ, hummus is beloved and considered a staple. This recipe shows how simple this classic dish is to make—and how the flavor of this homemade dip and spread far outshines anything from the store.

1. In a pot combine chickpeas, baking soda, and water, stir, and soak overnight at room temperature, covered.

2. The next day, drain the water and rinse the chickpeas in a colander.

3. In a large pot, combine the chickpeas and stock (or water if stock isn't available) and cook at a high simmer until the chickpeas are quite soft, about 1 hour.

4. In a blender or food processor, combine all of the remaining ingredients, except the chickpeas, and puree until achieving a perfectly smooth, creamy sauce; the ice water is the key to getting the correct consistency.

5. Add the warm, drained chickpeas to the tahini mixture and blend until perfectly smooth and not at all grainy, occasionally stopping to scrape down the sides of the bowl. This blending may take 3 minutes; keep going until the mixture is ultra-creamy and fluffy, adding a little water to make the hummus move.

6. Season to taste, adding more salt, lemon juice, and/or cumin as needed.

INGREDIENTS:

32	OZ. DRIED CHICKPEAS
3	TEASPOONS BAKING SODA
96	OZ. WATER
96	OZ. VEGETABLE STOCK OR CORN STOCK (SEE PAGE 729 OR PAGE 533)
8	OZ. TAHINI
2	TABLESPOONS ZA'ATAR (SEE PAGE 545)
2	TABLESPOONS SUMAC
2	TABLESPOONS CUMIN
2	TABLESPOONS SEA SALT
2	TABLESPOONS BLACK PEPPER
2	GARLIC CLOVES, GRATED
½	BUNCH CILANTRO, ROUGHLY CHOPPED
1	CUP EXTRA VIRGIN OLIVE OIL
1	CUP SESAME OIL
1	CUP ICE WATER
½	CUP FRESH LEMON JUICE

BABA GHANOUSH

YIELD: 12 SERVINGS / **ACTIVE TIME:** 15 MINUTES / **TOTAL TIME:** 1 HOUR AND 15 MINUTES

Though recipes may vary and this or that can be added to please any palate, there are some basic rules for preparing this eggplant dish. Like hummus, this spread can be enhanced with tahini and various spices.

1. Preheat the oven to 400°F.

2. On a sheet pan with a roasting rack, place the halved eggplants cut side up and roast for 50 minutes until they are soft when poked with a fork or knife. Remove from the oven and allow to cool for 10 minutes.

3. When the eggplants are cool to the touch, use a large spoon to scoop out the flesh of the eggplant; discard the skin.

4. Place scooped flesh of the eggplant in the bowl of a food processor, along with the garlic, lemon juice, salt, and tahini and blend for 1 minute, until the mixture is a smooth and creamy consistency. Season with additional lemon juice and salt to taste.

5. Transfer to a bowl, garnish with pomegranate seeds, parsley, and olive oil.

TIP: This is a simple iconic dish that can be prepared in a variety of ways. If you have access to a grill or open charcoal fire you can opt to char the eggplants over open flame to intensify their nutty and smoky aromas and flavors.

INGREDIENTS:

2	LARGE EGGPLANTS, HALVED
4	GARLIC CLOVES, SMASHED
4	TEASPOONS FRESH LEMON JUICE, PLUS MORE TO TASTE
1½	TEASPOONS SEA SALT, PLUS MORE TO TASTE
½	CUP TAHINI
¼	CUP POMEGRANATE SEEDS
2	TEASPOONS MINCED PARSLEY
¼	CUP EXTRA VIRGIN OLIVE OIL
	PITA BREAD (SEE PAGE 697), TO SERVE

Baba Ghanoush, page 161

ARUGULA SALAD WITH PICKLED BEETS & PRESERVED-LEMON VINAIGRETTE

YIELD: 4 SERVINGS / **ACTIVE TIME:** 20 MINUTES / **TOTAL TIME:** 3 HOURS AND 45 MINUTES

This is a bright salad perfect for almost any time of the year, although peppery arugula is usually best in spring and fall. The treat here is the vinaigrette, which enlivens all of the other ingredients.

1. Place each beet in its own small pot, cover with water, and simmer until a paring knife can easily pierce the beets, about 30 minutes. Cool beets, peel, and slice into thin half-moons. Reserve each beet in a separate bowl to ensure that the red beet slices don't stain the yellow ones.

2. Add the vinegar, sugar, and 1 cup water to a small pot, bring to a boil and then remove from heat. Divide the hot brine between the beets; let sit at room temperature until pickled, 3 to 4 hours.

3. Preheat the oven to 300°F.

4. In a small mixing bowl, whip the egg white until frothy, then add the pistachios and spices, toss to coat, and spread on a parchment-lined baking sheet. Bake until golden and fragrant, 15 minutes. Nuts will crisp as they cool.

5. In a medium bowl, combine the preserved lemon, oil, lemon juice, red pepper flakes, thyme, and salt and whisk well. Toss the arugula in the vinaigrette.

6. Arrange the pickled beets on a serving platter and place the dressed arugula on top of the beets. Sprinkle with the pistachios, drizzle with balsamic, and top with black pepper. Serve immediately.

INGREDIENTS:

PICKLED BEETS

1	LARGE RED BEET, SCRUBBED
1	LARGE YELLOW BEET, SCRUBBED
1	CUP RICE WINE VINEGAR
1	CUP GRANULATED SUGAR
1	EGG WHITE
½	CUP SHELLED RAW PISTACHIOS
½	TABLESPOON CREOLE OR CAJUN SEASONING
1	TABLESPOON MINCED PRESERVED LEMON
6	TABLESPOONS EXTRA VIRGIN OLIVE OIL
2	TABLESPOONS FRESH LEMON JUICE
¼	TEASPOON RED PEPPER FLAKES
1	SPRIG FRESH THYME, LEAVES FINELY CHOPPED
1	PINCH SALT
5	OUNCES (8 CUPS) ARUGULA
2	TABLESPOONS GOOD-QUALITY AGED BALSAMIC VINEGAR
	FRESHLY GROUND BLACK PEPPER, FOR SERVING

ITALIAN SWEET & SOUR FISH

YIELD: 4 SERVINGS / **ACTIVE TIME:** 10 MINUTES / **TOTAL TIME:** 30 MINUTES

This is a beloved Italian recipe for Rosh Hashanah. The red wine vinegar and honey combine to create that unmistakable contrast of flavors.

1. Preheat the oven to 400°F.

2. Season fish with salt and pepper, to taste, and place in a 9" x 13" pan.

3. In a small bowl, combine the vinegar, honey, oil, and 1 teaspoon salt, mix well, and pour mixture over the fish. Sprinkle raisins and pine nuts over the fish.

4. Bake until fish is no longer translucent throughout. For a very thin fish this will only take about 10 minutes. For a thicker fillet, such as halibut, this will take up to 20 minutes. Baste after 10 minutes if the fish is not yet ready.

5. Prior to serving, sprinkle with minced parsley. Serve hot or at room temperature.

INGREDIENTS:

4	LBS. WHITE-FLESHED FISH
1	TEASPOON SEA SALT, PLUS MORE TO TASTE
	BLACK PEPPER, TO TASTE
¼	CUP APPLE CIDER OR RED WINE VINEGAR
1	TABLESPOON HONEY
½	CUP AVOCADO OIL
⅓	CUP GOLDEN RAISINS, ROUGHLY CHOPPED
⅓	CUP PINE NUTS
2	TABLESPOONS MINCED PARSLEY, TO GARNISH

SEPHARDIC JEWELED ROSH HASHANAH RICE

YIELD: 4 SERVINGS / **ACTIVE TIME:** 25 MINUTES / **TOTAL TIME:** 1 HOUR AND 15 MINUTES

This gorgeous and fragrant dish has Persian origins. It is bejeweled with various nuts and dried fruits, making it perfectly adorned for a wedding celebration

1. In a small bowl, combine the salt, paprika, turmeric, cumin, and black pepper, mix well, and set aside.

2. Add 2 tablespoons oil to a pan with a lid over medium heat. Add the rice and the spice mix and stir well. Cook for about 4 minutes, stirring constantly and making sure the rice gets well coated with the oil and the spices.

3. Add the stock, bring to a boil, cover, and reduce heat to low. Cook for 20 minutes, remove from heat, and let it sit, covered, for 15 minutes.

4. Add 2 tablespoons oil and the onions to a pan over medium heat and cook for 20 minutes, stirring frequently, adding stock 1 tablespoon at a time to prevent from burning, if necessary.

5. Transfer onions to a plate and in the same skillet, heat remaining olive oil over low heat and add dried fruit, pomegranate juice, and pistachios and cook for 3 minutes, stirring frequently.

6. Once the rice is ready, fluff it with a fork, add onions, dried fruit, pistachios, lemon and orange zest, and toss well.

7. Right before serving sprinkle pomegranate seeds on the rice.

INGREDIENTS:

1½	TEASPOONS SEA SALT
1	TEASPOON SWEET PAPRIKA
½	TEASPOON TURMERIC
¼	CUMIN
⅛	TEASPOON FRESHLY GROUND BLACK PEPPER
4	TABLESPOONS EXTRA VIRGIN OLIVE OIL, PLUS 1 TEASPOON
1	CUP JASMINE RICE
1	CUP CHICKEN STOCK (SEE PAGE 722), PLUS MORE AS NEEDED
2	MEDIUM ONIONS, DICED
10	DRIED APRICOTS, QUARTERED
6	DRIED FIGS, QUARTERED
¼	CUP DRIED CHERRIES
¼	CUP SHELLED PISTACHIOS
1	TABLESPOON POMEGRANATE JUICE
1½	TEASPOONS LEMON ZEST
½	TEASPOON ORANGE ZEST
1	CUP POMEGRANATE SEEDS

DATE COCONUT ROLLS

YIELD: 12 SERVINGS / **ACTIVE TIME:** 30 MINUTES / **TOTAL TIME:** 2 HOURS

An essential for your Rosh Hashanah spread. The New Year prayer typically spoken before eating a date asks that the wicked cease.

1. In a food processor, combine the almonds and dates and pulse until a paste forms; it is okay is larger chunks of almond remain. Remove the balled up paste from the food processor and roll into 2" logs or balls.

2. Pour the coconut into a shallow dish and then roll and press the date mixture in the coconut. While rolling your hands may become sticky due to the sugar in the dates; rinse your hands with cold water to handle the mixture easily.

3. Refrigerate for at least an hour before serving.

INGREDIENTS:

1   CUP WHOLE ALMONDS

1   LB. PITTED DATES

1   CUP SHREDDED AND
     CHOPPED COCONUT
     (SWEETENED OR
     UNSWEETENED)

PASSOVER

MATZO BREI

YIELD: 2 SERVINGS / **ACTIVE TIME:** 10 MINUTES / **TOTAL TIME:** 20 MINUTES

Matzo Brei is eaten during Passover, when leavened bread is strictly forbidden. This recipe, which calls for dry matzo to be broken into pieces, softened in water or milk, mixed with eggs, and fried, is a great substitute for those who enjoy eggs and toast for breakfast.

1. In a large bowl, break matzo into fragments. Not too small! Sprinkle with a little boiling water—no more than ¼ cup.

2. While matzo is softening, beat the eggs. Pour over softened matzo, add salt and pepper, and mix well.

3. Add oil to a frying pan over medium heat. When the oil is hot, add the matzo mixture, stirring until the brei is dry but not crisp, about 7 to 10 minutes.

4. Serve with cinnamon and sugar, honey, or preserves (blackberry jam is particularly good). Matzo brei cools quickly. It can be reheated in the microwave.

INGREDIENTS:

6 SHEETS OF MATZO

   BOILING WATER

4 EGGS

   SEA SALT, TO TASTE

   WHITE PEPPER, TO TASTE

1 TABLESPOON AVOCADO
   OIL

CHAROSET

YIELD: 6 SERVINGS / **ACTIVE TIME:** 15 MINUTES / **TOTAL TIME:** 1 HOUR AND 15 MINUTES

This sweet apple-wine-nut mixture is eaten on Passover not just for its sweetness but to represent the mortar the slaves used in building the pyramids.

1. Place the walnuts in a skillet over low heat and cook until lightly browned, stirring occasionally.

2. In a large bowl, toss apples and walnuts with wine.

3. In a small bowl, mix the sugar and cinnamon and then sprinkle over apple mixture and toss to combine.

4. Refrigerate, covered, for 1 hour before serving. If desired, serve with matzo.

INGREDIENTS:

½   CUP FINELY CHOPPED WALNUTS

3   MEDIUM GALA OR FUJI APPLES, PEELED AND FINELY CHOPPED

2   TABLESPOONS SWEET RED WINE OR GRAPE JUICE

2   TABLESPOONS SUGAR

1   TEASPOON GROUND CINNAMON

    MATZO (OPTIONAL)

ROMANO BEANS WITH
MUSTARD VINAIGRETTE & WALNUTS

YIELD: 8 SERVINGS / **ACTIVE TIME:** 15 MINUTES / **TOTAL TIME:** 1 HOUR

Romano beans, also known as Italian pole beans, are wide and flat and have a less delicate texture than green beans but share their mild, sweet flavor.

1. Preheat the oven to 350°F.

2. Toast walnuts on a rimmed baking sheet, tossing once, until golden brown, 8 to 10 minutes. Let cool, then coarsely chop.

3. Cook the beans in a large pot of boiling salted water until bright green and tender, 8 to 10 minutes. Using a slotted spoon, transfer to a bowl of ice water and let cool. Drain and pat dry.

4. Meanwhile, in a large bowl, combine the vinegar, mustard, garlic, and 2 tablespoons oil and mix well. Let sit for 10 minutes for flavors to come together.

5. Add walnuts and beans to dressing. Finely zest lemon over beans and add parsley. Season with salt and lots of pepper and toss to coat. Transfer to a platter and drizzle with more oil.

INGREDIENTS:

1	CUP WALNUTS
3	LBS. ROMANO BEANS OR GREEN BEANS, TRIMMED
3	TABLESPOONS RED WINE VINEGAR
2	TABLESPOONS DIJON MUSTARD
1	GARLIC CLOVE, FINELY GRATED
2	TABLESPOONS EXTRA VIRGIN OLIVE OIL, PLUS MORE FOR DRIZZLING
	ZEST OF ½ LEMON
¾	CUP VERY COARSELY CHOPPED PARSLEY
	FRESHLY GROUND BLACK PEPPER, TO TASTE

GEFILTE FISH

YIELD: 12 TO 16 PIECES / **ACTIVE TIME:** 30 MINUTES / **TOTAL TIME:** 1 HOUR AND 30 MINUTES

Gefilte fish is one of those foods that your cousin dares you to try every year on Passover. Although opinions vary on this traditional Jewish food, white fish lovers can rejoice while noshing on this appetizer. In the Torah, it uses the word "blessing" three times with the first regarding the creation of fish. When a person eats fish on Shabbat, he or she is the beneficiary of a triple blessing. This recipe has been provided by Nana Tillie and Grandma Fannie.

1. In a large stockpot, combine water, wine, onion, carrot, lemon, bay leaves, and salt. Create an herb pouch with the thyme, parsley, peppercorns and fennel seeds and add to the pot. Cover the pot and bring to a simmer over medium-low heat for 30 minutes. Discard herb pouch. Remove 1 quart of broth and chill for later to cool cooked fish. Set aside the remainder of the broth.

2. Place fish and all remaining ingredients, except matzo meal and water, in a food processor and puree until smooth, about 2 to 3 minutes. When the mixture is well combined and smooth, transfer to a chilled bowl and add matzo meal hydrated by the water to create a binder. Mix until thoroughly incorporated and refrigerate for 1 hour.

3. In a separate bowl, fill with ice water and wet your hands in the water as you roughly shape 4 oz. portions of the fish mixture into ovals. Refrigerate the raw fish once formed.

4. Bring the cooking broth to a gentle simmer.

5. Working in batches, add one layer of the gefilte fish to the pot and poach until the fish turns opaque and its shape is set, about 5 minutes. Using a slotted spoon turn the fish over and continue to cook, until the fish is fully poached, about 12 to 15 minutes. Using a thermometer, check the temperature of the fish, it should read 135°F.

6. Remove the gefilte fish from the poaching liquid and transfer to a cold bowl, allowing the gefilte fish to cool in the cold reserved broth from earlier. Place the whole bowl on top of another bowl of ice for about 20 minutes until completely chilled. Place cooked fish in the refrigerator overnight before serving.

TIP: Keep all of the fish in a bowl in ice. The colder the fish is the better it will be to make the force meat.

INGREDIENTS:

COOKING BROTH
- 4 QUARTS WATER
- 2½ CUPS DRY WHITE WINE
- 1 MEDIUM ONION, THINLY SLICED
- 1 MEDIUM CARROT, PEELED AND SLICED INTO ROUNDS
- ½ LEMON, CUT INTO SLICES
- 2 BAY LEAVES
- 2 TABLESPOONS SEA SALT
- ½ BUNCH FRESH THYME
- ½ BUNCH FRESH FLAT LEAF PARSLEY
- ¼ TEASPOON WHOLE BLACK PEPPERCORNS
- ¼ TEASPOON WHOLE FENNEL SEEDS

FISH
- 1 LB. SKINLESS FILLETED COD, DICED INTO SMALL ½ INCH PIECES
- 1 LB. SKINLESS FILLETED WHITE FISH, DICED INTO SMALL ½" PIECES
- 1 LB. SKINLESS FILLETED PIKE, DICED INTO SMALL ½" PIECES
- 1 CUP GRATED ONION
- ½ CUP GRATED CARROT
- ½ CUP GRATED CELERY
- 1 LEMON, ZESTED
- 1 TABLESPOON MINCED FENNEL FRONDS
- 3 EXTRA-LARGE EGGS
- ½ CUP HEAVY CREAM
- 2 TABLESPOONS SUGAR
- 1 TEASPOON GARLIC POWDER
- 1 TABLESPOON SEA SALT
- 1½ TEASPOONS FRESH GROUND BLACK PEPPER
- ½ CUP MATZO MEAL
- ¼ CUP COLD WATER

OLIVE SALAD

YIELD: 6 SERVINGS / **ACTIVE TIME:** 15 MINUTES / **TOTAL TIME:** 15 MINUTES

A starter with Persian roots also popularized in Jewish Chilanga cuisine. This cold salad is made ahead by combining green olives, garlic, and pomegranate.

1. In a bowl, combine the olives, garlic, and pomegranate seeds and mix well.

2. In another bowl, add the pomegranate concentrate, ⅓ cup mint, and olive oil and mix until combined into a dressing. Pour the dressing over the olive mixture and stir well, until evenly coated. Add salt and pepper and mix well. Place the salad into an airtight container and refrigerate until serving.

3. Transfer the salad into a serving bowl and garnish with walnuts and remaining tablespoon of mint.

INGREDIENTS:

- 2 CUPS PITTED GREEN OLIVES
- 2 GARLIC CLOVES, FINELY CHOPPED
- 1 CUP POMEGRANATE SEEDS
- ⅓ CUP POMEGRANATE CONCENTRATE
- ⅓ CUP PLUS 1 TABLESPOON ROUGHLY CHOPPED MINT, DIVIDED
- ⅓ CUP OLIVE OIL
- 1 TEASPOON SEA SALT
- ¼ TEASPOON GROUND BLACK PEPPER
- 1 TEASPOON ROUGHLY CRUSHED ROASTED WALNUTS, FOR GARNISH

RUSTIC MATZO BALL SOUP

YIELD: 12 SERVINGS / **ACTIVE TIME:** 30 MINUTES / **TOTAL TIME:** 2 HOURS

This recipe has been shared by Lynn Krieger Gilden, lovingly known as Mom, Minama, and Grandma Lynn.

1. Place chicken in a large stockpot, add the stock, 1 teaspoon salt, and enough water to cover the chicken. Bring to a boil. Reduce heat and simmer until there is no more need for skimming the surface as foam rises.

2. Add the remainder of the ingredients and bring to a boil, then reduce heat and simmer for 1 hour and 30 minutes.

3. When done remove the chicken and set aside.

4. Add some of the contents of the pot to a food processor and puree. Place the puree into a clean pot and repeat until three-quarters of the pot is blended. Reserve the leftover carrots, onions, and celery to add to each soup bowl.

5. In a small bowl, whisk eggs and oil. Add the remainder of the ingredients and mix with a fork until combined. Cover and refrigerate for 15 minutes.

6. Remove and discard skin and bones from chicken; chop chicken and add to the blended soup. Stir in parsley, bring to a boil.

7. Using a teaspoon and wet hands, scoop 12 rounded matzo balls and gently add to the boiling soup.

8. Reduce heat, cover, and simmer for 25 minutes, or until a toothpick inserted into a matzo ball comes out clean; do not lift cover while simmering.

9. With a slotted spoon, carefully remove matzo balls and place 2 or 3 in each soup bowl.

INGREDIENTS:

SOUP

1	(4 LB.) WHOLE CHICKEN
2	LBS. CHICKEN LEGS
2	LBS. CHICKEN THIGHS
1	(14½ OZ.) CAN CHICKEN STOCK
1¾	TEASPOONS SEA SALT, DIVIDED
1	LB. CARROTS, CHOPPED
½	LB. PARSNIP, CHOPPED
6	CELERY RIBS, CHOPPED
3	MEDIUM SWEET ONIONS, CHOPPED
1	GARLIC CLOVE, MINCED
¼	TEASPOON BLACK PEPPER
¼	CUP MINCED PARSLEY
¼	TEASPOON CELERY SALT
¼	TEASPOON ONION POWDER

MATZO BALLS

4	EGGS
5	TABLESPOONS UNSALTED BUTTER
1½	TABLESPOONS SCHMALTZ (SEE PAGE 528)
⅓	CUP WATER
12	OZ. MATZO MEAL
¼	CUP DICED ONION,
1	TABLESPOON GARLIC POWDER
1	TEASPOON ONION POWDER
1	TEASPOON SEA SALT
1	TEASPOON BLACK PEPPER

TZIMMES CHICKEN
WITH APRICOTS, PRUNES & CARROTS

YIELD: 8 SERVINGS / **ACTIVE TIME:** 50 MINUTES / **TOTAL TIME:** 1 HOUR AND 40 MINUTES

This holiday-ready dinner has all the flavors of tzimmes, the traditional side dish made with stewed dried fruits and honey. Roasted on baking sheets with colorful young carrots, it feeds a crowd with minimal effort.

1. Arrange racks in the top and lower thirds of the oven and preheat it to 400°F.

2. Season chicken pieces with 2 teaspoons salt.

3. In a large bowl, combine the honey, oil, lemon juice, pepper, cinnamon, cumin, cayenne, and remaining 2 teaspoons salt and whisk well. Add chicken pieces, carrots, onion, garlic, apricots, prunes, and thyme and toss to combine.

4. Divide everything, except the chicken, between 2 rimmed baking sheets.

5. In a measuring cup, combine the wine with ½ cup water, then pour half over each sheet.

6. Cover sheets tightly with foil and roast for 15 minutes, then remove from the oven. Remove foil, divide chicken between sheets, and continue to roast, rotating sheets top to bottom halfway through, until carrots are fork-tender, chicken is golden brown, and an instant-read thermometer inserted into the thickest part of a breast registers 165°F, 30 to 35 minutes (if some pieces of chicken are finished before others, transfer them to a serving platter).

7. Transfer chicken mixture to a serving platter. Pour pan juices over. If desired, top with parsley before serving.

INGREDIENTS:

2 (4 LB.) WHOLE CHICKEN, BROKEN DOWN INTO 8 PIECES, WINGS AND BACKBONES RESERVED FOR ANOTHER USE

4 TEASPOONS SEA SALT, DIVIDED

½ CUP PLUS 2 TABLESPOONS HONEY

½ CUP AVOCADO OIL

½ CUP FRESH LEMON JUICE

2 TEASPOONS FRESHLY GROUND BLACK PEPPER

2 TEASPOONS CINNAMON

1 TEASPOON CUMIN

¼ TEASPOON CAYENNE PEPPER

2 LBS. CARROTS, PREFERABLY YOUNG CARROTS WITH GREENS ATTACHED, HALVED LENGTHWISE

1 LARGE RED ONION, CUT INTO ½" WEDGES

12 GARLIC CLOVES, PEELED

8 OZ. DRIED APRICOTS

8 OZ. DRIED PRUNES

20 SPRIGS FRESH THYME

1½ CUPS DRY WHITE WINE

PARSLEY LEAVES WITH TENDER STEMS, FOR SERVING (OPTIONAL)

CHEESECAKE

YIELD: 8 SERVINGS / **ACTIVE TIME:** 1 HOUR / **TOTAL TIME:** 10 HOURS

Considered one of the earliest recipes that the Central European Jewish community assimilated, now the world associates cheesecake with New York City. And who can blame them? It's rumored that the original deli cheesecake came from Lindy's on Broadway before being picked up by Jewish-owned Kraft as a way to sell their cream cheese. The rest is dense-yet-pillowy history when it comes to this rich dessert only made more perfect by a simple fruit topping.

1. Preheat the oven to 350°F.

2. Butter the bottom and side of a 9" springform pan.

3. Wrap the outside with aluminum foil, covering the bottom and extending it all the way up the side.

4. In a bowl, sift the flour, baking powder, and sea salt together.

5. In a bowl, using an electric mixer, beat the egg yolks on high for 2½ minutes.

6. With the mixer running, slowly add 2 tablespoons sugar and continue beating until thick, light-yellow ribbons form in the bowl, about 5 minutes more.

7. Mix in 1¼ teaspoons vanilla extract.

8. Sift the flour mixture over the batter and stir it in by hand, just until there are no remaining white flecks.

9. Blend in the melted butter.

10. In another bowl, beat the egg whites and cream of tartar together on high until frothy.

11. Gradually add the remaining sugar and continue beating until stiff peaks form.

12. Fold about one-third of the egg whites into the batter and then fold in the remaining egg whites.

13. Spread the batter over the bottom of the prepared pan and bake until just set and golden, about 10 minutes.

14. Remove pan from oven and set aside to cool.

15. In a bowl, using an electric mixer, beat 1 package of the softened cream cheese, ⅓ cup sugar, and the cornstarch together on low speed until creamy, about 3 minutes, scraping the bottom and sides of the bowl several times during the mixing process.

INGREDIENTS:

CRUST

1	TABLESPOON UNSALTED BUTTER, SOFTENED
⅓	CUP CAKE FLOUR, SIFTED
¾	TEASPOON BAKING POWDER
⅛	TEASPOON SEA SALT
2	EXTRA-LARGE YOLKS, SEPARATED
⅓	CUP GRANULATED WHITE SUGAR

CAKE

1¼	TEASPOONS PURE VANILLA EXTRACT, PLUS 1 TABLESPOON, DIVIDED
2	TABLESPOONS UNSALTED BUTTER, MELTED
¼	TEASPOON CREAM OF TARTAR
4	(8 OZ.) PACKAGES OF CREAM CHEESE
1⅔	CUPS GRANULATED SUGAR, DIVIDED
¼	CUP CORNSTARCH
2	EXTRA-LARGE EGGS
¾	CUP HEAVY WHIPPING CREAM
⅔	CUPS SOUR CREAM

16. Blend in the remaining cream cheese, 1 package at a time, beating well and scraping down the bottom of the bowl several times after each block.

17. Increase the mixer speed to medium and beat in the remaining sugar, then add the vanilla and mix again. Increase mixer speed and continue to blend batter

18. Blend in the eggs, 1 egg at a time, beating well after each egg.

19. Beat in the heavy whipping cream until just completely blended.

20. Preheat the oven to 350°F.

21. Gently spoon the batter over the crust.

22. Place the cake pan in a large shallow pan. Make a water bath by adding enough hot water so it comes halfway up the side of the springform pan. Bake for about 1 hour and 15 minutes.

23. The cheesecake edges should look golden brown, and the center should be a lighter golden. If the center looks too soft, bake for an additional 8 minutes.

24. Remove the cheesecake from the water bath, let cool for 2 hours, and then cover with plastic wrap and refrigerate overnight.

25. Serve cold with a fresh fruit compote.

HANNUKAH

Latkes, page 196

LATKES

YIELD: 12 SERVINGS / **ACTIVE TIME:** 20 MINUTES / **TOTAL TIME:** 45 MINUTES

Often served on Hanukkah, latkes are essentially fried potato pancakes topped with anything from sour cream to applesauce. The tradition of the latke is focused on the oil rather than the potato. It symbolizes the miracle of Hanukkah when, thousands of years ago, one night's oil lasted for eight nights.

1. Combine the potatoes and onion is a large cheesecloth-lined bowl and squeeze out as much liquid as possible.

2. Transfer the mixture to a large dry bowl, add the eggs, flour, salt, baking powder, and pepper, and mix until the flour is absorbed.

3. In a medium heavy-bottomed pan over medium-high heat, pour in about ¼" of oil.

4. Once the oil is hot, drop tablespoons of batter into the hot pan, being sure not to overcrowd the pan, and use a spatula to flatten and shape the drops into pancakes.

5. When the edges of the latkes are brown and crispy, about 5 minutes, flip, and cook until the second side is deeply browned, about another 5 minutes.

6. Transfer the latkes to a paper towel-lined plate to drain and sprinkle with salt while still warm.

7. Repeat with the remaining batter.

8. Serve with sour cream or applesauce.

INGREDIENTS:

1   LB. RUSSET POTATOES, GRATED

1   LARGE ONION, GRATED

3   LARGE EGGS

½   CUP ALL-PURPOSE FLOUR

2   TEASPOONS SEA SALT

1   TEASPOON BAKING POWDER

½   TEASPOON FRESHLY GROUND BLACK PEPPER

      AVOCADO OIL, FOR FRYING

POT ROAST

YIELD: 6 SERVINGS / **ACTIVE TIME:** 30 MINUTES / **TOTAL TIME:** 3 HOURS AND 30 MINUTES

Slow cooked until tender and delicious, this is comfort food at its finest, no matter the occasion.

1. Preheat the oven to 350°F and set a Dutch oven over high heat.

2. Season both sides of meat with salt and pepper. Add oil to the pot and sear meat on all sides until browned, about 3 to 4 minutes per side.

3. Remove roast from pan and set aside. Add garlic to pot and cook for 1 minute, and then deglaze the pot with red wine and stock. Add meat back to the pot.

4. Pour Worcestershire sauce over the meat and place the onion, carrots, celery, potatoes, and the rest of the ingredients on top of and around the meat.

5. Place a lid on the pan and transfer it to the oven. Cook 3 hours, or until meat reaches an internal temperature of 202°F and is fork-tender and easy to slice.

6. Season vegetables with additional salt and pepper to taste and serve hot.

INGREDIENTS:

1	(3-5 LB.) BEEF ROAST CHUCK OR BOTTOM ROUND
2	TEASPOONS SEA SALT
1	TEASPOON BLACK PEPPER
3	GARLIC CLOVES, PEELED AND SMASHED
1	CUP RED WINE
2	CUPS BEEF STOCK (SEE PAGE 721)
1	TABLESPOON WORCESTERSHIRE SAUCE
1	ONION, HALVED
1	LB. CARROTS, SLICED ON BIAS INTO SPEARS
½	HEAD OF CELERY, CUT INTO 3" SPEARS
1	LB. YUKON GOLD POTATOES, HALVED
2	TABLESPOONS TOMATO PASTE
1	TEASPOON SWEET PAPRIKA
¼	CUP PLUS 3 TABLESPOONS AVOCADO OIL
1	BAY LEAF
1	SPRIG FRESH ROSEMARY
2	CLOVES, WHOLE STUDDED INTO ONION
1	LEEK, HALVED

KEFTES DE ESPINACA

YIELD: 12 SERVINGS / **ACTIVE TIME:** 15 MINUTES / **TOTAL TIME:** 30 MINUTES

Small fried patties or croquettes, known as keftes, are popular in the Sephardic Jewish community. These are a delicious vegetarian take on the usually meaty kefte concept. Because keftes are pan fried in oil, they are often served for Hanukkah.

1. Add 1 tablespoon oil to a large skillet over medium heat. Sauté minced onion for 5 minutes until translucent. Add crushed garlic, sauté for 2 minutes longer.

2. Add half of the fresh spinach and allow the spinach to wilt and shrink slightly, then add remaining half and cover again, until all of the spinach has wilted.

3. Remove from heat and transfer the cooked mixture to a mesh strainer. With a spatula, gently press mixture in the strainer to remove excess moisture. Transfer mixture to a cutting board and roughly chop.

4. Place chopped mixture into a mixing bowl. Add remaining ingredients and mix well.

5. With an ice cream scoop or ¼ cup measuring cup, scoop the mixture into your hand and form smooth flat patties. Place them onto a sheet tray as you go.

6. Add remaining oil to the skillet over medium heat and bring to about 365°F. Place patties into the hot oil in small batches. Fry until brown, about 4 minutes on each side. Place on a paper towel or rack to drain.

7. Serve immediately.

INGREDIENTS:

½	CUP PLUS 1 TABLESPOON AVOCADO OIL
1	ONION, MINCED
½	TEASPOON CRUSHED GARLIC
10	OZ. FRESH SPINACH LEAVES
1	LARGE EGG
1	CUP MASHED RUSSET POTATOES
½	CUP PLAIN BREAD CRUMBS OR MATZO MEAL
1	TEASPOON SEA SALT
¼	TEASPOON BLACK PEPPER
1	PINCH CAYENNE (OPTIONAL)

BOUREKAS

YIELD: 12 SERVINGS / **ACTIVE TIME:** 1 HOUR / **TOTAL TIME:** 1 HOUR AND 50 MINUTES

The thin and flaky pastry is usually made from phyllo or yufka dough. The potato and cheese filling is simple enough to make, which is good news considering that these savory bites will be requested again and again.

1. Place the potatoes in a stockpot with enough cold water to cover by 1". Bring to a boil over medium-high heat and cook uncovered until the potatoes are tender and easily pierced with a fork, about 25 minutes.

2. Drain potatoes, place in a bowl, and mash with a potato masher. Set aside to cool.

3. Add oil to a skillet set over medium-high heat and sauté onion and garlic until soft and translucent, about 7 minutes. Remove from heat and set aside.

4. In a bowl, combine the nutmeg and cheeses and mix well.

5. Add the onion mixture and the cheese mixture to the potatoes, mix well, and season to taste with salt and pepper.

6. In a bowl, beat one of the eggs.

7. While stirring the cool potato mixture, slowly add the beaten egg. Mix well until the egg is totally integrated into the mashed potatoes.

8. Preheat the oven to 375°F.

9. Line a large baking sheet with parchment paper. Fill a bowl with water.

10. Cut puff pastry sheets into 5-inch squares.

11. Place a heaping tablespoon of filling in the center of each square.

12. Dip your fingers in the water and dampen the edges of the squares, then fold in half vertically to form a triangle pastry. Pinch the edges together to seal the filling inside.

13. Beat the second egg and brush it over the tops of the bourekas. Sprinkle sesame seeds on top.

14. Bake for 30 minutes, or until the bourekas are puffed and golden.

INGREDIENTS:

3   MEDIUM YUKON GOLD POTATOES, PEELED AND CUT INTO 1" PIECES

2   TABLESPOONS EXTRA VIRGIN OLIVE OIL

1   SMALL ONION, CHOPPED

1   GARLIC CLOVE, MINCED

⅛   TEASPOON GROUND NUTMEG

1   CUP RICOTTA CHEESE

1   CUP GRATED KASHKAVAL CHEESE

SEA SALT, TO TASTE

FRESHLY GROUND BLACK PEPPER, TO TASTE

2   LARGE EGGS

1   (14-16 OZ.) PACKAGE PUFF PASTRY (SHEETS OR PRE-CUT SQUARES)

TOASTED SESAME SEEDS, FOR SPRINKLING

SUFGANIYOT

YIELD: 21 SERVINGS / **ACTIVE TIME:** 45 MINUTES / **TOTAL TIME:** 3 HOURS

Potatoes aren't the only thing Jewish people deep-fry on Hanukkah. In Israel, sufganiyot—perhaps the most delicious jelly doughnuts you'll ever know—are an even more popular way of celebrating than latkes.

1. Sift the flour into a large mixing bowl. Add the salt and sugar and mix well. Add the yeast and mix.

2. Using a mixer fitted with a hook attachment, mix the flour mixture on low speed and add the egg and butter. Gradually add the warm milk and continue mixing for 8 to 10 minutes, until the dough is soft.

3. Shape the dough into a ball and place it in a clean, lightly oiled bowl. Cover with a clean kitchen towel or plastic wrap and let rise until doubled in size, about 2 hours.

4. Once the dough has risen, place dough on a lightly floured work surface and roll out the dough to a thickness of ¾". Using a 2" cookie cutter, cut circles out of the dough, as close to one another as possible.

5. Place the dough circles on a baking tray lined with parchment paper and cover with a clean kitchen towel. Allow to rise again for 20 minutes.

6. In the meantime, heat the oil in a Dutch oven until it reaches 325°F.

7. Gently add 4 dough circles into the oil and fry for 2 to 3 minutes on each side, until golden brown, but not too brown. Remove with a slotted spoon and place on a paper towel-lined plate. Repeat with remaining dough. Allow to cool slightly before filling.

8. Fill a piping bag with your desired filling. Using a sharp knife, make a small slit on the top of the sufganiyot. Place the piping bag inside the slit and fill until you can see the filling on top.

9. Sprinkle with powdered sugar before serving.

INGREDIENTS:

3½	CUPS ALL-PURPOSE FLOUR
½	TEASPOON SEA SALT
¼	CUP SUGAR
1	TABLESPOON DRY INSTANT YEAST
1	EGG
3½	TABLESPOONS UNSALTED BUTTER, CUBED
1¼	CUPS LUKEWARM MILK
1	QUART AVOCADO OIL
½	CUP STRAWBERRY OR RASPBERRY JAM, NUTELLA, OR READY-MADE VANILLA PUDDING
¼	CUP POWDERED SUGAR

SHABBAT DINNER

CHOLENT

YIELD: 4 SERVINGS / **ACTIVE TIME:** 15 MINUTES / **TOTAL TIME:** 24 HOURS

Consider this one of the world's oldest slow-cooked dishes, created from the necessity of not working—therefore, not cooking—on the Sabbath but still very much needing to eat. Cholent preparation can begin before sundown on Friday and be enjoyed as a hot lunch on Saturday. And while many people think of cholent as an Eastern European dish, its origins can actually be traced back to the Middle East, through North Africa, and into Spain. The end result is a plethora of cholent recipes: Iraqi tbit made with chicken, Moroccan lamb stew, and beef stew with beans and vegetables from Hungary. There are, of course, plenty of meat-free versions for vegetarians, too. A simple family recipe, such as this one, is sometimes all you need.

1. Grease the inside of your slow cooker with cooking spray.

2. Add meat, marrow bones, and potatoes to the slow cooker, followed by the onion, garlic, barley, beans, and the water they soaked in.

3. In a bowl, combine the ketchup, paprika, and 2½ cups water (or beer or stock), mix well, and add to the pot. Season with salt, pepper, and garlic powder and mix well. Add kishke on top.

4. Set the slow cooker to low and cook overnight. Check in the morning and add additional water or stock if it seems dry.

INGREDIENTS:

COOKING SPRAY, FOR GREASING

1½ LBS. FATTY STEW MEAT OR FLANKEN

4-5 MARROW BONES

2 LARGE YUKON GOLD OR RUSSET POTATOES, PEELED AND CUT INTO CHUNKS

1 WHOLE ONION, PEELED

3-4 GARLIC CLOVES, PEELED

2 CUPS PEARL BARLEY

1 CUP KIDNEY BEANS, SOAKED OVERNIGHT AND SOAKING WATER RESERVED

⅓ CUP KETCHUP

1 TABLESPOON PAPRIKA

3 CUPS WATER, PLUS MORE AS NEEDED

2 TEASPOONS SALT

1 TEASPOON PEPPER

1 TEASPOON GARLIC POWDER

1 LB. PACKAGED KISHKE

Roasted Shabbat Chicken with
Spring Vegetables, Page 212

ROASTED SHABBAT CHICKEN
WITH SPRING VEGETABLES

YIELD: 2 TO 6 SERVINGS / **ACTIVE TIME:** 30 MINUTES / **TOTAL TIME:** 2 HOURS

A beautifully roasted chicken with vegetables is an iconic and beloved Shabbat dinner. This recipe is simple enough to whip up when short on time, but always tastes as though it was prepared with love.

1. First, preheat the oven to 350°F and wash your chicken well and pat dry. Place on a rack in a roasting pan. The rack is important! It keeps the chicken from drying out and the veggies from burning.

2. Stuff your bird with the onion, lemon, and the garlic cloves. Then drizzle all over with ¼ cup oil, 1 tablespoon salt, 1 teaspoon pepper, and fresh herbs. Truss the chicken (tie the legs together).

3. Roast chicken for 1 hour and 20 minutes. Meanwhile, prep the vegetables. Clean the onions, cut the zucchini into spears, peel and quarter the turnips, and peel the carrots.

4. Toss in additional oil, salt, pepper, and herbs, just enough to coat the vegetables.

5. After 1 hour and 20 minutes, turn the heat up to 450°F to brown the chicken and add the veggies evenly on the rack.

6. Roast for another 30 minutes or so until the veggies are tender, and the internal temperature of the chicken near the thigh is 165°F and the juices run clear. Let rest covered in foil for 20 minutes.

INGREDIENTS:

- 1 (5 LB.) WHOLE CHICKEN, RINSED AND DRIED WELL AND THE INNARDS REMOVED
- ½ LEMON
- ½ WHITE ONION
- 3 GARLIC CLOVES PEELED
- ¼ CUP EXTRA VIRGIN OLIVE OIL, PLUS MORE FOR VEGETABLES
- 1 TABLESPOON SEA SALT, PLUS MORE FOR VEGETABLES
- 1 TEASPOON BLACK PEPPER, PLUS MORE FOR VEGETABLES
- 1 BUNCH FLAT LEAF PARSLEY
- 2 MEDIUM ZUCCHINI, WASHED AND CUT INTO SPEARS
- 1 BUNCH TURNIPS, PEELED AND QUARTERED
- 1 BUNCH CARROTS, ABOUT 25 PIECES, TRIMMED
- 1 CUP ROASTED ONIONS

ROASTED CAULIFLOWER

YIELD: 20 SERVINGS / **ACTIVE TIME:** 15 MINUTES / **TOTAL TIME:** 1 HOUR

The healthy benefits of cauliflower are turned decadent with this recipe. A combination of charred, fresh, sweet, and tangy that is sure to please.

1. Place a rack in the middle of the oven and preheat it to 375°F.

2. Place the whole heads of cauliflower directly on the middle rack and cook for 45 minutes, or until golden brown. Do not season or rub with oil.

3. When the cauliflower is browned and roasted, remove from the oven and allow it to cool enough to break it down into florets with a paring knife.

4. Heat a heavy-bottom sauté pan over medium-high heat and toast the mustard seeds in the pan for 30 seconds, then add the oil, Za'atar, turmeric, sumac, salt, and pepper. Shut off the flame and allow the spices to infuse into the oil for 2 minutes.

5. Turn the flame back on, heat the oil and lightly fry the onions for 15 seconds, then add the dates and cauliflower florets to the pan coating and season to taste.

6. Finish with the herbs, lemon juice, and zest, and season to taste.

INGREDIENTS:

8	CAULIFLOWER HEADS
1	TEASPOON BROWN MUSTARD SEEDS
¼	CUP EXTRA VIRGIN OLIVE OIL
3	TABLESPOONS ZA'ATAR (SEE PAGE 545)
2	TEASPOONS TURMERIC
1	TEASPOON SUMAC
2	TEASPOONS SEA SALT, PLUS MORE TO TASTE
1	TEASPOON BLACK PEPPER, PLUS MORE TO TASTE
4	OZ. RED ONIONS, SLICED
4	OZ. MEDJOOL DATES, PITS REMOVED AND DICED
4	TABLESPOONS MIX OF CHOPPED FRESH TARRAGON, PARSLEY, CHIVES, AND CILANTRO
¼	CUP FRESH LEMON JUICE
3	TEASPOONS LEMON ZEST

Roasted Cauliflower, page 213

WHITE WINE BRAISED LEEKS

YIELD: 12 SERVINGS / **ACTIVE TIME:** 25 MINUTES / **TOTAL TIME:** 1 HOUR AND 10 MINUTES

This dish is traditionally French in many ways. Pair it with roast chicken or fish, or simply enjoy on its own.

1. Thoroughly clean the leeks, trim the roots, and slice in half lengthwise.

2. Heat the olive oil in a pan over medium-high heat and season prepared leeks with sea salt and pepper to taste.

3. Place leeks cut-side down in the pan and sear until golden brown, 5 minutes.

4. Season again with sea salt and pepper and flip, allowing to cook for an additional 2 minutes, or until brown. Transfer leeks to a baking dish.

5. Preheat the oven to 400°F.

6. Add the avocado oil, shallots, garlic, thyme, lemon zest, salt, and pepper to the pan and cook until just brown, about 4 minutes.

7. Add wine and cook until reduced by half, about 10 minutes.

8. Add stock and bring to a boil. Once the mixture boils, remove from heat, and pour over leeks until they are almost but not quite submerged.

9. Put in the oven and allow to braise until tender, about 30 minutes.

INGREDIENTS:

6	LARGE LEEKS
½	CUP EXTRA VIRGIN OLIVE OIL
	SEA SALT, TO TASTE
	FRESHLY GROUND BLACK PEPPER, TO TASTE
2	TABLESPOONS AVOCADO OIL
4	SHALLOTS
2	GARLIC CLOVES, MINCED
1	TEASPOON DRIED THYME
1	TEASPOON LEMON ZEST
½	CUP WHITE WINE
2	CUPS CHICKEN STOCK (SEE PAGE 722)

SALTED HONEY APPLE UPSIDE-DOWN CAKE

YIELD: 6 SERVINGS / **ACTIVE TIME:** 20 MINUTES / **TOTAL TIME:** 1 HOUR AND 20 MINUTES

Milk and honey sound good, sure, but make that honey *salted* and now you're talking. This spin on the retro favorite upside-down cake is uplifted with just the right balance of sweet and savory.

1. Preheat the oven to 350°F.

2. In a small bowl, combine the flour, baking powder, ½ teaspoon salt, and cinnamon and whisk well.

3. In another small bowl, combine the sour cream, oil, and vanilla and whisk well.

4. In a medium bowl, combine the sugar and eggs and whisk until foamy, about 2 minutes.

5. Gently stir in half the flour mixture into the egg mixture, then stir in half the sour cream mixture. Stir in the remaining flour mixture and then the remaining sour cream mixture until just combined. Set aside.

6. Butter the bottom and sides of an 8" cast-iron skillet or spring-form pan and add honey, swirling the pan around to ensure it covers as much of the pan as possible. Sprinkle with ¼ teaspoon salt.

7. Arrange the sliced apples over the honey, overlapping them to fit in the pan. Pour the cake batter over the apples and tap the pan a few times to get rid of any large bubbles. Bake until the cake is golden brown and springs back when lightly touched with your finger, about 30 minutes.

8. Let the cake cool in the pan for 10 minutes, then run an offset spatula or knife around the pan and invert cake onto a cooling rack (or unmold then invert, if using a springform). Let cool for at least an additional 20 minutes before transferring to a platter and sprinkling with flaky salt.

9. To serve, if desired, whisk extra sour cream with honey to taste, and dollop on slices of cake.

INGREDIENTS:

- ½ TABLESPOON UNSALTED BUTTER
- ¾ CUP ALL-PURPOSE FLOUR
- 1 TEASPOON BAKING POWDER
- ¾ TEASPOON KOSHER SALT
- ½ TEASPOON CINNAMON
- ¼ CUP SOUR CREAM, PLUS MORE FOR SERVING (OPTIONAL)
- ¼ CUP AVOCADO OIL
- 2 TEASPOONS VANILLA EXTRACT
- ½ CUP GRANULATED SUGAR
- 2 EGGS
- ¼ CUP HONEY, PLUS MORE FOR SERVING (OPTIONAL)
- 1 BAKING APPLE, THINLY SLICED INTO ROUNDS (THE CORE IS EDIBLE, BUT SEEDS AND STEM SHOULD BE REMOVED)
- FLAKY SALT, FOR SERVING

Rosemary Rack Of Lamb with
Roasted Potatoes & Carrots, page 368

ENTREES

These beloved recipes are often considered the star of the show. When it comes to traditional Jewish cooking, a brisket, roasted chicken, or fish is at the heart of most meals, but read on to discover just how much variety there is.

ALICIOTTI CON INDIVIA

YIELD: 4 SERVINGS / **ACTIVE TIME:** 25 MINUTES / **TOTAL TIME:** 45 MINUTES

A classic Roman Jewish dish featuring anchovies baked in escarole or endives. The origins of this dish are linked with strict Papal laws that prohibited Roman Jews from consuming any other fish besides anchovies and sardines.

1. Preheat the oven to 350°F.

2. Place 1 tablespoon of olive oil in the bottom of a 9" x 13" baking dish. Sprinkle a teaspoon of chopped garlic over the oil. Place the escarole in the baking dish. Sprinkle the remaining garlic over the escarole.

3. Slice open the anchovies from head to tail. Place a layer of the anchovy fillets over the escarole so the flesh is on the escarole and the skin side is up. Sprinkle salt, pepper, red chili flakes, and olive oil over the anchovies. Tightly cover the baking dish with aluminum foil. Transfer into the oven and bake for about 20 minutes, until the greens are tender and the anchovies have softened.

4. Serve hot.

INGREDIENTS:

1	TABLESPOON, PLUS 1 TEASPOON OLIVE OIL
6	GARLIC CLOVES, FINELY CHOPPED
2	BUNCHES ESCAROLE, ROUGHLY CHOPPED
36	FRESH ANCHOVIES OR OIL AND VINEGAR MARINATED ANCHOVIES, SKIN-ON FILLETS
¼	TEASPOON SEA SALT
⅛	TEASPOON FRESHLY GROUND BLACK PEPPER
⅛	TEASPOON RED CHILI FLAKES

ALMODROTE

YIELD: 8 SERVINGS / **ACTIVE TIME:** 40 MINUTES / **TOTAL TIME:** 1 HOUR AND 45 MINUTES

A beautiful mainstay of Sephardic cuisine. Although it dates back to the Middle Ages, this delicious roasted eggplant and cheese pie remains perfectly comforting today.

1. Place the oven rack in the middle position and preheat to 425°F.

2. Rub a medium baking dish with the open-faced half of garlic clove, going over the entire surface of the dish a few times. Generously grease the dish with the butter and then sprinkle in the flour, coating the entire surface of the dish; tap out any excess flour over the sink.

3. Place the drained eggplant in a large mixing bowl. Taste the eggplant—if it is sweet, you can skip the zucchini; if it is a bit bitter, add the grated zucchini for balance. Add the eggs, 2½ cups of the cheese, and salt and mix vigorously with a fork or whisk, breaking up the eggplant, until well blended.

4. Spread the eggplant mixture evenly into the baking dish. Sprinkle the remaining cheese over the top.

5. Bake for 25 to 30 minutes, until well browned and crisp on top. Serve immediately or at room temperature with sour cream on the side.

INGREDIENTS:

1   GARLIC CLOVE, UN-PEELED AND HALVED LENGTHWISE

    UNSALTED BUTTER, FOR GREASING

2   TABLESPOONS ALL-PURPOSE FLOUR

    FLESH OF 5 MEDIUM EGGPLANTS (SEE PAGE 161)

1   SMALL LIGHT GREEN ZUCCHINI, GRATED AND LIQUID SQUEEZED OUT (OPTIONAL)

2   EGGS

3   CUPS KASHKAVAL CHEESE, GRATED

½   TEASPOON SEA SALT

    SOUR CREAM, FOR SERVING

Avikas, page 228

AVIKAS

YIELD: 6 SERVINGS / **ACTIVE TIME:** 1 HOUR / **TOTAL TIME:** 14 HOURS

This is the Jewish adaptation of a Greek stew and was regularly eaten by Jews in Greece on the Sabbath, since it could be slowly prepared overnight.

1. Add 1 tablespoon olive oil to a large pot over medium-high heat.

2. Season the meat with 1 teaspoon salt. Once the oil is hot, place the pieces of meat into the pot and sear on all sides until deep golden brown, about 3 minutes on each side. Transfer the meat to a plate.

3. Add the onions to the pot and sauté until golden, about 10 minutes, scraping the meat drippings on the bottom of the pot to incorporate. Add the tomato paste and cook for about 2 minutes until caramelized. Add the meat back into the pot, along with the beans, pepper and remaining salt. Cover with water and stir.

4. Bring the mixture to a boil and reduce to a gentle simmer. Add a lid slightly ajar and continue cooking the stew for about 1 hour and 30 minutes until the mixture cooks down into a stew like consistency and the beans and meat are tender.

5. Serve hot with white rice.

INGREDIENTS:

1	TABLESPOON OLIVE OIL
1	LB. CHUCK BEEF, CHOPPED INTO 2" CUBES
3	TEASPOONS SEA SALT, DIVIDED
1	YELLOW ONION, ROUGHLY CHOPPED
1	TABLESPOON TOMATO PASTE
½	CUP WHITE KIDNEY BEANS, SOAKED OVERNIGHT AND DRAINED
¼	TEASPOON GROUND BLACK PEPPER

BEEF MIXIOTE

YIELD: 4 SERVINGS / **ACTIVE TIME:** 40 MINUTES / **TOTAL TIME:** 24 HOURS

Traditional brisket, but with the enhanced flavor kick of chilies.

1. Devein and remove seeds from the dried chiles. Dry-roast them on a griddle along with the onion and garlic until fragrant and charred in spots, about 5 minutes.

2. Bring a small pot of water to a simmer, add the chilies, and soak until softened, about 15 minutes.

3. In a blender, combine the chilies, onion, garlic, oregano, and cloves with a cup of water and blend to a smooth puree.

4. In a deep bowl, combine the marinade with the meat. Cover well and refrigerate overnight.

5. The next day, remove the meat from the marinade, rub the surface with oil, and season with salt.

6. Preheat the oven to 350°F.

7. Line a baking dish with foil and banana leaves, and avocado leaves, if using. Place the meat in the center of the dish and pour any remaining marinade on top. Add the bay leaves. Fold the leaves over the top and wrap the whole thing in foil so that it's tightly packed. Pour about 2 cups water in the area between the pot and the foil.

8. Roast until the meat is tender and falls apart easily when pulled with a fork, about 4 hours. Check on the water in the pan during the cooking process and add more if it dries out.

9. Serve with warm tortillas, pickled red onions, and cilantro.

INGREDIENTS:

2	DRIED GUAJILLO CHILES
2	DRIED ANCHO CHILES
1	DRIED CHILE MORITA
1	DRIED CHILE NEGRO
1	MEDIUM WHITE ONION, HALVED
5	GARLIC CLOVES
1	TEASPOON GROUND OREGANO
¼	TEASPOON GROUND CLOVES
1½	LBS. BEEF SHOULDER, OR ANY OTHER STEW MEAT
¼	CUP AVOCADO OIL
1	TEASPOON SEA SALT
1	(14 OZ.) BAG BANANA LEAVES
15	AVOCADO LEAVES (OPTIONAL)
5	BAY LEAVES
2	CUPS WATER
	WARM TORTILLAS (SEE PAGE 737), FOR SERVING
	PICKLED RED ONIONS, FOR SERVING
	CILANTRO, FRESH PICKED, FOR SERVING

BEEF BRISKET

YIELD: 15 SERVINGS / **ACTIVE TIME:** 45 MINUTES / **TOTAL TIME:** 5 HOURS

Made with one of the toughest cuts of a butchered cow—and back in the shtetls of Eastern Europe the most inexpensive—this recipe yields a perfect brisket every single time, and is testament to the power of simple cooking.

1. Preheat the oven to 350°F.

2. Add oil to a 10 or 12" sauté pan over high heat. Place the trimmed brisket in the hot oil, fat-side down, and cook until browned, 5 to 7 minutes. Season the brisket with ½ teaspoon salt and ¼ teaspoon pepper. Turn over the brisket and brown the other side. Season this side with the same amount of salt and pepper. If the brisket is too large to fit the pan, cut off the tip and brown it separately.

3. Meanwhile, in a large mixing bowl, combine the onions, garlic, brown sugar, Worcestershire, mustard, vinegar, chili powder, paprika, remaining salt and pepper, ketchup, and 1¼ cups water. Use some of the water to rinse out the ketchup bottle. Stir until well blended.

4. Transfer the browned and seasoned brisket to a roasting pan or Dutch oven just big enough to hold the meat with about an inch of space around it. Place the bay leaves on top of the meat and pour the ketchup mixture over it.

5. Cover the roasting pan (using aluminum foil if the pan doesn't have a lid) and roast for 2 hours.

6. Remove from the oven and uncover. When the brisket is cool enough to handle, transfer it to a cutting board. Slice the brisket on an angle across the grain. The slices should be less than ¼" thick. As you slice the meat, transfer the slices back to the cooking liquid. When all of the meat is sliced, pour any juice on the cutting board back into the roasting pan, re-cover it, and return it to the oven for 1½ to 2 hours, or until the meat is tender enough to cut with a fork. Remove from the oven and let cool slightly before serving.

7. To store, lift the meat out of the gravy and store separately. To reheat, layer the meat with some of the gravy, cover, and bake in a 325°F oven for 30 to 45 minutes, or until warm.

INGREDIENTS:

5	TABLESPOONS AVOCADO OIL
1	WHOLE BEEF BRISKET (5-7 LBS.), TRIMMED OF EXCESS FAT
2	TEASPOONS SEA SALT
1	TEASPOON FRESHLY GROUND BLACK PEPPER
2	LARGE ONIONS, ROUGHLY CHOPPED
2	LARGE GARLIC CLOVES, MINCED
2	TABLESPOONS DARK BROWN SUGAR
2	TABLESPOONS WORCESTERSHIRE SAUCE
1	TABLESPOON DRY MUSTARD
1	TABLESPOON WHITE VINEGAR
1	TEASPOON CHILI POWDER
½	TEASPOON PAPRIKA
1	(14 OZ.) BOTTLE KETCHUP
1¼	CUPS WATER
2	LARGE BAY LEAVES

BOULETTES WITH CHICKEN & VEGETABLE SOUP & COUSCOUS

YIELD: 6 SERVINGS / **ACTIVE TIME:** 1 HOUR / **TOTAL TIME:** 2 HOURS AND 30 MINUTES

Boulettes, or "meatball" in French, is part of this hearty and warming meal that combines all of the comforting flavors of a chicken soup into a beautiful, textural dish.

1. Place the onion and cilantro in a food processor and process until a smooth paste is formed, about 5 minutes. Transfer the paste into a large bowl. Add the beef, breadcrumbs, salt, pepper, and 3 eggs. Mix well until all of the ingredients are evenly incorporated into the meatball mixture.

2. Take about 1½ tablespoons of mixture and shape it into an oval meatball. Place it onto a platter and continue shaping the remaining mixture into meatballs. Set aside.

3. To make the sauce, add oil to a wide and deep pan over medium-high heat. Add the onion and sauté for about 8 to 10 minutes, until browned. Add the tomato paste, 1 cup water, and salt and mix well. Reduce the heat to medium-low and simmer for about 3 minutes, until the tomato paste dissolves. Remove heat and set aside.

4. Place 2 cups flour in a wide and shallow bowl. Crack 3 eggs into another wide and shallow bowl and add 1 tablespoon water to the eggs. Beat the eggs well. Set aside.

5. Add about ¾" of oil to a wide and deep saucepan over medium-high heat. While the oil is heating up, start dredging the meatballs.

6. Take one meatball and gently place it into the bowl with flour, rolling it to cover all the edges with flour. Shake off any excess flour. Dip the floured meatball into the beaten eggs and roll the meatball so all the edges are covered with the egg. Shake off any excess eggs from the meatball. Repeat until all of the meatballs have been dredged.

7. Once the oil is sizzling in the pan, gently place the dredged meatballs in the oil, making sure not to overcrowd the pan. Fry the meatballs on each side until golden brown, about 3 to 5 minutes per side. Transfer the fried meatballs to a paper towel-lined plate and fry the remaining meatballs.

INGREDIENTS:

BOULETTES

1	YELLOW ONION, ROUGHLY CHOPPED
1	CUP ROUGHLY CHOPPED CILANTRO OR PARSLEY
1½	LBS. GROUND BEEF
½	CUP BREAD CRUMBS
3	TEASPOONS SEA SALT
1	TEASPOON FRESHLY GROUND BLACK PEPPER
6	EGGS
1	TABLESPOON WATER
2	CUPS ALL-PURPOSE FLOUR
	AVOCADO OIL, FOR FRYING

SAUCE

3	TABLESPOONS CANOLA OIL
1	YELLOW ONION, FINELY CHOPPED
1	TABLESPOON TOMATO PASTE
1	CUP WATER
1	TEASPOON SEA SALT

SOUP

3	TABLESPOONS AVOCADO OIL
6	CHICKEN DRUMSTICKS OR 4 CHICKEN BREASTS, SKIN ON AND BONE-IN
1	YELLOW ONION, FINELY CHOPPED
2	TEASPOONS GROUND CORIANDER
3	TEASPOONS GROUND CUMIN

8. Gently place the fried meatballs into the pan with the sauce that was set aside. Add enough water to just cover the meatballs three-quarters the way up.

9. Place the pan over medium-high heat and simmer until the water has reduced by half and the meatballs are cooked through, about 15 minutes. Set aside.

10. To prepare the soup, place 3 tablespoons oil in a large pot over medium heat. Once the oil is sizzling, add the chicken in one layer and sprinkle the onions around the meat. Sear the chicken on both sides until golden brown, about 5 minutes per side. Stir the onions occasionally until they are softened and lightly browned.

11. Meanwhile, in a bowl, combine the coriander, cumin, salt, pepper, 2 cloves, tomato paste, and ½ cup water and mix well.

12. Once the chicken is seared on both sides, add the spice and tomato paste mixture to the pot. Stir the chicken and onions in the sauce and cook for about 3 minutes. Reduce the heat to medium and add the carrots, turnips, squash, and potatoes.

13. Peel the whole onion, press 4 garlic cloves into the onion's surface, and add it into the pot.

14. Gently place the eggs, in their shells, in the pot over the vegetables. Add enough water to cover the eggs, chicken, and vegetables. Cook over a simmer and uncovered for 30 minutes.

15. Add the zucchinis, artichokes, and chickpeas and continue cooking for another 15 to 20 minutes, until the chicken, vegetables, and eggs are cooked through.

16. Transfer the eggs from the pot and remove their shells. Place the peeled eggs back into the soup and set the soup aside.

17. Place the couscous in a large heatproof bowl or baking dish. Add enough boiling water to just cover the couscous and let it sit for 10 to 15 minutes, or until tender. Once the couscous is ready use a fork to gently fluff and mix it.

18. To serve, place a small mound of couscous on each plate and top with a boulette, a piece of chicken, an egg, and some vegetables. If desired, add harissa for some spice. Serve hot.

2	TEASPOONS SEA SALT
½	TEASPOON FRESHLY GROUND BLACK PEPPER
6	WHOLE CLOVES, DIVIDED
2	TABLESPOONS TOMATO PASTE
½	CUP OF WATER
4	CARROTS, CHOPPED
3	SMALL TURNIPS, CHOPPED
2	CUPS CHOPPED BUTTERNUT SQUASH
4	SMALL YUKON GOLD POTATOES, PEELED AND CHOPPED
1	YELLOW ONION
7	EGGS
½	CUP MINCED CILANTRO
3	ZUCCHINIS, PEELED AND CHOPPED
6	HEARTS OF CANNED ARTICHOKES
2	CUPS CANNED CHICKPEAS, RINSED AND DRAINED

COUSCOUS

1	(6-8 OZ.) PACK STORE-BOUGHT COUSCOUS
1	TABLESPOON AVOCADO OIL
1	TEASPOON SEA SALT
	WARM WATER
1	TEASPOON HARISSA, FOR GARNISH (OPTIONAL)

Brisket with Pomegranate-Walnut Sauce &
Pistachio Gremolata, page 238

BRISKET WITH POMEGRANATE-WALNUT SAUCE & PISTACHIO GREMOLATA

YIELD: 8 SERVINGS / **ACTIVE TIME:** 30 MINUTES / **TOTAL TIME:** 30 HOURS

Tart pomegranate, acting as both marinade and sauce, brings brightness and balance to this rich brisket. The gremolata adds a touch of herbal freshness.

1. Season brisket all over with salt and pepper. Transfer to a large 2-gallon resealable plastic bag or bowl.

2. Add garlic, walnuts, honey, and 1 cup pomegranate juice to a blender and puree until very smooth. Add remaining pomegranate juice and blend until smooth. Pour marinade over the brisket. Seal bag or cover bowl tightly with foil. Refrigerate for at least 24 hours, and up to 48 hours.

3. Transfer brisket and marinade to roasting pan, cover tightly with foil, and let sit at room temperature 1 hour.

4. Preheat the oven to 275°F.

5. Bake brisket, covered, until meat shreds easily with 2 forks, about 5 hours; if meat is still tough, continue cooking, covered, for 1 hour.

6. Transfer brisket to a cutting board and cover loosely with foil.

7. Transfer cooking liquid to a saucepan and spoon off fat from the surface. Cook over medium-high heat, skimming off fat and foam as it surfaces, until reduced by two-thirds, about 2 cups of sauce. Season with salt and pepper, if necessary.

8. Add the mint, pistachios, garlic, lemon zest, salt, and pepper to a food processor and pulse until coarsely chopped. Drizzle in oil, pulsing until just combined; do not overprocess.

9. To serve, slice the brisket against the grain and transfer to a platter. Spoon sauce over and top with gremolata.

INGREDIENTS:

BRISKET AND MARINADE

1	(7 LB.) BEEF BRISKET WITH FAT TRIMMED TO ¼" THICKNESS
2	TEASPOONS SEA SALT, PLUS MORE TO TASTE
1	TEASPOON FRESHLY GROUND BLACK PEPPER, PLUS MORE TO TASTE
1	HEAD OF GARLIC, PEELED
1	CUP WALNUTS
2	TABLESPOONS HONEY
3	CUPS POMEGRANATE JUICE, DIVIDED

GREMOLATA

1½	CUPS MINT LEAVES
½	CUP SHELLED ROASTED AND SALTED PISTACHIOS
2	GARLIC CLOVES
2	TEASPOONS LEMON ZEST
¼	TEASPOON SEA SALT
⅛	TEASPOON FRESHLY GROUND BLACK PEPPER
2	TABLESPOONS EXTRA VIRGIN OLIVE OIL

BULGUR WITH FRIED ONIONS

YIELD: 6 SERVINGS / **ACTIVE TIME:** 30 MINUTES / **TOTAL TIME:** 55 MINUTES

You can follow the tradition of Syrian housewives of the past and make this dish on laundry day, when you're too busy to make a more elaborate meal. But when you realize how delicious and simple this texture-rich meal is, chances are you'll be looking for excuses to prepare it most any day of the week.

1. Add the oil to pot over medium heat. Add the noodles and sauté, stirring constantly, until lightly browned, about 2 minutes.

2. Add the bulgur and salt and cover with water by ½". Cook, covered, over medium-low heat for 20 to 25 minutes, until bulgur is tender. Remove from heat and let stand, covered, for 10 minutes.

3. Meanwhile, add the onions and oil to a cold medium sized pan and sauté over high heat for 20 minutes, until the onions are softened and golden brown. For a more charred onion, let the onions cook for an additional 5 minutes, stirring occasionally, until they are dark and start to get crispy.

4. Top the bulgur with the onions and chickpeas and serve at room temperature with cucumber mint yogurt and salad.

INGREDIENTS:

- ¼ CUP AVOCADO OIL
- ¼ CUP THIN VERMICELLI NOODLES
- 2 CUPS BULGUR WHEAT
- ½ TEASPOON SEA SALT, PLUS MORE TO TASTE
- 2¼ CUPS WATER, TO COVER
- 4 MEDIUM ONIONS, SLICED
- ½ CUP CANOLA OIL
- 1 (15 OZ.) CAN CHICKPEAS, DRAINED AND RINSED

CHICKEN STEW WITH POTATOES & RADISHES

YIELD: 4 SERVINGS / **ACTIVE TIME:** 30 MINUTES / **TOTAL TIME:** 2 HOURS AND 30 MINUTES

This one-pot comfort-food stew takes its flavor cues from chicken paprikash. Leave off the sour cream at the end if you prefer to keep dinner dairy-free.

1. Season chicken thighs all over with salt, to taste.

2. Add the oil to a large Dutch oven over medium-high heat. Working in 2 batches, cook chicken, skin-side down, until skin is golden brown, 8 to 10 minutes. Transfer chicken to a plate.

3. Cook onion in the same pot, stirring often, until softened and edges are browned, 8 to 10 minutes. Add garlic and cook, stirring often, until softened, about 2 minutes. Add paprika and cook, stirring, until fragrant, about 30 seconds.

4. Add tomatoes and smash with a wooden spoon until no pieces are bigger than ½". Bring to a simmer and cook until tomatoes are slightly thickened, 6 to 8 minutes.

5. Add stock, potatoes, and chicken and return to a simmer. Cook, stirring occasionally and adding more stock if needed to keep potatoes submerged, until chicken is very tender and potatoes are creamy, 1 hour and 15 minutes to 1 hour and 30 minutes. Remove from heat and season with salt and paprika, to taste.

6. Squeeze juice from lemon into a small bowl and stir in sour cream; season with salt. In another small bowl, combine radishes with a pinch of salt and toss.

7. Transfer stew to a platter and drizzle sour cream over, or serve alongside if you prefer. Top with radishes, drizzle with a little oil, and season with lots of pepper.

INGREDIENTS:

4   CHICKEN LEGS (THIGH AND DRUMSTICK), PATTED DRY

    SEA SALT, TO TASTE

2   TABLESPOONS EXTRA VIRGIN OLIVE OIL, PLUS MORE FOR DRIZZLING

1   LARGE ONION, CHOPPED

5   GARLIC CLOVES, THINLY SLICED

2   TABLESPOONS HUNGARIAN HOT OR SWEET PAPRIKA, PLUS MORE TO TASTE

1   (28 OZ.) CAN OF WHOLE PEELED TOMATOES

3   CUPS CHICKEN STOCK (SEE PAGE 722)

1½   LBS. BABY YUKON GOLD POTATOES

½   LEMON

¾   CUP SOUR CREAM

6   RADISHES, THINLY SLICED

    FRESHLY GROUND BLACK PEPPER, TO TASTE

CAST-IRON ROAST CHICKEN
WITH FENNEL & CARROTS

YIELD: 4 SERVINGS / **ACTIVE TIME:** 30 MINUTES / **TOTAL TIME:** 3 HOURS

Caramelized in the cooking juices released by the chicken, fennel and carrots have never tasted so good.

1. Pat the chicken dry with paper towels and season generously with salt, inside and out. Tie legs together with kitchen twine. Let sit for 1 hour to allow salt to penetrate, or refrigerate, uncovered, up to 1 day ahead.

2. Place a rack in the upper third of the oven and set a 12" cast-iron skillet, or 3 quart. enameled cast-iron baking dish, on the rack. Preheat the oven to 425°F.

3. In a large bowl, combine the fennel, carrots, and 2 tablespoons oil and toss to coat; season with salt and pepper, to taste.

4. Once the oven reaches temperature, pat chicken dry with paper towels and lightly coat with half of remaining oil. Drizzle remaining oil into the hot skillet; this helps keep the chicken from sticking and tearing the skin). Place chicken in the center of the skillet and arrange vegetables around it. Roast until fennel and carrots are golden brown and an instant-read thermometer inserted into the thickest part of the breast registers 155°F, about 50 to 60 minutes; the temperature will climb to 165°F as chicken rests. Let the chicken rest in the skillet at least 20 minutes, and up to 45 minutes.

5. Transfer chicken to a cutting board and carve. Serve with vegetables.

INGREDIENTS:

1 (3½-4 LB.) WHOLE CHICKEN

SEA SALT, TO TASTE

2 FENNEL BULBS, CUT INTO 6 WEDGES EACH

1 LB. SMALL CARROTS, CUT INTO 4"-LONG PIECES ON A DIAGONAL

3 TABLESPOONS AVOCADO OIL, DIVIDED

FRESHLY GROUND BLACK PEPPER, TO TASTE

Cast-Iron Roast Chicken
with Fennel & Carrots, page 243

CEDAR-PLANK SALMON

YIELD: 6 SERVINGS / **ACTIVE TIME:** 30 MINUTES / **TOTAL TIME:** 2 HOURS

A lovely pairing of woodsy and oceanic flavors, this salmon takes on a light smokiness from grilling on a cedar plank. A classic that adds color and simple sophistication to any table.

1. Immerse a cedar grilling plank in water for 2 hours.

2. Prepare grill for direct-heat cooking over medium-hot charcoal, or medium-high heat for gas.

3. In a bowl, combine the mustard, honey, rosemary, zest, salt, and pepper and mix well. Spread the mixture on flesh side of salmon and let stand at room temperature for 15 minutes.

4. Put salmon on the plank, skin-side down. Grill, covered with lid, until salmon is just cooked through and edges are browned, 13 to 15 minutes. Let salmon stand on plank 5 minutes before serving.

INGREDIENTS:

2 TABLESPOONS GRAINY MUSTARD

2 TABLESPOONS MILD HONEY OR PURE MAPLE SYRUP

1 TEASPOON MINCED ROSEMARY

1 TABLESPOON LEMON ZEST

½ TEASPOON SEA SALT

½ TEASPOON BLACK PEPPER

1 (2 LB.) SALMON FILLET WITH SKIN (1½" THICK)

CHICKEN WITH MEHSHI SFEEHA

YIELD: 6 SERVINGS / **ACTIVE TIME**: 30 MINUTES / **TOTAL TIME**: 3 HOURS

Chicken with stuffed eggplant has its roots in Syria. This hearty version is sure to fill up, and impress, the hungriest of diners at your table.

1. Preheat the oven to 400°F.

2. In a large bowl, combine beef, rice, allspice, 1 teaspoon salt, and water, mix well, and set aside.

3. To rehydrate the eggplant skins bring 6 cups water to a boil. Once boiling, carefully place the dried eggplant skins in the water and stir occasionally to make sure they are all submerged. Boil for about 5 minutes, or until soft. Drain the eggplants, sprinkle about ½ teaspoon salt on each eggplant skin and set aside to cool.

4. Using a teaspoon or your hands, stuff each eggplant skin with about 2 to 3 teaspoons of the meat mixture, and flatten the filling at the top edge of the eggplant skins. Set aside.

5. Lay the eggplant slices on paper towels and sprinkle with salt. Let stand for 30 minutes then pat dry. Add 2 tablespoons oil to a 10" skillet over medium-high heat. Once oil is hot, place a single layer of eggplant slices in the pan. Fry for about 2 to 4 minutes on each side until deep golden brown. Transfer eggplants with a slotted spoon to a paper towel-lined sheet tray to drain any excess oil. Continue frying the rest of the eggplant slices in batches.

6. Add 1 tablespoon oil to a Dutch oven over medium-high heat, coating the bottom of the pot evenly with the oil. Place the stuffed eggplants in a single layer on the bottom of the pot and sprinkle 1 teaspoon allspice on top. Lay the fried eggplant slices evenly over the stuffed eggplants.

7. Place the whole chicken over the eggplant slices, and coat the chicken evenly with the remaining oil. Rub the remaining allspice, a generous amount of salt, ras el hanout, paprika, and garlic all over the chicken. Place the chicken breast-side down. Add enough water to the pot to cover halfway up the stuffed eggplants, about ½ cup.

8. Roast uncovered in the oven for 1 hour and 30 minutes and up to 2 hours, flipping the chicken halfway between cooking, always ensuring that there is water in the pot to prevent the eggplants from burning. Remove from the oven, let the chicken and eggplants rest for 15 minutes.

9. To serve, arrange the chicken, stuffed eggplants, and fried eggplant sliced on a large serving platter. Serve hot.

INGREDIENTS:

1	LB. GROUND BEEF
¼	CUP SHORT GRAIN WHITE RICE, RINSED AND DRAINED
1	TEASPOON GROUND ALLSPICE
7	TEASPOONS SEA SALT, DIVIDED, PLUS MORE TO TASTE
1	TABLESPOON WATER
12	DRIED EGGPLANT SKINS
3	TABLESPOONS AVOCADO OIL, DIVIDED
1	EGGPLANT, SLICED INTO ½" ROUNDS CROSSWISE
2	TEASPOONS GROUND ALLSPICE, DIVIDED
1	(3 LB.) WHOLE CHICKEN
1	TABLESPOON RAS EL HANOUT
1	TEASPOON PAPRIKA
4-6	GARLIC CLOVES, MINCED

CHARRED CHICKEN
WITH SWEET POTATOES & ORANGES

YIELD: 4 SERVINGS / **ACTIVE TIME:** 30 MINUTES / **TOTAL TIME:** 2 HOURS AND 25 MINUTES

A topping of olives and feta is a salty, bright complement to the caramelized oranges and roasted sweet potatoes in this flavor-packed chicken dinner. If you're keeping the meal dairy-free, skip the cheese.

---

1. Preheat the oven to 450°F.

2. Place chicken in a large bowl and season with salt. Add garlic, 2 tablespoons lemon juice, and 2 tablespoons oil and toss to combine. Let sit at room temperature for at least 30 minutes, or cover and refrigerate for up to 12 hours.

3. Remove chicken from marinade, draining off any excess; discard marinade. Set chicken aside.

4. Prick the sweet potato all over with a fork and roast on a small foil-lined rimmed baking sheet until tender, about 1 hour. Let sit until cool enough to handle.

5. Once the potato comes out of the oven, start cooking the chicken. Add 1 tablespoon oil to a large skillet, preferably cast iron, over medium-high heat. Sear chicken, skin-side down, until the skin is very brown, about 5 minutes.

6. Transfer to the oven and roast, keeping skin side down, until cooked through, 18 to 22 minutes. About 1 minute before removing chicken from the oven, toss rosemary sprigs into the skillet.

7. When the chicken is done, set it on a plate skin-side up, along with the rosemary.

8. Set the skillet over medium-high heat and cook the orange slices until golden and slightly softened, about 30 seconds per side. Transfer to the plate with the chicken.

9. In a bowl, combine the chickpeas, olives, the remaining oil, and the remaining lemon and toss well; season to taste with salt.

10. To serve, tear open the sweet potato and arrange big sections of flesh on a large platter. Place chicken, along with any accumulated juices, around sweet potato, then top with orange slices, chickpea salad, and rosemary. Squeeze orange wedges over everything when at the table.

INGREDIENTS:

4	CHICKEN THIGHS, BONE-IN AND SKIN-ON
	SEA SALT, TO TASTE
4	GARLIC CLOVES, FINELY GRATED
3	TABLESPOONS FRESH LEMON JUICE, DIVIDED
5	TABLESPOONS AVOCADO OIL, DIVIDED
1	LARGE SWEET POTATO
3	LARGE SPRIGS FRESH ROSEMARY
1	BLOOD ORANGE, THINLY SLICED, PLUS WEDGES FOR SQUEEZING
1	(15 OZ.) CAN CHICKPEAS, DRAINED AND RINSED
½	CUP CASTELVETRANO OLIVES, PITTED
3	OZ. FETA CHEESE, CRUMBLED

Charred Chicken with Sweet Potatoes &
Oranges, page 249

CHEF'S SPECIAL SWEET & SOUR MEATBALLS

YIELD: 4 SERVINGS / **ACTIVE TIME:** 25 MINUTES / **TOTAL TIME:** 1 HOUR AND 10 MINUTES

Eat something, you look skinny. These meatballs are the kind of nosh that are hard not to fill up on. The richness from the meatballs and the sticky, satisfying sauce make it impossible not to go for seconds.

1. Drain the pineapple chunks over a bowl and reserve the juice.

2. In a medium pot, combine the tomato sauce, ketchup, vinegar, brown sugar, tomato paste, onion powder, ½ teaspoon salt, ¼ teaspoon garlic powder, and the reserved pineapple juice, mix well, and turn heat to low to let the sauce slowly warm.

3. Meanwhile, in a bowl, combine the ground beef and chicken, egg, 3 tablespoons matzo meal, paprika, ¼ teaspoon salt, ½ teaspoon garlic powder, black pepper, and cayenne and use a fork to mix well.

4. Form the meat mixture into small 1" meatballs. If the mixture seems too moist or sticky, add another tablespoon of matzo meal to the mixture. Place the meatballs into the warming sauce.

5. When all the meatballs are formed, bring the mixture to a boil and stir to cover the meatballs with sauce. Lower the heat to a low, even simmer and cover the pot. Cook for 40 minutes, stirring frequently, until the sauce thickens and meatballs cook all the way through. If the sauce seems to be reducing too fast or losing too much liquid, lower the heat and add a little water to thin it.

6. After 40 minutes, add the pineapple chunks to the sauce and stir to coat. Let the chunks warm in the sauce for 5 minutes before serving.

INGREDIENTS:

2	(20 OZ.) CANS OF SUGAR-FREE PINEAPPLE CHUNKS WITH JUICE
¾	CUP TOMATO SAUCE (SEE PAGE 733)
¾	CUP KETCHUP
½	CUP CIDER VINEGAR
¼	CUP BROWN SUGAR
2	TABLESPOONS TOMATO PASTE
1	TABLESPOON ONION POWDER
¾	TEASPOON SALT, DIVIDED
¾	TEASPOON GARLIC POWDER, DIVIDED
¾	LB. LEAN GROUND BEEF
¾	LB. DARK MEAT GROUND CHICKEN
1	LARGE EGG, BEATEN
3-4	TABLESPOONS MATZO MEAL
1	TEASPOON PAPRIKA
¼	TEASPOON BLACK PEPPER
1	PINCH CAYENNE, OR MORE TO TASTE

CHERMOULA SEA BASS

YIELD: 8 SERVINGS / **ACTIVE TIME:** 20 MINUTES / **TOTAL TIME:** 45 MINUTES

Chermoula is originally from Morocco but can be found throughout North Africa and the Middle East. This garlic and herb paste is perfect with rich, meaty sea bass. Have good pita or couscous at the ready, you are going to want to sop up the juices.

1. Preheat the oven to 425°F.

2. Rub the sea bass fillets with the chermoula. Place a 2' sheet of parchment paper on a work surface and fold in half lengthwise. Arrange 4 of the fillets along one edge of the seam. Fold the parchment over the fillets and fold the edges in to crimp and seal one large pouch around the fish. Repeat with a second sheet of parchment and the remaining fillets. Carefully transfer the pouches to a rimmed baking sheet. Bake until fish is cooked through and flakey, about 10 to 12 minutes.

3. Remove from the oven and carefully open the parchment pouches; be careful of the steam. Serve immediately with lemon wedges.

INGREDIENTS:

3   TABLESPOONS CHERMOULA SAUCE (SEE PAGE 517)

8   FILLETS MEDITERRANEAN SEA BASS, SKIN REMOVED

LEMON WEDGES, FOR SERVING

Chicken & Tomato Stew with
Caramelized Lemon, page 258

CHICKEN & TOMATO STEW
WITH CARAMELIZED LEMON

YIELD: 4 SERVINGS / **ACTIVE TIME:** 45 MINUTES / **TOTAL TIME:** 3 HOURS

Cooking lemon slices to just this side of burnt adds a layer of complex flavor and brightness to this comforting dish.

1. Pat chicken dry and season with salt. Let sit at room temperature for at least 15 minutes and up to 1 hour ahead, or cover and refrigerate for up to 24 hours.

2. Add 2 tablespoons oil in a large Dutch oven over medium-high heat and cook chicken until deep golden brown on both sides, about 6 minutes per side; adjust heat as necessary to avoid burning. Transfer chicken to a plate, leaving drippings behind.

3. Add onion to pot and cook, stirring often, until softened, 6 to 8 minutes. Add garlic and cook, stirring often until onion begins to brown around the edges, about 3 minutes. Stir in honey, tomato paste, turmeric, and cinnamon and cook until fragrant, about 2 minutes. Add tomatoes and juices and smash tomatoes with a wooden spoon until pieces are no larger than 1".

4. Return chicken to pot, pour in stock (it should barely cover chicken), and bring to a simmer. Reduce heat to low, mostly cover pot with lid, and gently simmer until chicken is tender and juices thicken, 1 hour and 10 minutes to 1 hour and 20.

5. Meanwhile, trim the top and bottom from the lemon and cut lengthwise into quarters; remove seeds and white pith in the center. Thinly slice quarters crosswise into quarter-moons.

6. Place the lemon pieces in a medium skillet, cover with water, and bring to a boil. Cook for 3 minutes, then drain and pat dry with paper towels. Transfer to a small bowl, sprinkle with sugar, and toss to coat.

7. Wipe out the skillet and heat 2 tablespoons oil over medium-high. Arrange lemon pieces in a single layer in the skillet. Cook, turning halfway through, until deeply browned in most spots, about 3 minutes. Transfer back to the bowl and season with salt.

8. Ladle stew into bowls and top with caramelized lemon, sesame seeds, and mint. Serve with flatbread.

INGREDIENTS:

4	CHICKEN LEGS (THIGH AND DRUMSTICK)
	SEA SALT, TO TASTE
4	TABLESPOONS EXTRA VIRGIN OLIVE OIL, DIVIDED
1	LARGE ONION, THINLY SLICED
6	GARLIC CLOVES, HALVED
2	TABLESPOONS HONEY
1	TABLESPOON TOMATO PASTE
¾	TEASPOON TURMERIC
½	TEASPOON CINNAMON
1	(14.5 OZ.) CAN OF WHOLE PEELED TOMATOES
3	CUPS CHICKEN STOCK (SEE PAGE 722)
1	LEMON
1-½	TEASPOONS SUGAR
1	TABLESPOON TOASTED SESAME SEEDS
½	CUP TORN MINT
	FLATBREAD, FOR SERVING

CHICKEN CURRY

YIELD: 6 SERVINGS / **ACTIVE TIME:** 15 MINUTES / **TOTAL TIME:** 30 MINUTES

An Indian Jewish favorite that combines all of the potent and powerful flavors of a curry with a sauce built around tomatoes and onions.

1. Heat oil in large skillet and stir in butter to melt.

2. Season chicken with salt and pepper.

3. Add flour to a wide bowl and dip the chicken in the flour to dust.

4. Sear the chicken in the skillet on both sides, about 2 minutes per side. Transfer the chicken to a plate; it will not be cooked through at this point.

5. Add the onions to the same skillet and cook until tender. Add the curry, cayenne, cinnamon, and cumin and cook until aromas are released. Add carrots and toss to coat.

6. Add stock and bring to a simmer.

7. Return the chicken to the skillet and stir in broccoli. Cover and simmer for 5 to 10 minutes to cook chicken.

8. Stir in cream, peas, and broccoli, cook until peas and cream warm through, and season to taste.

9. Serve with rice or bread.

INGREDIENTS:

2	TABLESPOONS AVOCADO OIL
1	TABLESPOON UNSALTED BUTTER
6	CHICKEN BREASTS, SKINLESS
½	TEASPOON SEA SALT
¼	TEASPOON WHITE PEPPER
	ALL-PURPOSE FLOUR, FOR DUSTING
1	CUP CHOPPED ONION
3	TEASPOONS BERBERE SPICE MIX (SEE PAGE 323)
½	TEASPOON CAYENNE PEPPER
1	TEASPOON CINNAMON
1	TEASPOON CUMIN
2	CARROTS, SLICED THIN ON DIAGONAL
1½	CUPS CHICKEN STOCK (SEE PAGE 722)
¼	CUP HEAVY CREAM
¾	CUP FROZEN PEAS
1	CUP BROCCOLI FLORETS

Chicken Curry, page 259

CHICKEN SCHNITZEL & CHERRY SAUCE

YIELD: 4 SERVINGS / **ACTIVE TIME:** 30 MINUTES / **TOTAL TIME:** 45 MINUTES

Crispy, perfectly breaded chicken schnitzel is usually a favorite for all ages. The cherry sauce, of Eastern European origin, adds a tart zing that pairs well with the richness of the fried breading.

1. Add cherries and enough water to just cover them to a pot over medium-high heat. Bring to a boil and lower heat to medium and simmer for about 7 to 10 minutes, until the cherries are tender and soft.

2. Add the wine, sugar, orange zest, ⅛ teaspoon salt, pepper, ginger, and star anise, stir, and cook for an additional 5 minutes.

3. In a small bowl, combine the cornstarch with 2 tablespoons water to make a slurry. Add the slurry to the cherries and mix well. Continue to simmer, stirring constantly until the liquid becomes glossy, thick, and clear, about 2 to 4 minutes. Transfer the sauce to a bowl and set aside.

4. Place the flour into a bowl. Place the beaten eggs into another bowl. In another bowl, combine the panko, bread crumbs, lemon zest, 2 teaspoons sea salt, and pepper and mix well.

5. Starting with one chicken breast at a time, coat the chicken in the flour and shake off any excess. Dip the chicken into the beaten eggs, coat on both sides and then press the chicken into the bread crumb mixture to coat on all sides. Transfer chicken to a plate or baking sheet. Repeat with the remaining chicken breasts.

6. Add the oil to a large skillet over medium-high heat. After about 1 minute, dip the tip of a chicken breast into the oil; if it sizzles, it is ready for frying. Place the chicken breasts into the pan and fry on both sides until golden brown, about 2 to 4 minutes on each side.

7. Transfer schnitzel to a paper towel-lined plate and immediately sprinkle it with the remaining salt.

8. Serve the schnitzel hot with a dollop of warm cherry sauce.

INGREDIENTS:

2	CUPS FRESH CHERRIES OR DEFROSTED FROZEN CHERRIES, PITTED
¼	CUP RED WINE
3-4	TABLESPOONS GRANULATED SUGAR
	ZEST OF 1 ORANGE
1	TEASPOON SEA SALT
1⅛	TEASPOONS FRESHLY GROUND BLACK PEPPER, DIVIDED
1	TABLESPOON FRESHLY GRATED GINGER
1	WHOLE STAR ANISE SEED
4	TABLESPOONS CORNSTARCH
1	CUP ALL-PURPOSE FLOUR
3	EGGS, BEATEN
1	CUP PANKO
1	CUP BREAD CRUMBS
	ZEST OF 1 LEMON
3	TEASPOONS FLAKY SEA SALT, DIVIDED
4	BONELESS CHICKEN BREASTS, POUNDED ¼" THICK
1	CUP AVOCADO OIL

CHICKEN WITH TAMARIND

YIELD: 6 SERVINGS / **ACTIVE TIME:** 20 MINUTES / **TOTAL TIME:** 2 HOURS

The sweet and tangy flavor of tamarind is what makes this traditional Georgian recipe so special.

1. Season all of the chicken pieces with salt and pepper.

2. Add the oil to a large heavy skillet over medium heat. Once the oil is hot, place the chicken pieces into the pan, skin-side down in one layer. Lower the heat to medium-low and slowly brown the chicken, for up to 1 hour, flipping the chicken every 15 minutes, or until the chicken is deep golden brown on all sides.

3. Add enough water to the skillet to cover the chicken pieces three-quarters the way up into the pan (about 4 cups). Increase the heat to medium-high and bring the mixture to a simmer. Add the apricots, apricot preserve, tamarind concentrate, and adobo sauce and stir. Reduce the heat and simmer for 30 to 40 minutes, or until the sauce reduces by a half and thickens and coats the back of a spoon.

4. Serve the chicken hot with a side of rice.

INGREDIENTS:

4	CHICKEN QUARTERS OR 8 CHICKEN PIECES OF YOUR CHOICE, BONE-IN SKIN-ON
1	TEASPOON SEA SALT
½	TEASPOON FRESHLY GROUND BLACK PEPPER
½	CUP AVOCADO OIL
¾	CUP ROUGHLY CHOPPED DRIED APRICOTS,
2	TABLESPOONS APRICOT PRESERVES
¾	CUP TAMARIND CONCENTRATE
2	TABLESPOONS ADOBO SAUCE
	WHITE RICE, TO SERVE

Chicken Schnitzel & Cherry Sauce, page 262

CHICKEN WITH TURMERIC, TAHINI, CHICKPEAS & ONIONS

YIELD: 4 SERVING / **ACTIVE TIME:** 25 MINUTES / **TOTAL TIME:** 1 HOUR AND 30 MINUTES

Musky turmeric and rich tahini enhance the flavors of this comforting and filling dish that can be served year-round.

1. Rub the chicken pieces with a generous amount of salt and pepper and put in a large resealable plastic bag with 1 cup of the tahini sauce. Seal the bag, leaving one corner open about ½". Massage the bag to coat all of the chicken pieces with sauce, then squeeze out as much air as you can and seal the bag completely. Let it sit out for 30 minutes, or refrigerate overnight.

2. Preheat the oven to 425°F.

3. On a large baking sheet, toss the chickpeas and half of the onion with the turmeric, cumin, coriander, and berbere. Drizzle with olive oil, season with salt and pepper, and toss everything to coat. Push everything to the edges of the pan and place the chicken pieces in the center in a single layer. Bake until the onions are crisp, the chicken skin is brown, and an instant-read thermometer registers 160°F when inserted into the thickest part of a thigh, about 50 minutes.

4. In a bowl, combine the remaining onion with the lemon juice and season with salt and pepper.

5. When the chicken is done, transfer it to a serving plate along with the chickpeas and onions. Drizzle with about 1 cup of the remaining tahini sauce and the hot sauce. Scatter the onion-lemon mixture and cilantro on top. Serve any remaining tahini sauce on the side.

INGREDIENTS:

1 (3½-4 LB.) WHOLE CHICKEN, CUT INTO PARTS, OR 3 LBS. BONE-IN, SKIN-ON CHICKEN PARTS

COARSE SEA SALT, TO TASTE

FRESHLY GROUND BLACK PEPPER, TO TASTE

2 CUPS TURMERIC TAHINI SAUCE, DIVIDED

2 (15 OZ.) CANS OF CHICKPEAS, DRAINED AND RINSED

1 MEDIUM RED ONION, THINLY SLICED, DIVIDED

1 TABLESPOON GROUND TURMERIC

1 TEASPOON CUMIN

1 TEASPOON CORIANDER

1 TEASPOON BERBERE SPICE MIX (SEE PAGE 323)

2 TABLESPOONS AVOCADO OIL, DIVIDED

1 TABLESPOON FRESH LEMON JUICE

HOT SAUCE, TO TASTE

LEAVES FROM ½ BUNCH CILANTRO, COARSELY CHOPPED

COJADA POTATO CASSEROLE

YIELD: 6 SERVINGS / **ACTIVE TIME:** 30 MINUTES / **TOTAL TIME:** 2 HOURS

A Sephardic version of the classic Spanish tortilla, this potato-and-egg casserole is a surefire crowd-pleaser.

1. Preheat the oven to 420°F.

2. Place the potatoes in a large pot, cover with cold water, and add 3 tablespoons salt. Bring to a boil over high heat and then reduce heat to medium-low and simmer until the potatoes are fork tender, about 30 to 40 minutes. Drain potatoes from the water and set aside to cool.

3. Grease an 11" x 5" casserole dish with 1 teaspoon oil and set aside.

4. Add 4 tablespoons oil to a saucepan over medium-high heat. Once oil is hot, add the onions and sugar and sauté until golden brown, about 15 minutes. Set aside.

5. Separate the egg yolks and egg whites. Reserve egg yolks. Place the egg whites in the bowl of a stand mixer with a whisk attachment and beat on low for 2 to 3 minutes. Increase speed to medium and whip the eggs for another 3 to 5 minutes until stiff peaks have formed. Set aside.

6. Peel the potatoes, discard the skins, and smash them with a fork until achieving a puree-like consistency.

7. Place the smashed potatoes into a large mixing bowl. Add the cooked onions, salt, pepper, cumin, ras el hanout, nutmeg, and egg yolks and mix well with a large fork. Gently fold in the egg whites.

8. Transfer the mixture to the prepared casserole dish. Smooth out the top layer with a spatula. Sprinkle 1 teaspoon of oil on top and bake for about 40 minutes, or until the cojada is golden brown on all edges.

INGREDIENTS:

3	LARGE RUSSET POTATOES
7	TABLESPOONS, PLUS 2 TEASPOONS AVOCADO OIL, DIVIDED
1	LARGE YELLOW ONION, FINELY CHOPPED
1	TEASPOON SUGAR
3	EGGS
1	TABLESPOON SEA SALT
¼	TEASPOON FRESHLY GROUND BLACK PEPPER
¼	TEASPOON CUMIN
¼	TEASPOON NUTMEG
½	TEASPOON RAS EL HANOUT

COLD ROAST SALMON
WITH SMASHED GREEN BEAN SALAD

YIELD: 10 SERVINGS / **ACTIVE TIME:** 20 MINUTES / **TOTAL TIME:** 40 MINUTES

Served chilled, this entire dish can be made a day ahead, and will keep you calm, cool, and collected at your holiday dinner.

1. Preheat the oven to 300°F.

2. Place salmon on a rimmed baking sheet and rub 2 tablespoons oil over each side. Season all over with black pepper, 2 teaspoons salt, and ¼ teaspoon red pepper flakes. Arrange skin-side down and roast until a tester, metal skewer, or thin-bladed knife inserted laterally through salmon flesh meets no resistance, about 20 to 25 minutes; the fish should be opaque throughout and just able to flake. Let cool.

3. While salmon is roasting, add lemon juice, 3 tablespoons oil, 2 teaspoons salt, and remaining ¼ teaspoon red pepper flakes to a large bowl and whisk to combine. Set aside.

4. Working in batches, place green beans in a large resealable plastic bag. Seal bag and whack beans with a rolling pin to split the skins and soften the insides without completely pulverizing the flesh. Add to the bowl with reserved dressing. Massage with your hands to break down beans further and coat. Let sit at room temperature for at least 1 hour.

5. Thinly slice the radishes lengthwise. Place in a large bowl of ice water, cover, and chill until ready to serve; this will allow you to get the prep out of the way and keep the radishes crisp and firm.

6. Just before serving, drain radishes and toss with marinated green beans. Add pistachios and season the salad to taste. Transfer to a platter and drizzle with oil and sprinkle with flaky salt.

7. Using 2 spatulas, carefully transfer salmon to another platter, leaving skin behind on the baking sheet. Drizzle with oil and squeeze juice from a lemon wedge or two over; sprinkle with flaky salt. Serve with more lemon wedges and Lemony Yogurt Sauce and/or Grilled Serrano Salsa Verde alongside.

INGREDIENTS:

1	(3½–3¾ LB.) WHOLE SIDE OF SALMON
7	TABLESPOONS AVOCADO OIL, DIVIDED, PLUS MORE FOR SERVING
	FRESHLY GROUND BLACK PEPPER, TO TASTE
4	TEASPOONS SEA SALT, DIVIDED, PLUS MORE TO TASTE
½	TEASPOON CRUSHED RED PEPPER FLAKES, DIVIDED
¼	CUP FRESH LEMON JUICE
2	LBS. GREEN BEANS, TRIMMED
1	BUNCH RADISHES, PREFERABLY FRENCH BREAKFAST, TRIMMED
1	CUP COARSELY CHOPPED SALTED AND ROASTED PISTACHIOS
	FLAKY SEA SALT, TO TASTE
	LEMON WEDGES, FOR SERVING
	LEMONY YOGURT SAUCE, FOR SERVING (SEE RECIPE)
	GRILLED SERRANO SALSA VERDE, FOR SERVING (SEE RECIPE)

LEMONY YOGURT SAUCE

1. In a medium bowl, combine all of the ingredients and whisk well.

GRILLED SERRANO SALSA VERDE

1. Prepare a grill for medium-high heat.

2. Skewer the chiles and grill, turning often, until charred and softened, about 6 minutes. Let cool; remove stems.

3. Meanwhile, pluck leaves from basil and leaves and tender stems from cilantro and parsley. You should have about 2 cups of each herb.

4. Add chiles, basil, cilantro, and parsley to a food processor and pulse until finely chopped. Add oil, vinegar, and salt and pulse until a thick, slightly textured sauce forms.

LEMONY YOGURT SAUCE

6	TABLESPOONS FRESH LEMON JUICE
1	GARLIC CLOVE, FINELY GRATED
1	TEASPOON SEA SALT
1	TEASPOON FRESHLY GROUND BLACK PEPPER
2	CUPS PLAIN WHOLE-MILK GREEK YOGURT

GRILLED SERRANO SALSA VERDE

6-8	SERRANO CHILES
1	BUNCH BASIL
1	BUNCH CILANTRO
1	BUNCH PARSLEY
1-¼	CUPS EXTRA VIRGIN OLIVE OIL
½	CUP SHERRY VINEGAR OR RED WINE VINEGAR
2½	TEASPOONS SEA SALT

CORNED BEEF WITH BARBEQUE SAUCE

YIELD: 6 SERVINGS / **ACTIVE TIME:** 20 MINUTES / **TOTAL TIME:** 3 HOURS AND 45 MINUTES

Corned beef isn't just for deli sandwiches. This recipe is well worth the time.

1. In a large pot, combine all of the beef ingredients and add enough water to completely cover the meat. Turn the heat on high and bring the mixture to a boil. Skim any scum that rises to the surface. Reduce heat to medium-low and simmer for 3 hours, or until the beef is tender and cooked through.

2. In a bowl, combine all of the sauce ingredients, mix well, and set aside.

3. Preheat the oven to 350°F.

4. Gently transfer and drain the beef onto a paper towel-lined cutting board and let cool for about 5 minutes, or until cool enough to handle. The liquid that is left behind in the pot is a beef broth that can be reserved for another dish.

5. Pat the beef dry and slice the beef against the grain into ½" thick slices. Use a large spatula or tongs to transfer the sliced corned beef onto a baking tray, while keeping its shape intact. Slightly fan out the beef slices on the baking tray and pour the sauce over the beef. Use a spatula or brush to evenly cover all the beef with sauce.

6. Cover the sauced beef with aluminum foil and roast it for 30 minutes, or until the beef is lightly browned and absorbs the sauce.

INGREDIENTS:

BEEF

4-5½	LBS. RAW PICKLED CORNED BEEF
2	TABLESPOONS SEA SALT
2	DRY BAY LEAVES
4	TABLESPOONS BROWN SUGAR
4	GARLIC CLOVES, PEELED
2	YELLOW ONIONS, PEELED

SAUCE

2	TABLESPOONS AVOCADO OIL
1	TABLESPOON YELLOW MUSTARD
½	CUP PACKED BROWN SUGAR
5	TABLESPOONS KETCHUP
3	TABLESPOONS APPLE CIDER VINEGAR
1	TABLESPOON SEA SALT
½	TEASPOON GROUND BLACK PEPPER

CROCKPOT SWEET & SOUR BRISKET

YIELD: 4 SERVINGS / **ACTIVE TIME:** 1 HOUR / **TOTAL TIME:** 10 HOURS

Put that wedding gift to use already! Your crockpot is a wonderful place to let your brisket tenderize, and this sauce will become a sticky family favorite.

1. Add 1 tablespoon oil to a large skillet over medium-high heat.

2. Sprinkle all sides of the brisket with salt and pepper. Place brisket in the hot skillet and brown on both sides, about 5 minutes per side. When the brisket is browned, add to the crock pot.

3. In the same skillet, add a touch more oil and sauté onions, carrots, celery, and garlic for 5 minutes.

4. In a bowl, combine the wine, stock, brown sugar, ketchup, and vinegar, whisk well, and set aside.

5. When vegetables are done add cranberries and cook for another minute. Pour in the wine mixture, add the parsley, and bring to a boil.

6. Carefully pour vegetables and sauce over the brisket and cook on high for 4 to 6 hours or on low for 8 to 10 hours.

7. When done, take out meat and let cool for 5 minutes, or until easy to handle. Cut, plate and spoon some vegetables over with a touch of gravy.

INGREDIENTS:

- 1 TABLESPOON, PLUS 1 TEASPOON AVOCADO OIL
- 3 LBS. BRISKET
- SEA SALT, TO TASTE
- FRESHLY GROUND BLACK PEPPER, TO TASTE
- 2 LARGE ONIONS
- 6 CARROTS, CUT INTO MATCHSTICKS
- 5 CELERY STALKS, CHOPPED
- 6 GARLIC CLOVES CHOPPED
- ¾ CUP RED WINE
- ¾ CUP CHICKEN OR BEEF STOCK (SEE PAGE 722 OR PAGE 721)
- ¼ CUP BROWN SUGAR
- ½ CUP KETCHUP
- 6 TABLESPOONS CIDER VINEGAR
- ¼ CUP DRIED CRANBERRIES
- 1 CUP CHOPPED FLAT-LEAF PARSLEY

Crispy Roast Chicken, page 274

CRISPY ROAST CHICKEN

YIELD: 4 SERVINGS / **ACTIVE TIME:** 45 MINUTES / **TOTAL TIME:** 1 HOUR AND 45 MINUTES

Rendered fat trickles down from the chicken as it roasts over a bed of sliced potatoes and onions. The result is a bird with deliciously crispy skin and juicy meat, a built-in side dish, and some well-earned kvelling.

1. Place a 12" cast-iron or stainless-steel skillet on a rack in the lower third of the oven and preheat it to 450°F.

2. Pull off any excess fat around cavities of chicken and discard. Using paper towels, thoroughly pat dry chicken inside and out. Arrange chicken breast-side up on a cutting board. Gently loosen skin covering breasts and thighs and tuck 4 herb sprigs under loosened skin; 1 sprig for each breast and thigh.

3. In a bowl, combine 1 tablespoon plus 1 teaspoon salt and pepper and mix well.

4. Using a metal skewer or paring knife, poke 20 to 30 holes all over chicken, paying special attention to the thickest parts of skin. Season chicken with salt mixture, placing a pinch inside the cavity, but primarily covering the outside of the bird. Then tie legs together with kitchen twine.

5. Cut remaining herb sprig crosswise into 3 or 4 pieces and place in a large bowl. Add potatoes, onions, oil, ½ teaspoon salt, and a generous pinch of pepper. Toss to combine.

6. Carefully remove the skillet from the oven. Transfer potato mixture to skillet (mixture will sizzle), then place chicken, breast-side up, on potato mixture. Return the skillet to the oven—remember, the handle is hot! Roast until an instant-read thermometer inserted into the thickest part of breast registers 165°F, 45 to 55 minutes.

7. Remove the skillet from the oven. Using tongs or a large wooden spoon inserted into the cavity, transfer chicken to a large plate. Give the potato mixture a stir, then return to the oven. Let the chicken rest for about 5 minutes.

8. Using a sharp knife, slash stretched skin between thighs and breasts to let steam escape. Carefully tilt bird and plate over a large bowl to drain juices; reserve juices. Let chicken rest until potatoes are fork-tender, 15 to 25 minutes more.

INGREDIENTS:

1	(4-4½ LB.) WHOLE CHICKEN
5	SPRIGS FRESH THYME, ROSEMARY, MARJORAM, OR SAGE
1	TABLESPOON PLUS 1½ TEASPOON SEA SALT
½	TEASPOON FRESHLY GROUND PEPPER, PLUS MORE TO TASTE
1¼	LBS. MEDIUM RED OR YUKON GOLD POTATOES, CUT INTO ½" WEDGES
2	SMALL ONIONS, CUT INTO ½" WEDGES, LEAVING ROOT END INTACT
1½	TABLESPOONS AVOCADO OIL

9. Tilt chicken and plate again over bowl with juices to drain any last bits, then transfer chicken to a cutting board and carve. If the juices have cooled and congealed, gently rewarm over low heat or for 10 seconds in the microwave.

10. Arrange chicken on a platter. Serve with roasted potatoes and onions alongside, spooning juices over.

TIP: If time allows, after patting dry and salting chicken, place on a wire rack set in a rimmed baking sheet, or on a V-rack set in a roasting pan, and refrigerate, uncovered, for at least 12 hours or up to 2 days. This dry brine will result in a flavorful juicy chicken with even crispier skin

Crockpot Carne con Papas, page 278

CROCKPOT CARNE CON PAPAS

YIELD: 6 SERVINGS / **ACTIVE TIME:** 1 HOUR / **TOTAL TIME:** 12 HOURS

Meat and potatoes made easy. Feed a crowd with this slow-but-simple recipe.

1. In a resealable plastic bag, combine beef, citrus juice, oregano, garlic, mustard, 3 tablespoons oil, salt, and pepper. Close the bag, making sure to remove all the air, and massage the ingredients together until well-combined. Refrigerate for 1 to 4 hours.

2. Once the meat has marinated, add the remaining oil to a large skillet over medium-high heat. Divide the beef into two sections, reserving the marinade liquid. Brown the first batch of beef for 3 minutes, and set aside. Lightly coat the second batch of beef in flour, and brown for 3 minutes. Set aside.

3. In the same skillet, add onion and bell peppers and cook for 3 minutes. Add tomatoes, tomato sauce, stock, and reserved marinade liquid, and deglaze the skillet using a wooden spoon. Stir in cumin and seasonings

4. Transfer the beef, vegetables, and sauce to a slow-cooker, and add in bay leaves and potatoes. Stir to combine, cover, and cook on low for 7 hours, or until beef is fork-tender. Season to taste.

5. Garnish with cilantro and serve with steamed white rice.

INGREDIENTS:

- 2 LBS. BEEF TOP ROUND OR STEW MEAT, CUT INTO 1" CHUNKS
- JUICE OF 3 SOUR ORANGES (OR 2 ORANGES AND 2 LEMONS)
- 1 TABLESPOON CHOPPED FRESH OREGANO
- 4 GARLIC CLOVES, FINELY MINCED
- 1 TABLESPOON SMOKED MUSTARD, OR DIJON
- 5 TABLESPOONS AVOCADO OIL, DIVIDED
- SEA SALT, TO TASTE
- FRESHLY GROUND BLACK PEPPER, TO TASTE
- 3 TABLESPOONS ALL-PURPOSE FLOUR
- 1 LARGE ONION, SLICED
- 1 GREEN BELL PEPPER COARSELY DICED
- 1 RED BELL PEPPER, COARSELY DICED
- 1 (14.5 OZ.) CAN OF DICED TOMATOES
- 1 (8 OZ.) CAN OF TOMATO SAUCE
- 2 CUPS BEEF STOCK (SEE PAGE 721)
- 1 TABLESPOON CHOPPED CILANTRO
- 1 TABLESPOON CUMIN
- 1 TABLESPOON OF A SPICE MIX WITH SALT, GROUND BLACK PEPPER, GARLIC POWDER, CORIANDER, CUMIN, OREGANO, AND ANNATTO SEEDS.
- 2 BAY LEAVES
- 2 LBS. SMALL WHITE POTATOES, HALVED
- CILANTRO, FOR GARNISH
- STEAMED WHITE RICE, FOR SERVING

DAFINA

YIELD: 4 SERVINGS / **ACTIVE TIME:** 20 MINUTES / **TOTAL TIME:** 24 HOURS

Served especially on Shabbat, this iconic slow-cooked Moroccan stew has a long history and no two variations are the same. For centuries, Jewish women around the world have prepared some kind of similar dish each week, usually prepping the ingredients Friday to be served for lunch the next day. Although recent generations have moved around the globe and reside in different countries, the tradition of this classic dish has prevailed and is a touchstone for many families.

1. Arrange the chickpeas on the bottom of a crockpot. Add the potatoes around the interior walls of the crockpot. Place the meat, chicken, whole eggs, and dates in the center.

2. Add all of the spices, garlic, and oil and mix very well but gently as to keep each ingredient in its place. Pour in enough water to cover everything by ¼".

3. Set the crockpot at a medium temperature and cook for 24 hours.

INGREDIENTS:

2	CANS OF CHICKPEAS, RINSED
12	LARGE RED POTATOES, PEELED
2	LBS. FLANKEN MEAT, BONE-IN
4	PIECES CHICKEN, BONE-IN
4	EGGS
4	PITTED DATES
1	TABLESPOON SEA SALT
1	TEASPOON BLACK PEPPER
1	TEASPOON PAPRIKA
1	TEASPOON CUMIN
1	TEASPOON TURMERIC
1	TEASPOON HONEY
1	TEASPOON CINNAMON
3-4	GARLIC CLOVES
2	TABLESPOONS AVOCADO OIL

DELICATA SQUASH PASTA
WITH BROWN BUTTER & SAGE

YIELD: 4 SERVINGS / **ACTIVE TIME:** 30 MINUTES / **TOTAL TIME:** 50 MINUTES

A delicious autumnal preparation that would be welcome at any Rosh Hashanah table. The brown butter is a simple way of adding an extra layer of gourmet sophistication to this dish.

1. Add the butter to a large skillet over medium heat and cook, swirling the pan occasionally, until butter turns caramel-brown and smells nutty, 2 to 3 minutes. Add sage and fry until crispy, 10 to 15 seconds. Remove from heat. Using a slotted spoon, transfer sage to paper towels to drain. Pour all but 2 tablespoons of the brown butter into a small bowl.

2. Cook panko and 4 sage leaves in the same skillet, stirring to break up sage, until mixture is toasty, about 2 minutes. Transfer to a plate.

3. Cook squash and 3 tablespoons of brown butter in the same skillet over medium heat, stirring frequently, until squash begins to brown, about 5 minutes. Add salt, ¼ teaspoon pepper, and ¾ cup water; cover pan and cook until squash begins to soften, about 5 minutes. Remove lid and continue cooking, stirring occasionally, until liquid has evaporated and squash is tender and caramelized, about 5 minutes more.

4. Meanwhile, bring a large pot of salted water to a boil and then the cook pasta, stirring occasionally, until al dente, 8 to 10 minutes. Drain, reserving ¾ cup pasta cooking liquid.

5. Add remaining 3 tablespoons brown butter to the skillet and stir until squash is evenly coated. Add ½ cup pasta cooking liquid and simmer until a thin sauce forms, about 1 minute; season with 1 teaspoon pepper. Add pasta, tossing to coat and adding pasta cooking water as needed to coat pasta. Remove from heat, top with half of the reserved sage, and stir to combine.

6. Transfer pasta to a large serving bowl or individual pasta bowls. Top with panko mixture, remaining sage, and a generous shaving of Parmesan.

INGREDIENTS:

1	STICK OF UNSALTED BUTTER
14	LARGE SAGE LEAVES
½	CUP PANKO
2	MEDIUM DELICATA SQUASH, HALVED LENGTHWISE, SEEDED, AND SLICED CROSSWISE INTO ¼" THICK HALF-MOONS
½	TEASPOON SEA SALT
1¼	TEASPOON FRESHLY GROUND BLACK PEPPER
12	OZ. THICK SPAGHETTI OR BUCATINI
¾	CUP WATER
¼	CUP THINLY SHAVED PARMESAN CHEESE

DOLMEH BEH

YIELD: 6 SERVINGS / **ACTIVE TIME:** 30 MINUTES / **TOTAL TIME:** 1 HOUR

A beautiful balance of both slightly sweet and sour, the cardamom adds an unexpected twist to this eye-catching beef and quince recipe.

1. Place the quinces and 2 cardamom pods in a medium pot and cover with water. Bring the water to a boil over high heat, reduce heat, and then simmer for 20 minutes, until the quinces are fork-tender. Drain and allow the quinces to cool. Cut each quince cross-wise into 1" pieces. Use a knife to remove the core from each piece, keeping the quince's ring shape intact. Discard the core and set aside the quince pieces.

2. Place the onion in a food processor and process until finely chopped, approximately 3 to 5 minutes. Transfer the onion to a large bowl and add the meat, tarragon, cilantro, pistachios, barberries, 1 teaspoon salt, and advieh. Knead the mixture together until combined. Divide the meat mixture into balls, the same number of balls as quince slices. Fill the center of each quince ring with a ball of the meat mixture. Set aside.

3. Using a mortar and pestle, ground the saffron and sugar into a powder. Transfer the powder to a small bowl and add the boiling water. Mix well and set aside for 15 minutes.

4. In a medium pot, combine saffron water with 2 cardamom pods, jalapeño, and lemon juice and bring the mixture to a boil over high heat. Add salt and pepper, remove from heat, and set aside.

5. Add the oil to a wide pot over medium heat. Once the oil is hot, place the stuffed quince pieces with the meat side down into the pot in one layer and sear until golden brown, about 3 to 5 minutes. Flip the quince pieces and pour the sauce over them until they are covered halfway. Place a lid on the pot and cook for 25 minutes, or until the quinces are tender and the meat is cooked. Occasionally, baste the quince with the sauce.

6. Transfer the stuffed quinces to a serving plate, pour sauce on top, and sprinkle with the chopped pistachios. Serve hot.

INGREDIENTS:

- 3 QUINCES
- 4 CARDAMOM PODS, DIVIDED
- 1 YELLOW ONION, PEELED AND HALVED
- 1 LB. GROUND BEEF OR LAMB
- 1 TABLESPOON FINELY CHOPPED TARRAGON
- ½ CUP FINELY CHOPPED CILANTRO
- ⅓ CUP FINELY CHOPPED ROASTED UNSALTED PISTACHIOS, PLUS MORE TO GARNISH
- 1½ TABLESPOONS BARBERRIES OR CRANBERRIES
- 2 TEASPOONS SEA SALT, DIVIDED
- 1 TEASPOON ADVIEH (PERSIAN SPICE MIX)
- 2 SAFFRON THREADS
- ⅛ TEASPOON SUGAR
- 2 TABLESPOONS BOILING WATER
- 2 CARDAMOM PODS
- 2 CUPS CHICKEN STOCK (SEE PAGE 722) OR WATER
- ½ JALAPEÑO, FINELY CHOPPED
- 1 TABLESPOON FRESH LEMON JUICE
- ¼ TEASPOON GROUND BLACK PEPPER
- 1 TABLESPOON AVOCADO OIL

EGGPLANT & CHORIZO BOUREKA

YIELD: 4 SERVINGS / **ACTIVE TIME:** 30 MINUTES / **TOTAL TIME:** 1 HOUR

Popular among Sephardic communities these filled pastries come in all sorts of shapes and can be filled with a dizzying array of ingredients.

1. Add 4 tablespoons oil to a pan over medium-high heat. Season the eggplant with salt and pepper and add the eggplant to the hot oil, tossing until it is all absorbed. Fry gently for 15 to 20 minutes, turning every so often, until the cubes are soft and the oil has released back into the pan. Using a slotted spoon, scoop out the eggplant and transfer it to a paper towel-lined plate.

2. Add the onion to the pan, fry gently for 10 minutes, until softened, then add the garlic and cumin. Fry for 30 seconds more, then transfer to a bowl and mix in the eggplant.

3. Add the chorizo to the pan and fry until golden and starting to crisp. Drain and mix with the rest of the ingredients in the bowl. Add the parsley and plenty of seasoning and allow to cool.

4. Heat the remainder of the oil to 350°F in a large non-stick sauté pan.

5. Place 2 sheets of boureka dough in a dish or bowl. Spoon a quarter of the filling into the center, making a well in the middle. Crack the egg into the well. Carefully fold one side of the pastry over the other and, using the corners, lift gently.

6. Place in the hot oil, pressing around the edges of the filing with a spatula to stop it escaping. Spoon some of the hot oil over the top.

7. Once it has been cooking for 30 seconds, and the underside is golden, flip it over carefully and cook on the other side.

8. Drain on a paper towel-lined plate and repeat to make 3 more. Serve in soft white rolls or pitas.

INGREDIENTS:

1¼ CUPS AVOCADO OIL, PLUS 4 TABLESPOONS, DIVIDED

1 EGGPLANT, CUBED

1 TEASPOON SEA SALT

1 TEASPOON BLACK PEPPER

1 LARGE ONION, FINELY SLICED

2 GARLIC CLOVES, FINELY SLICED

1 TEASPOON CUMIN SEEDS

7 OZ. CHORIZO, FINELY DICED

1 HANDFUL OF PARSLEY, CHOPPED

8 SHEETS OF BOUREKA DOUGH

4 EGGS

EGYPTIAN SHORT RIB & OKRA STEW

YIELD: 6 SERVINGS / **ACTIVE TIME:** 30 MINUTES / **TOTAL TIME:** 3 HOURS

The rice soaks up all of the delicious flavors from the short ribs and stew, turning this into a family favorite. Be prepared to serve seconds.

1. Preheat the oven to 350°F.

2. Slice meat into 2" cubes and season all sides with salt and pepper.

3. Add ¼ cup oil to a large heavy bottom pot over medium-high heat. Brown meat on all sides, about 5 minutes, adding garlic as meat is nearly browned.

4. Remove meat from the pot and add tomato paste. Cook for 30 seconds, stirring constantly. Add tomatoes in small batches, squeezing and juicing them into the pan before adding.

5. Add the water, lemon juice, paprika, 1 bay leaf, and 3 to 5 slices of jalapeño. Add meat back to pot, spacing evenly, and sprinkle it with the sugar. Turn down heat to low and simmer uncovered while preparing the okra.

6. Add 3 tablespoons of oil to pan over high heat. Once the oil is hot, add the okra, tossing until bright green and lightly blistered, 1 to 2 minutes. Remove from heat, toss with ¼ teaspoon salt and a squeeze of lemon juice.

7. Add okra to the pot, spacing evenly around the meat. Add 6 to 10 mint leaves, cover, and bake for 2 hours, checking every 30 minutes. If liquid reduces too much add water.

8. After 2 hours, the meat should be fork-tender. Turn on the broiler and broil, uncovered, for 10 to 12 minutes, until dark and caramelized.

9. Meanwhile, add 2 tablespoons oil to a small saucepan over high heat. Add the rice and toast, stirring until the grains are too hot to touch. Add 2 bay leaves, coriander, and boiling water, bring to a boil, then lower heat and simmer, covered, for 20 minutes.

10. Remove rice from heat and let stand for 10 minutes. Gently fluff rice with a spoon, then cover until ready to serve.

11. Remove from the stew from the oven. Season to taste and sprinkle with a handful of mint leaves. Serve warm with rice.

TIP: When choosing okra, make sure that it is crisp and not soggy; pierce the skin of the okra with a thumbnail to check for crispiness.

INGREDIENTS:

2¼	LBS. BONELESS SHORT RIBS
1	TEASPOON SEA SALT, PLUS MORE TO TASTE
½	TEASPOON BLACK PEPPER, PLUS MORE TO TASTE
¼	CUP PLUS 5 TABLESPOONS AVOCADO OIL
3	GARLIC CLOVES, PEELED AND SMASHED
4	TABLESPOONS TOMATO PASTE
¾	LB. VINE RIPE TOMATOES, QUARTERED
1½	CUPS WATER
	JUICE OF 1 MEDIUM LEMON, PLUS MORE TO TASTE
1	TEASPOON SWEET PAPRIKA
3	BAY LEAVES, DIVIDED
1	SMALL JALAPEÑO, SLICED INTO ⅛" ROUNDS
1	TEASPOON SUGAR
1	LB. OKRA, STEMS TRIMMED
1	BUNCH MINT
1	CUP BASMATI RICE
1	TEASPOON CORIANDER SEEDS
1½	CUPS BOILING WATER

EVERYTHING SPICED MALAWAH WITH FRIED EGG

YIELD: 1 SERVING / **ACTIVE TIME:** 15 MINUTES / **TOTAL TIME:** 15 MINUTES

Malawah is a buttery, flaky bread from Yemen. But topping it with Everything Spice and a fried egg is pure New York, of course.

1. In a small bowl, combine the sesame seeds, poppy seeds, minced garlic, dried onion, salt, and red pepper flakes, mix well, and set aside.

2. Add 1 teaspoon butter to a pan over medium heat. Add frozen malawah to the pan and cook according to directions, around 3 minutes. While the first side is cooking, gently sprinkle an even layer of the spice mixture on top, and press into dough. After 3 minutes, flip onto the second side and cook for another 3 minutes. Some of the spice mixture will fall off.

3. Fry eggs according to your taste in 1 teaspoon butter.

4. Top malawah with fried egg and sprinkle with fresh parsley if desired. Serve immediately.

INGREDIENTS:

1   TABLESPOON SESAME SEEDS

1   TABLESPOON POPPY SEEDS

1   TABLESPOON DRIED MINCED GARLIC

1   TABLESPOON DRIED ONION

2   TEASPOONS COARSE SEA SALT

¼   TEASPOON RED PEPPER FLAKES, OR MORE TO TASTE

2   TEASPOONS UNSALTED BUTTER

2   PIECES FROZEN MALAWAH BREAD

1   EGG

1   TEASPOON PARSLEY, TO GARNISH (OPTIONAL)

EYERLEKH MIT TZVIBLE

YIELD: 6 SERVINGS / **ACTIVE TIME:** 20 MINUTES / **TOTAL TIME:** 1 HOUR AND 30 MINUTES

This dish was born in the Eastern European shtetl and contains more potato than eggs and onion, but sometimes these things go without saying. If you truly want to follow tradition, enjoy this meal alongside good vodka.

1. Preheat the oven to 450°F.

2. Pierce the potatoes several times with a paring knife or fork and wrap each tightly in foil. Bake the potatoes until tender, about 1 hour. Set aside in the foil until cool enough to handle.

3. Meanwhile, slice the onions into ¼" rings and separate the pieces.

4. Heat the oil in a large skillet over medium-high heat. Working in batches, add the onion rings to the skillet and sauté until golden, flipping once with tongs, about 2 minutes per side. Transfer the onion rings to a large bowl. Add the garlic to the skillet and cook until golden, about 1 minute. Transfer to the bowl with the onions. Let the oil cool slightly, then drizzle it over the onion mixture, season with salt and pepper, and set aside.

5. Meanwhile, add the eggs to a small pot and just cover with water. Bring to a boil, reduce heat, and simmer the eggs for 7 to 8 minutes. Remove the eggs from heat and shock them in cold water to stop the cooking process.

6. To assemble the dish, remove the potatoes from the foil and break them into large bite-sized pieces. Add the potatoes to the bowl with the onion mixture and toss to coat. Peel the eggs and cut them once lengthwise and once crosswise into quarters. Add them to the bowl with the onions and potatoes. Fold in the scallions and season the mixture with salt and pepper, to taste. Serve at room temperature with smoked fish.

TIP: Cooking this recipe is all about timing. As the potatoes cook, be sure to move on to the next steps.

INGREDIENTS:

3   MEDIUM RUSSET POTATOES

3   LARGE YELLOW ONIONS

¼   CUP AVOCADO OIL

2   GARLIC CLOVES, THINLY SLICED

FINE SEA SALT, TO TASTE

FRESHLY GROUND BLACK PEPPER, TO TASTE

4   LARGE EGGS, AT ROOM TEMPERATURE

3   SCALLIONS, WHITE AND LIGHT GREEN PARTS ONLY, CUT INTO ½" PIECES

SMOKED FISH, LIKE WHITE ANCHOVIES, FOR SERVING

Fried Fish with Agristada Sauce, page 292

FRIED FISH WITH AGRISTADA SAUCE

YIELD: 6 SERVINGS / **ACTIVE TIME:** 30 MINUTES / **TOTAL TIME:** 1 HOUR

Agristada is a Sephardic lemon and egg sauce and always accompanies this recipe.

1. Place the fish in a shallow dish, pour the lemon juice on top, sprinkle ¼ teaspoon salt, and turn the fish until well coated. Let soak for 30 minutes, turning once or twice. Move the fillets to a colander, discarding the juice, and rinse well. Pat dry and then cut into 1" cubes.

2. Add enough oil to a large pan that it reaches about halfway up and set over medium-high heat.

3. In a shallow bowl, combine the flour with ¼ teaspoon salt, and whisk the eggs in another shallow bowl with the remaining ¼ teaspoon salt.

4. Cover each fish piece in flour from all sides, shaking off excess flour, then dip in the eggs from all sides, letting the excess drip off. Place a few pieces of fish in the oil, not overcrowding the pan, and fry on medium heat until well browned, 5 minutes on each side. Remove to a paper towel-lined deep dish and continue with the rest of the fish in batches.

5. Serve immediately with Agristada Sauce (see recipe).

INGREDIENTS:

2	LBS. COD FILLET OR RED MULLET FILLETS
½	CUP LEMON JUICE
¾	TEASPOON SALT, DIVIDED
	AVOCADO OIL, FOR FRYING
1	CUP ALL-PURPOSE FLOUR
2	EGGS

AGRISTADA SAUCE

4	EGGS
2	CUPS WARM WATER
2	TABLESPOONS ALL-PURPOSE FLOUR
¼	CUP AVOCADO OIL
⅓	CUP FRESHLY SQUEEZED LEMON JUICE
½	TEASPOON SEA SALT

AGRISTADA SAUCE

YIELD: 2 CUPS / **ACTIVE TIME:** 10 MINUTES / **TOTAL TIME:** 20 MINUTES

1. In a medium saucepan, whisk the eggs until evenly blended.

2. In a small bowl, vigorously mix the warm water with the flour, until there are no visible lumps, then strain it through a sieve or a strainer into the saucepan. Add the oil, lemon juice, and salt and place over medium-low heat, stirring constantly with a wooden spoon, until the sauce thickens, about 10 to 12 minutes. When it is about to boil, remove from heat, keep stirring for 1 more minute, then strain again into a glass dish.

3. Taste and add more lemon juice or salt if necessary. Cover with plastic wrap on the surface of the sauce to avoid a film on top. Cool to room temperature, refrigerate if not serving yet.

KIFTAHS

YIELD: 6 SERVINGS / **ACTIVE TIME:** 20 MINUTES / **TOTAL TIME:** 2 HOURS

Kiftahs are a staple meatball recipe with an easy-to-replicate mixture of ground meat, usually lamb or beef. The sour tomato sauce brightens this savory dish.

1. Add the tomatoes, water, prune juice, and 1 teaspoon salt to a pot over medium-high heat, bring to a boil, then lower the heat and simmer for 20 to 30 minutes, or until the flavors combine and the sauce thickens.

2. In a large bowl, combine beef, rice, 1 teaspoon salt, allspice and egg and use your hands to mix ingredients together to ensure that they are all well distributed. Shape about ½ tablespoon of the mixture into a ball and place it in the tomato sauce (which should still be simmering). Continue shaping and placing the meatballs into the sauce.

3. Partially cover the pot and simmer the meatballs for about 1 hour and 30 minutes, stirring occasionally. Taste sauce in the middle of cooking, and adjust for levels of salt, sweet, and sour.

4. Serve hot over white rice.

INGREDIENTS:

1	(28 OZ.) CAN OF CRUSHED TOMATOES
1	CUP WATER
¼	CUP PRUNE JUICE
2	TEASPOONS SALT, DIVIDED
1	LB. GROUND BEEF
¼	CUP SHORT-GRAIN RICE, RINSED AND DRAINED
1	TEASPOON GROUND ALLSPICE
1	EGG

GHORMEH SABZI

YIELD: 6 SERVINGS / **ACTIVE TIME:** 30 MINUTES / **TOTAL TIME:** 2 HOURS

Considered by many to be Iran's national dish, this beloved recipe combines fenugreek leaves, Omani limes, and minced herbs for a stew that is renowned for its mixture of sweet and sour flavors.

1. Place Persian limes in a medium heatproof bowl. Bring 1 cup water to a boil and pour over the limes. Let stand until ready to use.

2. In a large stockpot, combine the meat with the remaining 8 cups water. Bring to a boil and skim the foam off the top. Reduce the heat and simmer for 1 hour, skimming the foam as needed.

3. Add the beans to the pot and increase the heat to a boil for 5 minutes, continuing to skim any foam off the top. Add the dried Persian limes with their soaking liquid and reduce the heat to a low simmer; cover and cook for 1 hour.

4. Meanwhile, set a skillet over medium heat. Add the onion and cook without any oil until they begin to sweat, 5 minutes. Add 2 tablespoons oil and continue to cook until golden brown, 5 minutes more. Transfer to a large bowl and add all of the remaining ingredients.

5. Once the beans are tender, add the onion and herb mixture to the pot and stir to incorporate. Cover and continue to cook until the greens have wilted and the stew is fragrant, 20 to 30 minutes. Season to taste and serve.

INGREDIENTS:

12	DRIED BLACK PERSIAN LIMES, HALVED AND SEEDED
1	CUP BLACK EYED PEAS, SOAKED OVERNIGHT
9	CUPS WATER, DIVIDED
3	LBS. BEEF CHUCK, CUT INTO 1½" PIECES
2	MEDIUM ONIONS, ROUGHLY CHOPPED
5	TABLESPOONS AVOCADO, DIVIDED
8	CUPS CHOPPED PARSLEY, LEAVES AND TENDER STEMS
8	CUPS CHOPPED CILANTRO, LEAVES AND TENDER STEMS
1½	CUPS CHOPPED MINT, LEAVES
1	LEEK, GREEN PART ONLY, SLICED INTO ⅛" STRIPS
3	TABLESPOONS DRIED SAVORY
3	TABLESPOONS DRIED MINT
3	TEASPOONS FRESHLY GROUND BLACK PEPPER
2	TABLESPOONS SEA SALT, PLUS MORE TO TASTE
2½	TEASPOONS GROUND CUMIN

Hand-Rolled Couscous, page 298

HAND-ROLLED COUSCOUS

YIELD: 6 SERVINGS / **ACTIVE TIME:** 30 MINUTES / **TOTAL TIME:** 1 HOUR AND 15 MINUTES

The extra love and attention given to this staple is well worth the effort, trust us.

INGREDIENTS:

- 2¾ CUPS SEMOLINA FLOUR
- ½ CUP WATER, FOR SPRAYING
- 1½ TEASPOONS SEA SALT
- ⅓ CUP AVOCADO OIL
- 2 CUPS BEEF STOCK, CHICKEN STOCK, OR WATER (SEE PAGE 721 OR PAGE 722)

1. Pour the semolina into a large mixing bowl. Place ½ cup water in a sprayer and use it to moisten the semolina. Begin by spraying the surface, stirring the mixture with your hand, pressing down, and moving your palm in a circular motion. It is better to have too little moisture than too much because you don't want to create a dough. Continue to spray and mix until water is evenly incorporated into the semolina; it should form tiny granules without clumping—it is not necessary to use all of the water.

2. Depending on the texture of the mixture, sift it for uniformity and to remove any small clumps. To sift it, shake the moistened semolina through a strainer or colander with holes about ⅛" in diameter (better slightly larger than smaller) into another bowl. After most of it has passed through, stir to continue to pass it through, then press to pass as much as possible. There may be a small amount of doughy mixture that won't go through the strainer—as much as ⅓ cup—and this may be discarded.

3. Prepare a steamer by adding 4" to 5" water to the bottom and bringing it to a boil. Add the semolina and steam uncovered for 10 minutes, mixing about every 30 seconds to prevent clumping; after 10 minutes, the mixture won't clump any more. Cover and continue to steam for another 30 minutes, stirring about every 10 minutes.

4. Transfer the couscous to a bowl, sprinkle with salt, and drizzle with oil. Stir gently with a fork. The couscous may be covered and refrigerated at this point for up to 3 days.

5. To serve, bring 2 cups of water or stock to a boil and set aside. Steam the couscous one more time, covered, over boiling water, for another 15 to 20 minutes. Transfer to a bowl and add 1 to 2 cups of the liquid so it is moist but not wet. Fluff, and serve immediately, or if desired, pass once more through a large-holed sieve or colander.

LAMB STEW

YIELD: 10 SERVINGS / **ACTIVE TIME:** 30 MINUTES / **TOTAL TIME:** 1 HOUR

This lamb stew stand apart from others due to the heat from the berbere.

1. In a bowl, combine the wine, lemon juice, zest, berbere, paprika, and mustard and whisk well.

2. Season the lamb with salt and pepper.

3. In a large enameled cast-iron casserole dish, heat the olive until shimmering.

4. Add half of the lamb to the casserole dish and cook over moderately high heat, turning, until browned all over, 8 minutes. Using a slotted spoon, transfer the lamb to a medium bowl. Repeat with the remaining lamb.

5. Add the onions, garlic, rosemary, thyme, and a generous pinch each of salt and pepper to the casserole dish and cook over moderate heat, stirring occasionally, until the onions have softened, about 8 minutes.

6. Add the lamb and any accumulated juices to the casserole along with the wine mixture, tomatoes, pepper, and shallot. Cook over moderate heat, stirring, until the tomatoes and bell pepper have softened and the lamb is just cooked through, about 10 minutes.

7. Season to taste before serving.

INGREDIENTS:

2	TABLESPOONS RED WINE
1	TABLESPOON FRESH LEMON JUICE
½	TEASPOON LEMON ZEST
1	TABLESPOON BERBERE SPICE MIX (SEE PAGE 323)
1	TEASPOON SMOKED PAPRIKA
1	TEASPOON DIJON MUSTARD
3½	LBS. BONELESS LEG OF LAMB, CUBED
1	TEASPOON SEA SALT, PLUS MORE TO TASTE
½	TEASPOON FRESHLY GROUND BLACK PEPPER, PLUS MORE TO TASTE
¼	CUP EXTRA VIRGIN OLIVE OIL
2	RED ONIONS, THINLY SLICED
6	GARLIC CLOVES, MINCED
2	TEASPOONS FINELY CHOPPED ROSEMARY
2	TEASPOONS FINELY CHOPPED THYME
2	PLUM TOMATOES, DICED
1	ORANGE BELL PEPPER, DICED
1	LARGE SHALLOT, THINLY SLICED

HANDRAJO

YIELD: 16 SERVINGS / **ACTIVE TIME:** 1 HOUR AND 45 MINUTES / **TOTAL TIME:** 10 HOURS

This Sephardic pastry or pie is easy to love when the delicious eggplant, onion, and tomato filling combines with cheese and the slightly flaky crust.

1. Heat the oils in a large sauté pan over high heat. Add the eggplant cubes and garlic to the pan in an even layer, sprinkle with a ½ teaspoon salt, and sauté undisturbed for 5 minutes, until the eggplant starts to brown.

2. Add the onion and stir to combine. Cover with a lid, lowering the heat to medium, and cook for 10 minutes, until the vegetables are soft. Remove the lid and cook for 5 more minutes, until all of the liquid has evaporated.

3. Add the tomatoes, sugar, paprika, pepper, and the rest of the salt and mix well. Keep cooking for 5 more minutes, mixing from time to time and breaking up any large chunks with a wooden spoon, until the mixture is even and melded together. Season to taste.

4. Remove from heat, discard the garlic clove, and let cool completely before filling the dough; you can prepare in advance and refrigerate overnight.

5. When ready to bake the pastry, preheat the oven to 425°F and line a baking sheet with parchment paper.

6. Spread the puff pastry sheets on a clean work surface, and cut each sheet in half lengthwise; you should end up with 4 rectangles each one about 10" x 7".

7. Divide the filling between the 4 pieces (about ¾ cup each), spreading it on one half of the length of each rectangle, leaving about 1" of rim around it. Fold the other half of the dough over top of the filling, bringing the edges of the rectangle together. Using a fork, press down along each edge of the rectangle to seal the pastry together. Carefully move each pastry to the prepared baking sheet and brush with the whisked egg.

8. Place in the middle of the oven and bake for 20 to 25 minutes, until well browned and crisped.

9. Cut into individual portions on the diagonal, and serve. It doesn't need to be served with anything, but in Turkey there would always be amazingly rich yogurt on the table.

INGREDIENTS:

- ¼ CUP SUNFLOWER OIL
- 2 TABLESPOONS OLIVE OIL
- 2 MEDIUM EGGPLANTS, PEELED, WASHED IN WATER (TO ABSORB LESS OIL), CUT INTO ½" CUBES
- 1 GARLIC CLOVE
- 1 TEASPOON SEA SALT, DIVIDED, PLUS MORE TO TASTE
- 2 MEDIUM ONIONS, FINELY CHOPPED
- 3 MEDIUM TOMATOES, HALVED, GRATED, PEELS DISCARDED
- ½ TABLESPOON SUGAR
- ½ TEASPOON SWEET PAPRIKA
- ½ TEASPOON BLACK PEPPER
- 2 (28 OZ.) PACKAGES PUFF PASTRY, PREFERABLY BUTTER BASED, THAWED IN THE REFRIGERATOR OVERNIGHT
- 1 EGG, WHISKED

Jerusalem Mixed Grill, page 304

JERUSALEM MIXED GRILL

YIELD: 4 SERVINGS / **ACTIVE TIME:** 45 MINUTES / **TOTAL TIME:** 1 HOUR

This is a traditional and immensely popular sandwich that originated from the eponymous Holy City, at the Mahane Yehuda Market, according to some. It typically consists of grilled chicken hearts, liver, and spleen combined with ground lamb, or lamb fat, and onions. The mix is then seasoned with turmeric, garlic, black pepper, cumin, cilantro, and olive oil and grilled to perfection. Once ready, it is served in a baguette or pita bread as a sandwich with salads, hummus, and fries on the side.

1. Add 2 tablespoons oil to a skillet over medium heat. When it shimmers, add the sliced onions and a pinch of salt. Cook, stirring, until the onions begin to soften and turn translucent, about 7 minutes, then lower heat and continue to cook, stirring every few minutes, until the onions are deeply caramelized. This could take up to 45 minutes. Set aside.

2. Meanwhile, in a large bowl, combine the turmeric, cumin, fenugreek, baharat, cinnamon, and 2 teaspoons salt. Add the chicken—including the hearts and livers, if you're using them—and toss with the spices.

3. Add 2 tablespoons oil to a large skillet over high heat. When it shimmers, add the chicken and spread it out in an even layer. Let the meat sear, undisturbed, for about 2 minutes, then lower the heat to medium-high and cook, stirring once or twice, until chicken is cooked through, about 5 minutes. Add a squeeze of lemon juice.

4. Remove the chicken mixture from the skillet and stir in the caramelized onions. Serve with rice and salad or with pita, pickles, and plenty of hummus.

INGREDIENTS:

- ¼ CUP AVOCADO OIL
- 1 LARGE RED ONION, HALVED AND THINLY SLICED
- 2 TEASPOONS SEA SALT, PLUS MORE TO TASTE
- 2 TEASPOONS TURMERIC
- 1 TEASPOON CUMIN
- 1 TEASPOON GROUND FENUGREEK
- 1 TEASPOON BAHARAT
- 1 TEASPOON CINNAMON
- 2½ LBS. BONELESS, SKINLESS CHICKEN THIGHS, OR 1½ LBS. BONELESS, SKINLESS CHICKEN THIGHS, ½ LB. CHICKEN HEARTS, AND ½ LB. CHICKEN LIVERS, TRIMMED AND CUT INTO NICKEL-SIZE PIECES
- 1 LEMON, HALVED

MAMA KRAMER'S BRISKET

YIELD: 10 SERVINGS / **ACTIVE TIME:** 1 HOUR / **TOTAL TIME:** 16 HOURS

The Manischewitz or Concord grape juice not only flavors the tender, richly marbled point cut, but tenderizes each bite.

1. Season the brisket all over with pepper and salt, rubbing into the grain. Wrap tightly in plastic and refrigerate for at least 3 hours, and up to 3 days.

2. Place a rack in the lower third of the oven and preheat to 275°F.

3. Heat Schmaltz in a large roasting pan set over 2 burners on high. Unwrap brisket and sear on all sides, 7 to 10 minutes per side. Transfer to a baking sheet.

4. Reduce heat to medium-high. Add onions, carrots, and celery to pan and season with salt. Cook, stirring occasionally, until browned and just softened, 15 to 18 minutes. Add wine, bring to a boil, and cook until evaporated, 8 to 10 minutes. Add garlic, thyme, bay leaves, peppercorns, and stock and bring to a boil.

5. Nestle brisket into aromatics and cover tightly with foil; braise in oven until meat is very tender but still holds its shape, 3 to 4 hours. Let cool, and then refrigerate for at least 8 hours and up to 2 days.

6. Preheat the oven to 250°F. Remove solidified fat from the surface of braising liquid; discard. Transfer brisket to a platter. Strain braising liquid into a large measuring cup; discard solids. Return liquid to pan and cook over medium-high heat, stirring occasionally, until reduced by half, velvety, and intensely flavored, but not overly salty, about 30 minutes.

7. Return the brisket to the pan, cover with foil, and heat in the oven until warmed through, 60 to 90 minutes.

8. Transfer to a cutting board and slice against the grain. Arrange on a platter and pour braising liquid over.

INGREDIENTS:

1	(15 LB.) UNTRIMMED POINT- OR FLAT-CUT BEEF BRISKET
1	TABLESPOON FRESHLY GROUND BLACK PEPPER
¼	CUP PLUS 2 TEASPOONS SEA SALT, PLUS MORE TO TASTE
¼	CUP SCHMALTZ (SEE PAGE 528) OR AVOCADO OIL
2	LARGE ONIONS, ROUGHLY CHOPPED
5	LARGE CARROTS, PEELED AND ROUGHLY CHOPPED
5	CELERY STALKS, ROUGHLY CHOPPED
1½	CUPS MANISCHEWITZ CONCORD GRAPE WINE OR CONCORD GRAPE JUICE
2	HEADS OF GARLIC, HALVED CROSSWISE
8	SPRIGS FRESH THYME
4	BAY LEAVES
2	TABLESPOONS BLACK PEPPERCORNS
3	QUARTS CHICKEN STOCK (SEE PAGE 722)

KHACHAPURI

YIELD: 4 SERVINGS / **ACTIVE TIME:** 30 MINUTES / **TOTAL TIME:** 1 HOUR

Beloved bakeries from the Georgian-Israeli community have made Georgia's national dish one of Israel's most popular to-go breakfast and brunch nosh options. Shaped like a small boat, the khachapuri is stuffed to the brim with cheese and topped with a fried egg. Consider it the economical—and very tasty—start to a lazy weekend. Variations, from bean-based vegan to over-the-top seafood and garlic butter recipes, exist but the basis is leavened bread with cheese and egg.

1. In a medium bowl, combine yeast, sugar, and ⅔ cup warm water and let stand until foamy, about 10 minutes.

2. Add 1 tablespoon oil, flour, and 1 teaspoon salt to the yeast mixture and mix until a soft dough forms. Knead on a floured surface until the dough is smooth and elastic, about 4 minutes. Transfer to a lightly greased bowl, cover, and set in a warm place for 1 hour, or until doubled in size.

3. While the dough is rising, make the filling. Add 1 tablespoon oil to a large sauté pan. Cook kale with a pinch of salt until softened, cool, and then add ricotta, muenster, and remaining salt, to taste, and mix well.

4. When ready to bake, preheat the oven to 450°F.

5. Punch down the dough and divide in half. Roll out a piece of dough on a piece of parchment paper into a ⅛" thick oval. Spread half of the cheese mixture on the dough and leave a ½" border around the edge.

6. On one side of the oval, roll the dough up toward the cheese. Then do the same with the other side. Pinch the open ends together and twist to secure into a boat shape. Repeat with the other half of dough.

7. Transfer boats on paper to a pizza stone or baking sheet. Bake for 14 minutes, until golden brown. Then crack 1 egg onto the center of each piece. Return the khachapuri to the oven and bake another 3 to 4 minutes until the egg white is slightly set.

8. Place butter on bread, if desired, and serve immediately.

INGREDIENTS:

1	TEASPOON ACTIVE DRY YEAST
¼	TEASPOON GRANULATED SUGAR
⅔	CUP WARM WATER
2	TABLESPOONS AVOCADO OIL, DIVIDED
1¼	CUPS ALL-PURPOSE FLOUR, PLUS MORE FOR KNEADING AND DUSTING
1	TEASPOON SEA SALT, PLUS MORE TO TASTE
1½	CUPS CHOPPED KALE
1	CUP CRUMBLED RICOTTA CHEESE
2	CUPS GRATED MUENSTER CHEESE
2	EGGS
4	TABLESPOONS UNSALTED BUTTER, CUBED

KHORESH SIB

YIELD: 6 SERVINGS / **ACTIVE TIME:** 30 MINUTES / **TOTAL TIME:** 2 HOURS

A fragrant Persian lamb stew with just the right amount of sweetness thanks to a healthy dose of fruit. Some traditional recipes call for apples, but quince offers a bite and unique sweetness that is irresistible in this recipe.

1. Place the cut quince and the lime or lemon juice in a bowl, mix well, and set aside.

2. Add 2 tablespoons oil to a Dutch oven over medium heat. Add the onions and sauté for 5 to 6 minutes, until golden. Add the garlic, lamb meat, tomato, rose petals, cardamom, and turmeric and mix well. Cover with about 4 cups water and increase the heat to high to bring the mixture to a boil. Add salt and pepper to taste, cover the pot with a lid, reduce the heat to low, and simmer for 1 hour.

3. Meanwhile, add 3 tablespoons oil to a skillet over medium heat. Once the oil is hot add the quince, cinnamon, nutmeg, and cloves and mix, searing the quince on all sides until golden brown, about 5 minutes per side. Add the flour and mix well to coat all of the quince pieces.

4. Add the quince mixture into the pot with the meat, along with the apricots and sugar, and stir to combine. Continue cooking for another 20 minutes, covered, until the lamb and quince are tender. Season to taste before serving.

INGREDIENTS:

5	QUINCES OR RED APPLES, PEELED, CORED, AND QUARTERED
2	TABLESPOONS FRESH LEMON OR LIME JUICE
5	TABLESPOONS AVOCADO OIL, DIVIDED
1	YELLOW ONION, FINELY CHOPPED
3	GARLIC CLOVES, THINLY SLICED
1½	LBS. LAMB (NECK/ SHOULDER CUT), CUT INTO 1½" CUBES
1	TOMATO, FINELY CHOPPED
½	TEASPOON DRIED ROSE PETALS
⅓	TEASPOON GROUND CARDAMOM
1	TEASPOON GROUND TURMERIC
4	CUPS WATER
1½	TEASPOONS SEA SALT
¼	TEASPOON FRESHLY GROUND BLACK PEPPER
1	TEASPOON CINNAMON
⅛	TEASPOON GROUND NUTMEG
⅛	TEASPOON GROUND CLOVES
2	TABLESPOONS ALL-PURPOSE FLOUR
10	DRIED APRICOTS
2	TABLESPOONS SUGAR

Kuku Sabzi, page 312

KUKU SABZI

YIELD: 4 SERVINGS / **ACTIVE TIME:** 15 MINUTES / **TOTAL TIME:** 25 MINUTES

Whatever you call it—a Persian omelet or frittata—there's no denying that it's simply delicious. Many variations exist but filling it with as many chopped herbs as possible gives it an undeniably unique flavor.

1. In a large bowl, whisk together the eggs until smooth, then mix in the remaining ingredients, except the oil.

2. Add the oil to a 10" nonstick skillet over medium-low heat. Pour mixture into pan and let cook for 1 to 2 minutes. Reduce the heat to low and cook, covered, until the omelet begins to set and the bottom is lightly golden, 7 to 8 minutes. Flip the omelet using a spatula or slide it onto a plate to invert back into the pan and cook until set, 2 to 3 minutes more.

3. Transfer to a platter, slice, and serve.

INGREDIENTS:

4 EGGS

1 TEASPOON CUMIN

1 TEASPOON FRESHLY GROUND BLACK PEPPER

1 TEASPOON SEA SALT

5 SCALLIONS, THINLY SLICED

1 CUP CHOPPED PARSLEY, LEAVES AND TENDER STEMS

1 CUP CHOPPED CILANTRO, LEAVES AND TENDER STEMS

1 CUP CHOPPED DILL, LEAVES AND TENDER STEMS

2 TABLESPOONS AVOCADO OIL

LATKES WITH SHORT RIBS

YIELD: 6 SERVINGS / **ACTIVE TIME:** 1 HOUR / **TOTAL TIME:** 3 HOURS AND 30 MINUTES

Latkes are the perfect side dish year-round, not only for Hanukkah celebrations. Try this pairing and discover that the sauce and spice from the short ribs are ideally matched with crispy, golden potato pancakes.

STEW

1. Season the short ribs with salt and pepper.

2. Add oil to a large pot over medium-high heat. Once the oil is hot, gently add the short ribs and sear on all sides until golden brown, about 5 minutes per side.

3. Transfer the meat to a plate and reduce the heat to medium. Add the onions and garlic and sauté until soft, about 15 minutes.

4. Return the meat to the pot, along with the allspice and add enough water to cover the beef about three-quarters of the way up. Bring the mixture to a boil, then reduce the heat and simmer, covered, for about 3 hours, or until the meat is tender and the liquid has reduced to a stew-like consistency.

5. Grate the onion and potatoes and wrap them in a tea towel and squeeze out as much liquid as possible into a bowl. After about 5 minutes the potato starch in the liquid will settle at the bottom of the bowl. Gently drain out the water and then scrape off the potato starch from the bowl.

6. In a separate bowl, combine the potato starch, onions, potatoes, flour, eggs, salt, and pepper and mix well.

7. Preheat the oven to 400°F.

8. Add about 1" of oil to a large skillet over medium-high heat. Once the oil is sizzling, take 1½ tablespoons of the potato mixture into your palm and shape into a flat disk that is about 3" wide. Gently place the latke into the oil. Repeat the process, adding 4 or 5 more latkes to the pan, being sure to not overcrowd the pan. Fry the latkes on both sides until golden brown, about 5 minutes per side. Transfer to a paper towel-lined plate and continue frying the latkes in batches.

9. Once the stew is ready, arrange the latkes in one layer in a baking pan. Once the short ribs are cool enough to handle, shred the beef and discard the bones. Gently place a dollop of meat over each latke. Pour the stew liquids over the latkes. Place the baking pan in the oven and reduce the heat to 350°F. Bake for 15 minutes, or until the latkes have absorbed some of the stew and the flavors of the beef.

10. Serve hot with a few sprigs of fresh dill or parsley.

INGREDIENTS:

STEW

2	LBS. BONE-IN SHORT RIBS, CUT ACROSS THE BONE INTO 2½" PIECES
1½	TABLESPOONS SEA SALT
½	TEASPOON GROUND BLACK PEPPER
2	TABLESPOONS AVOCADO OIL
5	ALLSPICE BERRIES
1	YELLOW ONION, FINELY CHOPPED
2	GARLIC CLOVES, FINELY CHOPPED

LATKES

1	YELLOW ONION
4	LARGE RUSSET POTATOES
1	TABLESPOON ALL-PURPOSE FLOUR
½	CUP THINLY SLICED SCALLION
1	WHOLE EGG
1	EGG YOLK
1½	TABLESPOONS SEA SALT
½	TEASPOON FRESHLY GROUND BLACK PEPPER
	AVOCADO OIL, FOR FRYING
3-5	SPRIGS FRESH DILL OR PARSLEY

Leg of Lamb with
Garlic & Rosemary, page 316

LEG OF LAMB WITH GARLIC & ROSEMARY

YIELD: 8 SERVINGS / **ACTIVE TIME:** 30 MINUTES / **TOTAL TIME:** 2 HOURS AND 30 MINUTES

A classic recipe to recreate, and pass on, year after year. This beautifully seasoned leg of lamb is the star of any Passover table.

1. Pat the lamb dry and score fat by making shallow cuts all over with the tip of a sharp, small knife.

2. Using a mortar and pestle, pound the garlic to a paste with sea salt and stir together with rosemary, all of the spices, and pepper. Put lamb in a lightly oiled roasting pan, then rub paste all over lamb. Let stand at room temperature for 30 minutes.

3. Preheat the oven to 350°F.

4. Roast the lamb in the middle of the oven until an instant-read thermometer inserted 2" into the thickest part of meat registers 130°F, 1½ to 1¾ hours. Transfer to a cutting board and let stand 15 to 25 minutes (internal temperature will rise to about 135°F for medium-rare).

5. Add wine to pan and deglaze by boiling over moderately high heat, stirring and scraping up brown bits, about 1 minute. Season pan juices with salt and pepper and serve with lamb.

INGREDIENTS:

- 1   (7 LB.) SEMI-BONELESS LEG OF LAMB, FAT TRIMMED TO ¼" THICK, AND LAMB TIED
- 4   GARLIC CLOVES
- 1   TABLESPOON FINE SEA SALT
- 2   TABLESPOONS CHOPPED FRESH ROSEMARY
- 2   TABLESPOONS RAS EL HANOUT
- 2   TABLESPOONS SUMAC
- 2   TABLESPOONS BERBERE SPICE MIX (SEE PAGE 323)
- ½   TEASPOON BLACK PEPPER
- ¼   CUP DRY RED WINE OR BEEF STOCK (SEE PAGE 721)

MAHSHI LABAN

YIELD: 6 SERVINGS / **ACTIVE TIME:** 1 HOUR AND 30 MINUTES / **TOTAL TIME:** 2 HOURS AND 30 MINUTES

S tuffed zucchini is effortlessly rich and luxurious on its own. But add in a creamy yogurt-based sauce and this dish becomes next-level decadent.

1. Bring a small pot of water to a boil and then add 1 teaspoon salt and rice. Cook the rice for 5 minutes and drain; the rice should be partially cooked. Transfer the rice to a large mixing bowl and set aside.

2. Cut about ½" from both ends of the zucchinis crosswise. Partially peel all of the zucchinis with a striped pattern. Cut each zucchini in half crosswise. Using a zucchini corer or apple corer, carefully hollow out the inside of the zucchini, until the edges of the zucchini are about ¼" thick. Set the prepared zucchinis aside. Save the zucchini pulp for another dish, like zucchini bread.

3. Add the chickpeas, half the butter cubes, 1 teaspoon salt, and black pepper to the bowl with the rice and mix well, making sure the butter is well distributed. Set aside.

4. Preheat the oven to 350°F.

5. Using your hands, fill each piece of zucchini three-quarters of the way with the rice mixture. Once each zucchini is filled, place it side-by-side in one layer in the bottom of a large Dutch oven or any oven-proof pot. Sprinkle ½ teaspoon salt over the zucchini.

6. Evenly place the remaining butter over the stuffed zucchinis. Place any leftover stuffing into the pot to fill in any empty gaps. Place a small plate or pot lid that fits into the pot over the stuffed zucchinis to weigh them down. Cover the pot with its lid (in addition to the smaller sized plate or pot lid).

7. Place the pot over low heat on the stove and cook for about 10 minutes, until the zucchini releases some water.

8. In a bowl, mix 2 cups water with the juice of 1 lemon until dissolved. Remove the top lid of the pot and pour the lemon and water mixture over the stuffed zucchinis until the water reaches the level of the small plate or pot lid that is weighing down the zucchinis. Place the lid back onto the pot and transfer the pot to the oven. Cook for 1 hour or until the liquid is absorbed.

9. Remove the top pot lid and the small plate or pot lid. Set the oven to broil, or 500°F, and cook for another 5 to 7 minutes, or until the top of the zucchinis are golden brown.

10. Serve warm with a side of yogurt and cucumbers.

INGREDIENTS:

1 CUP SHORT GRAIN OR BASMATI RICE, RINSED AND DRAINED

2½ TEASPOONS SEA SALT, DIVIDED

9 ZUCCHINIS

¾ CUP CANNED CHICKPEAS, RINSED AND DRAINED

½ CUP SALTED BUTTER, SOFTENED AND CUT INTO ½" CUBES, DIVIDED

¼ TEASPOON FRESHLY GROUND BLACK PEPPER

2 CUPS WATER

1 LARGE LEMON

Mahshi Laban, page 317

MAHASHA

YIELD: 8 SERVINGS / **ACTIVE TIME:** 1 HOUR / **TOTAL TIME:** 2 HOURS

Many cultures have a variation of stuffed vegetables, but the combination of chicken, ginger, and coriander give mahasha its signature flavor.

1. Slice each tomato three-quarters of the way crosswise about ½" from the top, leaving the top attached. Scoop out the tomato seeds and meat from the inside and discard. Set aside.

2. Bring a medium pot of water to a boil. Peel the onions and cut off the onion root. Slice each onion lengthwise halfway through the center of the onion. Place the onions in the boiling water and cook for about 8 to 10 minutes, until the onion layers are soft and start to separate. Using a slotted spoon, gently remove the onions from the boiling water and let them cool until they can be handled easily. Keep the pot of water boiling over high heat. Gently separate each onion layer without tearing and set aside.

3. Place the rinsed and drained rice into the pot of boiling water and cook for about 5 minutes. Drain and discard the water.

4. In a bowl, combine the rice, chicken, 1 tablespoon lemon juice, 1 teaspoon salt, 1 teaspoon sugar, 1 teaspoon turmeric, celery leaves, mint, cilantro, garlic, ginger, cloves, cumin, and coriander and mix well.

5. Using your hands, place about 1 heaping tablespoon of the filling into the cavity of each tomato.

6. Lay out one onion layer. Place 1 heaping tablespoon of the filling on the left side of the inside of the onion layer. Starting with the edge closest to the filling roll the onion layer up into a sealed torpedo shape. Continue with the remaining onion layers.

7. Add the oil to a large Dutch oven over medium-low heat. Add 2 teaspoons turmeric, 2 teaspoons sugar, and ½ teaspoon salt and stir. Gently place all of the tomatoes along the outer edge of the pan, with their top side down in one layer. Gently place the onions into the middle of the pan seam-side down in the same layer as the tomatoes. Cover the pan and cook for 20 minutes. Uncover and sprinkle the remaining ½ teaspoon salt over the tomatoes and onions. Cover and continue cooking for 15 to 25 more minutes, until the filling is cooked through and the tomatoes and onions are tender.

8. Once ready, uncover the pan and sprinkle the remaining lemon juice over the vegetables. Transfer to a serving platter and serve hot.

INGREDIENTS:

10	TOMATOES, ON THE VINE
2	LARGE YELLOW ONIONS
1	LB. GROUND CHICKEN
1	CUP BASMATI RICE, RINSED AND DRAINED
⅓	CUP PLUS 1 TABLESPOON FRESH LEMON JUICE
2	TEASPOONS SEA SALT, DIVIDED
3	TEASPOONS GRANULATED SUGAR, DIVIDED
3	TEASPOONS TURMERIC, DIVIDED
5	CELERY LEAVES, FINELY CHOPPED
5-8	MINT LEAVES, FINELY CHOPPED
¼	CUP FINELY CHOPPED CILANTRO LEAVES
2-3	GARLIC CLOVES, FINELY GRATED
2	TEASPOONS FINELY GRATED GINGER
1	TEASPOON GROUND CLOVES
3	TEASPOONS CUMIN
5	TEASPOONS CORIANDER

FOR THE PAN

⅓	CUP AVOCADO OIL
2	TEASPOONS GROUND TURMERIC
2	TEASPOONS GRANULATED SUGAR
1	TEASPOON SEA SALT, DIVIDED
⅓	CUP FRESH LEMON JUICE

MESSER WOT

YIELD: 6 SERVINGS / **ACTIVE TIME:** 30 MINUTES / **TOTAL TIME:** 1 HOUR

Don't be afraid to play with the heat level while seasoning this vegetarian Ethiopian-based red lentil stew—it's meant to be spicy.

1. Place the onions, garlic, and ginger in a food processor and process for 3 to 5 minutes, until combined into a fine paste.

2. Add the oil to a pot over medium heat. Once the oil is hot, add the onion paste and sauté, stirring occasionally, for about 10 to 15 minutes, or until the mixture has softened, reduced, and become light brown.

3. Reduce the heat to medium-low and add the tomato paste, 1 cup water, Berbere Spice Mix, and salt. Cook for 15 minutes more, stirring occasionally, until the tomato paste starts to darken.

4. Add the lentils and 4 more cups of water to the pot. Stir well and increase the heat to high, bring the pot to a boil, stirring occasionally. Then, place a lid on the pot, reduce heat to low, and simmer for 35 to 40 minutes, stirring occasionally, until the lentils are soft and cooked through.

BERBERE SPICE MIX

1. Sift all of the spices into a bowl, mix well, and set aside.

INGREDIENTS:

2	RED ONIONS, QUARTERED
2	YELLOW ONIONS, QUARTERED
6	GARLIC CLOVES
1	2" PIECE FRESH GINGER, PEELED AND ROUGHLY CHOPPED
1	CUP AVOCADO OIL
1	(4½ OZ.) TOMATO PASTE TUBE
5	CUPS WATER, DIVIDED
2	TABLESPOONS BERBERE SPICE MIX (SEE RECIPE)
1½	TEASPOONS SEA SALT
2	CUPS RED LENTILS, RINSED AND DRAINED

BERBERE SPICE MIX

1	CUP HOT PAPRIKA OR CHILE POWDER
½	TABLESPOON GROUND CLOVES
1	TABLESPOON GROUND CARDAMOM
1	TABLESPOON GINGER POWDER
1	TABLESPOON ONION POWDER
1	TABLESPOON CORIANDER
1	TABLESPOON CUMIN
½	TABLESPOON CINNAMON
½	TABLESPOON GROUND NUTMEG
½	TABLESPOON GROUND FENUGREEK SEEDS
1	TABLESPOON BLACK PEPPER
1	TABLESPOON SEA SALT

MINA DE ESPINACA

YIELD: 6 SERVINGS / **ACTIVE TIME:** 30 MINUTES / **TOTAL TIME:** 1 HOUR AND 30 MINUTES

Matzo is truly the gift that keeps on giving. This pie—which, if you ask us, looks a lot like Jewish lasagna—uses softened matzo to create layers filled with a delicious cheese and spinach.

1. Place the potatoes into a pot. Cover with room temperature water, add 1 tablespoon salt, and bring to a boil over high heat. Reduce the heat to medium-low and cook for 20 to 25 minutes, until the potatoes can be easily pierced with a knife. Drain the potatoes and cool for about 5 minutes until the potatoes are still warm but easier to handle. Peel the potatoes; discard the peels.

2. In a large bowl, mash the potatoes with a potato ricer or fork, until smooth with no chunks. Add 1½ teaspoons salt, ¾ cup Parmesan, cream cheese, and the beaten eggs to the potatoes. Mix well with a spatula until the mixture is smooth and uniform. Set aside.

3. In a large bowl, combine the spinach with ¼ cup Parmesan and 1 teaspoon salt. Mix until the salt and cheese are evenly distributed with the spinach. Set aside.

4. Preheat the oven to 350°F. Grease a 10" circular springform baking pan with 1 teaspoon oil.

5. Fill a container large enough to fit one matzo sheet with water halfway up to the rim and ¼ teaspoon salt. Soak the matzo, one sheets at a time, in the water for about 30 seconds, until each sheet is flexible yet still firm enough to hold its shape. Gently place each soaked matzo on a kitchen towel and remove any excess moisture. Set aside.

6. Line the bottom of the baking pan with two matzos, one on top of the other. Trim any edges as needed and use the trimmings to fill in any gaps. Evenly spread half of the spinach-parmesan mixture on top of the matzos. Add another double layer of moistened matzos on top of the spinach and gently press the matzos into the spinach layer to make space for the remaining layers. Spread the second half of the spinach mixture over the matzo layer. Place another double layer of matzo over the second spinach layer. Gently press the matzos into the spinach to make room for the remaining layer. Spread the potato mixture evenly over the matzo layer. Use the back of a spoon or an offset spatula to make swirls on the surface of the potatoes to brown evenly in the oven. Sprinkle the remaining ¼ cup Parmesan on top of the potato mixture and drizzle 1½ tablespoons oil on top.

7. Bake the assembled mina for 35 to 45 minutes, until the mina is deeply golden brown.

8. Allow the mina to cool for about 5 minutes. Run the tip of a sharp knife along the outside edges of the mina to separate it from the pan. Unmold and serve hot.

INGREDIENTS:

- 2 RUSSET POTATOES
- 1 TABLESPOON PLUS 2¾ TEASPOONS SEA SALT, DIVIDED
- 1¼ CUPS GRATED PARMESAN CHEESE, DIVIDED
- 1 (8 OZ.) BLOCK CREAM CHEESE
- 2 EGGS, LIGHTLY BEATEN
- 1 LB. BABY SPINACH, REGULAR SPINACH OR DEFROSTED FROZEN SPINACH, FINELY CHOPPED
- 8 MATZO SHEETS
- 1½ TABLESPOONS PLUS 1 TEASPOON AVOCADO OIL, DIVIDED

MOROCCAN FISH & CRISPY RICE CAKE
WITH SAFFRON CRUST

YIELD: 6 SERVINGS / **ACTIVE TIME:** 1 HOUR / **TOTAL TIME:** 25 HOURS

This classical fish preparation defines Moroccan cuisine. Vibrant reds, yellows, and greens are matched with an equally colorful, spicy aroma, and are offset by delicate textures. Traditionally, the fish is assembled and marinated in the fridge overnight.

1. Make the rice cake: in a large saucepan, bring 4 cups water to a boil. Stir in the rice and 1 teaspoon salt. Reduce the heat to medium-low, cover, and cook for about 9 minutes. You don't want the rice to be fully cooked. Spoon the rice into a fine-mesh sieve placed over a bowl and let it stand until all of the liquid has drained.

2. Add oil to a large sauté pan over medium-high heat. Use a wooden spoon to swirl the saffron and paprika into the oil. When the oil starts to sizzle, carefully spoon in the rice, pressing it into the bottom of the pan to form a sort of "rice cake." Reduce the heat to medium, place a few paper towels over the rice, and cover the pan. Cook until the rice cake is nicely browned and crisp, 15 to 20 minutes. Using a spatula, lift the cake occasionally to make sure the rice isn't burning. When the cake is ready, uncover and let cool for a few minutes.

3. Remove the paper towels. Carefully invert a large plate over the top of the pan, invert the plate and pan together, and then lift off the pan. Serve right away. The rice cake can also be made up to 1 hour ahead and kept covered at room temperature. Just before serving, reheat in a 300°F oven.

4. Pour ¼ cup Paprika Oil into a large sauté pan. Add the garlic, cilantro stems, bell peppers, and chiles. Place the fish on top and add the preserved lemons. Pour 3 tablespoons Saffron Water evenly over the fish. Use your hands to rub the liquids into the fish. Season with salt and pepper. Cover the pan and refrigerate for up to 24 hours.

5. Remove the pan from the refrigerator, place over medium-high heat, and cook, covered, for 10 minutes. Reduce the heat to low, sprinkle the cilantro leaves over the fish, and cook, uncovered, for 10 minutes longer. The dish should look bright and bubbly. Serve immediately.

INGREDIENTS:

CRISPY RICE CAKE WITH SAFFRON CRUST

2   CUPS BASMATI RICE, WELL RINSED

    SEA SALT, TO TASTE

3   TABLESPOONS AVOCADO OIL

4   SAFFRON THREADS, CRUSHED

1   HEAPING TEASPOON SWEET PAPRIKA

MOROCCAN FISH

¼   CUP PAPRIKA OIL (SEE RECIPE)

4   GARLIC CLOVES, QUARTERED

1   BUNCH CILANTRO, STEMS RESERVED AND LEFT WHOLE, LEAVES CHOPPED

2   RED BELL PEPPERS, SEEDED AND FINELY DICED

3   DRIED RED CHILES

6   (6 OZ.) GROUPER OR TILAPIA FILLETS

1–2 PRESERVED LEMONS, CUT INTO SMALL PIECES

3   TABLESPOONS SAFFRON WATER (SEE RECIPE)

1   TEASPOON SEA SALT

1   TEASPOON FRESHLY GROUND PEPPER

    FRESH CILANTRO, TO GARNISH

Continued . . .

PAPRIKA OIL

1. In a glass jar combine the paprika and oil and shake until well blended. Set aside. This will serve as the base for your Moroccan cooking. Store in a dark pantry and always shake before using.

SAFFRON WATER

1. Preheat the oven to 425°F. Place the saffron on a small piece of aluminum foil and fold over to secure the saffron inside. Toast in the oven for no more than 1 minute.

2. Use your fingers to crumble the saffron into tiny pieces. Place in a small glass jar, pour in the boiling water, and shake until well blended. Set aside.

PAPRIKA OIL

½   CUP SWEET PAPRIKA

2   CUPS AVOCADO OIL

SAFFRON WATER

1   TABLESPOON SAFFRON THREADS

1   CUP BOILING WATER

MOROCCAN CORNISH HENS
WITH PINE NUT COUSCOUS

YIELD: 8 SERVINGS / **ACTIVE TIME:** 25 MINUTES / **TOTAL TIME:** 2 HOURS AND 40 MINUTES

The Cornish hens are massaged with a blend of spices that gives it that distinctive Moroccan flavor. The pine nuts in the couscous add an irresistible texture and richness.

1. Preheat the oven to 350°F.

2. Prepare the couscous according to the instructions on the packet.

3. Bake the pine nuts in the oven or dry-fry them until golden brown. When the couscous is ready, fold in the pine nuts. Separate ½ cup couscous and mix in 2 tablespoons oil. Set aside.

4. Add 1 tablespoon oil to a frying pan over medium-high heat. When the oil is hot, add the onions and cook until translucent. Add the ginger, garlic, mint, coriander, cumin, paprika, honey, tomatoes, chili flakes, and oregano and simmer for a few minutes to reduce the excess liquid from the tomatoes.

5. Season the Cornish hens with black pepper and stuff with couscous, being sure to pack it quite firmly.

6. Cover with warm onion and herb sauce, sprinkle remaining ½ cup couscous over the top of the Cornish hens and bake for 1½ hours, covered.

7. Roast, uncovered, for another 45 minutes. Baste every now and then. The couscous on top of the Cornish hens should be crispy.

INGREDIENTS:

- 2 CUPS COUSCOUS
- 4 OZ. PINE NUTS
- 3 TABLESPOONS AVOCADO OIL, DIVIDED
- SEA SALT, TO TASTE
- 2 ONIONS, CUT IN HALF AND THEN SLICED INTO SEMI-CIRCULAR RINGS
- 1 TEASPOON FRESHLY GRATED GINGER
- 4 GARLIC CLOVES, CRUSHED
- 1 TABLESPOON FINELY CHOPPED MINT LEAVES
- 1 TABLESPOON FINELY CHOPPED CILANTRO
- 1 TEASPOON CUMIN
- 1 TEASPOON PAPRIKA
- 1 TABLESPOON HONEY
- 1 (14 OZ.) CAN OF DICED TOMATOES
- 1 TEASPOON CHILI FLAKES
- 1 TEASPOON DRIED OREGANO
- 8 CORNISH HENS OR 2 WHOLE CHICKENS
- 1 TEASPOON COARSELY GROUND BLACK PEPPER

MOROCCAN LAMB SHANKS
WITH POMEGRANATE SAUCE

YIELD: 4 SERVINGS / **ACTIVE TIME:** 30 MINUTES / **TOTAL TIME:** 2 HOURS AND 30 MINUTES

If lamb weren't already succulent enough, the extra layer of fat around each shank adds richness when cooked. The ever-important pomegranate packs a tart punch, making this recipe layered and sophisticated.

1. Preheat the oven to 350°F.

2. Season the shanks with salt and pepper.

3. Add oil to a braising pot over medium-high heat and brown the shanks on all sides. Be sure to stand the shanks on the edges to brown all sides.

4. Remove the shanks and cook and stir the onion and garlic, over medium heat, until slightly softened, about 5 minutes. Add the spices, tomato paste, wine, and stock. Stir over medium heat for 5 minutes. Add the shanks to the pot, cover, and roast for 2 hours. Check the shanks every 30 minutes, turning them over in the sauce each time you check them.

5. When the lamb is nearly cooked, after 1½ hours, add the pomegranate juice. Continue cooking 30 minutes longer, or until the meat on the shank is buttery soft and nearly falling off the bone. When finished, the sauce will be thick and concentrated (you can thin it with a little water or stock if needed). Spoon the sauce over the shanks and serve alongside rice, noodles, or couscous.

INGREDIENTS:

4   (16 OZ.) LAMB SHANKS

     KOSHER SALT, TO TASTE

     FRESHLY GROUND BLACK PEPPER, TO TASTE

2   TABLESPOONS AVOCADO OIL

1   LARGE ONION, SLICED

6   GARLIC CLOVES, SMASHED

1   TEASPOON CINNAMON

1   TEASPOON CORIANDER

½   TEASPOON GROUND GINGER

1   TEASPOON CUMIN

2   DOZEN JUNIPER BERRIES

2   TABLESPOONS TOMATO PASTE

1   CUP SWEET RED WINE

2   CUPS BEEF STOCK (SEE PAGE 721)

1   CUP POMEGRANATE JUICE

MSOKI DE PESAJ

YIELD: 6 SERVINGS / **ACTIVE TIME:** 45 MINUTES / **TOTAL TIME:** 3 HOURS

The blend of braised lamb in a tomato-based stew makes this traditional Tunisian Passover dish a delicious dinner for cooler weather, as well.

1. Season the lamb with salt and pepper.

2. Add oil to a large pot over medium-high heat. When the oil is hot, sear the lamb until golden brown, about 3 to 5 minutes per side.

3. Add the onions, carrots, turnips, and garlic and sauté until soft and cooked, 15 to 20 minutes. Add the cinnamon stick and harissa and cook for about 5 more minutes.

4. Add the spinach, leeks, zucchini, fennel, celery, and red kale lettuce and continue cooking for another 15 minutes.

5. Add the fava beans, peas, artichoke hearts, parsley, cilantro, mint, and orange blossom water. Add enough water to reach three-quarters of the way up the vegetables. Simmer, uncovered, for about 2 hours, stirring occasionally, until the liquid has reduced to one-quarter the original amount.

6. Serve hot with rice.

INGREDIENTS:

- 2½ **LBS. LAMB SHOULDER MEAT, CHOPPED INTO 3" CUBES**
- 1 **TABLESPOON KOSHER SALT**
- ½ **TEASPOON FRESHLY GROUND BLACK PEPPER**
- 2 **TABLESPOONS AVOCADO OIL**
- 2 **LARGE YELLOW ONIONS, CHOPPED**
- 2 **CARROTS, CHOPPED**
- 1 **TURNIP, CHOPPED**
- 1 **GARLIC CLOVE, MINCED**
- 1 **CINNAMON STICK**
- 2 **TEASPOONS HARISSA**
- 2 **LBS. SPINACH LEAVES, FINELY CHOPPED**
- 2 **LEEKS, FINELY CHOPPED**
- 1 **ZUCCHINI, CHOPPED**
- 1 **FENNEL, CHOPPED**
- 3 **CELERY STALKS, CHOPPED**
- **HALF OF 1 RED KALE LETTUCE HEART, FINELY CHOPPED**
- 1½ **CUPS FRESH OR FROZEN FAVA BEANS, DEFROSTED**
- 1 **CUP FRESH OR FROZEN GREEN PEAS, DEFROSTED**
- 4 **FRESH OR FROZEN ARTICHOKE HEARTS, DEFROSTED AND CUT INTO WEDGES LENGTHWISE**
- ¼ **BUNCH PARSLEY, FINELY CHOPPED**
- ¼ **BUNCH CILANTRO, FINELY CHOPPED**
- ¼ **BUNCH MINT LEAVES, FINELY CHOPPED**
- 2 **TEASPOONS ORANGE BLOSSOM WATER**

ONION MAHSHI

YIELD: 4 SERVINGS / **ACTIVE TIME:** 30 MINUTES / **TOTAL TIME:** 1 HOUR AND 30 MINUTES

This dish can be found throughout the Middle East, but is generally considered of Lebanese origin. The onions are generously stuffed with beef and rice, then roasted to aromatic perfection.

1. Fill up a large pot halfway with water and bring to a boil over high heat.

2. Peel and cut off the roots of the onions. Make a lengthwise slit to reach the center of each onion, cutting only halfway through the onions.

3. Once the water is boiling, add the onions to the pot and boil for 10 to 15 minutes, or until the onions soften and their layers start separating. Drain the onions and set aside until cool enough to handle.

4. In a bowl, combine the beef, allspice, rice, and 1½ tablespoons salt and mix well.

5. Gently peel the layers of each onion making sure each layer stays intact and does not tear.

6. Place about 1 to 2 tablespoons of the meat mixture into one end of the inside of a piece of onion. Roll up the onion layer to seal the meat mixture and create a torpedo shape. Repeat, filling and shaping the remaining onion layers with the meat mixture.

7. Preheat the oven to 360°F.

8. In a bowl, combine the pomegranate molasses, water, 1 teaspoon salt, and sugar and mix well.

9. Pack the stuffed onions tightly in a medium-sized baking pan, placing them in two layers if needed.

10. Pour the sauce over the onions. Add enough water to cover three-quarters of the way up the onions. Cover the baking pan with aluminum foil and bake for 30 minutes, or until the rice and meat is cooked. Uncover and continue cooking for another 15 to 20 minutes, until the sauce thickens.

INGREDIENTS:

4	LARGE YELLOW ONIONS
1	LB. GROUND BEEF
1	TABLESPOON ALLSPICE
¾	CUP ARBORIO RICE
1½	TABLESPOONS SEA SALT, PLUS 1 TEASPOON, DIVIDED
½	CUP POMEGRANATE MOLASSES
½	CUP WATER
1	TEASPOON SUGAR

Oven-Poached Salmon,
page 336

OVEN-POACHED SALMON

YIELD: 4 SERVINGS / **ACTIVE TIME:** 10 MINUTES / **TOTAL TIME:** 30 MINUTES

No matter how it's prepared, it's hard not to love salmon. This simple oven-poached version is a go-to weeknight favorite.

1. Preheat the oven to 350°F.

2. In a medium bowl, whisk together the mayonnaise and salt.

3. Lay out a sheet of heavy-duty aluminum foil roughly 12" square and place one salmon fillet in the center, skin-side down. Slather 1 tablespoon of the mayonnaise mixture all over the salmon, including the skin, coating the fish evenly. Return the salmon to the center of the foil. Lay a small bunch of dill sprigs on top of the salmon and arrange 4 lemon wheels across the top in a line. Carefully fold up the edges of the foil to make a packet, and crimp the seams; this will help keep the steam inside and keep the fish moist when cooking. Repeat the process with the remaining fillets. At this point the packets are ready to cook, but they can be refrigerated overnight.

4. Space the salmon packets evenly on a large rimmed baking sheet. Bake for 20 minutes and remove from the oven. Immediately open each packet, being careful of the hot steam. The salmon will easily pull away from the skin, if desired, or it can be carefully removed whole with a flat spatula.

5. The salmon can be served hot right away, at room temperature, or cold. Sprinkle with chopped fresh dill and serve with lemon wedges.

INGREDIENTS:

¼ CUP MAYONNAISE

1 TABLESPOON PLUS 1 TEASPOON SEA SALT

4 (6 OZ.) SKIN-ON SALMON FILLETS, PATTED DRY

1 BUNCH FRESH DILL, SEPARATED INTO 4 SMALLER BUNCHES, PLUS 1 TABLESPOON ROUGHLY CHOPPED

16 LEMON WHEELS, ABOUT ⅛" THICK

1 LEMON, CUT INTO WEDGES

OSHI BAKHSH

YIELD: 6 SERVINGS / **ACTIVE TIME:** 15 MINUTES / **TOTAL TIME:** 1 HOUR

Bakhsh is a green rice pilaf that gets its color from coriander and other herbs and Oshi Bakhsh is considered the most recognizable dish of Bukharian Jewish cuisine.

1. Place the lamb in a large pot over medium heat and add 2 cups water. Cook the meat, breaking and crumbling it frequently with a wooden spoon until it is cooked and becomes brown, about 10 minutes.

2. Add the cilantro, mint, and oil and stir well, then add the rice and salt and stir again. Increase the heat to high and bring the mixture to a boil. Cover the pot with a small kitchen towel or paper towel and place the lid above the towel. Reduce the heat to low and cook until all of the liquids are absorbed and the rice is done, about 35 to 40 minutes.

3. To serve, transfer to a wide serving platter and sprinkle with pomegranate seeds, mixing some into the rice and sprinkling the rest on top. Serve hot with some lemon wedges on the side.

INGREDIENTS:

- 1¼ LBS. GROUND LAMB
- 2 CUPS WATER
- 2 BUNCHES CILANTRO, FINELY CHOPPED
- 1 BUNCH MINT LEAVES, FINELY CHOPPED
- ¼-½ CUP AVOCADO OIL
- 1½ CUPS BASMATI RICE, RINSED AND DRAINED
- 2-3 TEASPOONS COARSE SEA SALT
- 1 CUP POMEGRANATE SEEDS
- 1 LEMON, CUT INTO WEDGES, FOR SERVING

Pastrami, page 340

PASTRAMI

YIELD: 10 SERVINGS / **ACTIVE TIME:** 1 HOUR / **TOTAL TIME:** 7 DAYS

Have the rye ready because you're going to be piling your sandwiches high. The smoking process is what gives pastrami its distinctive and unforgettable flavor.

1. Make the brine by adding sea salt, sugars, honey, pink salt, garlic, mustard seed, coriander, and water to a large container and whisk until all of the sugar and salt is dissolved. Refrigerate for 1 hour.

2. Rinse the brisket and place in the container, making sure it is completely submerged. Use a plate or bowl to weigh it down. Cure it in the refrigerator for 5 to 7 days, depending on size and thickness of the brisket. Agitate every other day, flipping the meat over. To check for full cure, make an incision through the fattest part of the brisket, looking for a consistent pink color through the meat. If there is a darker or gray color in the center, continue to brine.

3. In a bowl, combine coarse pepper and coarse coriander and mix well.

4. Remove brisket from the brine and pat dry with paper towels. In a bowl or on a large cookie sheet, coat brisket evenly in the pepper and coriander mix. For best results, refrigerate overnight uncovered, so the surface can dry a bit and get a better crust upon cooking.

5. Preheat the oven to 225°F. Soak the wood chips in water for 1 hour. In a cast-iron skillet, ignite wood chips with a kitchen torch and place in the bottom of the oven. Place the brisket on a cookie sheet and place on the top shelf of the oven. Cook for 4 to 6 hours or until the center reaches 170°F. Remove from the oven, cool, and wrap in plastic wrap.

6. When ready to serve, the easiest home method is to slice cold and steam in a vegetable steamer for about 15 minutes, until tender. Alternatively, heat the oven to 350°F, place brisket in a large roasting pan on a roasting rack. Add 1 cup hot water to the bottom of the pan. Cover and seal the entire rack/pan tightly with plastic wrap, then a layer of tin foil. Place in the oven for 1 hour or until meat is tender. You should be able to insert a carving fork and rotate it with little effort. Slice against the grain to serve.

INGREDIENTS:

6½	TABLESPOONS FINE SEA SALT
5	TABLESPOONS WHITE SUGAR
1¼	TABLESPOONS BROWN SUGAR
1¼	TABLESPOONS HONEY
1¼	TABLESPOONS PINK SALT (SODIUM NITRITE) OR SALTPETER
1	TEASPOON CHOPPED GARLIC
½	TEASPOON MUSTARD SEED
¼	TEASPOON CORIANDER
6⅓	CUPS WARM WATER
1	(5-8 LBS.) BEEF BRISKET FLAT PORTION ("FIRST CUT"), WITH LARGE FAT CAP UNTRIMMED
¼	CUP COARSE FRESHLY GROUND PEPPER
¼	CUP COARSE GROUND CORIANDER
½	CUP HICKORY OR OAK WOOD CHIPS

POACHED FISH IN PEPPER SAUCE

YIELD: 6 SERVINGS / **ACTIVE TIME**: 15 MINUTES / **TOTAL TIME**: 30 MINUTES

This recipe is versatile and can be made with any type of white fish or salmon. Take the spice factor to a new level by adding harissa sauce or more chili powder, hot paprika, or red pepper flakes. A delightful main course for lunch over the Passover holiday.

1. Cut the fish into 2" x 5" pieces. Set aside.

2. Add oil to a large frying pan over medium-low heat. Add the garlic and onions and cook for 5 minutes. Add the peppers and cook for another 4 minutes.

3. Stir in the paprika, salt, black pepper, and chili powder or heat of choice. Add the water, increase the heat to medium-high, and bring to a boil.

4. Reduce the heat to low, place the fish slices on top of the garlic, onions, and peppers, cover, and cook for 5 minutes.

5. Use a fork to place some of the peppers and onions on top of the fish. Cover and cook for another 5 minutes. Taste the sauce and add more salt if necessary.

6. Sprinkle with the cilantro and serve.

INGREDIENTS:

2	LBS. WHITE FISH (SUCH AS TILAPIA, HALIBUT, OR FLOUNDER)
3	TABLESPOONS AVOCADO OIL
2	GARLIC CLOVES, THINLY SLICED
2	MEDIUM ONIONS, HALVED AND THINLY SLICED
1	RED PEPPER, CORED, SEEDED, AND THINLY SLICED
1	ORANGE PEPPER, CORED, SEEDED, AND THINLY SLICED
1	YELLOW PEPPER CORED, SEEDED, AND THINLY SLICED
¼	TEASPOON PAPRIKA
¾	TEASPOON SEA SALT
	BLACK PEPPER, TO TASTE
¼-½	TEASPOON YOUR CHOICE OF CHILI POWDER, HOT PAPRIKA, CRUSHED RED PEPPER FLAKES
1½	CUPS WATER
⅔	CUP CHOPPED CILANTRO LEAVES

Pirozhki, page 344

PIROZHKI

YIELD: 24 PIES / **ACTIVE TIME:** 50 MINUTES / **TOTAL TIME:** 3 HOURS

This Russian hand pie is similar to its Polish cousin, the pierogi, in that it's a little dumpling-shaped morsel packed full of irresistible flavors, like potato and eggs. But Pirozhki is less delicate and easier to pack up and eat on the go due to its outer layer of fried or baked yeast dough.

1. In a large bowl, combine all of the dough ingredients and mix with a wooden spoon until well combined. If using a stand mixer, knead with dough hook attachment until dough is soft and pliable—it should pull away from the bowl sides while kneading. If the dough is too sticky, add a few tablespoons of flour. If kneading by hand, knead for 3 to 4 minutes on a lightly floured surface, careful to not add too much extra flour, until smooth.

2. Place the dough in a large greased bowl and allow it to rise, covered in plastic wrap, in a warm spot for 1 hour and 30 minutes until light, well-risen, and almost doubled in size.

3. While the dough is rising, make the filling. Add oil to a skillet over medium-high heat and sauté the scallions until they are soft but still bright green; season with salt and pepper. Set aside.

4. Cut cooked, cooled potatoes into large cubes, add to a large bowl and crush lightly with a fork to break up into smaller pieces. Add scallions, dill, and egg to the potatoes and mix well, until achieving the consistency of chunky mashed potatoes. Taste and season with salt and lots of pepper. Set aside.

5. Line 2 large baking sheets with parchment paper. Once dough has risen, transfer from the bowl onto a lightly floured surface and divide into 4 equal pieces. Then, divide each of those into 6 pieces. Working quickly, roll each piece into a ball and place on baking sheets. Cover with a slightly damp kitchen towel to rest for 15 mins.

6. Working with one ball at a time, and adding flour as needed to prevent sticking, roll each ball out into a 3½" circle with a flour-dusted rolling pin. Place 2 tablespoons of filling in the center of each dough round, then bring the 2 sides of the dough up and around the filling at the top of the round, pinching the dough closed around the filling as you move down the center to close up and encase the filling. For a fancier pleat, start by pinching the dough at the top to seal and create a starting point. Then, carefully pull each side up and over the filling to meet the dough on the other side, then pinch to seal as you pleat. Work your way down the center by alternating sides as you pull and pinch one side over

INGREDIENTS:

DOUGH

2¼ TEASPOONS INSTANT DRY YEAST

3¾ CUPS ALL PURPOSE FLOUR

2½ TABLESPOONS SUGAR

1½ TEASPOONS SEA SALT

½ CUP WARM WATER

2 LARGE EGGS

½ CUP SOUR CREAM

4 TABLESPOONS UNSALTED BUTTER, SOFTENED

FILLING

2 TABLESPOONS SUNFLOWER OIL

6-8 SCALLIONS, THINLY SLICED

4 MEDIUM YUKON GOLD POTATOES, PEELED, BOILED, AND COOLED

3 TABLESPOONS FINELY CHOPPED DILL

3 LARGE HARD-BOILED EGGS, FINELY CHOPPED

SEA SALT, TO TASTE

BLACK PEPPER, TO TASTE

the other to create a decorative, braided pleat. Keep these under a towel as you finish each one so they do not dry out or crack.

7. When all pirozhki are pleated and sealed, cover with a light cotton towel or pillowcase and allow to rest again and rise slightly for 20 to 30 minutes.

8. Preheat the oven to 375°F.

9. In a bowl, prepare the egg wash by whisking together 2 egg yolks with 2 tablespoons milk.

10. After the final rise, uncover the pirozhki and make sure they are spaced at least an inch apart across the 2 baking sheets. Brush each one well with the egg wash and bake for 20 minutes or until they are golden all over. Cool on a rack for 5 to 10 minutes and serve warm or at room temperature.

Polenta Medallions, page 348

POLENTA MEDALLIONS

YIELD: 36 LATKES / **ACTIVE TIME:** 25 MINUTES / **TOTAL TIME:** 50 MINUTES

Ashkenazi roots with a gourmet twist. Delight your taste buds, and dinner guests, with these polenta-based latkes.

1. Add 2 tablespoons oil to a large skillet over medium-high heat. Add onions and sauté until tender, 3 to 4 minutes. Add stock and bring to a boil.

2. Add polenta slowly, whisking constantly. Reduce heat to medium and continue to cook, stirring constantly, until polenta comes away from sides of pan, about 20 minutes. Season with salt and pepper.

3. While still hot, spread polenta about 1" thick onto an oiled baking pan. Cool, cover, and refrigerate until cold and firm, several hours or overnight.

4. Using a 2" round scalloped cookie cutter, cut polenta into rounds and transfer to a large platter.

5. Add 2 tablespoons oil to a nonstick skillet over medium-high heat. Cook the polenta rounds, turning occasionally, until brown and crispy on both sides, 8 minutes. Drain on paper towels and repeat with remaining rounds, adding additional oil as needed.

6. Serve immediately with sauce of your choosing or reheat just before serving.

INGREDIENTS:

- 4   TABLESPOONS AVOCADO OIL, DIVIDED
- ½   CUP CHOPPED ONIONS
- 4 ½ CUPS VEGETABLE STOCK (SEE PAGE 729) OR WATER
- 1 ½ CUPS POLENTA OR YELLOW CORNMEAL
- ½   TEASPOON SEA SALT

      FRESHLY GROUND BLACK PEPPER, TO TASTE

POMEGRANATE & HONEY GLAZED CHICKEN

YIELD: 4 SERVINGS / **ACTIVE TIME:** 20 MINUTES / **TOTAL TIME:** 1 HOUR AND 20 MINUTES

This sweet and tangy sauce is so tasty you'll want to try it on everything. To really get this dish to sing, be sure not to crowd the pan when browning the chicken because you want the sauce to glaze the crisp skin.

1. Add 2 tablespoons oil to a large pan over medium-high heat. When the oil is hot, add onion and cook until soft and translucent. Add garlic and sauté for 2 to 3 minutes, being sure not to let it turn brown.

2. Add pomegranate molasses, juice, honey, stock, and spices, mix well, and bring to boil. Lower heat and simmer, uncovered, for about 20 minutes, or until the sauce is reduced by about half the volume and slightly thickened. Taste sauce and adjust seasoning, to taste. Remove sauce from heat and pour into a bowl. Set aside.

3. Rinse chicken parts, pat dry, season with salt and pepper.

4. Add 2 tablespoons oil to the same pan and place chicken parts skin-side down. Brown on one side and flip to second side. Do not crowd chicken in the pan as this causes chicken to steam rather than brown.

5. Lower heat, pour prepared sauce over the chicken. Cover pan and simmer for 35 to 40 minutes.

6. Transfer the cooked chicken to a platter and garnish with parsley and pomegranate.

INGREDIENTS:

1	(4 LB.) CHICKEN, BROKEN DOWN, BREASTS HALVED IF LARGE
4	TABLESPOONS AVOCADO OIL, DIVIDED
1	LARGE ONION, CHOPPED
3	GARLIC CLOVES, MINCED
½	CUP POMEGRANATE MOLASSES
½	CUP SWEETENED POMEGRANATE JUICE
½	CUP HONEY
2	CUPS VEGETABLE STOCK OR CHICKEN STOCK (SEE PAGE 729 OR PAGE 722)
1	TEASPOON CUMIN
½	TEASPOON GINGER
⅛	TEASPOON ALLSPICE
½	TEASPOON TURMERIC
	SEA SALT, TO TASTE
	BLACK PEPPER, TO TASTE
2	TABLESPOONS PARSLEY, TO GARNISH
2	TABLESPOONS POMEGRANATE SEEDS, TO GARNISH

Pomegranate & Honey Glazed Chicken,
page 349

POMEGRANATE BRISKET
WITH CRANBERRY SUCCOTASH

YIELD: 4 SERVINGS / **ACTIVE TIME:** 30 MINUTES / **TOTAL TIME:** 3 HOURS AND 30 MINUTES

This brisket is slowly smoked until it nearly falls apart. The tender meat is then smothered in a sweet and tangy sauce, making it irresistible.

1. Preheat the oven to 275°F.

2. Season brisket on all sides with salt and pepper.

3. Add avocado oil to a large Dutch oven over medium-high heat and brown the brisket on all sides, about 5 minutes per side.

4. Remove the brisket to rest, and add onions and garlic to the pot. Sauté until browned, about 5 minutes.

5. Add brisket back in over the vegetables fat-side down and cover with pomegranate juice, red wine, and enough stock so the brisket is covered about three-quarters of the way. Add in rosemary and thyme.

6. Cover the brisket and braise in the oven for 3 hours, or until fork-tender.

7. Once cooked, remove brisket to rest and heat pan juices over medium-high heat, until reduced by at least half and sauce is thickened. Strain and season to taste.

8. In a bowl, combine the corn and cranberries and mix well.

9. In a separate bowl, whisk together extra virgin olive oil, honey, and red wine vinegar. Toss with corn mixture and add in cilantro and salt to taste.

10. Once the brisket has cooled, slice against the grain and top with sauce and succotash.

INGREDIENTS:

1	(4 LB.) BRISKET
	SEA SALT, TO TASTE
	BLACK PEPPER, TO TASTE
2	TABLESPOONS AVOCADO OIL
2	MEDIUM WHITE ONIONS, CHOPPED
2	GARLIC CLOVES, MINCED
2	CUPS POMEGRANATE JUICE
½	CUP DRY RED WINE
1-2	CUPS CHICKEN STOCK (SEE PAGE 722)
2	SPRIGS FRESH ROSEMARY
2	SPRIGS FRESH THYME
2	EARS CORN, SHUCKED AND REMOVED FROM THE COB
1	CUP DRIED CRANBERRIES
2	TABLESPOONS EXTRA VIRGIN OLIVE OIL
2	TEASPOON HONEY
2	TEASPOONS RED WINE VINEGAR
¼	CUP MINCED CILANTRO

PORCINI-RUBBED BEEF RIB ROAST

YIELD: 10 SERVINGS / **ACTIVE TIME:** 30 MINUTES / **TOTAL TIME:** 5 HOURS AND 30 MINUTES

Using dried porcini mushrooms as the base of the rub for this dramatic centerpiece roast gives it a pleasantly surprising earthy flavor.

1. Add the mushrooms, salt, peppercorns, and marjoram to a spice mill or mini food processor and pulse until coarsely ground.

2. Pat meat dry, then rub mushroom mixture all over. Transfer to a wire rack set inside a rimmed baking sheet. Let sit at room temperature 1 hour (for even more flavor, chill, uncovered, overnight, then let sit at room temperature 1 hour before roasting).

3. Preheat the oven to 225°F. Roast meat until an instant-read thermometer inserted into the center registers 120°F, about 4 hours. Tent with foil and let rest at room temperature at least 30 minutes and up to 1 hour.

4. Increase oven temperature to 500°F. Remove foil and roast meat until browned and crisp, 5 to 10 minutes. Immediately transfer to a cutting board. Cut off ribs in 1 piece, then slice into individual ribs. Carve roast into ½" slices and arrange on a serving platter along with ribs. Season with salt and serve with Horseradish-Yogurt Sauce, if desired.

HORSERADISH-YOGURT SAUCE

1. In a bowl, combine all of the ingredients and whisk well. Refrigerate before serving.

INGREDIENTS:

- ⅓ CUP DRIED PORCINI MUSHROOMS
- 2 TABLESPOONS SEA SALT
- 1 TABLESPOON WHOLE BLACK PEPPERCORNS
- 1 TEASPOON MARJORAM OR OREGANO LEAVES
- 1 (10 LB.) BONE-IN 4-RIB ROAST
- FLAKY SEA SALT, FOR SERVING
- HORSERADISH-YOGURT SAUCE (SEE RECIPE), FOR SERVING

HORSERADISH-YOGURT SAUCE

- 4 CUPS GREEK-STYLE YOGURT, PREFERABLY FULL-FAT
- 1 (6 OZ.) JAR OF PREPARED HORSERADISH
- 2 GARLIC CLOVES, FINELY GRATED
- 2 TEASPOONS SEA SALT
- ¾ TEASPOON CRUSHED RED PEPPER FLAKES
- ½ TEASPOON FRESHLY GROUND BLACK PEPPER

RACK-ROASTED CHICKEN

YIELD: 2 SERVINGS / **ACTIVE TIME:** 1 HOUR / **TOTAL TIME:** 24 HOURS

Roasting a chicken directly on your oven rack gives it a crispier skin on all sides. Add a tray of vegetables underneath it to catch all the delicious drippings. Trust us, you'll never roast the same again.

1. In a large pot, combine the salt, sugar, and peppercorns. Squeeze in juice from lemon and add lemon to the pot along with 2 quarts water. Bring to a boil, stirring to dissolve salt and sugar. Remove pot from heat and stir in 2 quarts ice water. Add chickens to brine, weight with a plate to keep submerged, if needed, and cover. Refrigerate for 12 to 24 hours.

2. Remove chickens from brine; pat dry. Place in a large baking dish and refrigerate, uncovered, 3 to 12 hours (longer is better) to dry skin in order to cook a crispier bird.

3. Place racks in the upper and lower thirds of the oven and preheat to 425°F.

4. Arrange potatoes and shallots in a roasting pan or baking dish just large enough to fit them all in a single crowded layer. Drizzle with oil and season with a little salt and pepper, then toss to coat. Place the pan on the lower rack, then set chickens, breast-side up and tail facing the oven door, directly on the rack above the vegetables. Roast chicken and vegetables until a thermometer inserted into the thickest part of chicken thigh registers 165°F, 35 to 45 minutes.

5. Insert a long-handled wooden spoon into the chicken's cavity and carefully tilt the bird toward you to allow juices in the cavity to drain into the pan below. Remove vegetables from the oven, then, using a spoon, remove chicken from the oven and place on top of vegetables. Let rest 10 minutes before carving.

INGREDIENTS:

5	OZ. SEA SALT, PLUS MORE TO TASTE
¼	CUP SUGAR
1	TEASPOON BLACK PEPPERCORNS
1	LEMON, HALVED
2	(2½ LB.) CHICKENS
1½	LBS. SMALL FINGERLING POTATOES
1	LB. SMALL SHALLOTS, PEELED
2	TABLESPOONS AVOCADO OIL
	FRESHLY GROUND PEPPER, TO TASTE

RED WINE-BRAISED OXTAIL

YIELD: 6 SERVINGS / **ACTIVE TIME:** 30 MINUTES / **TOTAL TIME:** 3 HOURS

Consider this a new weekend favorite for colder times of year. Serve this cozy dish in shallow bowls over the vegetables with plenty of sauce spooned all over

1. Preheat the oven to 350°F.

2. Season the oxtail with salt and pepper.

3. Add oil to Dutch oven over medium-high heat. Working in 2 batches, dust the oxtail with a little flour, berbere, and baharat and brown on all sides, about 8 minutes per batch. Transfer the oxtail to a plate. Pour off all but 3 tablespoons drippings from pot.

4. Add onions, carrots, and celery to pot and stir often, until onions are browned, about 5 minutes. Add the remaining flour and tomato paste; cook, stirring constantly, until well combined and deep red, 2 to 3 minutes.

5. Stir in wine, then add short ribs with any accumulated juices. Bring to a boil; lower heat to medium and simmer until wine is reduced by half, about 25 minutes.

6. Add all of the herbs, garlic, and stock and bring to a boil; cover and transfer to the oven.

7. Cook until oxtail is tender, 2 to 2½ hours. Transfer oxtails to a platter.

8. Strain sauce from pot into a measuring cup. Spoon fat from surface of sauce and discard; season sauce to taste with salt and pepper.

9. Serve in shallow bowls with vegetables of choice, sauce spooned over.

INGREDIENTS:

5	LBS. BONE-IN BEEF OXTAIL, CUT CROSSWISE, DE-JOINTED
	SEA SALT, TO TASTE
	FRESHLY GROUND BLACK PEPPER, TO TASTE
3	TABLESPOONS AVOCADO OIL
3	TABLESPOONS ALL-PURPOSE FLOUR
1	TABLESPOON BERBERE SPICE MIX (SEE PAGE 323)
1	TABLESPOON BAHARAT
3	MEDIUM ONIONS, CHOPPED
3	MEDIUM CARROTS, CHOPPED
2	CELERY STALKS, CHOPPED
1	TABLESPOON TOMATO PASTE
1	(750 ML) BOTTLE DRY RED WINE (PREFERABLY CABERNET SAUVIGNON)
10	SPRIGS FRESH FLAT LEAF PARSLEY
8	SPRIGS FRESH THYME
4	SPRIGS FRESH OREGANO
2	SPRIGS FRESH ROSEMARY
2	BAY LEAVES
1	HEAD OF GARLIC, HALVED CROSSWISE
4	CUPS BEEF STOCK (SEE PAGE 721)

ROASTED APRICOT CHICKEN
WITH MINT & SAGE BUTTERNUT SQUASH

YIELD: 6 SERVINGS / **ACTIVE TIME:** 30 MINUTES / **TOTAL TIME:** 2 HOURS

Another beautiful recipe to add to your Rosh Hashanah table. The mint and sage add unexpected flavor and depth to the butternut squash.

1. Preheat the oven to 375°F.

2. In a large bowl, combine the cinnamon, cumin, turmeric, paprika, 1 teaspoon sea salt, and oil and mix well. Add the chicken to the bowl and, using your hands, work the rub into the chicken, ensuring the entire chicken is coated.

3. In a deep cast-iron pot, combine the tomatoes, apricots, garlic, raisins, and stock and mix well. Place the chicken on top of the veggies and place the pot in the oven for 50 minutes, or until the chicken reaches an internal temperature of 150°F.

4. Transfer the chicken to a cutting board and let rest for 15 minutes.

5. Place the pot with the veggies over medium-low heat and simmer for 10 to 15 minutes, or until reduced by half and thickened.

6. In a bowl, combine the squash with the avocado oil, 2 teaspoons salt, sage, and mint and toss to coat. Spread out in an even layer on a baking sheet and roast for 15 minutes, or until knife-tender.

7. Using a large knife and fork, carve the chicken meat from the carcass. Cut the chicken into bite-size pieces and mix thoroughly into the simmering sauce. Remove from the heat and serve over the roasted butternut squash.

INGREDIENTS:

CHICKEN AND RUB

1	TEASPOON CINNAMON
½	TEASPOON CUMIN
1	TEASPOON TURMERIC
1½	TEASPOONS SPANISH PAPRIKA
3	TEASPOONS SEA SALT, DIVIDED
1	TEASPOON OLIVE OIL
1	(4-6 LB.) WHOLE CHICKEN
3	PLUM TOMATOES, DICE
1	CUP CHOPPED DRIED TURKISH APRICOTS
4	LARGE GARLIC CLOVES, MINCED
¼	CUP GOLDEN RAISINS
3	CUPS CHICKEN STOCK (SEE PAGE 722)
1	BUTTERNUT SQUASH, PEELED, CUT IN HALF, DESEEDED, AND DICED
1	TEASPOON AVOCADO OIL
1	TABLESPOON CHOPPED FRESH SAGE
1	TABLESPOON CHOPPED FRESH MINT

ROAST CHICKEN WITH HARISSA & SCHMALTZ

YIELD: 4 SERVINGS / **ACTIVE TIME:** 1 HOUR / **TOTAL TIME:** 25 HOURS

The real magic begins when the Schmaltz starts sizzling in the pan. Its richness is matched and balanced with high-heat harissa.

1. Add the garlic, sugar, coriander seeds, salt, and 8 cups water to a large saucepan over high heat and bring to a boil, stirring to dissolve sugar and salt. Transfer to a large bowl and add 1 cup ice. Let cool.

2. While brine is cooling, bone chicken breasts, leaving leg and thigh quarters intact. Start by cutting off wing tips; discard. Place chicken, skin-side down, on a cutting board. Working with 1 chicken half at a time, angle the blade of a thin, sharp knife flush against breast bone and cut along bone to separate the rib cage from flesh. The only bones remaining should be in the wing, thigh, and drumstick. Repeat on the other side; save bones for making stock.

3. Place chicken halves in cooled brine. Cover tightly and refrigerate for 12 hours.

4. Transfer chicken to a rimmed baking sheet or baking pan and pick off coriander seeds. Spread Three-Chile Harissa all over chicken. Cover tightly and refrigerate for at least 1 hour and up to 12 hours.

5. Preheat the oven to 400°F.

6. Add Schmaltz to a large cast-iron pan over medium heat. Carefully place chicken halves, skin-side down, in the pan, making sure all the skin is in the fat. Cook until the skin darkens and starts to crisp, about 5 minutes. Transfer skillet to oven and roast chicken until skin is very dark and meat is more than halfway cooked through, 20 to 25 minutes.

7. Remove the skillet from the oven and carefully turn chicken. Return to the oven and roast, skin-side up, until an instant-read thermometer inserted into the thickest part of thigh registers 165°F, 8 to 12 minutes.

8. Transfer chicken to a large platter, placing skin-side up. Drizzle some of the Schmaltz over chicken and serve remaining Schmaltz alongside.

Continued . . .

INGREDIENTS:

3	GARLIC CLOVES, SMASHED, PEELED
⅓	CUP SUGAR
¼	CUP CORIANDER SEEDS
1	CUP KOSHER SALT, PLUS MORE TO TASTE
8	CUPS WATER
1	(4-4½ LB.) CHICKEN, HALVED AND BACKBONE REMOVED
1	CUP THREE-CHILE HARISSA (SEE RECIPE)
¼	CUP SCHMALTZ (SEE PAGE 528)

THREE-CHILE HARISSA

3	OZ. DRIED GUAJILLO CHILES, SEEDS REMOVED AND TORN INTO 1" PIECES
1	OZ. CHIPOTLE CHILES, SEEDS REMOVED AND TORN INTO 1" PIECES
1	TABLESPOON NIGELLA SEEDS
1	TEASPOON CORIANDER SEEDS
2	GARLIC CLOVES
1	TABLESPOON CUMIN
1	TEASPOON KOSHER SALT
½	TEASPOON ALEPPO PEPPER
½	CUP OLIVE OIL
2	TABLESPOONS WHITE WINE VINEGAR

THREE-CHILE HARISSA

1. Place guajillo and chipotle chiles in a large heatproof bowl and pour in boiling water to cover. Let chiles soak until softened, 40 to 45 minutes; drain.

2. Grind nigella seeds and coriander seeds in a spice mill or with a mortar and pestle. Transfer to a food processor and add garlic, cumin, salt, and Aleppo pepper and pulse until garlic is very finely chopped. Add rehydrated chiles and pulse until they are chopped. Add oil and vinegar and pulse just until mixture has the texture of a coarse paste.

Ropa Vieja, page 364

ROPA VIEJA

YIELD: 8 SERVINGS / **ACTIVE TIME:** 40 MINUTES / **TOTAL TIME:** 3 HOURS

Yes, this is one of Cuba 's national dishes. But the recipe itself is over five hundred years old and originates from the Sephardic Jews, who prepared it to be eaten on the Sabbath.

1. Place the meat, 2 bay leaves, sliced garlic, 1½ onions, and stock in a pressure cooker set to high heat. Cook until the meat is tender and easy to shred, about 35 to 40 minutes. If you do not have a pressure cooker, place ingredients in an oven-safe pot with a lid and braise at 325°F, until meat is tender and easy to shred, 2 to 2½ hours. Once meat is braised, shred with a fork.

2. Add ¼ cup oil to a medium pot over high heat. Add the peppers and sauté for 5 minutes to soften. Add the remaining onion and sauté for 3 to 5 more minutes. Add the tomato puree, wine, cumin, paprika, salt, and pepper. Cover and cook over medium heat for 15 minutes, until the sauce thickens.

3. Add the shredded meat and remaining bay leaf and stir to combine with the sauce. Cover and cook for 5 minutes. Taste and adjust for seasoning.

4. Add 1 tablespoon oil and crushed garlic clove to a saucepan over medium heat. Add rice and mix to coat with oil. Add 4 cups of water and ½ teaspoon of salt.

5. Cover and simmer over medium heat for 15 minutes. Turn off heat and let sit for 5 more minutes. Fluff before serving alongside meat, avocado, and tostones.

INGREDIENTS:

- 2   LBS. FLANK STEAK
- 3   BAY LEAVES, DIVIDED
- 2   YELLOW ONIONS, SLICED AND DIVIDED
- 4   CUPS CHICKEN STOCK (SEE PAGE 722)
- ¼   CUP PLUS 1 TABLESPOON AVOCADO OIL
- 1   MEDIUM RED BELL PEPPER, SLICED
- 1   MEDIUM GREEN BELL PEPPER, SLICED
- 3   GARLIC CLOVES, SLICED PLUS 1 CLOVE, CRUSHED
- 28   OZ. CAN OF TOMATO PUREE
- 1½   CUPS WHITE WINE
- 1   TEASPOON CUMIN
- ½   TEASPOON SMOKED PAPRIKA
- 1   TEASPOON SEA SALT
- ⅛   TEASPOON FRESHLY GROUND BLACK PEPPER
- 2   CUPS OF JASMINE RICE

     SLICED AVOCADO, FOR SERVING

     TOSTONES, FOR SERVING

SABICH

YIELD: 6 SERVINGS / **ACTIVE TIME**: 20 MINUTES / **TOTAL TIME**: 1 HOUR

Israelis will happily stuff anything they can into a pita. Sure, falafel, burika, and shawarma are commonplace, but the sabich is arguably the most representative of the country's history. It was originally a dish eaten by Iraqi Jews on Shabbat morning but has now become a popular daily staple. The pita is stuffed with fried eggplant slices, hard-boiled eggs, tahini sauce, and Israeli salad—a combination of finely diced cucumbers, tomatoes, onion, and peppers. To be enjoyed on every street corner in Israel, or in the comfort of your own home.

1. Preheat the oven to 425°F.

2. Arrange the eggplant rounds in a single layer on a wire rack set over a baking sheet. Sprinkle both sides with salt and leave to sweat for at least 20 minutes, or up to 1 hour. Thoroughly wipe the water from the eggplant slices using a paper towel and pat dry.

3. Generously brush both sides of the eggplant with oil and place on a baking sheet, being careful not to overcrowd. Roast the eggplant for 20 minutes, flipping halfway through until browned and golden.

4. Create your spread.

INGREDIENTS:

2   MEDIUM EGGPLANTS, SLICED INTO 1" ROUNDS

2   TEASPOONS SEA SALT

    AVOCADO OIL

SERVE WITH ANY, OR ALL, OF THE FOLLOWING:

6-8   PITA OR LAFFA (SEE PAGE 697 OR PAGE 571)

8   LARGE HARD-BOILED EGGS, QUARTERED

    ISRAELI CHOPPED SALAD

    TAHINI

    PARSLEY

    PICKLES

    OLIVES

    HOT PEPPERS

    PIECES OF COOKED POTATO

    ZHOUG (SEE PAGE 700)

    AMBA

Sabich, page 365

ROSEMARY RACK OF LAMB
WITH ROASTED POTATOES & CARROTS

YIELD: 2 SERVINGS / ACTIVE TIME: 30 MINUTES / TOTAL TIME: 1 HOUR AND 30 MINUTES

This elegant dinner of lamb, miso butter–basted potatoes, and honey-glazed carrots is the perfect size for a small, intimate dinner party. But only make if you're prepared to be everyone's favorite new chef.

1. Preheat the oven to 425°F.

2. Rub lamb with garlic, rosemary, pepper, and ½ teaspoon salt.

3. In a small bowl, combine miso, paprika, 4 tablespoons butter, and ½ teaspoon salt, mix well, and set aside.

4. Peel the potatoes. Working with one potato at a time, slice a thin sliver off one long side to make a flat bottom. Trim ends off, then slice vertically every ¹⁄₁₆", cutting down to ¼" from the bottom. To make sure you do not cut all the way through the potato, line it with chopsticks on each side to stop your knife. Brush potatoes with miso butter, fanning slices open to get butter between each slice. Transfer to a rimmed baking sheet and roast for 15 minutes.

5. Remove the baking sheet from the oven and brush potatoes with more miso butter. Arrange lamb on baking sheet alongside potatoes and roast, brushing potatoes with miso butter halfway through, until an instant-read thermometer inserted into the thickest part of the lamb registers 125°F for medium-rare, and the potatoes are fork-tender, 20 to 25 minutes.

6. Transfer lamb to a cutting board and let rest for 10 minutes, and continue roasting the potatoes if needed.

7. Meanwhile, in a bowl, combine the honey, coriander, the remaining 1 tablespoon butter, and ¼ teaspoon salt, mix well, and then brush over carrots. Arrange carrots on a baking sheet and roast until lightly browned and fork-tender, 15 to 20 minutes.

8. Slice lamb between each rib. Brush potatoes with remaining miso butter, top carrots with parsley, and serve alongside lamb.

INGREDIENTS:

1	(1-1½ LB.) RACK OF LAMB, FAT CAP SCORED
1	GARLIC CLOVE, FINELY CHOPPED
2	TEASPOONS CHOPPED ROSEMARY
⅛	TEASPOON FRESHLY GROUND BLACK PEPPER
1¼	TEASPOONS SEA SALT, DIVIDED
1	TABLESPOON WHITE MISO PASTE
¼	TEASPOON SMOKED PAPRIKA
5	TABLESPOONS UNSALTED BUTTER, SOFTENED, DIVIDED
2	MEDIUM YUKON GOLD POTATOES
1	TEASPOON HONEY
¼	TEASPOON GROUND CORIANDER
½	LB. MEDIUM CARROTS, PEELED
1	TABLESPOON FINELY CHOPPED PARSLEY

SEITAN BRISKET

YIELD: SERVINGS: 6 / **ACTIVE TIME:** 30 MINUTES / **TOTAL TIME:** 2 HOURS

When the family gathers for any High Holiday or Shabbat, make sure that everyone, including the vegetarians at the table, can partake. The chewy texture and savory appeal of seitan is perfect for creating a meat-free brisket.

1. Preheat the oven to 375°F.

2. Add oil, onions, carrots, celery, and tamari to a heavy baking dish, stir to coat, and bake for 40 minutes.

3. Remove the dish from the oven and distribute seitan on top of the veggies.

4. In a bowl, combine stock, 1½ tablespoons juice/wine, 2 tablespoons brown sugar, and caraway seeds, mix well, and pour over seitan and veggies. Grind black pepper over top, cover tightly with foil, and return to the oven. Bake for an additional 40 minutes.

5. Remove pan, uncover, and ladle out as much of the cooking liquid as possible into a large measuring cup.

6. Add the oil to a skillet over medium heat. Add flour and cook, whisking constantly, for 3 minutes. Slowly whisk in reserved cooking liquid and stir constantly until smooth and thick, 2 to 3 minutes. If you don't have enough cooking liquid, add stock to substitute. Stir in half the garlic. Spread sauce onto the seitan, stirring to blend. Add salt to taste, if needed.

7. Raise oven temperature to broil. Prepare the glaze by combining the remaining juice/wine, remaining brown sugar, miso, and remaining garlic in a bowl and mixing well. Spoon the glaze over the seitan. Return to the oven and broil, uncovered, until bubbling hot, and deeply browned, 5 to 10 minutes. Serve hot.

INGREDIENTS:

- 2 TABLESPOONS AVOCADO OIL
- 2 MEDIUM ONIONS, SLICED VERTICALLY
- 2 MEDIUM CARROTS, SLICED INTO 1" PIECES
- 2 CELERY STALKS, CHOPPED ROUGHLY
- ½ TABLESPOON TAMARI
- 15 OZ. SEITAN, SLICED
- 1¾ CUPS PAREVE "CHICKEN"-FLAVORED STOCK OR VEGETABLE STOCK (SEE PAGE 729)
- ¾ CUP PLUS 1½ TABLESPOONS GRAPE JUICE OR FRUITY RED WINE, DIVIDED
- 3½ TABLESPOONS BROWN SUGAR, DIVIDED
- 1 TEASPOON CARAWAY SEEDS
- FRESHLY GROUND BLACK PEPPER, TO TASTE
- 3 TABLESPOONS AVOCADO OIL
- ¼ CUP UNBLEACHED ALL-PURPOSE FLOUR
- 2 GARLIC CLOVES, MINCED AND DIVIDED
- 1½ TABLESPOON MISO PASTE
- 1 TEASPOON SEA SALT, TO TASTE

SHAKSHUKA WITH SPINACH & LAMB MEATBALLS

YIELD: 4 SERVINGS / **ACTIVE TIME:** 20 MINUTES / **TOTAL TIME:** 40 MINUTES

The addition of lamb meatballs transforms what is traditionally a breakfast or light dinner staple into a hearty feast. And although there are many components, it's a one-pot wonder perfect for midweek meals.

1. In a medium bowl, combine spices for lamb meatballs, add lamb, and mix well. Roll lamb into small meatballs, about 1" in diameter.

2. Add 1 tablespoon oil to a large pan over medium heat. Brown meatballs on all sides, around 2 to 3 minutes. Remove from the pan and set aside. Leave liquid and lamb bits in the bottom of the pan for flavor.

3. Add another tablespoon oil to the same pan along with garlic and cook 1 minute, scraping up brown bits. Add tomato paste and spices and continue to cook for 3 to 4 minutes, until fragrant.

4. Add tomatoes and meatballs and simmer, covered, for 15 minutes.

5. After 15 minutes, add spinach on top and cook for another 3 to 4 minutes, until spinach has wilted completely. Stir.

6. When sauce has thickened slightly, crack eggs into small glass bowls and then gently add to tomato sauce. Cover and cook for 3 to 5 minutes, until whites have set and yolk is to your liking.

7. Serve immediately after drizzling tahini over the top and sprinkling with fresh parsley.

INGREDIENTS:

MEATBALLS

½	TEASPOON CUMIN
¼	TEASPOON PAPRIKA
¼	TEASPOON CINNAMON
¼	TEASPOON CORIANDER
¼	TEASPOON SALT
⅛	TEASPOON PEPPER
1	PINCH RED PEPPER FLAKES
2	TABLESPOONS CHOPPED PARSLEY
¾	LB. GROUND LAMB
1	TABLESPOON AVOCADO OIL

SHAKSHUKA

2-3	TABLESPOONS AVOCADO OIL
3	GARLIC CLOVES, MINCED
1	TABLESPOON TOMATO PASTE
1	TABLESPOON PAPRIKA
1	TEASPOON CUMIN
1	PINCH CARAWAY SEEDS
1	(28 OZ.) CAN OF DICED TOMATOES
1	TEASPOON SEA SALT
½	TEASPOON PEPPER
2-4	LARGE EGGS
2	CUPS FRESH SPINACH
¼	CUP TAHINI, FOR SERVING
	FRESH PARSLEY SPRIGS, FOR SERVING

Shakshuka, page 376

SHAKSHUKA

YIELD: 6 TO 8 SERVINGS / **ACTIVE TIME**: 30 MINUTES / **TOTAL TIME**: 5 HOURS

Shakshuka was brought to Israel by the Tunisian and Libyan Jews as part of the Jewish exodus from Arab and Muslim countries, and it became part of the culture due to Israel's African Jewish population. Eggs are poached or baked in a sauce with tomatoes, chili peppers, onions, cumin, or whatever else your heart so desires. Tunisian in origin, shakshuka (which translates to "shaken" in Hebrew and "a mixture" in Arabic) is commonly eaten for breakfast but can be enjoyed as a light dinner as well.

1. Add oil, tomatoes, garlic, peppers, paprika, salt, and 2 cups water to a large skillet over medium-high heat. Bring to a simmer and then lower to the lowest possible flame and cook for 4 to 5 hours; this may require using the smallest burner on the stove. Stir occasionally and add water, 1 cup at a time, as necessary until a deeply flavorful, thick, jam-like base forms.

2. To finish, gently crack the egg over the sauce. Cover and cook over medium-high heat until the whites are set but the yolk is still runny, about 5 minutes.

3. Serve immediately with homemade bread.

INGREDIENTS:

½ CUP OLIVE OIL

5 LBS. TOMATOES, GRATED

1 HEAD OF GARLIC, CLOVES PEELED AND SMASHED

2 WHOLE GREEN CHILI PEPPERS, LIKE POBLANO, SERRANO, OR JALAPEÑO

1 TABLESPOON PAPRIKA

1 TABLESPOON SEA SALT

1 EGG

SHAWARMA-SPICED BRAISED LEG OF LAMB

YIELD: 8 SERVINGS / **ACTIVE TIME:** 30 MINUTES / **TOTAL TIME:** 30 HOURS

There's always something impressive about the size and shape of a leg of lamb. We prefer a bone-in version, as it lends flavor to the meat as it braises. But a boneless tied leg of lamb is a little more manageable and cooks more quickly.

1. Grind cumin, caraway, and coriander seeds in a spice mill or with a mortar and pestle to a powder. Transfer to a small bowl and stir in chiles, garlic, oil, paprika, and cinnamon.

2. Trim excess fat from lamb and remove any membrane. Lightly score flesh with a knife and pat dry with paper towels. Season lamb very generously with salt and pepper; place on a wire rack set inside a rimmed baking sheet and apply the rub. Refrigerate for 12 to 24 hours.

3. Let the lamb come to room temperature, about 1 hour.

4. Preheat the oven to 450°F.

5. Roast lamb until well browned all over, 20 to 25 minutes. Remove from the oven and reduce oven temperature to 250°F.

6. Meanwhile, grind caraway and coriander seeds in a spice mill or with a mortar and pestle to a powder.

7. Heat oil in a large Dutch oven over medium; if lamb doesn't fit in the pot you have, set a roasting pan over two burners instead. Add onion and cook, stirring occasionally, until translucent, 5 to 7 minutes.

8. Add ancho chile powder, chipotle chile powder, turmeric, black pepper, and cinnamon and stir to coat onion. Cook, stirring, until spices are fragrant, about 2 minutes. Add tomatoes and broth and bring liquid to a simmer; season lightly with salt.

9. Carefully place the lamb in the pot and add just enough water to cover if it is not submerged. Cover pot and braise lamb in the oven until meat is very tender and bone wiggles easily in the joint, about 5 hours. If using a roasting pan, add water as needed so liquid comes halfway up the side of the leg, cover with foil, and turn lamb once during braising.

10. Transfer lamb to a platter and tent with foil to keep warm while making the sauce.

11. Place cooking vessel over medium-high heat and bring braising liquid to a boil; cook, stirring often to prevent sticking, until reduced by half, 25 to 30 minutes. Taste sauce and season to taste. Spoon over lamb.

INGREDIENTS:

RUB
- 2 TABLESPOONS CUMIN SEEDS
- 2 TEASPOONS CARAWAY SEEDS
- 2 TEASPOONS CORIANDER SEEDS
- 2 THAI CHILES, FINELY CHOPPED
- 4 GARLIC CLOVES, FINELY GRATED
- ½ CUP AVOCADO OIL
- 1 TABLESPOON PAPRIKA
- ½ TEASPOON GROUND CINNAMON

LAMB
- 6 LB. BONE-IN LEG OF LAMB, SHANK ATTACHED, FRENCHED
- SEA SALT, TO TASTE
- FRESHLY GROUND BLACK PEPPER, TO TASTE
- ½ TEASPOON CARAWAY SEEDS
- ½ TEASPOON CORIANDER SEEDS
- ¼ CUP AVOCADO OR GRAPESEED OIL
- 1 LARGE ONION, THINLY SLICED
- 1 TABLESPOON ANCHO CHILE POWDER
- 1 TABLESPOON CHIPOTLE CHILE POWDER
- 1 TEASPOON GROUND TURMERIC
- ½ TEASPOON FRESHLY GROUND BLACK PEPPER
- ½ TEASPOON GROUND CINNAMON
- 1 (28 OZ) CAN CRUSHED TOMATOES
- 4 CUPS LOW-SODIUM CHICKEN BROTH
- 1 TEASPOON SEA SALT

Shashlik, page 380

SHASHLIK

YIELD: 12 SERVINGS / **ACTIVE TIME:** 20 MINUTES / **TOTAL TIME:** 6 HOURS

This Georgian version of shish kabobs gained popularity throughout Eastern Europe, and is often associated with Russian cuisine, as well. Many families have a secret recipe that involves different blends of spices, but this combination is our favorite.

1. In a large bowl, combine the red wine, red wine vinegar, pomegranate molasses, oil, salt, sugar, black pepper, coriander, oregano, garlic cloves, and onion. Place the lamb cubes in a non-reactive container or large resealable bag and cover with the marinade. Refrigerate for at least 6 hours, but no longer than 14 hours.

2. Remove meat from the marinade, discarding all solids. Thread the meat onto heavy, flat metal skewers—6 to 8 cubes per skewer—and season with salt and pepper.

3. Grill over medium-high heat for 7 to 8 minutes per side, rotating them as needed until cooked through and evenly charred on all sides.

4. Serve immediately with sliced raw onion and pomegranate molasses and adjika.

INGREDIENTS:

- 2 CUPS MEDIUM-BODIED RED WINE
- ½ CUP RED WINE VINEGAR
- ¼ CUP POMEGRANATE MOLASSES, PLUS MORE FOR SERVING
- ¼ CUP AVOCADO OIL
- 1 TABLESPOON SEA SALT, PLUS MORE FOR SERVING
- 1 TABLESPOON SUGAR
- 2 TEASPOONS FRESHLY CRACKED BLACK PEPPER, PLUS MORE FOR SERVING
- 1 TEASPOON GROUND CORIANDER
- ½ TEASPOON DRIED OREGANO
- 12 LARGE GARLIC CLOVES, PEELED AND SMASHED
- 1 MEDIUM YELLOW ONION, HALVED LENGTHWISE AND SLICED INTO THICK ½" RINGS, PLUS MORE FOR SERVING
- 6 LBS. BONELESS LEG OF LAMB, CUT INTO 2-3" CUBES
- ADJIKA (GEORGIAN PEPPER PASTE), FOR SERVING

SHEET PAN TZIMMES-ROASTED CHICKEN THIGHS

YIELD: 2 SERVINGS / **ACTIVE TIME:** 20 MINUTES / **TOTAL TIME:** 55 MINUTES

A sheet pan makes this recipe both easy to prepare and a cinch to clean up. Apricots, prunes, and honey make this a sweet and savory dish perfect for Rosh Hashanah or Sabbath.

1. Preheat the oven to 425°F.

2. Pat dry the chicken with paper towels. Season well on both sides with generous amounts of salt and pepper and set aside, skin-side up, on a sheet pan.

3. In a small bowl, combine oil, lemon juice, honey, cinnamon, red pepper flakes, and ½ teaspoon salt and mix well.

4. Remove two garlic cloves from the head and set aside. Arrange the vegetables, prunes, and remaining garlic on the pan with the chicken and drizzle the oil mixture over, tossing everything to coat.

5. Bake, tossing vegetables in the chicken fat halfway though, until vegetables are browned and chicken is cooked through, 35 to 45 minutes, depending on how large the thighs are; an instant-read thermometer should register 165°F. If the vegetables are done before the chicken, remove them to a plate and finish cooking chicken.

6. Before serving, grate remaining cloves of garlic into a small bowl and mix with parsley. Season with salt and pepper. Sprinkle this mixture over the chicken and vegetables.

INGREDIENTS:

- 1 LB. BONE-IN, SKIN-ON CHICKEN THIGHS
- ½ TEASPOON SEA SALT, PLUS MORE TO TASTE
- FRESHLY GROUND BLACK PEPPER, TO TASTE
- 3 TABLESPOONS AVOCADO OIL
- ¼ CUP FRESH LEMON JUICE, PLUS LEMON WEDGES FOR SERVING
- 2 TABLESPOONS HONEY
- ¼ TEASPOON CINNAMON
- ½ TEASPOON RED PEPPER FLAKES, PLUS MORE FOR SERVING
- ½ LB. BABY YUKON GOLD (OR ANY WAXY) POTATOES (HALVED IF LARGER THAN 1½")
- 1 MEDIUM SWEET POTATO, CUT INTO WEDGES THE SIZE OF THE POTAOES
- ½ LB. CARROTS, SCRUBBED AND HALVED LENGTHWISE
- 1 HEAD OF GARLIC, CUT IN HALF CROSSWISE
- 1 MEDIUM RED ONION, UNPEELED, QUARTERED THROUGH ROOT END
- ½ CUP PRUNES
- ½ CUP CHOPPED PARSLEY, LEAVES AND STEMS
- TOASTED CHALLAH OR COUNTRY BREAD, FOR SERVING

SHEIKA

YIELD: 6 SERVINGS / **ACTIVE TIME:** 20 MINUTES / **TOTAL TIME:** 1 HOUR AND 30 MINUTES

In Eastern Europe, sheika was traditionally made solely from the skin of a chicken neck, but today some chefs utilize skin from the entire chicken. The filling is a simple mixture of flour and onions.

1. Rinse the chicken and cut off and reserve any fat you can find. Loosen the skin of the chicken by rubbing your fingers under the skin and separating. Remove the skin in one giant piece.

2. In a large bowl, sift the flour over onions and mix to combine.

3. Cut the reserved fat into small pieces and place in the bowl with the flour and onions. Add the Schmaltz and 1 teaspoon salt. Mix until combined.

4. Using a needle and thread, sew the edges of the skin of the chicken together to make a cavity for the filling. Stuff the skin with the onion and flour mixture and stitch to enclose completely.

5. Place the stuffed skin in a large stockpot and cover with cold water. Add 2 teaspoons salt, bring to a boil, and then lower to a simmer and cook for 40 minutes.

6. Remove from the pot and slice once cool enough to handle. Serve immediately.

INGREDIENTS:

SKIN AND FAT OF 1 (3-4 LB.) WHOLE CHICKEN

1¼ CUPS ALL-PURPOSE FLOUR

3 MEDIUM ONIONS, CHOPPED

½ CUP SCHMALTZ (SEE PAGE 528)

3 TEASPOONS SEA SALT, DIVIDED

SKILLET ROAST CHICKEN
WITH FENNEL, PARSNIPS & SCALLIONS

YIELD: 6 SERVINGS / **ACTIVE TIME:** 20 MINUTES / **TOTAL TIME:** 1 HOUR

A beautifully browned bird and seasonal vegetables cook in a single skillet for an effortless dinner. Swap in carrots, quartered onions, or tiny potatoes--anything goes.

1. Preheat the oven to 425°F. Heat 1 tablespoon oil in a large ovenproof skillet over medium-high. Season chicken inside and out with salt and pepper and cook, breast-side down, until a beautiful golden brown. Use tongs to gently rotate chicken, being careful not to tear skin, and brown on all sides, 12 to 15 minutes total; transfer to a plate. Reserve skillet.

2. Toss fennel, parsnips, scallions, and lemon zest in skillet with remaining 2 tablespoons oil; season with salt and pepper. Place chicken, breast-side up, on top of vegetables. Roast until an instant-read thermometer inserted into the thickest part of chicken thigh registers 165°F, 35 to 40 minutes. (You can also check doneness by cutting into thigh meat right at the joint. If the juices run clear, the bird is ready.) Transfer chicken to a cutting board and let rest at least 10 minutes before carving.

3. Serve chicken and vegetables with pan juices for spooning over and lemon wedges.

INGREDIENTS:

3	TABLESPOONS AVOCADO OIL, DIVIDED
1	(3½–4-LB.) CHICKEN
1	TEASPOON SEA SALT AND FRESHLY GROUND BLACK PEPPER
1	FENNEL BULB, SLICED LENGTHWISE ½" THICK
2	LARGE PARSNIPS, PEELED, SLICED ½" THICK ON THE DIAGONAL
1	BUNCH SCALLIONS
3	WIDE STRIPS LEMON ZEST
	LEMON WEDGES (FOR SERVING)

SKEWERS OF CHICKEN & LAMB FAT

YIELD: 8 SERVINGS / **ACTIVE TIME:** 35 MINUTES / **TOTAL TIME:** 45 MINUTES

D iet, schmiet. A little fat never hurt anyone—it only makes these skewers more succulent and delicious.

1. Light the charcoal or fire up the grill.

2. Assemble 10 skewers, alternating two chicken cubes followed by one lamb fat cube three times for a total of 9 pieces per skewer.

3. Brush the skewers with oil and season each with ¼ teaspoon of paprika and sea salt.

4. When the grill is ready, place the skewers on the grill and roast until they are browned and the fat is golden and very aromatic, about 10 to 12 minutes.

5. Serve immediately.

INGREDIENTS:

- 2¼ LBS. BONELESS, SKINLESS CHICKEN THIGHS, CUT INTO 1" CUBES
- ¾ LB. LAMB FAT, CUT INTO ¾" CUBES
- 1 TABLESPOON AVOCADO OIL
- 2½ TEASPOONS HIGH QUALITY SWEET PAPRIKA, DIVIDED
- 1 TEASPOON SEA SALT

SLOW-COOKED SHORT RIBS
WITH GREMOLATA

YIELD: 8 SERVINGS / **ACTIVE TIME:** 25 MINUTES / **TOTAL TIME:** 15 HOURS

English short ribs are cut lengthwise along the bone, so the meat sits on top. With a day or two of notice, any butcher should be able to cut them to order. The gremolata is a pungent, bright addition.

1. Season short ribs generously with salt and pepper; place in a large roasting pan and chill, uncovered, 12 hours.

2. Preheat the oven to 325°F. Toast breadcrumbs on a rimmed baking sheet, tossing halfway through, until golden brown, 8 to 10 minutes. Let cool.

3. Add 1 cup water to the roasting pan. Cover pan with foil and cook until meat is tender, 2½ to 3 hours. Uncover pan and increase oven temperature to 400°F. Roast until ribs are browned on top, 25 to 30 minutes longer.

4. When short ribs are almost done, mix garlic, parsley, horseradish, lemon zest and juice, breadcrumbs, and 2 tablespoons oil in a small bowl; season gremolata with salt and pepper.

5. Meanwhile, heat remaining 1 tablespoon oil in a large skillet over medium-high heat. Cook lemons, cut side down, until golden brown, about 4 minutes. Top short ribs with gremolata and serve with seared lemons.

INGREDIENTS:

6	10" ENGLISH-STYLE BONE-IN BEEF SHORT RIBS (ABOUT 10 LBS.)
1½	TEASPOONS SEA SALT
1	TEASPOON FRESHLY GROUND PEPPER
½	CUP COARSE FRESH BREADCRUMBS
2	GARLIC CLOVES, FINELY GRATED
1	CUP CHOPPED FRESH FLAT-LEAF PARSLEY
½	CUP GRATED PEELED HORSERADISH OR 2 TABLESPOONS PREPARED HORSERADISH
1	TABLESPOON FINELY GRATED LEMON ZEST
1	TABLESPOON FRESH LEMON JUICE
3	TABLESPOONS AVOCADO OIL, DIVIDED
4	LEMONS, HALVED

SLOW-ROASTED CHICKEN
WITH ALL THE GARLIC

YIELD: 4 SERVINGS / **ACTIVE TIME:** 20 MINUTES / **TOTAL TIME:** 3 HOURS

When we say "all the garlic," we mean as much as you can take. Before you let out an "Oy, gavelt," let us point out that any alliums, like green garlic bulbs, are perfectly at home in the oven. When smothered in olive oil and seasoned with salt, their robust flavor softens and sweetens to perfection.

1. Preheat the oven to 325°F.

2. Trim dark tops from green garlic and place in chicken cavities; loosely tie legs together with kitchen twine.

3. Halve green garlic bulbs and pale-green parts.

4. Place chicken in a 2 quart baking dish; season with salt and pepper.

5. Tuck green garlic, garlic cloves, and lemon wedges around (make sure everything fits snugly to keep garlic from getting too dark); pour oil over.

6. Roast, turning garlic and lemon occasionally, until chicken is very tender and garlic is soft and deeply caramelized, 2½ to 3 hours.

7. Serve chicken with garlic and lemon alongside.

INGREDIENTS:

4	GREEN GARLIC BULBS
1	(3½–4 LBS.) CHICKEN
1	TEASPOON SEA SALT
½	TEASPOON FRESHLY GROUND PEPPER
1	CUP PEELED GARLIC CLOVES
1	LEMON, CUT INTO 8 WEDGES, SEEDS REMOVED
½	CUP AVOCADO OIL

SLOW-ROASTED CHICKEN
WITH HONEY-GLAZED CARROTS & GINGER

YIELD: 4 TO 6 SERVINGS / **ACTIVE TIME:** 30 MINUTES / **TOTAL TIME:** 3 HOURS

Cooking chicken in a lidded pot over low heat lets the bird gently steam, resulting in meat that's juicier than if left uncovered. When dinner time approaches, crank up the oven to crisp the skin.

1. Preheat the oven to 250°F. Season chicken generously with salt inside and out. Place the head of garlic inside the cavity; tie legs together if desired. Let sit at least 5 minutes or chill, uncovered, up to 2 days.

2. Combine carrots, shallots, ginger, butter, and honey in a large Dutch oven or other heavy pot; season lightly with salt. Place chicken on top, nestling into vegetables so the lid will sit tight. Cover; bake until an instant-read thermometer inserted into the thickest part of breast registers 155°F, about 2 hours. Uncover and let rest for 30 minutes.

3. Meanwhile, cook oil and sliced garlic in a small saucepan over medium until garlic is lightly browned, 6 to 8 minutes. Add red pepper flakes and let cool. Stir in lime juice; season dressing with salt.

4. Increase oven temperature to 450°F. Place chicken on a rimmed baking sheet and roast until skin is browned and crisp, 10 to 14 minutes.

5. Meanwhile, place the pot over medium-high heat; bring juices to a simmer. Cook, reducing heat as needed, until vegetables are glazed, 10 to 12 minutes. Keep warm over low heat until chicken is done.

6. Serve chicken on top of vegetables with dressing drizzled over.

INGREDIENTS:

- 1   (3-½–4 LB.) CHICKEN
- 1   TEASPOON SEA SALT
- 1   HEAD OF GARLIC, HALVED CROSSWISE, PLUS 4 CLOVES, THINLY SLICED
- 1½   LB. CARROTS, SCRUBBED, CUT IN HALF
- 8   SMALL SHALLOTS, PEELED
- 1   (2") PIECE GINGER, UNPEELED, THINLY SLICED
- 2   TABLESPOONS UNSALTED BUTTER
- 1   TABLESPOON HONEY
- 2   TABLESPOONS AVOCADO OIL
- 1   TEASPOON CRUSHED RED PEPPER FLAKES
- ¼   CUP FRESH LIME JUICE

SLOW-ROASTED LAMB SHOULDER
WITH BRUSSELS SPROUTS & CRISPY KALE

YIELD: 4 TO 6 SERVINGS / **ACTIVE TIME:** 25 MINUTES / **TOTAL TIME:** 3 HOURS AND 25 MINUTES

The biggest wow factor of this impressive Rosh Hashanah roast is how easy it is to make. Rub the lamb with a mix that includes fennel, cumin, garlic, oregano, and brown sugar, then roast for several hours.

1. Preheat the oven to 350°F. Place the fennel and cumin seeds in a mortar and pound with a pestle until fine. Add the garlic, oregano, brown sugar, 1 teaspoon salt, vinegar and 2 tablespoons of the oil and mix to combine. Rub the lamb with the spice mixture and place in a large roasting pan. Add the water and cover with aluminum foil.

2. Roast for 2 hours, remove the foil and spoon over the cooking liquid. Roast for 40 more minutes or until golden brown.

3. Place the Brussels sprouts, 1 teaspoon salt, pepper and the remaining oil in a large bowl and toss to combine. Transfer to a lightly greased rimmed baking sheet lined with non-stick parchment paper and roast for 15 to 20 minutes or until golden. Add the almonds and kale and roast for 5 more minutes or until the kale is crisp.

4. Serve the lamb with the greens.

INGREDIENTS:

1	TABLESPOON FENNEL SEEDS
1	TABLESPOON CUMIN SEEDS
2	GARLIC CLOVES, CRUSHED
6	SPRIGS FRESH OREGANO
¼	CUP BROWN SUGAR
1	TEASPOON SEA SALT, PLUS 1 TEASPOON, DIVIDED
¼	CUP MALT VINEGAR
¼	CUP AVOCADO OR GRAPESEED OIL
1	(4½ LB.) BONE-IN LAMB SHOULDER
1	CUP WATER
1	LB. BRUSSELS SPROUTS, TRIMMED AND HALVED
½	TEASPOON FRESHLY GROUND BLACK PEPPER
½	CUP SMOKED ALMONDS, CHOPPED
5¼	OZ. BABY KALE LEAVES

Spaghetti Al Tonno, page 392

SPAGHETTI AL TONNO

YIELD: 4 TO 6 SERVINGS / **ACTIVE TIME:** 20 MINUTES / **TOTAL TIME:** 1 HOUR

This staple of Cucina Ebraica, or Jewish Italian cuisine, is a salty and savory marriage of tuna, capers, onions, and an anchovy-based tomato sauce.

1. Heat the oil in a medium-sized saucepan over medium-low heat and sauté the garlic and chopped onions just until the onions are soft, while stirring often for about 5 minutes. Add the chili flakes.

2. Add in the passata bottle of strained tomatoes, salt, and pepper and stir well.

3. Fill the bottle of passata three-quarters full with water. Give it a good swirl and add this to the sauce.

4. Bring the sauce to a boil then lower the heat, cover, and simmer for about 45 minutes or until the sauce thickens.

5. While the sauce is slowly simmering, bring a large pot of water to boil.

6. Salt the water and cook the pasta. Cook for about 5 minutes until al dente, pasta is tender but still has a bite to it.

7. Add the drained tuna to the tomato sauce and allow to simmer for about 5 minutes.

8. When ready, drain the pasta and toss with some of the tomato sauce.

9. Plate the pasta and top with more sauce and a sprinkle of chopped parsley.

INGREDIENTS:

2 TABLESPOONS AVOCADO OIL

3 GARLIC CLOVES, FINELY CHOPPED

1 SMALL YELLOW ONION, FINELY CHOPPED

⅛ TEASPOON RED CHILI FLAKES

24 OZ. TOMATO PASSATA (STRAINED TOMATOES)

6 OZ. ITALIAN OIL PACKED TUNA, DRAINED

SALT AND PEPPER, TO TASTE

16 OZ. PACKAGE OF SPAGHETTI

4 SPRIGS FRESH PARSLEY, CHOPPED

SPINACH PESTO STUFFED SALMON

YIELD: 6 SERVINGS / **ACTIVE TIME:** 10 MINUTES / **TOTAL TIME:** 25 MINUTES

Stuffed salmon is a perfect dinner most nights of the week as it is simple to make yet always impressive. The spinach pesto stuffing is soon to be a favorite flavor combination that you'll likely add to many other dishes.

1. Add spinach, water, garlic, and salt to a sauté pan over medium heat and cook until all of the liquid evaporates.

1. Add the lemon zest and juice and pine nuts, and mix well.

2. Preheat the oven to 350°F.

3. Slice through the middle of each salmon fillet and stuff the salmon with the spinach mixture.

4. In a bowl, combine the mustard, honey, lemon juice, and chili flakes and mix well.

5. Brush the salmon with mustard sauce and bake for 20 minutes.

INGREDIENTS:

1	CUP FROZEN SPINACH
⅛	CUP WATER
2	GARLIC CLOVES, MINCED
1	TEASPOON SEA SALT
½	TEASPOON BLACK PEPPER
	ZEST AND JUICE OF HALF A LEMON
⅓	CUP MINCED PINE NUTS
6	SALMON FILLETS
2	TABLESPOONS DIJON MUSTARD
2	TABLESPOONS HONEY
1	TABLESPOON LEMON JUICE

Spayty, page 396

SPAYTY

YIELD: 4 TO 6 SERVINGS / **ACTIVE TIME:** 20 MINUTES / **TOTAL TIME:** 1 HOUR AND 20 MINUTES

This is a Shabbat meal prepared by the community of Baghdadi Jews living in India. The bamboo gives this dish an earthy flavor and pleasant texture.

1. Place the chicken pieces into a large bowl and sprinkle and rub all sides with 1½ teaspoons sea salt, ½ teaspoon pepper, and ½ teaspoon turmeric. Set aside for about 30 minutes.

2. Place the oil into a large pot over medium heat. Add the cloves, cardamom, cinnamon, coriander, and cumin. Fry for about 30 seconds or until fragrant.

3. Place all the chicken pieces into the pot with the skin side down. Sear the chicken until golden brown, about 5 minutes on each side. Transfer the chicken onto a plate.

4. Place the potatoes into the pot with the oil and spices and fry the potatoes until golden brown on all sides, flipping them occasionally.

5. Meanwhile, place the onion, ginger, and garlic into a food processor. Process the mixture until a paste is formed, about 2 minutes. Add the paste to the pot with the fried potatoes. Add the paprika and remaining ½ teaspoon of ground turmeric. Cook until golden, about 4 to 6 minutes. Place the chicken pieces back into the pot with the skin side up. Add the coconut cream, vinegar, water, and bamboo shoots into the pot. Cover the pot and cook on medium-low heat for about 40 minutes, until the chicken is cooked through.

6. Sprinkle garam masala over the curry and serve hot.

INGREDIENTS:

1   (3 LB.) CHICKEN CUT INTO 8 PIECES

1½   TEASPOONS SEA SALT

½   TEASPOON GROUND BLACK PEPPER

1   TEASPOON GROUND TURMERIC, DIVIDED

4   TABLESPOONS AVOCADO OIL

3   CLOVES

3   CARDAMOM PODS

1   CINNAMON STICK

5   TEASPOONS GROUND CORIANDER

3   TEASPOONS GROUND CUMIN

8   SMALL-MEDIUM POTATOES, PEELED

1   LARGE ONION

1   PIECE OF FRESH GINGER (2 TABLESPOONS)

2   GARLIC CLOVES

1   TEASPOON PAPRIKA

2   CUPS COCONUT CREAM

2   TEASPOONS WHITE VINEGAR

½   CUP WATER

1   (8 OZ.) CAN OF BAMBOO SHOOTS, DRAINED AND CUT INTO THIN SLICES LENGTHWISE

1   TEASPOON GARAM MASALA

SPINACH RISSOLES WITH LEMON SAUCE

YIELD: 4 SERVINGS / **ACTIVE TIME:** 30 MINUTES / **TOTAL TIME:** 30 MINUTES

These Bulgarian spinach patties are hearty enough to hold up when fried. The acidity from the lemon sauce balances out the richness from the frying process.

1. Make the sauce by combining the stock, lemon juice, ½ teaspoon salt, and ¼ teaspoon pepper in a small saucepan, bring to a simmer, and keep warm.

2. In a large bowl mix the spinach, eggs, flour, bread crumbs, and remaining salt and pepper and mix well. The mixture should be solid, to hold up when fried; add flour and bread crumbs by the tablespoon if it is too loose.

3. Add ¼" oil to a pan over medium-high heat.

4. With a large cooking spoon, or wet hands, scoop from the spinach mixture and gently place in the hot oil. Keep on one side until firm and browned, about 4 to 5 minutes, then flip to the other side for 4 minutes. Remove from the pan to a paper towel-lined plate and continue in batches with the remaining spinach mixture.

5. When done frying, remove the pan from heat and carefully drain most of the oil, leaving about 1 tablespoon with no spinach bits.

6. Carefully slide the spinach rissoles into the sauce, partially overlapping, to allow all of them to cook together and immerse in the sauce. Simmer for 5 minutes until most of the sauce is absorbed, rearranging them once in the middle to allow even cooking. Serve immediately.

INGREDIENTS:

½	CUP CHICKEN STOCK (SEE PAGE 722)
½	CUP FRESHLY SQUEEZED LEMON JUICE
1½	TEASPOONS SEA SALT, DIVDED
½	TEASPOON BLACK PEPPER, DIVIDED
1⅓	LBS. REGULAR SPINACH LEAVES, RINSED AND DRIED OR PRE-WASHED AND THEN FINELY CHOPPED
5	EGGS, ROOM TEMPERATURE, WHISKED
⅔	CUP ALL-PURPOSE FLOUR
⅔	CUP BREAD CRUMBS
1	TEASPOON SEA SALT
¼	TEASPOON BLACK PEPPER
	AVOCADO OIL, FOR FRYING

STUFFED LAMB

YIELD: 6 TO 8 SERVINGS / **ACTIVE TIME:** 40 MINUTES / **TOTAL TIME:** 2 HOURS AND 50 MINUTES

This stuffed lamb recipe is ideal for a more decadent Passover spread. The complex sauce is rich and delicately sweet and spicy.

SAUCE

1. Combine the tomatoes, tomato paste, tamarind concentrate, oil, sugar, garlic, chiles, and onion in a medium saucepan and cook over low heat until the tomatoes break down and the sauce reduces, about 1 hour and 30 minutes.

2. Add the olives and cilantro, then cook until the olives soften, another 30 minutes.

3. Season with salt to taste and set aside.

STUFFING

1. Heat the oil in a heavy-bottomed pan over medium heat and sweat the onions and garlic until translucent, 4 to 5 minutes. Add the ground lamb, rice, chiles, tomato, and nutmeg, then stir, breaking up the ground lamb, until the lamb is browned, 3 to 4 minutes. Season with salt to taste.

2. Add the broth to the mixture and bring to a simmer. Cook until the liquid almost completely evaporates, 10 to 12 minutes. Add the water and return to a simmer. Cook again until the water almost completely evaporates, about 8 minutes. Reduce the heat to low and cover the pan. Cook until the rice is tender, about 5 minutes more. Fluff with a fork and check for seasoning.

INGREDIENTS:

SAUCE

2	LBS. (8 SMALL) ROMA TOMATOES, HALVED LENGTHWISE AND QUARTERED
½	CUP TOMATO PASTE
3	TABLESPOONS TAMARIND CONCENTRATE
1	TABLESPOON AVOCADO OIL
1	TABLESPOON SUGAR
4	GARLIC CLOVES, MINCED
2	SMALL DRIED CHILE DE ÁRBOL
1	LARGE YELLOW ONION, ROUGHLY CHOPPED
1½	CUPS PITTED KALAMATA OLIVES
1	CUP FRESH CILANTRO LEAVES
	SEA SALT, TO TASTE

STUFFING

2	TABLESPOONS AVOCADO OIL
1	LARGE YELLOW ONION, FINELY CHOPPED
3	GARLIC CLOVES, MINCED
1½	LBS. GROUND LAMB
1	CUP LONG-GRAIN WHITE RICE
5	SMALL DRIED CHILE DE ÁRBOL
1	SMALL PLUM TOMATO, ROUGHLY CHOPPED
1	PINCH FRESHLY GRATED NUTMEG
	SEA SALT, TO TASTE
2	CUPS BEEF BROTH
1	CUP WATER

BRAISED LAMB

1. Preheat the oven to 375°F. Butterfly the lamb shoulder so that it is one, large piece, even in thickness (you can ask the butcher to do this for you). Season both sides generously with salt.

2. Place 1 cup of stuffing in a row down the center of the lamb and roll into a log. Tie the lamb into a roast with twine. Reserve the remaining stuffing for serving.

3. Heat the oil in a 6-quart Dutch oven over medium-high heat. Sear the lamb, turning as needed, until browned on all sides, 15 to 18 minutes. Transfer the lamb to a plate.

4. Reduce the heat to medium and add the celery, carrots, and onion to the pan. Cook until the vegetables are slightly brown, 6 to 8 minutes. Add the broth and deglaze, scraping up any browned bits on the bottom of the pan with a wooden spoon.

5. Return the lamb to the pot and bring to a simmer. Cover the pot and transfer to the oven. Braise until the lamb is tender and reads 145°F on a thermometer, around 50 to 55 minutes. Transfer the lamb to a platter and cover with foil to rest.

POTATOES

1. Place the potatoes and cilantro stems in a medium saucepan. Strain the braising liquid, discarding the vegetables and transfer to pot with the potatoes. Bring to a boil and cook until the potatoes are tender when pierced with a knife, 20 minutes.

2. Layer the remaining stuffing on a large platter. Slice the lamb, discarding the twine and arrange over the stuffing. Scatter the potatoes around the lamb and spoon some of the braising liquid over top. Serve with the tomato-olive sauce on the side.

BRAISED LAMB

1	(3½ LB.) LAMB SHOULDER
2	TABLESPOONS AVOCADO OR GRAPESEED OIL
4	CELERY STALKS, ROUGHLY CHOPPED
2	LARGE CARROTS, ROUGHLY CHOPPED
1	LARGE YELLOW ONION, ROUGHLY CHOPPED
3	CUPS BEEF BROTH
	SEA SALT, TO TASTE

POTATOES

1	LB. SMALL NEW POTATOES, PREFERABLY MULTI-COLOR
½	CUP CILANTRO STEMS

STUFFED SADDLE OF LAMB

YIELD: 4 SERVINGS / **ACTIVE TIME:** 30 MINUTES / **TOTAL TIME:** 1 HOUR AND 30 MINUTES

The quince and pomegranate in this recipe add lovely sweetness that balances out the heat from the jalapeño and the richness of the lamb.

1. Place the ground lamb in a mixing bowl, and add the garlic, jalapeño, cilantro, bread crumbs, allspice, half the ginger, half of the onion, egg, ¾ teaspoon sea salt, and a pinch of black pepper.

2. Mix well, and set in the refrigerator to cool.

3. Peel the quince and halve them.

4. Put the halves in a bowl of cold water, with the juice of the half lemon.

5. Use a spoon to hollow out the quince halves so that you are left with a ⅔" thick shell.

6. Reserve the scooped out flesh.

7. Fill the hallowed quince halves with the lamb mix.

8. Place the reserved quince flesh in a blender and pulse until well blended.

9. Heat the extra virgin olive oil in a frying pan.

10. Transfer the blended quince to the pan, along with the remaining ginger, onion, and cardamom seeds.

11. Sauté for 12 minutes, until the onion has softened.

12. Add the molasses, 1 tablespoon fresh lemon juice, sugar, stock, ½ teaspoon sea salt, and ¼ teaspoon black pepper and mix.

13. Add the quince halves to the sauce, facing upwards, and lower the heat to a gentle simmer.

14. er the pan and cook for about 30 minutes.

15. Remove the lid and simmer for 3 to 5 minutes to reduce the sauce, until it has thickened.

16. Finish with chopped cilantro and pomegranate seeds over the top.

INGREDIENTS:

1½	LBS. GROUND LAMB
2	CLOVE GARLIC, CRUSHED
1	JALAPEÑO, CHOPPED
½	BUNCH CILANTRO, CHOPPED
½	CUP BREAD CRUMBS
1	TEASPOON GROUND ALLSPICE
2	TABLESPOONS GRATED FRESH GINGER
2	MEDIUM ONIONS, FINELY CHOPPED
1	LARGE EGG
2	TEASPOONS SEA SALT
1	TEASPOON FRESH GROUND BLACK PEPPER
4	QUINCE
	JUICE FROM ½ LEMON, PLUS 1 TABLESPOON
3	TABLESPOONS EXTRA VIRGIN OLIVE OIL
2	TABLESPOONS CARDAMOM SEEDS
2	TEASPOONS POMEGRANATE MOLASSES
2	TEASPOONS GRANULATED WHITE SUGAR
2	CUPS BEEF STOCK (SEE PAGE 721)
¼	TEASPOON NUTMEG
¼	CUP POMEGRANATE SEEDS

SUMAC CHICKEN & RICE

YIELD: 6 SERVINGS / **ACTIVE TIME:** 20 MINUTES / **TOTAL TIME:** 1 HOUR AND 20 MINUTES

This is an easy favorite to make for Shabbat. The brightly colored sumac adds a surprising splash of color and flavor to this simple meal.

SPICE MIX

1. Make the spice rub by combining the sumac, lemon zest, salt and white pepper in a small bowl.

CHICKEN AND RICE

1. Preheat the oven to 400°F with the rack in the middle.

2. Rub spice mix under the skin and on top of the pieces of chicken.

3. In a roasting pan, combine the rice, pine nuts, berberis, turmeric, salt and 2 tablespoons of oil until the rice is a beautiful yellow color. Press the rice down so it's pretty flat.

4. Top the rice with the slices of red onion and lay the chicken pieces on top of the onions. Top each piece of chicken with a lemon slice.

5. If you are assembling ahead of time and roasting later, this is the point you will want to cover the roasting pan with tin foil or lid and set in the fridge.

6. Pour the stock around the chicken onto the rice. Drizzle the chicken with a decent amount of oil.

7. Cover the roasting pan tightly with tin foil and place it in the oven. Roast for 40 minutes. Remove the foil and continue roasting for an additional 20-25 minutes until the chicken is cooked through and the rice has soaked up all of the liquids.

INGREDIENTS:

SPICE MIX

¼	CUP SUMAC
	ZEST FROM 1 LEMON
1	TEASPOON SEA SALT
¼	TEASPOON WHITE OR BLACK PEPPER

CHICKEN AND RICE

6	PIECES BONE-IN, SKIN-ON CHICKEN LEGS (DRUMSTICK & THIGH) OR CHICKEN BREAST
3	CUPS BASMATI OR JASMINE RICE
½	CUP PINE NUTS
3	TABLESPOONS BERBERIS, DRIED CRANBERRIES, OR CHERRIES
1	TEASPOON TURMERIC
½	TEASPOON SEA SALT
2	TABLESPOONS AVOCADO OIL
1	RED ONION, CUT IN ½" THICK SLICES
1	LEMON, CUT IN ¼" ROUND SLICES
4½	CUPS CHICKEN STOCK (SEE PAGE 722)

TACO DE GRIBENES

YIELD: 6 SERVINGS / **ACTIVE TIME:** 30 MINUTES / **TOTAL TIME:** 2 HOURS

Chicken crackling, duck egg, caramelized onions, and mustard salsa verde . . . need we say more?

1. Preheat the oven to 350°F.

2. Line a baking sheet with parchment paper and have another piece of parchment paper ready to cover the chicken skins.

3. Loosen the skin by placing your fingers underneath and gently lifting it up. Make shallow cuts round the joints where the wings and drumsticks are attached to the body and lift and peel off the skin. Remove the skin from the breast and the back of the chicken and cut as needed. Remove the remaining skin from the thighs and wings.

4. Pat dry the skins using a paper towel. Lay the skins on the parchment paper in a single layer, season with salt and spices and top with another piece of parchment paper.

5. Bake for 40 minutes, or until golden brown and crispy. Set aside.

6. Add 1 tablespoon butter to a frying pan over medium-high heat. Crack the duck eggs into the pan, add 2 tablespoons water to the pan, and place a lid on top. Steam the eggs until the tops are white but the yolks are soft.

7. Add 2 tablespoons butter and oil to a pan over medium-high heat. Once the oil is shimmering add the onions and stir to coat. Spread out the onions and let cook, stirring occasionally. After 10 minutes, sprinkle some salt over the onions. Let cook for 30 minutes to an hour more, stirring every few minutes, until deeply golden brown.

8. Warm tortillas in a slightly greased pan

9. Then top the tortillas with the egg, crackling, Salsa Verde, cilantro, onion and finish with a squeeze of lime.

INGREDIENTS:

	CHICKEN SKINS FROM AT LEAST 2 CHICKENS
½	TABLESPOON PLUS ⅛ TEASPOON SEA SALT, DIVIDED
⅛	TEASPOON FRESHLY GROUND BLACK PEPPER
⅛	TEASPOON PAPRIKA,
⅛	TEASPOON GARLIC POWDER
⅛	TEASPOON ONION POWDER
⅛	TEASPOON CHILI POWDER
2	DUCK EGGS
3	TABLESPOONS UNSALTED BUTTER, DIVIDED
	WATER, AS NEEDED
1	TABLESPOON EXTRA VIRGIN OLIVE OIL
1	MEDIUM SWEET ONION, SLICED
12	MINI FLOUR TORTILLAS, WARMED
¾	CUP DICED RED ONION
½	CUP CHOPPED CILANTRO LEAVES
	SALSA VERDE (SEE PAGE 269 OR PAGE 540)
1	LIME, CUT INTO WEDGES

TOMATOES REINADOS

YIELD: 6 SERVINGS / **ACTIVE TIME:** 45 MINUTES / **TOTAL TIME:** 1 HOUR 15 MINUTES

This recipe has Turkish origins. The "royal" tomatoes are first stuffed with beef and the pan-seared face down, searing the meat.

1. Cut about ¼" off the top of the tomatoes crosswise. Scoop out the seeds and meat from the tomatoes.

2. Soak a loaf of bread in water for about 10 minutes and drain.

3. In a mixing bowl, place the ground beef, bread, salt, and pepper. Mix until combined well. Stuff each tomato with about 1 tablespoon of the beef mixture, using your palms to flatten out the top of the filled tomatoes.

4. Add ½ cup oil to a saucepan over medium-high heat. Add the beaten egg into a small bowl. Add the flour into another small bowl and set aside.

5. Starting with one stuffed tomato, dip the top of the tomato into the flour, shake off any excess flour, and then dip the top of the tomato into the egg wash and place on a plate. Repeat with the remaining tomatoes.

6. Once the oil is hot, place the tomatoes into the pot with the top of the tomato down into the oil. Fry the tomatoes until their tops are golden brown. Transfer the fried tomatoes into another skillet. Place them into the pan with the fried side up. Add 1 cup water into the pan or enough to cover three-quarters of the tomatoes. Place the pan over medium high heat and bring the water to a boil and reduce the heat to low. Cover the pan and cook the tomatoes over a gentle simmer until the meat is cooked, the tomatoes are tender and about one-quarter of the water remains, about 45 minutes.

7. Serve hot.

INGREDIENTS:

10	TOMATOES
1	LOAF WHITE BREAD
1	LB. GROUND BEEF
1½	TEASPOONS SEA SALT
¼	TEASPOON GROUND BLACK PEPPER
1	EGG, BEATEN
½	CUP ALL-PURPOSE FLOUR
½	CUP AVOCADO OIL
1	CUP WATER

TSYPLYONOK TABAKA

YIELD: 2 SERVINGS / **ACTIVE TIME:** 1 HOUR / **TOTAL TIME:** 10 HOURS

This Russian dish of pressed and pan-fried Cornish hens is wonderful for Hanukkah. The walnut-garlic sauce is both pungent and lightly sweet.

1. In a bowl, combine all of the ingredients for the wet rub and mix well.

2. Rinse and pat dry the chickens. Spatchcock each chicken: cut out the backbone of each bird using poultry shears; open like a book, remove the breast bones, and flatten with the palm of your hand.

3. Cover them in plastic wrap and use the flat side of a meat mallet to pound the chickens and flatten them further, especially in bony areas. Put the chickens in individual gallon resealable plastic bags.

4. Pour half of the spice paste into each bag and rub chickens all over and under the skin where it pulls away easily.

5. Separate the sliced onions across the 2 bags, and spread around all sides of the chickens.

6. Push out the air and seal. Refrigerate for 6 to 8 hours, preferably overnight.

7. Remove the chickens from the refrigerator and wipe off excess juices, discard any excess rub, garlic, and onions. Blot the chickens with paper towels to dry them as well as you can. Set over clean paper towels and let sit for 30 minutes at room temperature before cooking.

8. Preheat the oven to 200°F to keep cooked chicken warm while cooking remaining chicken, if necessary. Have a lined sheet pan with a rack ready to transfer the chicken to the oven.

9. Prepare a large cast-iron pan that will fit a flattened bird, allowing the complete surface area of the chicken to be in direct contact with the pan. You will also need something to weigh down the chicken evenly. A smaller sized cast iron pan that fits inside the larger one, filled with a heavy mortar and pestle, or large cans of tomatoes works well. You can also use a foil wrapped brick or two, or a round Dutch oven weighted with cans or water-filled jars.

10. Cut a piece of parchment paper that will fit completely over the chicken in the large pan you'll be cooking the bird in and set aside.

INGREDIENTS:

WET RUB

1	CUP AVOCADO OIL
6	GARLIC CLOVES, HEAVILY SMASHED
1	TABLESPOON TURMERIC
1	TABLESPOON SMOKED PAPRIKA
1	TABLESPOON FRESHLY GROUND PEPPER
1	TABLESPOON GARLIC POWDER
	JUICE AND PEEL OF ONE LEMON (PEEL TO BE IN STRIPS, MADE WITH A VEGETABLE PEELER)
	JUICE AND PEEL OF ONE ORANGE (PEEL TO BE IN STRIPS, MADE WITH A VEGETABLE PEELER)
1	MEDIUM WHITE ONION, SLICED INTO THIN RINGS

CHICKEN

2	(1½-2 LB.) CORNISH HENS, POUSSINS, OR SMALL CHICKENS
6	GARLIC CLOVES, PEELED AND SMASHED
1	HANDFUL EACH OF ROUGHLY CHOPPED DILL, CILANTRO, TARRAGON, FLAT-LEAF PARSLEY, MIXED
6	TABLESPOONS CLARIFIED BUTTER, DIVIDED
2	TABLESPOONS AVOCADO OIL, DIVIDED
	JUICE FROM ½ A LEMON
	WALNUT-GARLIC SAUCE (SEE PAGE 543), FOR SERVING

11. Heat 2 tablespoons clarified butter in the large cast-iron pan over medium-high heat. Rub the chicken all over with oil, salt, and pepper.

12. Add to the hot pan, skin-side up. Cover with parchment paper and weigh down. Do not touch it or move it around. After 12 to 15 minutes, remove the weights and parchment and flip the chicken over, skin-side down. Replace parchment paper and weights and cook for 12 to 15 minutes more. Do not touch it or move it around so as not to tear or disturb the skin until it's crispy and pulls away from the pan by itself. It is done when a thermometer inserted into the thickest part of the breast reads 165°F, or juices run clear when pierced with the tip of a knife.

13. Remove chicken from pan, place skin side up and transfer to lined sheet pan. Place in a warm oven while making the second one the same way.

14. While both chickens are warming, melt the remaining 2 tablespoons clarified butter in a small saucepan with smashed garlic cloves and a squeeze of lemon juice. Warm through until fragrant. Remove chickens from the oven and pour any juices from the chickens into the butter mixture.

15. Arrange chickens on a serving platter or on a clean sheet tray, drizzle with warmed butter and garlic mixture, and generously top with chopped mixed herbs.

16. Serve with pickled vegetables, fermented cabbage slaw, and Walnut Garlic Sauce.

TURKISH COFFEE-RUBBED BRISKET

YIELD: 6 SERVINGS / **ACTIVE TIME:** 30 MINUTES / **TOTAL TIME:** 30 HOURS

If you love the deeply rich flavors associated with Turkish coffee, prepare to fall in love with how this rub transforms brisket. The recipe tenderizes the meat and adds a dark, smokey layer to every bite.

1. Preheat the oven to 400°F.

2. Place onions, potatoes, carrot, fennel, and garlic in a heavy roasting pan. Toss with oil, 1 teaspoon salt, and ½ teaspoon pepper.

3. In a small bowl, combine coffee, cinnamon, cardamom, remaining 1 tablespoon salt, and 1 teaspoon pepper and mix well. Rub all over brisket and nestle brisket into vegetables. Roast until vegetables are lightly browned, 45 minutes.

4. Cover tightly with foil, lower oven to 300°F, and roast until fork-tender, 5 hours for first cut and 6 hours for second cut. As the brisket cooks, check on it every 45 minutes, adding ¼ cup water to the pan if it starts to look dry.

5. When the brisket is cooked, remove roasting pan from oven, cool to room temperature, and refrigerate with the vegetables until fat is solid, 8 to 24 hours.

6. Transfer brisket to a cutting board and slice across the grain. Skim and discard fat in the roasting pan. Return brisket slices to the roasting pan with the vegetables and cooking juices.

7. To serve, preheat the oven to 300°F. Transfer the roasting pan to the oven and heat brisket until liquid is melted and the brisket and vegetables are just warmed through, 15 to 20 minutes.

8. Transfer the brisket and vegetables to a serving dish, cover with foil, and reserve. Set the roasting pan over two burners on the stovetop and simmer the liquid over medium heat until thickened, 10 to 15 minutes. Pour the thickened pan juices over the brisket and serve.

INGREDIENTS:

- 2   ONIONS, QUARTERED
- 2   LARGE POTATOES, SCRUBBED AND CUT INTO 1" THICK WEDGES
- 1   LARGE CARROT, PEELED AND CUT INTO 2" PIECES
- 1   FENNEL BULB, CUT INTO 1½" THICK WEDGES
- 1   GARLIC HEAD, SLICED IN HALF CROSSWISE
- 2   TABLESPOONS AVOCADO OIL
- 1   TABLESPOON PLUS 1 TEASPOON SEA SALT, DIVIDED
- 1½   TEASPOONS FRESHLY GROUND BLACK PEPPER, DIVIDED
- 1   TABLESPOON FINELY GROUND TURKISH COFFEE OR ESPRESSO
- 1   TABLESPOON SMOKED CINNAMON OR REGULAR CINNAMON
- 1   TEASPOON GROUND CARDAMOM
- 1   (3½-4 LB.) BRISKET

TURKISH EGGPLANT DOLMA

YIELD: 6 TO 8 SERVINGS / **ACTIVE TIME:** 30 MINUTES / **TOTAL TIME:** 1 HOUR AND 30 MINUTES

The beautiful display of dried eggplants that can be found in Turkish markets is used most often for dishes such as these. For this preparation, fresh eggplant is used, stuffed with a mixture of meat.

1. Preheat the oven to 350°F.

2. In a large bowl, cover the torn bread with ½ cup of the water and mash with your hands into a paste. Add the beef, salt, cumin, and pepper and mix by hand until well incorporated. Set aside.

3. Remove the tops and bottoms of each eggplant, then thinly slice each lengthwise into ¼" slices, discarding the end pieces; you want both sides of each slice to be the white flesh of the eggplant with the skin on the outside edges to hold it together when cooking).

4. In a large bowl, whisk the eggs with salt and pepper, then toss in the eggplant slices to coat completely. Transfer the slices to a colander to drain for 5 minutes.

5. Meanwhile, add oil to a large skillet over medium-high heat and prepare a sheet pan, lined with paper towels. Working in batches, fry a few slices of the eggplant, flipping once, until golden and softened, 2 to 3 minutes per side. Transfer the slices to the prepared sheet pan to drain and repeat until all the eggplant is fried, adding more oil to the pan if needed as you fry.

6. Once the eggplant slices have cooled, work one at a time to stuff them by placing 2 tablespoons of the beef mixture at the base of each slice, then rolling them lengthwise. Place each roll next to each other in a 9" x 13" inch baking dish.

7. In a medium bowl, stir the remaining ½ cup water with the tomato sauce, tamarind concentrate and sugar. Season with salt and pepper, then pour over the eggplant to coat. Bake until the edges of the eggplant are golden and the filling is fully cooked, 35 to 40 minutes.

8. Remove from the oven and garnish with feta and chopped parsley, then serve.

INGREDIENTS:

3   SLICES WHOLE WHEAT BREAD, CRUSTS REMOVED AND ROUGHLY TORN

1   CUP WATER, DIVIDED

2   LBS. GROUND BEEF

2   TEASPOONS SEA SALT, PLUS MORE TO TASTE

2   TEASPOONS GROUND CUMIN

1   TEASPOON FRESHLY GROUND BLACK PEPPER, PLUS MORE TO TASTE

2   EGGPLANTS (PREFERABLY WITH AN ELONGATED SHAPE)

4   EGGS

¼   CUP AVOCADO OIL, PLUS MORE AS NEEDED

1   CUP TOMATO SAUCE (SEE PAGE 733)

2   TABLESPOONS TAMARIND CONCENTRATE

1   TABLESPOON GRANULATED SUGAR

CRUMBLED FETA CHEESE, FOR GARNISH

CHOPPED PARSLEY LEAVES, FOR GARNISH

TURMERIC CHICKEN WITH TOUM

YIELD: 2 TO 4 / **ACTIVE TIME:** 1 HOUR / **TOTAL TIME:** 16 HOURS

Turmeric adds not only a visual brightness to any dish, but a light and tangy zing to the palate. The health benefits of turmeric also leave you feeling properly nourished after a meal such as this.

1. In a bowl, combine the ground turmeric, orange peel, fennel, cumin, coriander, garlic, and fresh turmeric. Then add the orange juice, orange blossom water, and yogurt and stir to combine.

2. Season the cavity of the chicken with salt and pepper. Rub some of the marinade inside the cavity of the chicken.

3. Using kitchen twine, tie the legs together.

4. Evenly season the outside of the chicken with salt and pepper. Place the chicken on a sheet pan and let it sit, uncovered, at room temperature for 30 minutes. Then rub the marinade all over the outside; it may seem like a lot but use it all. Transfer the sheet pan, uncovered, to the refrigerator and marinate overnight.

5. When ready to cook, remove the chicken from the refrigerator and let sit at room temperature for 2 hours prior to cooking.

6. Preheat the oven to 450°F.

7. Place the chicken breast-side up on the rack of a roasting pan. Roast for 40 to 50 minutes, until the meat between the leg and thigh feels tender to the touch or using an instant-read thermometer placed in the thigh, the temperature reaches 160° to 165°F (if the skin is browning too quickly, decrease the heat to 375°F).

8. Remove the chicken from the oven and let rest for 15 minutes to let the juices redistribute. Cut off the kitchen twine, carve, and serve with a side of Toum.

INGREDIENTS:

1 TABLESPOON GROUND TURMERIC

2 TEASPOONS GROUND DRIED ORANGE PEEL

1 TEASPOON GROUND FENNEL SEEDS

¾ TEASPOON GROUND CUMIN

1½ TEASPOONS GROUND CORIANDER

1 GARLIC CLOVE, GRATED

1" PIECE FRESH TURMERIC, PEELED AND GRATED

1 TABLESPOON FRESHLY SQUEEZED ORANGE JUICE

1 TABLESPOON PLUS 1 TEASPOON ORANGE BLOSSOM WATER

¾ CUP WHOLE MILK GREEK YOGURT

1 (3½ LB.) WHOLE CHICKEN

1 TABLESPOON PLUS 2½ TEASPOONS SEA SALT

1 TEASPOON FRESHLY GROUND BLACK PEPPER

TOUM (SEE PAGE 430), FOR SERVING

VEGETABLE TANZIA

YIELD: 6 SERVINGS / **ACTIVE TIME:** 45 MINUTES / **TOTAL TIME:** 1 HOUR AND 45 MINUTES

This festive dish is a favorite for Moroccan Jews on Rosh Hashanah. Tanzia is a perfect way of adding sweetness to your new year.

1. Add 6 tablespoons oil to a large skillet over medium heat. Add the onions and 1 teaspoon salt and cook, stirring frequently, until caramelized and deep golden brown, about 30 minutes.

2. Transfer the onions to a large bowl. Add the prunes, apricots, figs, walnuts, sugar, and cinnamon, mix well, and season with salt and pepper, to taste.

3. Preheat the oven to 375°F.

4. Place the potatoes, turnips, and butternut squash on a roasting pan and rub with the remaining oil, then toss the vegetables with the turmeric, and season well with salt and pepper. Spread out the vegetables on the pan and spoon the fruit mixture over and around the vegetables.

5. Add 1½ cups of water to the pan. Roast the vegetable mixture until well browned and cooked through, stirring them once halfway through cooking for even browning and adding more water if needed, about 1 hour.

6. While the vegetables are roasting, toast the almonds in a dry medium skillet over medium-low heat, stirring often, until lightly browned, about 6 to 8 minutes. Set aside.

7. Transfer the vegetables and fruit-nut mixture to a large serving platter and sprinkle with the toasted almonds. Serve immediately.

INGREDIENTS:

8   **TABLESPOONS AVOCADO OIL**

2   **LBS. YELLOW ONIONS, THINLY SLICED**

1   **TEASPOON SEA SALT, PLUS MORE TO TASTE**

½   **CUP PITTED PRUNES, HALVED**

½   **CUP DRIED APRICOTS, HALVED**

½   **CUP DRIED FIGS, STEMMED AND HALVED**

½   **CUP SHELLED WALNUT HALVES AND PIECES**

2   **TABLESPOONS SUGAR**

1   **TEASPOON CINNAMON**

    FRESHLY GROUND BLACK PEPPER, TO TASTE

1   **LB. SWEET POTATOES, PEELED AND CUT INTO 2" PIECES**

1   **LB. TURNIPS, PEELED AND CUT INTO 2" PIECES**

2   **LBS. BUTTERNUT SQUASH, PEELED, DESEEDED, AND CUT INTO 2" PIECES**

½   **TEASPOON GROUND TURMERIC**

½   **CUP BLANCHED SLIVERED ALMONDS, TO GARNISH**

Vegetable Tanzia,
page 409

WHITE SHAKSHUKA

YIELD: 4 SERVINGS / **ACTIVE TIME:** 15 MINUTES / **TOTAL TIME:** 45 MINUTES

One of the beautiful things about shakshuka is that you can truly add almost anything to the pot to accentuate its color, flavor, and heartiness. White Shakshuka features a tomato sauce filled with garlic and labneh, making this a beautifully satisfying meatless meal.

1. Add oil to an 8" skillet over medium heat. Add the onion and sauté until golden, 10 to 12 minutes. Add the garlic and 3 tablespoons herbs and sauté 1 minute more. Season with salt and pepper to taste.

2. Stir Labneh into the onion mixture and spread evenly in the pan. Cook until Labneh begins to steam and bubbles form at the edges, about 15 minutes.

3. Using the back of a spoon, create 8 depressions in the mixture and gently nestle an egg yolk in each. Cook until the yolks begin to grow firm and opaque at the edges but remain soft in the centers, 3 to 5 minutes more.

4. Sprinkle with the remaining tablespoon of the herbs, season with salt and pepper, and serve immediately in the pan with warm pita.

INGREDIENTS:

¼ CUP AVOCADO OIL

1 LARGE YELLOW ONION, CHOPPED

4 GARLIC CLOVES, FINELY CHOPPED

4 TABLESPOONS COARSELY CHOPPED HYSSOP LEAVES (OR A MIX OF COARSELY CHOPPED MINT, OREGANO, SAGE, OR THYME)

SEA SALT, TO TASTE

FRESHLY GROUND BLACK PEPPER, TO TASTE

1 LB. LABNEH (SEE PAGE 530)

8 LARGE EGGS YOLKS

WARM PITA, FOR SERVING

WINE-BRAISED BRISKET
WITH BUTTERNUT SQUASH

YIELD: 6 SERVINGS / **ACTIVE TIME:** 30 MINUTES / **TOTAL TIME:** 5 HOURS AND 30 MINUTES

Like most briskets, this recipe calls for hours of braising. But swap the red wine for white and the more traditional potatoes for butternut squash, and you've got a lighter, brighter brisket—and hopefully, a lighter, brighter new year.

---

1. Preheat the oven to 300°F.

2. In a large bowl, combine tomatoes, stock, wine, salt, and pepper and mix well.

3. Add oil to a large Dutch oven over medium heat. Sear the meat, 2 to 3 minutes on each side, or until it is evenly browned. Remove the meat and set aside.

4. Line the bottom of the Dutch oven with onion slices. Place the brisket on top of the onion and pour the tomato mixture over the meat, making sure that the liquid covers the meat entirely. If you are using a larger pot and the liquid does not cover the meat and vegetables, add water until it does. Add the thyme sprigs.

5. Cover and place in the oven for 3½ hours, checking every hour or so to make sure the liquid is still covering the meat. If at any point it isn't, pour hot water into the Dutch oven to make sure the meat remains covered.

6. After 3½ hours, add the squash, making sure to submerge it under the liquid. Cook for 1 hour more, then remove the pot from the oven. Let stand at least 45 minutes before slicing.

7. Brisket tastes even better the next day, reheated in the oven. To serve, scoop out about 3 cups of liquid from the Dutch oven and place in a small saucepan. Cook over medium-low heat until it has reduced into a sauce. Serve the brisket and squash on a platter, with the sauce ladled over the top, and garnish with fresh herbs.

INGREDIENTS:

1½ CUPS CANNED DICED TOMATOES

4 CUPS BEEF, CHICKEN, OR VEGETABLE STOCK (SEE PAGE 721, PAGE 722, OR PAGE 729)

1 (750-ML) BOTTLE WHITE WINE

1 TABLESPOON SEA SALT

1 TEASPOON FRESHLY GROUND BLACK PEPPER

1 TABLESPOON AVOCADO OR GRAPESEED OIL

2½ LBS. SECOND CUT BRISKET (ALSO CALLED DECKLE)

1 LARGE ONION, SLICED

HANDFUL OF FRESH THYME SPRIGS

1 LARGE BUTTERNUT SQUASH, PEELED, DESEEDED, AND CHOPPED

CHOPPED FRESH HERBS, FOR SERVING

ZA'ATAR CHICKEN WITH GARLICKY YOGURT

YIELD: 4 SERVINGS / **ACTIVE TIME:** 20 MINUTES / **TOTAL TIME:** 1 HOUR AND 30 MINUTES

Bright and savory za'atar-studded chicken pieces roasted and piled onto a yogurt smeared-platter with lemon wedges, roasted red onions, and roasted garlic . . . if your mouth isn't watering, check your pulse.

1. Preheat the oven to 325°F.

2. Pat chicken legs dry with paper towels. Arrange chicken, onions, halved garlic heads, and lemon in a 13" x 9" baking dish; season generously with salt. Pour in oil and toss everything to coat. Turn garlic cut-side down and nestle it in so it is in contact with the baking dish.

3. Roast, rotating pan halfway through, until meat is almost falling off the bone, 50 minutes to 1 hour.

4. Meanwhile, finely grate 1 garlic clove into a small bowl. Add yogurt, a big pinch of salt, and 1 tablespoon water and mix well. Set aside yogurt sauce.

5. Remove the baking dish from the oven and transfer onions, garlic, and lemon to a plate. Increase oven temperature to 425°F and continue to roast chicken until skin is golden brown, 10 to 15 minutes more.

6. Transfer chicken to a cutting board and let rest for 10 minutes. Set aside the pan with juices.

7. Finely grate remaining garlic clove into another small bowl. Add Za'atar, coriander, lemon zest, and lime zest. Pour reserved juices in the pan into this mixture until you've reached an oily consistency, about ⅓ cup. Season to taste.

8. Spread yogurt sauce over a platter and arrange chicken legs on top. Scatter onions, garlic, and lemon around and drizzle with za'atar oil.

INGREDIENTS:

2½ LBS. CHICKEN LEGS, THIGHS AND DRUMSTICKS

2 MEDIUM RED ONIONS, CUT INTO 1" THICK WEDGES

2 HEADS OF GARLIC, HALVED CROSSWISE, PLUS 2 CLOVES

1 LEMON, QUARTERED, SEEDS REMOVED

SEA SALT, TO TASTE

⅓ CUP AVOCADO OIL

1½ CUPS PLAIN WHOLE-MILK GREEK YOGURT

3 TABLESPOONS ZA'ATAR (SEE PAGE 545)

1 TEASPOON CORIANDER

1 TEASPOON GRATED LEMON ZEST

1 TEASPOON GRATED LIME ZEST

Noodle Kugel, page 464

SIDES

Potatoes, noodles, roasted vegetables, and more. The side dishes are often as beloved as the entrees they accompany—and are often just as satisfying.

ASH-ROASTED BEETS

YIELD: 20 SERVINGS / **ACTIVE TIME:** 10 MINUTES / **TOTAL TIME:** 40 MINUTES

A lesson in the dynamics of simplicity, it is amazing how the flavor profile of these beets changes when cooked differently.

FOR OVEN ROASTED

1. Preheat the oven to 425°F.

2. Cut off root ends and place the root down on a baking sheet covered with half of the salt.

3. Drizzle the oil over tops of beets and then sprinkled with the remaining salt.

4. Roast for 30 to 40 minutes, or until you can pierce the beets with a knife.

FOR ASH ROASTED

1. Preheat the oven to 425°F.

2. Follow basic washing steps from above and make dough of flour, salt, and water, using 1 cup flour, a pinch of salt, and 2 to 3 tablespoons water; this dough is not meant to be consumed.

3. Roll out the dough to the size of a baking sheet.

4. Place the dough over the beets and press dough around the tops of beets like a blanket.

5. Roast for 30 to 40 minutes, or until you can pierce the beets with a knife.

FOR COAL ROASTED

1. Make sure to start with new coals; remove and discard any old ashes. Place the coals in a pyramid shape to provide good air circulation. Light the coals, and after approximately 30 minutes, the coals should be ashy and gray. Once the coals have become ashes, place sprigs of thyme on them for a nice aroma.

2. Bury the whole, unpeeled, scrubbed beets in the coals and bake them for approximately 20 to 30 minutes, or until the skin burns, rotating the beets occasionally. Check for doneness. The inside should be very soft. If not done, cook for an additional 10 minutes. Remove the beets from the ashes. Once they're cool enough to handle, brush the ashes from the skin. Let cool to room temperature before using.

INGREDIENTS:

10	LBS. BEETS, WASHED & SCRUBBED
2	CUPS KOSHER SALT
1	CUP EXTRA VIRGIN OLIVE OIL

AUTUMN KALE SALAD

YIELD: 6 SERVINGS / **ACTIVE TIME:** 25 MINUTES / **TOTAL TIME:** 1 HOUR

Celebrate the colors and flavors of fall with bright orange squash. The sweet golden raisins contrast the dark, vegetal kale and a pungent roasted garlic dressing gives it all a savory kick.

1. Preheat the oven to 400°F.

2. Trim about 1" off the head of the garlic, exposing the cloves. Drizzle 1 teaspoon olive oil on the garlic skins and rub it in. Wrap the garlic in aluminum foil, place on a baking sheet, and roast for 30 to 40 minutes, or until the individual cloves are completely soft. Remove from the oven and set aside.

3. As the garlic roasts, prepare to roast the squash. In a bowl, combine the slices of squash with 2 tablespoons oil, 1 teaspoon salt, and the black pepper and toss to coat. Spread out the squash on a large baking sheet and roast for about 20 minutes, flipping halfway through, until the pieces are browned and cooked through. Set aside to cool.

4. In a small bowl, stir together the remaining 4 tablespoons oil, vinegar, lemon juice, honey, remaining 1 teaspoon salt, and the cayenne, if using. Squeeze out the roasted garlic into the dressing. Stir well, breaking up the garlic. Set aside.

5. Slice the kale into thin strips, place it in a large bowl, and add the dressing a bit at a time, using your hands to massage the kale leaves gently until the volume is reduced and they look softened and shiny; there might be leftover dressing. Add the raisins, nuts, and squash pieces and toss.

6. Serve the salad at room temperature, topped with shaved Parmesan, if desired.

INGREDIENTS:

½	HEAD GARLIC
6	TABLESPOONS EXTRA VIRGIN OLIVE OIL, PLUS 1 TEASPOON, DIVIDED
1	SMALL DELICATA SQUASH, SEEDS REMOVED AND THINLY SLICED
2	TEASPOONS SEA SALT, DIVIDED
1	PINCH FRESHLY GROUND BLACK PEPPER
2	TABLESPOONS APPLE CIDER VINEGAR
2	TABLESPOONS FRESH LEMON JUICE
1	TEASPOON HONEY
1	PINCH CAYENNE PEPPER OR HOT PAPRIKA (OPTIONAL)
1	LARGE HEAD LACINATO KALE, THICKEST RIBS REMOVED
½	CUP GOLDEN RAISINS
½	CUP CHOPPED HAZELNUTS OR ALMONDS, TOASTED
	SHAVED PARMESAN CHEESE (OPTIONAL)

BEET CHIPS WITH SPICY HONEY MAYONNAISE

YIELD: 8 SERVINGS / **ACTIVE TIME:** 30 MINUTES / **TOTAL TIME:** 1 HOUR

Sprinkled with a little salt, these crunchy chips are delicious on their own. But take them to the next decadent level when paired with a sweet and spicy pareve mayonnaise.

1. Add the oil to a large, wide pot over high heat.

2. Cut the root end off the beets and use a mandolin to cut ⅛" thick slices.

3. Set up a cooling rack over paper towels near the pot.

4. Once oil reaches 375°F, slip one layer of beets into the pot and fry until golden and the bubbling and sizzling stops, about 3 to 4 minutes.

5. Remove the cooked beets with a slotted spoon and immediately sprinkle with salt and pepper and let cool on the rack. The chips will crisp up as they cool.

6. As the beets fry, prepare the dipping sauce: in a small bowl, combine the mayonnaise, honey, and Sriracha and mix well. Chill for at least 10 minutes before serving alongside freshly made beet chips.

INGREDIENTS:

BEET CHIPS

1 QUART VEGETABLE OIL

3 MEDIUM BEETS, WASHED AND DRIED WELL

SEA SALT, TO TASTE

COARSE BLACK PEPPER, TO TASTE

SPICY HONEY MAYONNAISE

¼ CUP MAYONNAISE

3 TEASPOONS HONEY

2-3 TEASPOONS SRIRACHA, OR TO TASTE

BLACK-EYED PEAS
WITH TURMERIC & POMEGRANATE

YIELD: 4 SERVINGS / **ACTIVE TIME:** 20 MINUTES / **TOTAL TIME:** 1 HOUR

As are many a recipe featuring pomegranate, this dish is of Persian origin. The acidity of the pomegranate balances the black-eyed peas and turmeric in this warm, bright stew.

1. If using dried black-eyed peas, soak them overnight in enough water to cover them by at least 1".

2. When ready to cook the peas, fill a medium pot with water and bring to a boil. Add peas, cover the pot, reduce the heat to low, and simmer until peas are fork-tender, between 45 minutes and 1½ hours. Cooking time varies drastically and depends on the age of your peas, so check them regularly.

3. Meanwhile, heat the olive oil in your smallest sauté pan over medium-high heat. Add the turmeric and shallots, and cook for 3 to 4 minutes, until shallots are soft, fragrant, and browned in spots. Add salt, stir to combine, and remove from heat.

4. When peas are soft but still retaining their shape, drain them, transfer them to a bowl, and pour the shallot mixture over the peas, making sure to scrape the sauté pan for all those little bits of turmeric and shallot clinging to the bottom. Stir to incorporate, taking care not to smush the peas too much.

5. Add soy sauce and pomegranate syrup and toss to combine.

6. Right before serving, fold in pomegranate seeds, fresh herbs, and lime juice. Serve at room temperature or slightly chilled.

INGREDIENTS:

- 1 HEAPING CUP BLACK-EYED PEAS
- 2 TABLESPOONS OLIVE OIL
- 1 TEASPOON FRESH GRATED TURMERIC ROOT OR ¼ TEASPOON GROUND TURMERIC
- 1 LARGE SHALLOT, MINCED
- ¾ TEASPOON SALT
- 1 TEASPOON SOY SAUCE
- 2 TEASPOONS POMEGRANATE SYRUP*
- ½ CUP POMEGRANATE SEEDS
- 2-3 TABLESPOONS CHOPPED PARSLEY, CHIVES, OR A MIXTURE
- JUICE OF ½ LIME

* IF POMEGRANATE SYRUP IS UNAVAILABLE, DOUBLE THE LIME JUICE.

CELERY SLAW WITH SEEDS & DATES

YIELD: 8 SERVINGS / **ACTIVE TIME:** 1 HOUR / **TOTAL TIME:** 3 HOURS

Even the most skeptical celery eaters will be surprised by the cool, sweet, crunchy, chewy, and savory flavors and textures that are packed into this side dish recipe.

1. Place mustard seeds in a small heat-proof jar or bowl. Combine the vinegar, sugar, and salt in a small saucepan over medium-high heat and bring to a simmer, stirring to dissolve sugar and salt. Pour brine over mustard seeds and let cool, about 2 hours.

2. Add oil and shallot to a small saucepan over medium heat and bring to a simmer. Cook for 1 minute, being sure that the shallot doesn't take on any color. Let cool, then pour oil through a fine-mesh sieve into a small bowl; discard cooked shallot.

3. Add vinegar, soy sauce, and sugar to the small bowl of shallot oil and whisk to combine; season vinaigrette with salt.

4. Trim ends from cucumbers and very thinly slice lengthwise on a mandoline to creat long ribbons, or use a vegetable peeler or sharp knife.

5. In a large bowl, combine cucumbers, arugula, celery, celery leaves, and dates and mix well.

6. Drizzle half of dressing over slaw and add 2 tablespoons drained pickled mustard seeds (save remaining mustard seeds for another use) and toss again to coat. Taste and season to taste.

7. Transfer the slaw to a platter and top with sesame seeds; serve with remaining vinaigrette alongside.

INGREDIENTS:

PICKLED MUSTARD SEEDS
- ¼ CUP BROWN MUSTARD SEEDS
- ⅓ CUP UNSEASONED RICE VINEGAR
- 2 TABLESPOONS SUGAR
- ½ TEASPOON SEA SALT

CELERY SLAW
- ⅓ CUP OLIVE OIL
- 1 SMALL SHALLOT, THINLY SLICED
- ¼ CUP UNSEASONED RICE VINEGAR
- 2 TABLESPOONS SOY SAUCE
- 1 TEASPOON SUGAR
- SEA SALT, TO TASTE
- 2 PERSIAN CUCUMBERS
- 8 CUPS MATURE ARUGULA, TOUGH STEMS TRIMMED
- 4 CELERY STALKS, THINLY SLICED ON A DIAGONAL, PLUS 1 CUP CELERY LEAVES
- 10 MEDJOOL DATES, SLICED
- TOASTED SESAME SEEDS, FOR SERVING

CHALLAH STUFFING

YIELD: 10 SERVINGS / **ACTIVE TIME:** 20 MINUTES / **TOTAL TIME:** 1 HOUR

Thanks to Tina Kuritzky, lovingly known as Nana, for this recipe.

1. Preheat the oven to 350°F.

2. Add the olive oil and butter to a skillet over medium heat and sauté the onions, until golden brown; set aside.

3. Sauté the mushrooms in the same onion pan over medium heat until tender, about 5 minutes; season with salt and pepper to taste.

4. Place the cubed bread in a large bowl and add 1 to 2 cups boiled water to the bowl, using enough to moisten all the cubes. Add corn flake crumbs, eggs, cooked mushrooms and onions, dill, salt, and pepper and mix well.

5. Transfer the stuffing to a baking dish and cook for 35 to 40 minutes, until the top is golden brown.

INGREDIENTS:

1	TEASPOON EXTRA VIRGIN OLIVE OIL
1	STICK OF UNSALTED BUTTER
4	VIDALIA ONIONS, SLICED
1	LB. MUSHROOMS, SUCH AS CREMINI, SHIITAKE, AND OYSTER, TRIMMED AND THINLY SLICED
1	TEASPOON SEA SALT, PLUS MORE TO TASTE
1	TEASPOON FRESHLY GROUND PEPPER, PLUS MORE TO TASTE
1	CHALLAH (SEE PAGE 129), CUBED
1	CUP CORN FLAKE CRUMBS
3	EGGS
1	TEASPOON DILL

CHARRED SWEET POTATOES WITH TOUM

YIELD: 4 SERVINGS / **ACTIVE TIME:** 1 HOUR AND 30 MINUTES / **TOTAL TIME:** 3 HOURS

The sweetness of fingerling sweet potatoes halved and caramelized is matched with pungent perfection when served on a bed of toum, a fluffy white garlic sauce.

1. Chill oil in freezer for 30 minutes; this helps the sauce emulsify.

2. Combine garlic, lemon juice, ¼ cup cold oil, and 1 tablespoon ice water in a blender and pulse until smooth. With the motor running, very gradually and steadily stream in ½ cup oil. Scrape down sides and continue to blend, slowly adding remaining ¼ cup oil, until a slightly thick sauce forms; it should cling to a spoon. Add 1 more tablespoon ice water, season with salt, and pulse again to combine. This whole process will take 8 to 10 minutes. Take your time! Transfer Toum to a medium bowl.

3. Place a rack in bottom third of oven and preheat to 400°F. Place sweet potatoes in a large heavy skillet, preferably cast iron. The pan should be large enough so that sweet potatoes cover only half of the pan. Pour in just enough water to barely coat the bottom of the pan. Cover tightly with foil and bake sweet potatoes until tender, 30 to 35 minutes. Transfer to a cutting board and let cool; reserve skillet. Slice sweet potatoes in half lengthwise.

4. Return reserved skillet to oven and heat for 20 minutes. Remove skillet from oven and swirl 2 tablespoons butter around in pan to coat. Add sweet potatoes, cut side down, and roast until edges are browned underneath and crisp, 18 to 25 minutes.

5. Spoon some Toum on a plate or in shallow bowl and arrange sweet potatoes on top (save extra Toum for another use). Combine the remaining 2 tablespoons butter with honey in the skillet and place over medium heat to warm. Drizzle honey butter over sweet potatoes. Sprinkle with nigella seeds, if using, and sea salt.

INGREDIENTS:

1	CUP AVOCADO OR GRAPESEED OIL
⅓	CUP GARLIC CLOVES
2	TABLESPOONS FRESH LEMON JUICE
2	TABLESPOONS ICE WATER
	SEA SALT, TO TASTE
1½	LBS. SMALL SWEET POTATOES, SCRUBBED
4	TABLESPOONS UNSALTED BUTTER, DIVIDED
2	TABLESPOONS HONEY
2	TEASPOONS NIGELLA SEEDS (OPTIONAL)
	FLAKY SEA SALT, TO TASTE

COUSCOUS WITH SEVEN VEGETABLES

YIELD: 6 SERVINGS / **ACTIVE TIME:** 20 MINUTES / **TOTAL TIME:** 50 MINUTES

A Sephardic New Year is incomplete without this dish. The bounty of easy-to-prepare vegetables represents the hopeful bounty on its way to you in the coming year.

1. Heat the oil in a Dutch oven over medium heat. Add the onions and sauté until softened, about 5 minutes; season with salt and pepper.

2. Add the garlic and tomatoes and sauté until softened, about 5 minutes. Add the tomato paste and spices, and stir to combine. Sauté the mixture for a few additional minutes until fragrant, stirring frequently to prevent burning.

3. Add the peppers, zucchini, turnips, carrots, and squash, as well as the stock or water. Bring to a boil, reduce heat, and cover. Simmer until vegetables are tender, about 10 to 15 minutes.

4. Remove cover and add chickpeas. Simmer until chickpeas are heated through and stew is thickened, another 5 to 10 minutes.

5. Meanwhile, make couscous according to package directions.

6. Just before serving, add the ras el hanout to the stew; season to taste.

7. To serve, spread the couscous on a platter or shallow dish with a well in the middle. Spoon the vegetable stew over the couscous. Garnish with chopped parsley and slivered almonds, if using.

INGREDIENTS:

- 3 TABLESPOONS AVOCADO OR GRAPESEED OIL
- 1 LARGE YELLOW ONION, DICED
- SEA SALT, TO TASTE
- BLACK PEPPER, TO TASTE
- 2 GARLIC CLOVES, MINCED
- 2 TOMATOES, SEEDED AND DICED
- 1 TABLESPOON TOMATO PASTE
- 2 TEASPOONS CUMIN
- 1 TEASPOON PAPRIKA
- 1 TEASPOON GROUND GINGER
- 1 TEASPOON CINNAMON
- ¼ TEASPOON CAYENNE
- 2 RED PEPPERS, CHOPPED
- 2 ZUCCHINIS, HALVED AND CUT INTO WEDGES
- 2-3 SMALL TURNIPS, PEELED AND CUT INTO WEDGES
- 1 BUNCH CARROTS, PEELED AND CHOPPED
- 1 BUTTERNUT SQUASH, PEELED AND CUBED
- 4 CUPS VEGETABLE STOCK (SEE PAGE 729) OR WATER
- 1 (15 OZ.) CAN CHICKPEAS, RINSED AND DRAINED
- 2 TEASPOONS RAS EL HANOUT
- 2 TABLESPOONS CHOPPED FLAT-LEAF PARSLEY
- HANDFUL SLIVERED ALMONDS (OPTIONAL)
- 1 BOX INSTANT COUSCOUS

Couscous with Seven
Vegetables, page 431

COLESLAW

YIELD: 12 SERVINGS / **ACTIVE TIME:** 30 MINUTES / **TOTAL TIME:** 12 HOURS

How many families have their own version of this classic side dish? We find our recipe hits all the creamy and crunchy notes that you want a good coleslaw to have.

1. In a large bowl, mix together the cabbage and carrots.

2. In a separate bowl, combine the remainder of the ingredients and whisk.

3. Add the dressing to the cabbage and carrots and mix well.

4. Cover and refrigerate overnight before serving.

INGREDIENTS:

2	LBS. GREEN CABBAGE, FINELY GRATED
1	LB. RED CABBAGE, FINELY GRATED
3	CARROTS, FINELY GRATED
⅓	CUP MAYONNAISE
⅓	CUP SOUR CREAM
⅓	CUP APPLE CIDER VINEGAR
⅓	CUP WHITE GRANULATED SUGAR
½	CUP LOOSELY PACKED COARSELY CHOPPED PARSLEY LEAVES
2	TABLESPOONS DIJON MUSTARD OR COARSE GROUND MUSTARD
1	TEASPOON CELERY SEEDS
2	TEASPOONS ONION POWDER
2	TEASPOONS SEA SALT
¼	TEASPOON FRESHLY GROUND PEPPER

CREAMY POTATO & LEEK GRATIN

YIELD: 8 SERVINGS / **ACTIVE TIME:** 20 MINUTES / **TOTAL TIME:** 1 HOUR AND 30 MINUTES

Cutting leeks into large pieces gives them a presence equal to disks of potato. Cooking the vegetables separately before combining—the leeks are braised in butter, the spuds are simmered in milk and cream—preserves their distinct flavors. Serve this one with a side of salmon or perhaps a whole branzino.

1. Preheat oven to 400°F with rack in middle.

2. Generously butter a 3-quart shallow baking dish.

3. Cut a round of parchment paper to fit just inside a 12" heavy skillet, then set parchment aside.

4. Halve leeks lengthwise, then cut crosswise into 1½" pieces. Wash leeks and pat dry.

5. Add the butter, leeks, ½ teaspoon salt, and ¼ teaspoon pepper to the 12" skillet and cook over medium heat, covered with parchment round, until tender, stirring occasionally, about 10 to 12 minutes.

6. Meanwhile, peel potatoes and slice crosswise 1⁄16" thick with a mandoline. Transfer to a large heavy pot with cream, milk, thyme, salt, and pepper and bring to a boil over medium heat, stirring occasionally; the liquid will thicken. Stir in the cooked leeks, then transfer to the prepared baking dish.

7. Bake, uncovered, until potatoes are tender, 45 minutes to 1 hour. Let stand 10 minutes before serving.

INGREDIENTS:

3	**LBS. LEEKS, WHITE AND PALE GREEN PARTS ONLY**
3	**TABLESPOONS UNSALTED BUTTER, PLUS MORE FOR GREASING**
1½	**TEASPOONS SEA SALT**
1	**TEASPOON BLACK PEPPER**
2	**LBS. RUSSET POTATOES**
1½	**CUPS HEAVY CREAM**
1	**CUP WHOLE MILK**
2	**TEASPOONS THYME LEAVES**

CRISPY BABY YUKON GOLD POTATOES

YIELD: 10 SERVINGS / **ACTIVE TIME:** 25 MINUTES / **TOTAL TIME:** 55 MINUTES

A classic side to any meat is punched up with a mix of fresh thyme and nutmeg to keep things interesting.

1. Preheat the oven to 450°F and arrange racks in upper and lower thirds of oven.

2. In a large bowl, toss potatoes with oil, thyme, salt, pepper, and nutmeg until coated.

3. Arrange in an even layer, cut side down, on two rimmed baking sheets. Roast potatoes, rotating sheets front to back and top to bottom halfway through, until crisp and golden brown on the bottom, about 25 minutes.

4. Serve with Horseradish-Yogurt Sauce, if desired.

HORSERADISH-YOGURT SAUCE

1. In a medium bowl, combine all of the ingredients and whisk well. Refrigerate before serving.

INGREDIENTS:

4 LBS. BABY YUKON GOLD POTATOES, HALVED

3 TABLESPOONS AVOCADO OR GRAPESEED OIL

1 TABLESPOON CHOPPED THYME LEAVES

2 TEASPOONS SEA SALT

½ TEASPOON FRESHLY GROUND BLACK PEPPER

¼ TEASPOON FRESHLY GRATED NUTMEG

HORSERADISH-YOGURT SAUCE, FOR SERVING (SEE RECIPE)

HORSERADISH-YOGURT SAUCE

4 CUPS GREEK-STYLE YOGURT, PREFERABLY FULL-FAT

1 (6 OZ.) JAR PREPARED HORSERADISH

2 GARLIC CLOVES, FINELY GRATED

2 TEASPOONS SEA SALT

¾ TEASPOON CRUSHED RED PEPPER FLAKES

½ TEASPOON FRESHLY GROUND BLACK PEPPER

EGYPTIAN LENTILS & RICE

YIELD: 8 SERVINGS / **ACTIVE TIME:** 1 HOUR / **TOTAL TIME:** 2 HOURS

This dish, also known as koshari, is humble yet hearty. This is a wonderful side dish but is also ideal for vegetarians as the lentils are packed with protein.

1. Add oil to a large saucepan over medium heat, add the garlic and ginger, and cook briefly. Add the cinnamon stick and cook briefly.

2. Add the tomatoes, cumin, coriander and cayenne pepper, bring to a boil, lower the heat, and simmer for about 30 minutes.

3. Remove the cinnamon stick and set aside.

4. Preheat the oven to 225°F.

5. Cook the pasta until al dente. Drain and set aside.

6. Cook the lentils in lightly salted water for about 20 minutes or until tender. Drain and set aside.

7. Combine the rice with 1 cup water in a small saucepan over high heat, bring to a boil, and then reduce heat to low, cover, and cook for 18 to 20 minutes. Remove from heat but keep the cover on the pan to keep the rice warm.

8. Heat 2 tablespoons of the oil in a large sauté pan over low-medium heat, add the onions, and cook, stirring occasionally, for about 30 minutes or until golden brown. Remove the onions to a bowl and place in the oven to keep warm.

9. If necessary, reheat the tomato sauce.

10. In the same pan used for the onions, add ½ tablespoon oil and the cooked pasta and cook over medium heat, without stirring, for about 2 minutes, or until the bottom is crispy. Stir and cook for another 2 minutes to crisp the pasta. Remove the pasta to a serving dish.

11. Add ½ tablespoon oil to the pan. Add the lentils and cook for 1 to 2 minutes or until lightly crispy. Spoon the lentils on top of or alongside the pasta. Add the rice to the serving dish.

12. Add ½ tablespoon oil to the pan. Add the chickpeas and cook briefly to warm them. Spoon the chickpeas onto the serving dish.

13. Spoon the caramelized onions onto the serving dish. Spoon the tomato sauce on top or serve separately.

INGREDIENTS:

TOMATO SAUCE

2	TABLESPOONS AVOCADO OR GRAPESEED OIL
1	LARGE GARLIC CLOVE, CHOPPED
1	TEASPOON FINELY CHOPPED GINGER
1	(2") CINNAMON STICK
1	(28 OZ.) CAN CHOPPED ITALIAN STYLE TOMATOES, INCLUDING LIQUID
½	TEASPOON GROUND CUMIN
¼	TEASPOON GROUND CORIANDER
⅛	TEASPOON CAYENNE PEPPER

KOSHARI

6	OZ. SMALL PASTA, SUCH AS ELBOWS OR FARFALLE
½	CUP LENTILS
½	CUP WHITE RICE
3½	TABLESPOONS AVOCADO OR GRAPESEED OIL
2	LARGE ONIONS, SLICED
1	CUP CANNED CHICKPEAS, RINSED AND DRAINED

Egyptian Lentils & Rice, page 439

CRUNCHY SALTY LEMONY SALAD

YIELD: 4 SERVINGS / **ACTIVE TIME:** 30 MINUTES / **TOTAL TIME:** 30 MINUTES

A light and refreshing start to the holiday meal, this salad hits every spot on the palate and is extra pleasing due to its crunchy texture.

1. Using a mandoline or very sharp knife, thinly slice beets, cucumbers, and radish.

2. Arrange sliced vegetables on a serving platter, scatter cheese on top.

3. Finely grate lemon zest over salad, then slice open lemon and squeeze some juice over the salad.

4. Drizzle with oil and season with salt and pepper.

INGREDIENTS:

2   SMALL CHIOGGIA BEETS, TRIMMED AND PEELED

2   PERSIAN CUCUMBERS

1   MEDIUM WATERMELON RADISH, TRIMMED

1   OZ. PARMESAN, PECORINO, ASIAGO, OR OTHER HARD CHEESE, SHAVED

1   LEMON

    OLIVE OIL, FOR DRIZZLING

    FLAKY SEA SALT, TO TASTE

    FRESHLY GROUND BLACK PEPPER, TO TASTE

GRAIN SALAD WITH OLIVES & WHOLE-LEMON VINAIGRETTE

YIELD: 8 SERVINGS / **ACTIVE TIME:** 15 MINUTES / **TOTAL TIME:** 1 HOUR

Look for Castelvetrano olives for this recipe; their buttery flesh and mild flavor will convert the most olive-averse.

INGREDIENTS:

- 2 **CUPS FARRO OR SPELT**
- **SEA SALT, TO TASTE**
- 2 **CUPS GREEN OLIVES**
- 1 **LEMON, PLUS MORE JUICE IF DESIRED**
- 2 **MEDIUM SHALLOTS, FINELY CHOPPED**
- **FRESHLY GROUND BLACK PEPPER, TO TASTE**
- ½ **CUP OLIVE OIL**
- 2 **CUPS COARSELY CHOPPED MINT AND/OR CILANTRO**
- 2 **CUPS COARSELY CHOPPED PARSLEY**

1. Toast the grains in a large, wide pot over medium heat, stirring often, until golden brown, about 4 minutes; it should start to smell like popcorn. Remove pot from heat and pour in cold water to cover grains by 1" and throw in a generous handful of salt. Set pot over medium-high heat and bring water to a boil. Reduce heat and simmer, skimming surface occasionally of any foam that may rise to the top, until grains are tender but still have some bite, 25 to 35 minutes. Drain and transfer grains to a large bowl.

2. Meanwhile, using the side of a chef's knife, coarsely crush olives to break them up into large craggy pieces; discard pits. Place olive pieces in a large bowl.

3. Halve the lemon and after removing the seeds finely chop it, peel and all. Combine chopped lemon and the shallots with the olives, toss to combine, and season with salt and pepper. Let mixture stand for 5 minutes to allow shallots to slightly pickle and flavors to meld.

4. Heat oil in a small saucepan over medium. Add olive mixture and cook, swirling occasionally, until ingredients are warmed through and shallots are slightly softened, about 4 minutes.

5. Scrape vinaigrette into bowl with farro and toss to combine. Taste grain salad and season with salt, pepper, and a little lemon juice if desired.

6. Just before serving, fold herbs into the salad.

GREEN BEANS WITH ZA'ATAR & LEMON

YIELD: 8 SERVINGS / **ACTIVE TIME:** 15 MINUTES / **TOTAL TIME:** 30 MINUTES

Life's too short, prep your green beans quickly. Stack a handful of them together on a cutting board and trim the stem ends off all of them at the same time for this delicious side dish.

1. Add the stock to a large skillet over medium-high heat and bring to a simmer. Add the green beans, cover pan, and cook, tossing occasionally, until crisp-tender, 5 to 7 minutes. Uncover pan, add butter, and toss to coat.

2. Remove pan from heat and stir in the za'atar, lemon zest, salt, and pepper.

INGREDIENTS:

¼   CUP CHICKEN STOCK (SEE PAGE 722)

2   LBS. GREEN BEANS, STEM ENDS TRIMMED

2   TABLESPOONS UNSALTED BUTTER

1   TABLESPOON ZA'ATAR (SEE PAGE 545)

    GRATED ZEST OF 1 LEMON

    SEA SALT, TO TASTE

    FRESHLY GROUND BLACK PEPPER, TO TASTE

Green Beans with Za'atar & Lemon, page 445

HONEY-CARROT HALWA

YIELD: 2 SERVINGS / **ACTIVE TIME**: 15 MINUTES / **TOTAL TIME**: 20 MINUTES

Carrot Halwa is an Indian dish that is usually prepared as a dessert for special occasions or festivals, but can also work as a side when paired with a rich, earthy roasted meat.

1. Melt the butter in a medium saucepan, then add the carrots and cardamom and cook over medium heat until the carrots start to soften, about 5 minutes.

2. Add the milk and honey, bring to a simmer, and cook until the milk has reduced and the carrots are very soft. Season with salt and serve.

INGREDIENTS:

1   TABLESPOON UNSALTED BUTTER

½   LB. CARROTS, PEELED AND GRATED

¼   TEASPOON GROUND CARDAMOM

1   CUP WHOLE MILK

¼   CUP HONEY

     SEA SALT, TO TASTE

HONEY-ROASTED CARROTS
WITH TAHINI YOGURT

YIELD: 4 SERVINGS / **ACTIVE TIME:** 10 MINUTES / **TOTAL TIME:** 50 MINUTES

Make this holiday side extra vibrant by using different-colored carrots. The sauce is sure to be a favorite, so make enough for everyone to get a great big dollop on the side.

1. Preheat the oven to 425°F.

2. In a small bowl, combine the tahini, yogurt, lemon juice, garlic, and salt, whisk, and set aside.

3. In a large bowl, combine the honey, oil, coriander and cumin seeds, thyme, salt, and pepper and mix well. Add the carrots and toss to coat.

4. Arrange the carrots on a large baking sheet and roast for 40 minutes, stirring gently once or twice, until cooked through and glazed.

5. Transfer the carrots to a large serving platter or individual plates. Serve warm or at room temperature, with a spoonful of sauce on top, garnished with the cilantro.

INGREDIENTS:

3 TABLESPOONS TAHINI PASTE

⅔ CUP GREEK YOGURT

2 TABLESPOONS FRESH LEMON JUICE

1 GARLIC CLOVE, CRUSHED

SEA SALT, TO TASTE

3 TABLESPOONS HONEY

2 TABLESPOONS AVOCADO OR RAPESEED OIL

1 TABLESPOON CORIANDER SEEDS, TOASTED AND LIGHTLY CRUSHED

1½ TEASPOON CUMIN SEEDS, TOASTED AND LIGHTLY CRUSHED

3 SPRIGS FRESH THYME

BLACK PEPPER, TO TASTE

3 LBS. LARGE CARROTS, PEELED AND EACH CUT CROSSWISE INTO TWO 2½" BATONS

1½ TABLESPOONS COARSELY CHOPPED CILANTRO LEAVES, TO GARNISH

HONEY-ROASTED VEGETABLE SALAD

YIELD: 4 SERVINGS / **ACTIVE TIME:** 30 MINUTES / **TOTAL TIME:** 1 HOUR

Roasted carrots, cauliflower florets, and chopped pumpkin sizzle to sweet perfection in the oven. Top with yogurt sauce and scattered mint, and prepare to amaze with this sweet, sour, and savory side dish.

1. Preheat the oven to 400°F. Line a large roasting pan with non-stick baking paper.

2. Using a sharp knife, carefully peel and chop the pumpkin into ¾" pieces, discarding the seeds.

3. Trim and cut the cauliflower into florets, halving any large ones.

4. Trim and gently scrub the carrots.

5. Place the vegetables in the prepared pan and drizzle with the oil and honey. Sprinkle with the cumin, salt, and pepper and use tongs to toss to combine.

6. Roast for 25 to 30 minutes or until the vegetables are tender and golden.

7. Remove the pan from the oven and add the spinach and mint, if using, and mix.

8. In a small bowl, combine the yogurt, lemon juice, salt, and pepper and mix well.

9. To serve, transfer the vegetables to a salad bowl and drizzle with the dressing.

INGREDIENTS:

1	(1¾ LB.) PUMPKIN OF YOUR CHOOSING
1	SMALL HEAD CAULIFLOWER
1	BUNCH BABY HEIRLOOM CARROTS
2	TABLESPOONS EXTRA VIRGIN OLIVE OIL
1	TABLESPOON HONEY
1	TEASPOON GROUND CUMIN
	SEA SALT, TO TASTE
	FRESHLY CRACKED BLACK PEPPER, TO TASTE
4	CUPS BABY SPINACH LEAVES
1	CUP MINT LEAVES (OPTIONAL)
½	CUP PLAIN GREEK-STYLE YOGURT
1	TABLESPOON FRESH LEMON JUICE

POTATO & SCHMALTZ KUGEL

YIELD: 6 SERVINGS / **ACTIVE TIME:** 20 MINUTES / **TOTAL TIME:** 1 HOUR AND 20 MINUTES

There are many variations of potato pudding. This one has a crisp crust and a moist, soft interior. Schmaltz and gribenes add richness and savory flavor, but you can also use vegetable oil and grated carrot if you're going meatless.

1. Preheat the oven to 375°F. Heat an 8" or 9" square baking dish in the oven.

2. Coat the bottom and sides of the baking dish with ¼ cup of the Schmaltz or oil and return to the oven until very hot, about 15 minutes.

3. Place the potatoes in a large bowl of lightly salted cold water; this keeps them from discoloring.

4. Place the onions into a large bowl and then grate the potatoes into the onions, stirring to mix.

5. Stir in the eggs, remaining ¼ cup schmaltz or oil, salt, pepper, and, if desired, Gribenes or carrot. Add enough matzo meal or flour to bind the batter.

6. Pour into the heated dish and bake until golden brown, about 1 hour. Although this is best when warm, the leftovers can be served at room temperature.

INGREDIENTS:

½ CUP SCHMALTZ (SEE PAGE 528) OR AVOCADO OIL

2 LBS. RUSSET POTATOES, PEELED

1 CUP CHOPPED YELLOW ONIONS

3 LARGE EGGS, LIGHTLY BEATEN

1 TEASPOON SEA SALT

FRESHLY GROUND BLACK PEPPER, TO TASTE

¼ CUP GRIBENES (SEE PAGE 528) OR GRATED CARROT, OPTIONAL

⅓ CUP MATZO MEAL OR ALL-PURPOSE FLOUR

Kasha Varnishkes, page 456

KASHA VARNISHKES

YIELD: 6 SERVINGS / **ACTIVE TIME:** 30 MINUTES / **TOTAL TIME:** 1 HOUR

This dish is all about texture. Perfect al dente farfalle gets an extra bite from the kasha in this recipe that is filling and fuss-free.

1. Melt Schmaltz in a large skillet over medium heat, add onions, and sauté, stirring frequently, until onions are turning brown. Using a slotted spoon, transfer onions to a bowl; set aside both the onions and the skillet.

2. Cook the pasta in the stock until al dente. Drain, reserving liquid, and set aside.

3. In a large bowl, lightly beat the egg and then add the kasha; mix until coated.

4. Warm a medium skillet that has a lid, turn kasha into the pan, and cook, stirring often, until kasha has separated into individual grains.

5. Deglaze the skillet that was used to cook the onions with the reserved stock and then pour the contents of the skillet into the pan with the kasha. Stir, bring to a boil, stir again, reduce heat to simmer, cover, and cook until tender, about 30 minutes.

6. Toward the end of cooking, set cover slightly askew to allow any liquid to fully evaporate.

7. In a large saucepan, combine onions, pasta, and kasha, mixing well.

8. Season to taste and garnish with parsley.

INGREDIENTS:

4   TABLESPOONS SCHMALTZ (SEE PAGE 528)

2   LARGE ONIONS, SLICED

½   LB. FARFALLE

2   CUPS CHICKEN STOCK (SEE PAGE 722)

1   CUP KASHA

1   LARGE EGG, AT ROOM TEMPERATURE

    SEA SALT, TO TASTE

    FRESHLY GROUND BLACK PEPPER

1   TABLESPOON CHOPPED PARSLEY

LEEKS BRAISED IN WHITE WINE

YIELD: 12 SERVINGS / **ACTIVE TIME:** 25 MINUTES / **TOTAL TIME:** 1 HOUR

This dish is traditionally French in many ways. Pair it with roast chicken or fish, or simply enjoy on its own.

1. Thoroughly clean the leeks, trim the roots, and slice in half lengthwise.

2. Heat the olive oil in a pan over medium-high heat and season prepared leeks with sea salt and pepper to taste.

3. Place leeks cut-side down in the pan and sear until golden brown, 5 minutes.

4. Season again with sea salt and pepper and flip, allowing to cook for an additional 2 minutes, or until brown. Transfer leeks to a baking dish.

5. Preheat the oven to 400°F.

6. Add the avocado oil, shallots, garlic, thyme, lemon zest, salt, and pepper to the pan and cook until just brown, about 4 minutes.

7. Add wine and cook until reduced by half, 10 minutes.

8. Add stock and bring to a boil. Once the mixture boils, remove from heat, and pour over leeks until they are almost but not quite submerged.

9. Put in the oven and allow to braise until tender, about 30 minutes.

INGREDIENTS:

6	LARGE LEEKS
½	CUP EXTRA VIRGIN OLIVE OIL
	SEA SALT, TO TASTE
	FRESHLY GROUND BLACK PEPPER, TO TASTE
2	TABLESPOONS AVOCADO OIL
2	CUPS CHICKEN STOCK (SEE PAGE 722)
½	CUP WHITE WINE
1	TEASPOON DRIED THYME
1	TEASPOON LEMON ZEST
4	SHALLOTS
2	GARLIC CLOVES, MINCED

LEEKS WITH THYME & POMEGRANATE

YIELD: 4 SERVINGS / **ACTIVE TIME:** 15 MINUTES / **TOTAL TIME:** 1 HOUR AND 15 MINUTES

Not only is this side dish delectable, but its color contrasts immediately beautify your table. The braised leeks and thyme are favorite fall flavors.

1. Preheat the oven to 375°F.

2. Cut leeks lengthwise down the middle and make sure they have been well cleaned; if they need to be rinsed in water make sure to pat dry.

3. Arrange the leek halves cut-side down in a snug single layer in a shallow 8" square baking dish and nestle the thyme sprigs among the leeks.

4. In a small bowl, combine the olive oil, wine, and pomegranate juice, mix well, and drizzle over the leeks. Sprinkle evenly with the salt.

5. Cover the baking dish tightly with aluminum foil. Braise the leeks in the oven until completely tender and easy to pierce with a fork, about 45 minutes. Uncover the dish and continue to braise until the leeks are caramelized, about 15 minutes more.

6. Serve the leeks warm or at room temperature. Before serving, sprinkle the pomegranate seeds over the leeks.

INGREDIENTS:

6	MEDIUM LEEKS, WHITE AND LIGHT GREEN PARTS
15	SMALL SPRIGS FRESH THYME
¼	CUP OLIVE OIL
1	TABLESPOON DRY WHITE WINE
2	TABLESPOONS POMEGRANATE JUICE
½	TEASPOON SEA SALT
¼	CUP POMEGRANATE SEEDS

MACARONI SALAD

YIELD: 10 SERVINGS / **ACTIVE TIME:** 1 HOUR / **TOTAL TIME:** 1 HOUR

What could be more iconic of a picnic, barbecue, potluck, or deli lunch? Macaroni salad should be easy to prepare, and even easier to devour.

1. Cook the macaroni, drain well, rinse with cold water, and drain again.

2. In a large bowl, combine the cooked pasta with the celery, onion, carrots, pickle, red pepper, and parsley and mix well.

3. In a small bowl, combine the mayonnaise, mustard, sugar, vinegar, sour cream, and salt and whisk.

4. Pour dressing over pasta and toss to coat well.

5. Season to taste with salt and pepper and serve.

INGREDIENTS:

- 2 CUPS ELBOW MACARONI
- ⅓ CUP DICED CELERY
- ¼ CUP MINCED RED ONION
- ¼ CUP GRATED CARROTS
- 1 TABLESPOON CHOPPED SOUR PICKLE
- ⅓ CUP CHOPPED RED BELL PEPPER
- 1 TABLESPOON CHOPPED CURLY LEAF PARSLEY
- ½ CUP MAYONNAISE
- ¾ TEASPOON DRY DIJON MUSTARD
- 1½ TEASPOONS WHITE GRANULATED SUGAR
- 1½ TABLESPOONS CIDER VINEGAR
- 3 TABLESPOONS SOUR CREAM
- ½ TEASPOON SEA SALT
- FRESHLY GROUND BLACK PEPPER, TO TASTE

MARINATED OLIVES

YIELD: 8 SERVINGS / **ACTIVE TIME:** 20 MINUTES / **TOTAL TIME:** 2 HOURS AND 20 MINUTES

The recipe for marinating is just the beginning. Once you feel comfortable with the process, you can begin adding an assortment of different herbs and spices to make it your own.

1. Rinse the darker olives so their juices don't discolor the other olives, and then drain all the other olives in a colander, place them in a large bowl, and set aside.

2. Heat a small dry pan over medium-high heat and, once hot, add the coriander and fennel seeds. Roast until very fragrant, about 3 minutes, mixing the seeds occasionally. Add the oil and vinegar and heat for a minute.

3. Remove from heat and add all of the remaining ingredients, except for the olives. Let stand until the marinade has cooled down.

4. Pour the marinade over the olives, stir to combine, and then place the olives in a wide-mouthed jar with a lid. Cover and shake the jar to coat the olives.

5. Refrigerate for 2 hours or for up to 2 weeks, shaking the jar a few times a day to redistribute the seasonings.

INGREDIENTS:

1½   LBS. ASSORTED KALAMATA, BLACK, GREEN, AND SPANISH OLIVES

2   TEASPOONS LIGHTLY CRACKED CORIANDER SEEDS

1   TEASPOON LIGHTLY CRACKED FENNEL SEEDS

¾   CUP EXTRA VIRGIN OLIVE OIL

2   TABLESPOONS RED WINE VINEGAR

4   GARLIC CLOVES, THINLY SLICED

1½   TEASPOONS MINCED ROSEMARY

1½   TEASPOONS MINCED THYME

4   BAY LEAVES, BROKEN INTO PIECES

1   DRIED SMALL RED CHILI, MEMBRANE AND SEEDS REMOVED, CHOPPED

FRESH LEMON RIND STRIPS

MUJADARA

YIELD: 6 SERVINGS / **ACTIVE TIME:** 30 MINUTES / **TOTAL TIME:** 1 HOUR AND 30 MINUTES

The vegetarian base of cooked lentils, brown rice, and caramelized crispy onions is enhanced with garnishes of herbs and roasted peanuts.

1. Heat the olive oil in a very large nonstick skillet over low heat; if you only have smaller skillets, divide the oil and onions between two. When the oil shimmers, add the onions and cook, stirring frequently, until golden, 15 to 20 minutes. Season with salt and pepper, to taste.

2. Meanwhile, bring the water to a boil in a large saucepan and add the lentils. Simmer, uncovered, for 20 minutes, then add the rice and half the cooked onions. Season with salt and pepper to taste. Simmer, covered, over very low heat until the lentils and rice are tender, about 20 minutes more. You may need to add more water toward the end; check after 15 minutes. Remove from the heat and let rest, covered, for 5 minutes.

3. While the rice and lentils are cooking, cook the onions remaining in the skillet over low heat, stirring often, until dark brown and nearly crisp, 15 to 20 minutes.

4. Serve hot or at room temperature, with browned onions sprinkled on top. Add a dollop of the yogurt or sour cream, if desired.

INGREDIENTS:

- ⅓ CUP OLIVE OIL
- 4-5 LARGE ONIONS, HALVED AND THINLY SLICED
- SEA SALT, TO TASTE
- BLACK PEPPER, TO TASTE
- 4½ CUPS WATER
- 1½ CUPS BROWN OR GREEN LENTILS, SORTED AND RINSED
- 1¼ CUPS LONG-GRAIN WHITE RICE
- PLAIN YOGURT OR SOUR CREAM, FOR SERVING (OPTIONAL)

NOODLE KUGEL

YIELD: 12 SERVINGS / **ACTIVE TIME:** 20 MINUTES / **TOTAL TIME:** 1 HOUR AND 40 MINUTES

Kugel is served as part of festive meals in Ashkenazi Jewish homes. In particular, it's eaten on the Shabbat and other holidays. While noodle kugel and potato kugel dishes are served at holiday meals, matzo kugel is a common alternative served at Passover seders.

1. Preheat the oven to 350°F.

2. Add 1 teaspoon salt to a large pot of water and bring to a boil and cook the egg noodles, stirring occasionally, until al dente, about 5 minutes. Drain the noodles.

3. Generously butter a 13" x 9" glass baking dish.

4. Cut the butter into a few big pieces and transfer to a small bowl and microwave until butter is melted, about 1 minute. Let cool slightly.

5. In a large bowl, whisk 8 large eggs and sugar until sugar is dissolved and eggs are frothy, about 2 minutes.

6. Add cottage cheese, sour cream, vanilla extract, cinnamon, and remaining salt to egg mixture. Whisk vigorously to combine.

7. Pour in melted butter and whisk again to combine. Add the warm noodles and dried fruit to the bowl and use a spatula to toss until coated.

8. Transfer noodle mixture to prepared baking dish.

9. Bake kugel, rotating pan halfway through, until custard has souffléed, top is browned, and noodles on the surface are crispy, about 50 minutes.

10. Let cool at least 20 minutes before slicing.

INGREDIENTS:

12	OZ. EXTRA-WIDE EGG NOODLES
2	TEASPOONS SEA SALT, DIVIDED
½	CUP UNSALTED BUTTER, PLUS MORE FOR GREASING
8	LARGE EGGS
½	CUP SUGAR
1	LB. COTTAGE CHEESE
1	LB. SOUR CREAM
2	TEASPOONS VANILLA EXTRACT
1	TEASPOON GROUND CINNAMON
¼	CUP DRIED CRANBERRIES
¼	CUP DRIED CHERRIES

Potato Tahdig,
page 468

POTATO TAHDIG

YIELD: 6 SERVINGS / **ACTIVE TIME:** 20 MINUTES / **TOTAL TIME:** 1 HOUR AND 45 MINUTES

If you can't get enough of the crispy rice that sticks to the bottom of the pan, prepare to be amazed. The starch from the potatoes adds extra crisp and crunch to this filling tahdig.

1. Drain the rice from the water.

2. Add water and salt to a large pot or Dutch oven over high heat and bring the water to a boil.

3. Boil the rice for 6 to 8 minutes, or until it's toothsome and some of the rice rises to the top of the water. Strain the rice and set aside.

4. In a non-stick pan prepared with oil, place the potato slices in one layer to cover the bottom of the pan. Cook the potatoes over medium heat for 10 to 15 minutes until they are crispy and golden brown.

5. Add the boiled rice on top of the potatoes in a pyramid shape and poke three holes around the top of the mound with the back of a wooden spoon.

6. Reduce the heat to low, pour 2 teaspoons oil over the rice and gently cover the rice with a dish towel.

7. Cook the rice on the stovetop, or in a 350°F oven, for 20 minutes.

8. Steep the saffron threads in 2 to 3 tablespoons of hot water and pour over the rice just before serving.

9. Flip the rice over onto a flat plate when it is ready to serve to reveal the potato crust. Serve hot.

INGREDIENTS:

- 2 CUPS LONG-GRAIN WHITE BASMATI RICE, RINSED 5 TIMES IN COLD WATER AND SOAKED UNCOVERED IN COLD WATER FOR 1 HOUR, OR OVERNIGHT
- 2 TABLESPOONS SEA SALT
- 2 TEASPOONS AVOCADO OIL
- 1-2 MEDIUM-SIZED POTATOES, SKIN ON, THINLY SLICED INTO ½" PIECES
- 2 TEASPOONS OLIVE OIL
- ½ TEASPOON SAFFRON

POTATO KUGEL

YIELD: 12 SERVINGS / **ACTIVE TIME:** 10 MINUTES / **TOTAL TIME:** 2 HOURS AND 10 MINUTES

There are many variations of potato pudding. This one has a crisp crust and a moist, soft interior. Schmaltz and gribenes add richness and savory flavor, but you can also use vegetable oil and grated carrot if you're going meatless.

1. Place a 9" x 13" baking dish in the oven and preheat it to 400°F, letting the dish heat up inside.

2. In a large mixing bowl, beat the eggs with the salt and pepper until well combined.

3. Add the potatoes and onions to the eggs, and add the oil, potato starch, and baking powder and mix well.

4. Take the preheated baking dish out of the oven. Quickly pour in 3 tablespoons Schmaltz, then spread around the fat to cover the bottom and sides of the hot dish.

5. Carefully but quickly add the potato mixture, smoothing it out so that it is evenly distributed.

6. Drizzle the remaining Schmaltz across the top.

7. Bake, uncovered, for 45 minutes to 1 hour, or until the kugel is creamy in the center and the whole top is a rich, crunchy brown.

INGREDIENTS:

5	LBS. RUSSET POTATOES, PEELED AND GRATED
4	EGGS
1	TABLESPOON SEA SALT
½	TEASPOON FRESHLY GROUND PEPPER
1	LARGE SWEET ONION, GRATED
6	TABLESPOONS EXTRA VIRGIN OLIVE OIL
6	TABLESPOONS POTATO STARCH
¼	TEASPOON BAKING POWDER
4	TABLESPOONS SCHMALTZ (SEE PAGE 528)

POTATO SALAD

YIELD: 8 SERVINGS / **ACTIVE TIME:** 15 MINUTES / **TOTAL TIME:** 45 MINUTES

Let's not fight over who's Bubbe does it better. Potato salad is a classic side dish that should be so thick, creamy, and delicious that your mouth is too full to argue.

1. Place potatoes in a large pot, cover them with water by 2", bring to a boil, and cook, covered, for 30 minutes, stirring occasionally.

2. Drain potatoes, rinse under very cold water, and let cool.

3. Cut potatoes into large chunks and place in a large serving bowl.

4. Add vinegar, salt, and pepper and gently toss.

5. In a medium bowl, add mayonnaise, mustard, and parsley and whisk. Add to potatoes and gently combine.

6. In a small bowl, combine celery, pickles, scallions, peppers, parsley, caraway seeds, and horseradish, mix well, and add to potato mixture. Toss gently.

7. Refrigerate until ready to serve.

8. Taste and season to taste. Top with dill before serving.

INGREDIENTS:

- 2   **LBS. RED POTATOES**
- 2   **TABLESPOONS RED WINE VINEGAR**
- ½   **TEASPOON SEA SALT**
- ½   **TEASPOON FRESHLY GROUND BLACK PEPPER**
- 2   **TABLESPOONS SPICY BROWN MUSTARD**
- ½   **CUP MAYONNAISE**
- ½   **CUP DICED CELERY**
- ¼   **CUP CHOPPED SWEET PICKLES**
- 3   **SCALLIONS, THINLY SLICED**
- ½   **CUP CHOPPED ORANGE BELL PEPPER**
- 2   **TABLESPOONS CHOPPED FLAT LEAF PARSLEY**
- 1   **TEASPOON CARAWAY SEEDS**
- 1   **TABLESPOON HORSERADISH**
- 1   **SPRIG FRESH DILL, FOR GARNISH**

RICE WITH BARBERRIES

YIELD: 6 SERVINGS / **ACTIVE TIME:** 20 MINUTES / **TOTAL TIME:** 2 HOURS

The combination of rice and barberries is a classic Persian flavor combination. The barberries add a bright acidity that matches the richness of the saffron.

1. Place the barberries, saffron, and water into a small pot and set aside for 1 hour, stirring the mixture every 5 minutes. Add oil and sugar to the pot and place it over low heat.

2. Cook for 10 minutes, stirring occasionally, until the sugar has dissolved and the sauce is bright orange in color. Remove from heat and set it aside.

3. Place the rice in a large bowl and cover it completely with room temperature water. Soak for 30 minutes, rinse, drain, and refill the water every 10 minutes until the water runs clear.

4. Fill a large pot with water three-quarters of the way up and add 1 heaping tablespoon salt. Place the pot over high heat and bring to a boil. Add the rice to the boiling water and cook for 7 minutes, until it is partially cooked. Rinse and set the rice aside in a bowl.

5. Add oil and turmeric to a 9" non-stick pot. Mix the turmeric and oil to combine. Cover the bottom of the pan with one layer of potato slices. Lightly and gently place the par cooked rice on top of the potatoes, do not mix the rice in the pot or pack it in. Using the back tip of a wooden spoon, make four evenly dispersed holes into the rice that reach the bottom of the pot (to release the steam during cooking). Place a kitchen towel over the pot, and place the lid above, tie the towel on top of the lid to keep it away from the flame. Place the pot over medium-high heat and cook the rice for about 15 minutes. Reduce the heat to low and continue cooking the rice for an additional 25 minutes.

6. Remove the pot from the heat and remove the lid and towel. To turn out the tahdig, place a large flat platter on top of the pot and, using a kitchen towel, hold the top of the pot with one hand and the plate with another to flip the pot and invert the tahdig onto the plate. Pour the barberry-and-saffron sauce over the tahdig and rice and serve immediately.

INGREDIENTS:

¾	CUP BARBERRIES
7	THREADS SAFFRON
¼	CUP BOILING WATER
1	TABLESPOON AVOCADO OR GRAPESEED OIL
1	TABLESPOON SUGAR
2¼	CUPS BASMATI RICE
3	TABLESPOONS SEA SALT, DIVIDED
6	TABLESPOONS AVOCADO OIL
½	TEASPOON GROUND TURMERIC
1	LARGE RUSSET POTATO, PEELED AND CUT CROSSWISE INTO ¼" SLICES

Rice with Barberries, page 471

ROASTED BRUSSELS SPROUTS
WITH WARM HONEY GLAZE

YIELD: 4 SERVINGS / **ACTIVE TIME:** 15 MINUTES / **TOTAL TIME:** 35 MINUTES

By preheating the baking sheet, you'll ensure that every sprout in this goes-with-anything side has that irresistible crispy edge. The warm honey glaze adds a sticky sweetness that always seems to pair beautifully with brussels sprouts.

1. Place a rack in the bottom third of the oven and set a rimmed baking sheet on top; preheat the oven to 450°F. In a large bowl, combine the brussels sprouts and oil, toss well, and season with salt and pepper, to taste.

2. Carefully remove baking sheet from oven. Using tongs, arrange brussels sprouts, cut side down, on the hot baking sheet. Roast on the bottom rack until tender and deeply browned, 20 to 25 minutes.

3. Meanwhile, bring honey to a simmer in a small saucepan over medium-high heat. Reduce heat to medium-low and cook, stirring often, until honey is a deep amber color but not burnt (it will be foamy), about 3 minutes. Remove from heat; add vinegar and red pepper flakes, if using, and whisk until sauce is smooth (it will bubble quite aggressively when you first add the vinegar).

4. Set the saucepan over medium heat, add butter and ½ teaspoon salt, and cook, whisking constantly, until glaze is glossy, bubbling, and slightly thickened, about 4 minutes.

5. Transfer brussels sprouts to a large bowl. Add glaze and toss to coat. Transfer to a serving platter and top with scallions and lemon zest.

INGREDIENTS:

- 1½ LBS. BRUSSELS SPROUTS, TRIMMED AND HALVED
- ¼ CUP AVOCADO OIL
- ½ TEASPOON SEA SALT, PLUS MORE TO TASTE
- FRESHLY GROUND BLACK PEPPER, TO TASTE
- ¼ CUP HONEY
- ⅓ CUP SHERRY VINEGAR OR RED WINE VINEGAR
- ¾ TEASPOON CRUSHED RED PEPPER FLAKES (OPTIONAL)
- 3 TABLESPOONS UNSALTED BUTTER
- 3 SCALLIONS, THINLY SLICED ON A BIAS
- 1 TEASPOON FINELY GRATED LEMON ZEST

ROASTED BRUSSELS SPROUTS

YIELD: 20 SERVINGS / **ACTIVE TIME:** 10 MINUTES / **TOTAL TIME:** 40 MINUTES

These brussels sprouts have a bright citrus pop and a wonderful, far from ordinary tang from the ginseng.

1. Preheat the oven to 400°F.

2. In a large bowl combine all of the ingredients, except the vinegar, and use your hands to make sure each sprout is coated.

3. Arrange on a baking sheet evenly. Roast for 30 to 40 minutes, or until each sprout center is tender

4. Before serving, drizzle with the vinegar.

INGREDIENTS:

5	LBS. BRUSSELS SPROUTS, HALVED
¼	CUP EXTRA VIRGIN OLIVE OIL
¼	CUP FRESH LEMON JUICE
3	TABLESPOONS LEMON ZEST
2	TABLESPOONS SEA SALT
1	TABLESPOON BLACK PEPPER
1	TABLESPOON PINE NUTS
¼	TEASPOON ASHWAGANDHA (INDIAN GINSENG)
4	TABLESPOONS MIX OF CHOPPED FRESH TARRAGON, PARSLEY, CHIVES, AND CILANTRO
	AGED BALSAMIC VINEGAR, TO TASTE

ROASTED PLUMS WITH TAHINI DRESSING

YIELD: 4 SERVINGS / **ACTIVE TIME:** 20 MINUTES / **TOTAL TIME:** 2 HOURS AND 20 MINUTES

The rich and incredibly creamy tahini and lemon dressing cuts the sugary dessert-worthy sweetness of the roasted plums.

1. Preheat the oven to 400°F.

2. Line a baking sheet with parchment paper. Arrange the fruit, cut-side up, on the prepared baking sheet. Drizzle with oil and season with 1 teaspoon salt and pepper. Sprinkle the fruit with all but a pinch of the fresh herbs.

3. Place the baking sheet in the oven and immediately reduce the heat to 250°F. Roast until the fruit is very soft and juicy and starting to caramelize, about 2 hours. (Alternatively, turn off the oven after 1 hour and leave the fruit in the oven overnight. This will produce a leathery result.)

4. In a medium bowl, combine 3 tablespoons lemon juice, the tahini, ¾ cup water, ½ teaspoon salt, and the ice cube and whisk vigorously until the mixture comes together. It should lighten in color and thicken enough that it holds an edge when the whisk is dragged through it.

5. Remove the ice cube if any remains and adjust the seasoning, adding more lemon juice and salt, to taste.

6. To serve, layer a plate with the roasted fruit, then drizzle with the tahini dressing. Sprinkle with the reserved fresh herbs and a pinch of flaky sea salt.

INGREDIENTS:

2   **LBS. PLUMS, HALVED AND PITTED**

2   **TABLESPOONS AVOCADO OIL**

1½   **TEASPOONS SEA SALT, PLUS MORE AS NEEDED**

  FRESHLY CRACKED BLACK PEPPER, TO TASTE

1   **TABLESPOON FRESH THYME AND/OR OREGANO LEAVES**

  FLAKY SEA SALT, TO GARNISH

6   **TABLESPOONS FRESH LEMON JUICE, PLUS MORE AS NEEDED**

1   **CUP RAW TAHINI**

½   **TEASPOON SEA SALT, PLUS MORE AS NEEDED**

1   **ICE CUBE**

Roasted Pepper Salad, page 480

ROASTED PEPPER SALAD

YIELD: 6 SERVINGS / **ACTIVE TIME:** 10 MINUTES / **TOTAL TIME:** 30 MINUTES

Roasted pepper salad is a classic Moroccan dish. Consider it the perfect accompaniment for your summer barbecues.

1. Place the peppers directly on the flames of a gas stovetop over medium-high heat, flipping them occasionally until charred on all sides and tender inside, about 10 minutes. Set the peppers aside until cool enough to handle. Peel the charred skins from the peppers and scoop out the seeds. Slice the cleaned peppers lengthwise into slices that are ¼" thick. Set aside.

2. Add 1 tablespoon of oil to a saucepan over medium heat and sauté the onions until translucent, about 5 to 7 minutes. Set aside to cool.

3. In a large bowl, place the peppers, onions, ½ cup oil, vinegar, salt, pepper, cumin, and cilantro and mix well.

4. Serve at room temperature.

INGREDIENTS:

3	RED PEPPERS
2	YELLOW PEPPERS
1	GREEN PEPPER
½	CUP AVOCADO OIL, PLUS 1 TABLESPOON
½	ONION, THINLY SLICED
1	TEASPOON WHITE VINEGAR
¼	TEASPOON SEA SALT
⅛	TEASPOON GROUND BLACK PEPPER
½	TEASPOON CUMIN
¼	BUNCH CILANTRO LEAVES, ROUGHLY CHOPPED

SEARED RADICCHIO & ROASTED BEETS

YIELD: 8 SERVINGS / **ACTIVE TIME:** 15 MINUTES / **TOTAL TIME:** 1 HOUR

In this autumnal salad, roasting beets over high heat yields charred skin, which is a nice contrast to the sweet flesh.

1. Preheat the oven to 450°F.

2. Toss the beets with 1 tablespoon oil on a foil-lined rimmed baking sheet; season with kosher salt. Roast, tossing once, until skins are charred and beets are tender, 40 to 50 minutes. Let cool.

3. Meanwhile, add 2 tablespoons oil to a large skillet over medium-high heat and cook radicchio wedges on cut sides until browned, about 2 minutes per side. Transfer to a platter.

4. Add pomegranate juice to the hot skillet, bring to a boil, and cook until thickened and syrupy, about 5 minutes. Stir in vinegar and season with sea salt.

5. To serve, tear open the beets and place around radicchio; spoon the warm dressing over. Top the salad with pomegranate seeds, flaky sea salt, and drizzle with remaining 2 tablespoons oil.

INGREDIENTS:

6	MEDIUM BEETS, SCRUBBED
5	TABLESPOONS AVOCADO OIL, DIVIDED
	KOSHER SALT, TO TASTE
2	SMALL HEADS OF RADICCHIO, CUT INTO LARGE WEDGES THROUGH ROOT END
1	CUP POMEGRANATE JUICE
2	TABLESPOONS RED WINE VINEGAR
	SEA SALT, TO TASTE
½	CUP POMEGRANATE SEEDS
	FLAKY SEA SALT, TO GARNISH

SHAVED RADISH SALAD WITH WALNUTS & MINT

YIELD: 6 SERVINGS / **ACTIVE TIME:** 20 MINUTES / **TOTAL TIME:** 1 HOUR AND 20 MINUTES

Mandolines were made for recipes like this. Even slices will make this simple fall salad look like the work of a pro.

1. Preheat the oven to 375°F.

2. Wash beets under cold water and cut off the top and bottom. Cut the beets in half and toss with olive oil, salt, and pepper, to taste.

3. Lay out a large piece of tinfoil, top with a piece of parchment paper, and wrap and seal beets. Roast the foil package for 1 hour or until beets are tender when poked with a fork.

4. Turn down the oven to 350°F.

5. Using rubber gloves or paper towels, rub the beets so the skins slide right off. Set aside to cool before slicing.

6. Toast walnuts on a baking sheet, tossing once, until golden brown, about 10 minutes. Let cool and then crush the walnuts to small pieces.

7. In a blender, combine lemon juice, mustard, lemon zest, honey, and poppy seeds and pulse until fully mixed. Season to taste and set aside.

8. Layer the radishes and beets on a large plate and top with walnuts, Parmesan cheese, mint, lemon juice, and lime zest. Drizzle with dressing and season to taste.

INGREDIENTS:

1   CHIOGGIA BEET

1   GOLDEN BEET

¾   CUP EXTRA VIRGIN OLIVE OIL, PLUS MORE AS NEEDED

     SEA SALT, TO TASTE

     FRESHLY GROUND BLACK PEPPER, TO TASTE

¼   CUP WALNUTS

¼   CUP FRESH LEMON JUICE

1   TABLESPOON DIJON MUSTARD

½   TABLESPOON LEMON ZEST

1   TABLESPOON HONEY

1   TABLESPOON POPPY SEEDS

1   WATERMELON RADISH, THINLY SLICED

3   RADISHES, THINLY SLICED

½   CUP SHAVED PARMESAN CHEESE

1   BUNCH CHOCOLATE MINT

½   TABLESPOON LIME ZEST

SHAVED CARROT & RADISH SALAD
WITH HERBS & TOASTED PUMPKIN SEEDS

YIELD: 8 SERVINGS / ACTIVE TIME: 10 MINUTES / TOTAL TIME: 20 MINUTES

This salad is all about highlighting the mixture of green herbs: parsley, cilantro, dill, mint, tarragon, and/or basil. Crunchy radishes and carrot ribbons make for a colorful presentation.

1. Peel carrots and shave lengthwise into ribbons with a vegetable peeler.

2. Heat 1 tablespoon oil in a skillet over medium and add pumpkin seeds and cumin and cook, stirring, until lightly toasted and fragrant, 5 minutes. Transfer to paper towel-lined plate, season with salt, to taste, and let cool.

3. In a medium bowl, combine lemon juice, honey, pepper, and ¾ teaspoon salt and whisk until honey dissolves. Slowly whisk in remaining oil until emulsified.

4. In a salad bowl, combine carrots, radishes, and dressing and mix well. Then fold in the herbs and half of the pumpkin seeds.

5. Season to taste and before serving top the salad with remaining pumpkin seeds.

INGREDIENTS:

- 2 LBS. CARROTS
- ¼ CUP AVOCADO OIL, DIVIDED
- 1 CUP RAW SHELLED PUMPKIN SEEDS
- ½ TEASPOON CUMIN
- ¾ TEASPOONS SEA SALT, PLUS MORE TO TASTE
- 3 TABLESPOONS FRESH LEMON JUICE
- 1 TEASPOON HONEY
- ¼ TEASPOON FRESHLY GROUND BLACK PEPPER
- 10 RADISHES, THINLY SLICED
- ¾ CUP TORN PARSLEY
- ¾ CUP TORN CILANTRO
- ¾ CUP TORN DILL
- ¾ CUP TORN CHOCOLATE MINT
- ¾ CUP TORN TARRAGON
- ¾ CUP TORN BASIL
- ½ CUP CHOPPED CHIVES

Shaved Carrot & Radish Salad with Herbs & Toasted Pumpkin Seeds,
page 483

SHAVED FENNEL SALAD

YIELD: 4 SERVINGS / **ACTIVE TIME:** 20 MINUTES / **TOTAL TIME:** 40 MINUTES

If the rest of the meal is rich and filling, you need a Rosh Hashanah salad like this one for balance. Crunchy fennel and croutons are dressed with all the acidity and zing you need, thanks to lemon juice and zest, vinegar, mint, and red pepper flakes.

1. Preheat the oven to 400°F.

2. Place bread on a baking sheet and brush with 3 tablespoons oil and season with salt. Cook until nicely browned, about 10 minutes.

3. Place walnuts on a separate baking sheet and bake until walnuts are golden brown, about 15 minutes. Let cool, then coarsely chop walnuts.

4. In a bowl, combine vinegar, garlic, thyme, parsley and red pepper flakes and mix well. Whisk 3 tablespoons oil into the vinegar mixture, then add croutons and chopped walnuts. Season with salt and toss to coat and let croutons soften slightly; set aside.

5. Remove the stalks and fronds from fennel bulbs. Remove fronds from stalks and coarsely chop; thinly slice stalks. Place in a bowl. Cut the fennel bulbs in half and thinly slice. Add to the same bowl along with the mint.

6. Zest the lemon half over the salad, then squeeze in juice. Season with salt and toss to combine.

7. Divide reserved crouton mixture among plates and top with half of the Parmesan.

8. Arrange fennel salad over the croutons and top with remaining Parmesan and drizzle with oil.

INGREDIENTS:

- 2 **CUPS CUBED COUNTRY BREAD**
- ½ **CUP WALNUTS**
- 6 **TABLESPOON AVOCADO OIL, PLUS MORE FOR DRIZZLING**
-   **SEA SALT, TO TASTE**
- 3 **TABLESPOONS SHERRY VINEGAR**
- 1 **GARLIC CLOVE, FINELY GRATED**
- ¼ **TEASPOON CRUSHED RED PEPPER FLAKES**
- 2 **FENNEL BULBS, WITH FRONDS**
- ¾ **CUP MINT LEAVES**
- ½ **LEMON**
- ½ **TEASPOON FRESH LEMON JUICE**
- ⅛ **TEASPOON CHOPPED THYME LEAVES**
- 1 **TABLESPOON CHOPPED FLAT-LEAFED PARSLEY**
- 3 **TABLESPOON SHAVED PARMESAN CHEESE**

Sheet-Pan Roasted Squash & Feta Salad,
page 490

SHEET-PAN ROASTED SQUASH & FETA SALAD

YIELD: 4 SERVINGS / **ACTIVE TIME:** 15 MINUTES / **TOTAL TIME:** 40 MINUTES

Feta and bread get roasted alongside winter squash, then tossed with pleasantly bitter greens for a salad that's equal parts warm and cold, soft and crunchy, and sweet and savory. A perfect side dish but hearty enough to eat on its own.

1. Preheat the oven to 400°F.

2. Halve squash lengthwise, deseed, and cut into ¼" thick slices.

3. Toss squash, 1 teaspoon salt, black pepper, and 2 tablespoons oil on a baking sheet and arrange in an even layer. Roast until squash is beginning to brown on one side, about 15 minutes.

4. Remove the baking sheet from the oven, turn the squash, and then arrange the bread and feta over the squash. Return to the oven and roast until bread is lightly toasted and feta is soft and warmed through, about 10 minutes.

5. In a large bowl, combine vinegar, honey, thyme, remaining oil, and ½ teaspoon salt and whisk well.

6. In a small, combine the paprika and cayenne, mix well, and set aside.

7. Add radicchio and hot squash mixture to the bowl with the dressing and toss to coat.

8. Transfer to a platter and sprinkle with the spice blend.

INGREDIENTS:

- 1½ LBS. ACORN SQUASH
- ¼ TEASPOON FRESHLY GROUND BLACK PEPPER
- ½ CUP AVOCADO OIL, DIVIDED
- 1½ TEASPOONS SEA SALT, DIVIDED
- 4 CUPS CUBED FRENCH BREAD
- ½ LB. GREEK FETA
- ¼ CUP SHERRY WINE VINEGAR
- 1 TEASPOON HONEY
- 1 TEASPOON THYME LEAVES
- ½ TEASPOON HUNGARIAN SWEET PAPRIKA
- ½ TEASPOON CAYENNE PEPPER
- 1 HEAD OF RADICCHIO OR ½ HEAD OF ESCAROLE, LEAVES SEPARATED, TORN INTO LARGE PIECES

SLOW-COOKED CHERRY TOMATOES WITH CORIANDER & ROSEMARY

YIELD: 6 SERVINGS / **ACTIVE TIME:** 10 MINUTES / **TOTAL TIME:** 1 HOUR

Douse ripe cherry tomatoes in lots of olive oil and slow-roast until they come completely. Serve with your brisket, your chicken, or whatever main dish feels right.

1. Place a rack in the middle of the oven and preheat to 350°F.

2. In a shallow baking dish, combine the tomatoes, garlic, rosemary, oil, coriander seeds, sugar, and toss to coat.

3. Turn garlic cut-side down and then roast tomatoes, tossing 2 or 3 times, until golden brown and very tender, about 50 minutes.

4. Let cool slightly, then add vinegar and stir to combine.

INGREDIENTS:

1½   LBS. HEIRLOOM CHERRY TOMATOES

½   HEAD OF GARLIC

2   SPRIGS FRESH ROSEMARY

½   CUP AVOCADO OIL

¾   TEASPOON CORIANDER SEEDS

½   TEASPOON SUGAR

¾   TEASPOON SEA SALT

1   TABLESPOON RED WINE VINEGAR

Slow-Cooked Cherry Tomatoes with Coriander & Rosemary, page 491

SPLIT PEAS WITH BERBERE

YIELD: 8 SERVINGS / **ACTIVE TIME:** 15 MINUTES / **TOTAL TIME:** 24 HOURS

Ethiopian berbere is hot, spicy, and tangy, so serve this soup with rice or another starch to balance the heat.

1. In a large saucepan, cover the soaked split peas with water and bring to a simmer. Cook until the peas are soft, about 1 hour, adding water if necessary.

2. Heat a large stockpot over high heat. Add the onion and sauté until it begins to brown, about 3 minutes. Add ½ cup water and simmer until the water has evaporated, 2 to 5 minutes. Add the oil and berbere and sauté until fragrant. Add the garlic and sauté for 1 minute, then add the tomato and bell pepper. Cover and continue to cook until vegetables begin to soften, about 3 minutes.

3. Add the peas, with any remaining water from the pot, ½ cup water, and the salt. Bring to a boil, then lower to a simmer. Cook, stirring occasionally, until the sauce thickens, about 1 hour. If it dries out too much before it's ready, add water.

4. Season to taste before serving.

INGREDIENTS:

2   LBS. DRIED GREEN SPLIT PEAS, SOAKED OVERNIGHT AND DRAINED

1   LARGE ONION, CHOPPED

¼   CUP AVOCADO OIL

3   TABLESPOONS BERBERE SPICE MIX (SEE PAGE 323)

8-10 GARLIC CLOVES, CHOPPED

1   TOMATO, CUBED

1   RED BELL PEPPER, CUBED

2   TEASPOONS SEA SALT

SPAETZLE

YIELD: 4 SERVINGS / **ACTIVE TIME:** 10 MINUTES / **TOTAL TIME:** 20 MINUTES

These noodles of German and Alsatian origin are known for their egg-yolk yellow color and odd, curly shape. They make a perfect side dish to almost any meat and are best served with lots of butter.

1. In a bowl, combine flour, salt, nutmeg, and pepper. Add eggs and milk and stir until a thick batter forms.

2. Add stock to a Dutch oven and bring to a boil.

3. Drop batter by ½ teaspoonfuls into boiling liquid. Cook until spaetzle rises to the surface; remove to ice water.

4. Drain well.

5. Melt the butter in a skillet over medium heat and then heat spaetzle until lightly browned. Serve with schnitzel (see page 262) or Parmesan cheese.

INGREDIENTS:

1	CUP ALL-PURPOSE FLOUR
½	TEASPOON SALT
½	TEASPOON GROUND NUTMEG
1	DASH WHITE PEPPER
2	EGGS, LIGHTLY BEATEN
¼	CUP MILK
4	QUARTS CHICKEN STOCK (SEE PAGE 722) OR WATER
2	TABLESPOONS UNSALTED BUTTER
1	TABLESPOON GRATED PARMESAN CHEESE

Spaetzle, page 495

STUFFED MATZO BALL SOUP
WITH CHICKEN & APPLES

YIELD: 6 SERVINGS / **ACTIVE TIME:** 40 MINUTES / **TOTAL TIME:** 1 HOUR AND 5 MINUTES

S tuffing matzo balls is a great way to diversify this classic dish. These have a filling of ground chicken laced with fennel, almond syrup, and pepper—and there are nigella seeds and fragrant cubeb in the outer layer.

1. In a bowl, combine the matzo meal, oil, salt, pepper, and sesame seeds. Add 1 cup boiling Chicken Broth and mix well.

2. Add the egg, mixing quickly to avoid partially cooking it.

3. Using wet hands, form the dough into 14 equal portions; flatten and set aside

4. In a bowl, combine the chicken, fennel, almond extract, sea salt, and pepper and mix well. Using wet hands, roll the mixture into 14 balls.

5. Place a ball of filling on the flattened matzo-meal and fold the edges together to form a ball. Repeat with remaining filling and dough.

6. Bring a pot of chicken stock to a boil.

7. Gently add the stuffed matzo balls, reduce heat, cover, and simmer until matzo balls are cooked through and float, about 25 minutes.

8. Meanwhile, heat the Schmaltz in a saucepan over medium heat. Add the apples and sauté until slightly softened, about 5 minutes. Add the brandy and stir, scraping up any bits on the bottom of the pan, until most of the brandy has evaporated, about 2 minutes.

9. Remove apples from the pan and set aside.

10. In a pot, heat the broth until just simmering.

11. Divide the apples among soup bowls, then ladle broth and matzo balls into each bowl. Garnish with sesame seeds.

INGREDIENTS:

MATZO BALL DOUGH

1¼	CUPS MATZO MEAL
2	TABLESPOONS EXTRA VIRGIN OLIVE OIL
2	TEASPOONS SEA SALT
¼	TEASPOON FRESHLY GROUND BLACK PEPPER
1	TABLESPOON TOASTED OR BLACK SESAME SEEDS
1	LARGE EGG
1	CUP CHICKEN BROTH (SEE RECIPE)

FILLING

¼	LB. GROUND CHICKEN
⅛	TEASPOON GROUND FENNEL
1	DROP ALMOND EXTRACT
¼	TEASPOON SEA SALT
⅛	TEASPOON FRESHLY GROUND BLACK PEPPER

CHICKEN BROTH

⅓	CUP SCHMALTZ (SEE PAGE 528)
2	GRANNY SMITH APPLES, PEELED AND DICED
2	GOLDEN DELICIOUS APPLES, PEELED AND DICED
2½	TABLESPOONS APPLE BRANDY
3½	CUPS CHICKEN STOCK (SEE PAGE 722)
2	TEASPOONS TOASTED OR BLACK SESAME SEEDS

SWEET POTATO & TAHINI DIP WITH ZA'ATAR

YIELD: 8 SERVINGS / **ACTIVE TIME:** 15 MINUTES / **TOTAL TIME:** 1 HOUR AND 15 MINUTES

The base of this dip is so simple—but the homemade za'atar really helps the flavors stand out.

1. Toast the sesame seeds in a skillet over low heat until golden and fragrant, about 3 minutes. Transfer to a bowl, add the thyme, sumac, and salt. Stir and set aside.

2. Preheat the oven to 400°F.

3. Pierce the sweet potatoes all over with a fork and wrap in foil. Place on a baking sheet and roast until the flesh gives easily when pressed, about 1 hour. Unwrap and set aside to cool completely.

4. Peel the sweet potatoes and place them in a food processor, along with the tahini, water, lemon juice, lime zest, hot sauce, black pepper, and 2 tablespoons of Za'atar. Puree until completely smooth. Season to taste.

5. Scrape the dip into a small serving bowl, drizzle with the oil, and sprinkle with Za'atar.

INGREDIENTS:

1 TABLESPOON RAW BLACK SESAME SEEDS

1 TABLESPOON MINCED THYME

1 TABLESPOON SUMAC

¼ TEASPOON SEA SALT, PLUS MORE TO TASTE

1 LB. SWEET POTATOES

2 TABLESPOONS TAHINI

2 TABLESPOONS WATER

1 TABLESPOON FRESH LEMON JUICE

1 TEASPOON LIME ZEST

3 DASHES TABASCO

FRESHLY GROUND BLACK PEPPER, TO TASTE

1 TEASPOON EXTRA VIRGIN OLIVE OIL

1 TABLESPOON ZA'ATAR (SEE PAGE 545)

Swiss Chard & Herb Fritters,
page 502

SWISS CHARD & HERB FRITTERS

YIELD: 25 FRITTERS / **ACTIVE TIME:** 15 MINUTES / **TOTAL TIME:** 25 MINUTES

These golden-brown fritters are bursting with a generous helping of Swiss chard, parsley, cilantro, and dill.

1. Bring a large pot of water with 1 teaspoon salt to a boil, add chard, and simmer for 5 minutes. Remove from the pot and drain well, patting leaves dry.

2. Place chard in a food processor with onion, cilantro, dill, parsley, caraway, coriander, nutmeg, sugar, flour, garlic, harissa, pepper, eggs, and ½ teaspoon salt and pulse until well blended. Fold in the feta by hand.

3. Heat oil in a large sauté pan over medium-high heat. When oil is hot, spoon in 1 heaping tablespoon of mixture for each fritter. Press down gently on the fritter to flatten.

4. Cook 2 minutes per side, until golden brown.

5. Transfer to a baking sheet lined with paper towels.

6. Add oil as needed and repeat until all of the mixture is made.

7. Serve warm with lemon wedges.

INGREDIENTS:

1¼	SWISS CHARD, STEMS REMOVED
1½	TEASPOONS SEA SALT, PLUS MORE TO TASTE
3	ONIONS, GRATED
1	BUNCH CILANTRO
1	BUNCH DILL
1	BUNCH CURLY LEAF PARSLEY
½	TEASPOON GROUND CARAWAY
1	TABLESPOON GROUND CORIANDER
1½	TEASPOONS GRATED NUTMEG
½	TEASPOON GRANULATED WHITE SUGAR
3	TABLESPOONS ALL-PURPOSE FLOUR
2	GARLIC CLOVES, CHOPPED
1	TABLESPOON HARISSA PEPPER PASTE
¼	TEASPOON FRESHLY GROUND PEPPER
6	LARGE EGGS, DIVIDED
½	CUP CRUMBLED FETA CHEESE
1	TABLESPOON AVOCADO OIL, PLUS MORE AS NEEDED
	LEMON WEDGES, TO SERVE

TAHDIG

YIELD: 8 SERVINGS / **ACTIVE TIME:** 5 MINUTES / **TOTAL TIME:** 45 MINUTES

It's okay if you burn your rice, just learn to do it the Persian way! Tahdig means "bottom of the pot" in Farsi, but all you need to know is that this pilaf lets the little bits of burnt rice from the bottom of the pot shine. Tahdig is incredibly versatile, so there are recipes for dairy-eating vegetarians and vegans. Try potato tahdig for extra starchiness.

1. Combine the rice and water in a saucepan and bring to a boil. Reduce the heat to medium-low, add salt, and stir. Cover the pot and allow to simmer for 20 minutes or until rice is tender.

2. In a large skillet or sauté pan, heat the olive oil over medium heat. Be sure to coat the sides and the bottom of the pan. Add the cooked rice and press down with the back of a large spoon to compact it, ensuring it is evenly spread throughout the pan.

3. Cover and cook for about 20 minutes on medium heat, or until you hear it crack and sizzle.

4. Once the rice is done, remove the lid and carefully flip the rice over onto a serving dish, so the crusted rice is now on the top. The rice should have a thick layer of brown, crispy rice. Serve immediately.

INGREDIENTS:

2	CUPS UNCOOKED RICE OF YOUR CHOICE
4	CUPS WATER
½	TEASPOON SEA SALT
3	TABLESPOONS AVOCADO OIL OR UNSALTED BUTTER

ZA'ATAR OKRA & LEMONS

YIELD: 4 SERVINGS / **ACTIVE TIME:** 20 MINUTES / **TOTAL TIME:** 20 MINUTES

If you've ever been put off by slimy okra, try this high-heat recipe that keeps the pods crispy.

1. Add oil to a large skillet over high heat. When the oil begins to shimmer, add the okra and lemon, season with salts, and cook, stirring frequently, until the okra and lemon begin to char.

2. Remove pan from heat, add Za'atar, stir to incorporate, transfer to a serving bowl, and garnish with parsley.

INGREDIENTS:

2 TABLESPOONS AVOCADO OIL

1 LB. OKRA, TRIMMED

1 LEMON, CUT INTO WEDGES

SEA SALT, TO TASTE

ZA'ATAR (SEE PAGE 545), TO TASTE

PARSLEY, TO GARNISH

ZUCCHINI MAHSHI

YIELD: 6 SERVINGS / **ACTIVE TIME:** 1 HOUR / **TOTAL TIME:** 2 HOURS

The zucchinis are cut in half vertically and hollowed out, an easy task to do with a melon scoop. Fill them to the brim with beef and rice for a delicious summer dinner.

1. Remove the zucchini stems and peel the zucchini in a striped pattern. Using an apple corer, core out the center cavity of each zucchini, leaving about ½" of zucchini meat on the edges.

2. In a bowl, combine the beef, rice, allspice, and 1½ tablespoons salt and mix well.

3. Stuff the cavity of each zucchini with enough meat to fill it up with ¼" space on each side; the filling will expand as it cooks.

4. In a bowl, combine the lemon juice, pomegranate molasses, tomato paste, sugar, and salt and mix well.

5. Place 1 tablespoon of oil into a wide pot over medium heat. Once the oil is hot, place the stuffed zucchini into the oil and sear on all sides until golden brown, about 3 minutes per side.

6. Pour the sauce over the zucchini. Add enough water to cover the zucchini about three-quarters of up the way. Place a lid on the pot and cook over medium to medium-low heat or on a simmer for about 40 minutes, or until the meat and rice is cooked through and the sauce reduces and thickens.

INGREDIENTS:

8-10 ZUCCHINI

1 TABLESPOON AVOCADO OIL

1 LB. GROUND BEEF

¾ CUP ARBORIO RICE

1 TABLESPOON ALLSPICE

1½ TABLESPOONS SEA SALT, PLUS 1 TEASPOON

½ CUP LEMON JUICE

¼ CUP POMEGRANATE MOLASSES

2 TABLESPOONS TOMATO PASTE

1 TEASPOON SUGAR

WATER, AS NEEDED

Skewers of Chicken & Lamb Fat,
page 385

CONDIMENTS

We're not just talking pickled this and that! Condiments for Jewish cooking include rich labneh, spice blends like za'atar, and much more.

CHAROSET

YIELD: 6 SERVINGS / **ACTIVE TIME:** 15 MINUTES / **TOTAL TIME:** 1 HOUR AND 15 MINUTES

This sweet apple-wine-nut mixture is eaten on Passover not just for its sweetness but to represent the mortar the slaves used in building the pyramids.

1. Place the walnuts in a skillet over low heat and cook until lightly browned, stirring occasionally.

2. In a large bowl, toss apples and walnuts with wine.

3. In a small bowl, mix the sugar and cinnamon and then sprinkle over apple mixture and toss to combine.

4. Refrigerate, covered, for 1 hour before serving. If desired, serve with matzo.

INGREDIENTS:

½ CUP FINELY CHOPPED WALNUTS

3 MEDIUM GALA OR FUJI APPLES, PEELED AND FINELY CHOPPED

2 TABLESPOONS SWEET RED WINE OR GRAPE JUICE

2 TABLESPOONS SUGAR

1 TEASPOON GROUND CINNAMON

MATZO (OPTIONAL)

CHAMPAGNE VINAIGRETTE

Elegant simplicity in a bottle. Bring any salad to life with this dressing, or roasted vegetables.

1. In a bowl, combine all of the ingredients, except for the oil, and mix well.

2. Whisk in oil and refrigerate to store.

INGREDIENTS:

⅔   CUP CHAMPAGNE VINEGAR

¼   CUP WATER

2   TABLESPOONS DIJON
     MUSTARD

½   TEASPOON SEA SALT

½   TEASPOON BLACK PEPPER

2   TABLESPOONS HONEY

1½   CUPS EXTRA VIRGIN OLIVE
     OIL

CHERMOULA SAUCE

YIELD: 1 GALLON / **ACTIVE TIME:** 5 MINUTES / **TOTAL TIME:** 10 MINUTES

Traditionally used with fish, this flavorful North African sauce can be used on anything your palate deems tasty.

1. Bloom the saffron by placing it in ¼ cup water. Once it has been hydrated remove saffron from the water. Do not use the water in the sauce or it will be too loose, however you might want to save it and use it in a tomato sauce.

2. In a large bowl, combine all of the ingredients and mix well with a rubber spatula. Make sure to use a rubber spatula to get every last drop of sauce in a storage container.

INGREDIENTS:

1   TABLESPOON SAFFRON THREADS

1   GALLON MAYONNAISE

1   TABLESPOON RAS EL HANOUT

1   TABLESPOON BERBERE SPICE MIX (SEE PAGE 323)

2   TABLESPOONS ZA'ATAR (SEE PAGE 545)

1   TABLESPOON SUMAC

2   CUPS MIX OF FRESH TARRAGON, PARSLEY, CHIVES, AND CILANTRO

1   TABLESPOON DRIED OREGANO

1   TABLESPOON FINE SEA SALT

1   TABLESPOON FINE BLACK PEPPER

Chermoula Sauce,
page 517

CHIMICHURRI SAUCE

YIELD: 2 CUPS / **ACTIVE TIME:** 10 MINUTES / **TOTAL TIME:** 10 MINUTES

Add flavor to meat, rice, vegetables, or anything else with this fresh herb-heavy condiment.

1. Place all ingredients in a blender and puree until thick and smooth.

2. Refrigerate to store.

INGREDIENTS:

2	TABLESPOONS FRESH LEMON JUICE
1	TABLESPOONS FRESH LIME JUICE
1	JALAPEÑO PEPPER, DESTEMMED
¼	CUP PINEAPPLE CHUNKS
¼	CUP GARLIC CLOVES
¼	CUP RED WINE VINEGAR
½	BUNCH CILANTRO, LEAVES AND STEMS
¼	BUNCH BASIL, LEAVES AND STEMS
¼	BUNCH PARSLEY, LEAVES AND STEMS
¼	BUNCH OREGANO, NO STEMS
¼	BUNCH MINT, LEAVES AND STEMS
1	TEASPOON DRIED OREGANO
2	TEASPOONS FINE SEA SALT
1	TEASPOON BLACK PEPPER
2	CUPS AVOCADO OIL

CILANTRO-LIME VINAIGRETTE

YIELD: 2 QUARTS / **ACTIVE TIME:** 5 MINUTES / **TOTAL TIME:** 5 MINUTES

Be sure to try this on grilled vegetables. Between the char and fish sauce it's a double umami taste treat.

1. Place all of the ingredients in a Vitamix and blend until smooth and able to fit through a squeeze bottle cap.

2. Refrigerate to store.

INGREDIENTS:

2 QUARTS SAFFLOWER OIL

1 CUP CHIMICHURRI (SEE PAGE 521)

½ CUP FISH SAUCE

½ CUP HONEY

1 CUP FRESH LIME JUICE

2 BUNCHES CILANTRO, LEAVES AND STEMS

2 TABLESPOONS SEA SALT

1 TABLESPOON BLACK PEPPER

GINGER CARROT VINAIGRETTE

YIELD: 2 GALLONS / **ACTIVE TIME:** 10 MINUTES / **TOTAL TIME:** 10 MINUTES

This is a riff on the salad dressing so often used in Japanese restaurants.

1. Place water, carrots, and ginger in a Vitamix blender and puree for 2 minutes.

2. Add remaining ingredients and puree until smooth and color has a deep orange hue, about 3 minutes. Season to taste.

INGREDIENTS:

6	OZ. WATER
8	CARROTS, ROUGHLY CHOPPED
1	OZ. FRESH GINGER
4	OZ. RICE WINE VINEGAR
4	OZ. MIRIN
8	OZ. SESAME OIL
12	OZ. EXTRA VIRGIN OLIVE OIL
4	OZ. MIX OF FRESH TARRAGON, PARSLEY, CHIVES, AND CILANTRO
1	TABLESPOON SEA SALT, PLUS MORE TO TASTE
1	TABLESPOON BLACK PEPPER, PLUS MORE TO TASTE

DUKKAH

YIELD: 1 CUP / **ACTIVE TIME:** 15 MINUTES / **TOTAL TIME:** 15 MINUTES

If you love za'atar on everything from hummus and pita to roasted potatoes, then you'll love dukkah, an Egyptian spice blend that's used in a similar way.

1. Heat a cast-iron skillet over medium heat. Add pistachios and almonds and toast for 1 to 2 minutes, stirring frequently until golden; remove from heat if they start to burn. Turn the heat off and add sesame seeds, stirring frequently for a few minutes to toast as the pan cools down. Pour into a bowl and set aside.

2. Add the mint, thyme, poppy seeds, and sumac to the bowl of nuts.

3. Next, heat the cast-iron skillet again over medium heat. When hot, add fennel seeds and toast for 30 seconds, or until fragrant. Then add the cumin and coriander and cook for an additional 30 more seconds, or until they start to pop. Pour these into another bowl, separate from the nuts.

4. Return the pan to the heat and toast the nigella seeds and peppercorns for 1 minute. Add those to the bowl of fennel, cumin, and coriander.

5. When the spices have cooled, transfer the bowl of fennel, cumin, coriander, nigella seeds, and peppercorns to a spice grinder, food processor, or coffee grinder (if you use a coffee grinder, make sure you've cleaned it out first!) and pulse until the mixture is as coarse or fine as you'd like.

6. Pour the ground spices into the bowl of nuts and seeds, and mix with a fork until it's thoroughly combined. Store in an airtight container for a month or so, or store in an airtight container in the freezer for up to 4 months. Enjoy with olive oil and bread, labneh, salad, or whatever you can think of!

INGREDIENTS:

- ¼ CUP CHOPPED ALMONDS
- ¼ CUP CHOPPED PISTACHIOS
- 2 TABLESPOONS SESAME SEEDS
- 1½ TABLESPOONS DRIED MINT
- 1½ TABLESPOONS DRIED THYME
- 2 TABLESPOONS POPPY SEEDS
- 1 TABLESPOON SUMAC
- 1 TABLESPOON FENNEL SEEDS
- 1 TABLESPOON CUMIN SEEDS
- 1 TABLESPOON CORIANDER SEEDS
- 1 TEASPOON BLACK NIGELLA SEEDS
- 1 TEASPOON BLACK PEPPERCORNS
- 1 TABLESPOON SALT

Gribenes & Schmaltz, page 528

GRIBENES & SCHMALTZ

YIELD: ½ CUP SCHMALTZ / 2 CUPS GRIBENES / **ACTIVE TIME:** 15 MINUTES / **TOTAL TIME:** 1 HOUR AND 30 MINUTES

Are we being dramatic when we say you can't make truly authentic Ashkenazi cuisine without Schmaltz? Schmaltz is so simple—just rendered chicken or goose fat—and yet it is crucial for making so many a dish delicious. For some, cooking without it is schande. For us, we simply love how good it makes everything from latkes to liver and matzo balls taste. And speaking of yummy fat, don't forget Jewish Bacon. Need we say more? These fried bits of chicken skin are so scrumptious, it's nearly sinful.

1. In a large nonstick skillet over medium heat, toss chicken skin and fat with salt and 1 tablespoon water and spread out in one layer. Cook over medium heat for about 15 minutes, until fat starts to render and skin begins to turn golden at the edges.

2. Add onion, if using, and cook 45 minutes to 1 hour longer, tossing occasionally, until chicken skin and onions are crispy and richly browned, but not burned.

3. Strain through a sieve. Reserve the Schmaltz and store in refrigerator for up to 6 months.

4. If you want the gribenes to be crispier, return to the skillet and cook over high heat until done to taste. Drain gribenes on a paper-towel-lined plate before serving.

INGREDIENTS:

- ¾ LB. CHICKEN SKIN AND FAT, DICED (USE SCISSORS, OR FREEZE THEN DICE WITH A KNIFE)
- ¾ TEASPOON KOSHER SALT
- ½ MEDIUM ONION, PEELED AND CUT INTO ¼" SLICES

MAROR

YIELD: 1 CUP / ACTIVE TIME: 10 MINUTES / TOTAL TIME: 10 MINUTES

On Passover, Jews eat horseradish to remember the bitterness of their forebears' lives as slaves in ancient Egypt. Regular horseradish is too mild to do justice to the experience, so making your own maror is a must. The great news is that it's so easy, you can eat it year-round instead of buying the bottled stuff. Just watch out for your eyes and don't come kvetching to us if you breathe in the fumes.

1. Combine all of the ingredients in a food processor or blender, and then process until the mixture is pureed. Cover the horseradish and refrigerate to store.

INGREDIENTS:

1	CUP PEELED AND CUBED HORSERADISH ROOT
¾	CUP RED OR WHITE WINE VINEGAR (DEPENDING ON YOUR PREFERENCE FOR COLOR)
2	TEASPOONS SUGAR
¼	TEASPOON SALT

ISRAELI YOGURT SAUCE

YIELD: 1 GALLON / ACTIVE TIME: 5 MINUTES / TOTAL TIME: 5 MINUTES

This works very well with plain yogurt, but it is even better if you use homemade labneh.

1. In a large mixing bowl, combine all of the ingredients and mix well.

INGREDIENTS:

4	QUARTS PLAIN YOGURT OR LABNEH (SEE PAGE 530)
4	OZ. EXTRA VIRGIN OLIVE OIL
4	OZ. FRESH LEMON JUICE
1	TABLESPOON ZA'ATAR (SEE PAGE 545)
1	TEASPOON CUMIN
1	TEASPOON SUMAC
1	TABLESPOON SEA SALT
1	TABLESPOON BLACK PEPPER
2	TEASPOONS OREGANO
2	TEASPOONS BASIL
2	TEASPOONS PARSLEY
2	TEASPOONS GARLIC POWDER
3	TABLESPOONS CHOPPED DILL

LABNEH

YIELD: 2½ CUPS / **ACTIVE TIME:** 10 MINUTES / **TOTAL TIME:** 25 TO 48 HOURS

Congratulations, you're about to pull off the easiest recipe for homemade cheese! This is a strained yogurt cheese, dried and prepared either as a buttery spread or shaped into balls. Native to the Middle East, labneh cheese is a popular food in Israel. Creamy labneh is usually spread out onto a pita bread or a bagel, and blends well with lemon juice, olive oil, zaatar, and herbs like marjoram, oregano, thyme, and sesame seeds.

1. Add the yogurt to a large bowl and season it with the salt; the salt helps pull out excess whey, giving you a creamier, thicker cheese.

2. Place a fine-mesh strainer on top of a medium-sized bowl. Line the strainer with cheesecloth or a linen kitchen towel, letting a few inches hang over the side of the strainer. Spoon the seasoned yogurt into the cheesecloth and gently wrap the sides over the top of the yogurt, protecting it from being exposed to air in the refrigerator.

3. Store everything in the refrigerator for 24 to 48 hours, discarding the whey halfway through if the bowl beneath the strainer becomes too full.

4. Remove the labneh from the cheesecloth and store it in an airtight container.

5. To serve as a dip, press a dent in the center of the cheese, drizzling the olive oil into the center and sprinkling it with Za'atar.

INGREDIENTS:

- 32 OZ. WHOLE COW'S MILK YOGURT OR GREEK YOGURT
- ½ TEASPOON SALT
- 1 TABLESPOON OLIVE OIL, FOR SERVING
- 1-2 TEASPOONS ZA'ATAR (SEE PAGE 545)

POMEGRANATE VINAIGRETTE

YIELD: 1 GALLON / **ACTIVE TIME:** 30 MINUTES / **TOTAL TIME:** 30 MINUTES

Not only does this add flavor to anything it covers, but it also provides color.

1. Pour the pomegranate juice into a small saucepan over medium-high heat and reduce to ¼ cup. Let cool.

2. Combine all of the ingredients, except the oil, in a blender and puree.

3. With the blender on, drizzle in the oil to make an emulsion.

INGREDIENTS:

1	BOTTLE OF POMEGRANATE JUICE REDUCED TO ¼ CUP
4	OZ. RED WINE VINEGAR
2	TABLESPOONS DIJON MUSTARD
2	TABLESPOONS HONEY
1	TABLESPOON ZA'ATAR (SEE PAGE 545)
2	TEASPOONS SUMAC
2	TABLESPOONS SEA SALT
1	TABLESPOON BLACK PEPPER
1	TABLESPOON FRESH OREGANO
1	TABLESPOON FRESH BASIL
1	TABLESPOON FRESH PARSLEY
1	TABLESPOON FRESH MINT
24	OZ. EXTRA VIRGIN OLIVE OIL

ROASTED CORN SAUCE

YIELD: 20 SERVINGS / **ACTIVE TIME:** 30 MINUTES / **TOTAL TIME:** 1 HOUR

M ake the most of sweet summer corn by using all of it. The cobbs possess an amazing amoung of milky flavor.

1. Preheat the oven to 500°F.

2. Arrange the corn cobbs on sheet trays, season with salt and pepper, and then roast for 8 minutes, until the corn is lightly cooked through. Keep the oven on and allow the corn to cool.

3. Shuck the corn and remove the kernels from the cobbs and set aside.

4. Roast the cobbs again for an additional 8 minutes and then add to 1 gallon of boiling water along with carrots, celery, onion, and sachet d'épices to make a stock.

5. In a saucepan, sweat the remaining ingredients and then place them in a blender with corn kernels. Blend until thick and smooth; the sauce should coat the back of a spoon. Use the corn stock to adjust the consistency of the sauce.

INGREDIENTS:

10	EARS OF CORN, ROASTED ON THE COBB THEN SHUCKED
2	TABLESPOONS SEA SALT
1	TABLESPOON BLACK PEPPER
2	CARROTS, CHOPPED
2	CELERY STALKS, CHOPPED
1	YELLOW ONION, QUARTERED
1	SACHET D'ÉPICES (SEE PAGE 745)
1	TABLESPOON AJI AMARILLO POWDER
2	TABLESPOONS FRESH LEMON JUICE
4	YELLOW BELL PEPPERS, DESEEDED
2	YELLOW BANANA PEPPERS
1	GARLIC CLOVE
1	CUP BRUNOISE RED ONION
3	TABLESPOONS RICE WINE VINEGAR
2	TABLESPOONS AJI-MIRIN
1	CUP MIX OF FRESH TARRAGON, PARSLEY, CHIVES, AND CILANTRO
3	TABLESPOONS SESAME OIL
4	TABLESPOONS EXTRA VIRGIN OLIVE OIL

Relish Tray, page 537

RELISH TRAY

YIELD: 2 SERVINGS / **ACTIVE TIME:** 30 MINUTES / **TOTAL TIME:** 2 HOURS AND 30 MINUTES

This retro-style platter of pickled vegetables and crudités will make it feel like you're at Bubbe's, even if you can't be.

1. Arrange pickled carrots, celery, radishes, cornichons, and olives on a tray of crushed ice.

QUICK PICKLED CARROTS

1. Bring vinegar, sugar, salt, peppercorns, mustard seeds, and 2 cups water to a boil in a medium pot over high heat, stirring occasionally. Reduce heat to medium-low and simmer for 10 minutes.

2. Place carrots in a heatproof resealable container or jar (divide among several containers if necessary). Pour hot brining liquid over carrots. Let cool to room temperature, then cover and chill at least 2 hours before serving.

INGREDIENTS:

½   RECIPE QUICK PICKLED CARROTS (SEE RECIPE)

5   CELERY STALKS, CUT INTO 4"-5" LOGS

1   BUNCH RADISHES, HALVED IF LARGE

1   CUP CORNICHONS, DRAINED

1   CUP PITTED BLACK OLIVES, DRAINED

QUICK PICKLED CARROTS

2   CUPS APPLE CIDER VINEGAR

½   CUP SUGAR

2   TABLESPOONS KOSHER SALT

1   TABLESPOON BLACK PEPPERCORNS

1   TABLESPOON MUSTARD SEEDS

1½   LBS. MEDIUM CARROTS, PEELED, QUARTERED AND SLICED CROSSWISE INTO 3" SEGMENTS

SAFFRON TOMATO COULIS

YIELD: ½ GALLON / **ACTIVE TIME:** 5 MINUTES / **TOTAL TIME:** 25 MINUTES

Add this any white fish to make a simple weeknight meal feel like you're eating in a restaurant.

1. Add the oil, onion, garlic, bay leaves, salt, and pepper to a saucepan over medium heat and sweat until translucent.

2. Deglaze with wine and bring to simmer, add saffron water and tomato and cook for 5 minutes.

3. Season to taste.

INGREDIENTS:

2	TABLESPOONS EXTRA VIRGIN OLIVE OIL
¼	CUP MINCED ONIONS
¼	CUP SLICED GARLIC
3	BAY LEAVES
3	TABLESPOONS SEA SALT
2	TABLESPOONS BLACK PEPPER
½	CUP WHITE WINE
1	(6 OZ.) CAN SAN MARZANO DICED TOMATOES
3	TEASPOONS SAFFRON, SOAKED IN 1 CUP WATER

SAFFRON TOMATO FENNEL BROTH

YIELD: ½ GALLON / **ACTIVE TIME:** 5 MINUTES / **TOTAL TIME:** 25 MINUTES

This can be consumed hot, but also works as a cool palate cleanser, especially during the summer.

1. Add the olive oil, onions, parsnips, celery, fennel, garlic, bay leaves, salt, and pepper to a saucepan over medium heat and sweat until the onions are translucent.

2. Deglaze with wine and bring to simmer.

3. Add saffron water, tomato juice, and all of the fresh herbs and return to a simmer for 10 minutes.

4. Add lemon juice, vinegar, and salt and pepper, to taste.

INGREDIENTS:

- 2 TABLESPOONS EXTRA VIRGIN OLIVE OIL
- 1 CUP SMALL DICED ONIONS
- ½ CUP SMALL DICED PARSNIPS
- ½ CUP SMALL DICED CELERY
- ½ CUP SMALL DICED FENNEL (RESERVE FRONDS AND STALK)
- ¼ CUP SLICED GARLIC
- 3 BAY LEAVES
- 3 TABLESPOONS SEA SALT, PLUS MORE AS NEEDED
- 2 TABLESPOONS BLACK PEPPER, PLUS MORE AS NEEDED
- 2 CUPS WHITE WINE
- 2 TEASPOONS SAFFRON, SOAKED IN 1 QUART WATER
- 2 (64 OZ.) CANS SACRAMENTO TOMATO JUICE
- ½ OZ. OREGANO
- ½ OZ. BASIL
- ½ OZ. PARSLEY
- 1 OZ. FRESH LEMON JUICE
- 1 OZ. RED WINE VINEGAR

SALSA VERDE

YIELD: 8 SERVINGS / **ACTIVE TIME:** 5 MINUTES / **TOTAL TIME:** 5 MINUTES

Capers and mint place this squarely in the tradition of Italian cuisine, although you can use this sauce on anything.

1. In a blender, combine the parsley, mint, capers, anchovies, garlic, mustard, and vinegar and pulse until finely chopped, being sure not to overblend.

2. Add the oil and blend to combine.

3. Season with salt and pepper.

INGREDIENTS:

1	CUP FLAT LEAF PARSLEY
¼	CUP CHOCOLATE MINT
2	TABLESPOONS CAPERS
3	ANCHOVY FILLETS
1	GARLIC CLOVE, CHOPPED
1	TABLESPOON DIJON MUSTARD
2	TABLESPOONS RED WINE VINEGAR
1	CUP EXTRA VIRGIN OLIVE OIL
1	TEASPOON SEA SALT
½	TEASPOON FRESHLY GROUND BLACK PEPPER

TOMATO JAM

YIELD: ½ GALLON / **ACTIVE TIME:** 30 MINUTES / **TOTAL TIME:** 1 HOUR AND 30 MINUTES

This savory spread is amazing on sandwiches.

1. Wash the tomatoes and pat dry. Cut into large dice

2. Place all of the ingredients in a blender and puree until thick and smooth.

3. Prepare jars and hot water baths (see page 749 for additional canning instructions)

4. Pour the puree into a large pot. Bring to a boil, being sure to stir often once it starts to thicken.

5. The cooking can take 1 hour depending on how high your heat goes and the size of the pot. When the mixture hits 215°F, place jam into sterilized jars, wipe rims clean, and place sterilized rings and lids on jars.

6. Place in a hot water bath covered by 1" to 2" of water for 10 minutes. Remove and place on the towel covered counter overnight. Check lids for sealing. Label and store in the pantry for up to 1 year.

INGREDIENTS:

20   LBS. GREEN TOMATOES, CHOPPED

20   LBS. TOMATILLOS, PEELED AND CHOPPED

3   LBS. SUGAR

¼   CUP FRESH LEMON JUICE

¼   CUP FRESH LIME JUICE

2   JALAPEÑOS, DESTEMMED

½   CUP PINEAPPLE CHUNKS

1   GARLIC CLOVE

3   TABLESPOONS RICE WINE VINEGAR

3   TABLESPOONS AJI-MIRIN

4   BUNCHES CILANTRO, LEAVES AND STEMS

4   BUNCHES PARSLEY, LEAVES AND STEMS

2   BUNCHES OREGANO, LEAVES ONLY

2   BUNCHES MINT, LEAVES AND STEMS BLANCHED AND SHOCKED

2   BUNCHES BASIL, LEAVES AND STEMS BLANCHED AND SHOCKED

1   CUP FINE SEA SALT

¼   TABLESPOON BLACK PEPPER

WALNUT-GARLIC SAUCE

YIELD: 6 CUPS / **ACTIVE TIME:** 10 MINUTES / **TOTAL TIME:** 10 MINUTES

Dress up any pasta with this rich sauce, or use it as a dip for raw vegetables and pita.

1. Place the walnuts, garlic cloves, salt, and pepper into a food processor and pulse a few times until a very coarse, crumbly mixture forms. Do not over process.

2. Remove the walnuts from the processor into a bowl. Stir in the parsley, dill, honey, vinegar, and olive oil. If too thick, add a teaspoon more each of olive oil and vinegar. Sauce should resemble pesto—thick, but pourable.

3. Season to taste with more salt and pepper if desired.

4. Pour sauce into a jar and cover until ready to serve.

TIP: Making this sauce at least a few hours in advance and allowing it to sit covered at room temperature will allow the flavors to marry and the overall texture to improve significantly. It can also be prepared 1 day in advance and refrigerated. Bring to room temperature and stir well before serving.

INGREDIENTS:

1½ CUPS TOASTED WALNUTS, FULLY COOLED

10 GARLIC CLOVES, PEELED

1 TEASPOON SEA SALT

1 TEASPOON FRESHLY GROUND BLACK PEPPER

2 CUPS CHOPPED FLAT LEAF PARSLEY LEAVES

1 CUP CHOPPED DILL FRONDS

1 TEASPOON HONEY

2 TABLESPOONS RED WINE VINEGAR

1½ CUPS EXTRA VIRGIN OLIVE OIL

ZA'ATAR

YIELDS: 8 OZ. / **ACTIVE TIME**: 5 MINUTES / **TOTAL TIME**: 5 MINUTES

There are many variations on this Middle Eastern seasoning, but they all share in common a mixture of earthy dried herbs and crunchy toasted seeds. You'd be wise to double, or quadruple this recipe because once you have it in your kitchen, you'll want to try it on everything.

1. In a large mixing bowl, combine all of the ingredients and mix thoroughly.

INGREDIENTS:

1	TABLESPOON CUMIN
1	TABLESPOON SUMAC
1	TABLESPOON THYME
2	TEASPOONS HEMP SEEDS
2	TEASPOONS CRUSHED TOASTED SUNFLOWER SEEDS
2	TABLESPOONS SESAME SEEDS
2	TABLESPOONS SEA SALT
1	TABLESPOON BLACK PEPPER
2	TABLESPOONS OREGANO
2	TABLESPOONS BASIL
2	TABLESPOONS PARSLEY
1	TABLESPOON GARLIC POWDER
1	TABLESPOON ONION POWDER

BREAD

*B*read in its many forms is considered a blessing to any table. From challah to laffa, here are the many bread recipes to break and eat with family and friends.

BALSAMIC APPLE DATE CHALLAH

YIELD: 2 LOAVES / **ACTIVE TIME:** 35 MINUTES / **TOTAL TIME:** 6 HOURS

This beloved loaf of bread is made fashionable in this recipe that is intensified with a combination of sweet-and-sour balsamic-glazed apples and dates.

1. In a small bowl, combine the yeast, 1 teaspoon sugar, and lukewarm water. Stir and allow to stand until it becomes foamy on top, about 10 minutes.

2. In a large bowl or stand mixer fitted with whisk attachment, mix together 1½ cups flour, salt, remaining sugar, honey, vanilla, cinnamon, and nutmeg. Add the foamy water and yeast mixture to the flour mixture along with oil and mix thoroughly.

3. Add another cup of flour and the eggs and whisk until smooth.

4. Switch to the dough hook attachment if you are using a stand mixer. Add another 1½ cups flour and then remove from the bowl and place on a floured surface. Knead remaining flour into dough, continuing to knead for around 10 minutes.

5. Place dough in a greased bowl, cover with a damp towel, and allow to rise for 3 to 4 hours.

6. To make the filling, combine the apples, dates, salt, cinnamon stick, water, red wine, and sugar in a medium saucepan and bring to a boil. Lower heat to medium and simmer until the mixture is reduced, about 10 minutes. Add the vinegar and simmer for another 3 minutes.

7. Remove from heat and allow to cool for 5 minutes. Remove cinnamon sticks and place the filling in a food processor fitted with the blade attachment and pulse until smooth.

8. After the challah is done rising, cut the dough in half. To be as precise as possible, use a scale to measure the weight.

9. Using a rolling pin, roll out the first ball into a rectangle. Spread around half, perhaps slightly less, of the filling in an even layer, leaving ½" all around without filling. Working quickly, start rolling up the dough toward you. Try and keep the roll relatively tight as you go. Pinch the end when you finish.

INGREDIENTS:

DOUGH

1½	TABLESPOONS YEAST
½	CUP SUGAR, PLUS 1 TEASPOON, DIVIDED
1¼	CUPS LUKEWARM WATER
4½-5	CUPS BREAD FLOUR
½	TABLESPOON SALT
3	TABLESPOONS HONEY
2	TEASPOONS VANILLA
1	TEASPOON CINNAMON
¼	TEASPOON NUTMEG
¼	CUP VEGETABLE OIL
2	WHOLE EGGS

FILLING

3	GALA APPLES, PEELED, CORED, AND DICED
1	CUP PITTED AND CHOPPED DATES
½	TEASPOON SALT
1	CINNAMON STICK
¼	CUP WATER
¼	CUP RED WINE
1	TABLESPOON SUGAR
2	TABLESPOONS BALSAMIC VINEGAR

TOPPING

1	EGG, BEATEN
1	TEASPOON HONEY
	COARSE SEA SALT, TO TASTE (OPTIONAL)
	CINNAMON SUGAR, TO TASTE (OPTIONAL)

10. Create a pinwheel shaped-challah by snaking the dough around and around in a circle around itself. When finished, tuck the end under the challah neatly and pinch lightly. This doesn't have to be perfect—remember, as long as it tastes good, almost no one (maybe except that judgmental great aunt) will care what it looks like. Place the loaf on a baking sheet to proof for the second rise before baking.

11. Repeat with the other half of the dough.

12. Preheat the oven to 350°F.

13. Allow challahs to rise another 45 minutes, or until you can see that both loaves have grown. Beat 1 egg with 1 teaspoon honey. Brush liberally over each challah. Top challah with coarse sea salt and cinnamon sugar, if desired.

14. Bake for 25 to 30 minutes, or until the middle looks like it has just set, and the color is golden.

Bialy, page 554

BIALY

YIELD: 12 BIALYS / **ACTIVE TIME:** 1 HOUR / **TOTAL TIME:** 10 HOURS

When it comes to the difference between bagels and bialys, why choose sides? All we know is that the little indentation in the top means more room for extra garlic, onions, or seeds, which we are clearly all for.

DOUGH

1. Combine the flour, salt, yeast, and onion powder in the bowl of a stand mixer and mix well by hand. Add the water and mix, using the dough hook attachment, until just combined, 1 or 2 minutes at low speed. Stop the mixer, cover the bowl, and let rest for 20 minutes.

2. Uncover the bowl and continue kneading at medium speed for 8 minutes, or until the dough is smooth and elastic.

3. Cover and refrigerate the dough overnight for a slow, cool rise to develop the dough's flavor.

4. The next day, divide the dough into 12 pieces (they'll weigh just under 4 ounces each) and round each into a ball. Place on a lightly oiled baking sheet, cover with greased plastic, and let rise at room temperature for 1 hour, or until puffy.

5. Preheat the oven to 475°F.

6. Pulse the onion in a food processor until very finely chopped, but not liquid. Add in the poppy seeds, salt, and pepper.

7. Heat the oil in a saucepan and cook the onion mixture for a few minutes over medium-low heat until the liquid cooks off and the onion is very slightly caramelized. Remove from heat and let cool.

8. Lightly sprinkle 2 baking sheets with cornmeal. Take each dough ball and stretch it into a bagel shape about 6" to 7" in diameter, without puncturing the center, and being sure to leave a wide, flat indentation where the hole would be. Place a few inches apart on the prepared baking sheets, 6 per pan. Place a scant teaspoon of the onion filling in the indentation and spread it out with your fingers. Don't overfill; a little goes a long way.

9. Bake for 8 to 10 minutes, until light golden brown. Remove the bialys from the oven and serve warm; or cool on a rack and save for toasting later.

TIP: Resist the temptation to be generous with the onions; the moisture in them can keep the center of the bialy from cooking at the same speed as the edges, causing the center to puff up like a topknot.

INGREDIENTS:

DOUGH

7	CUPS UNBLEACHED BREAD FLOUR
2¾	TEASPOONS SALT
1¼	TEASPOONS INSTANT YEAST
½	TEASPOON ONION POWDER
2¼	CUPS WATER

FILLING

1	MEDIUM ONION, PEELED AND QUARTERED
1	TEASPOON POPPY SEEDS
⅛	TEASPOON SALT
3–4	GRINDS COARSELY GROUND BLACK PEPPER
1	TABLESPOON OLIVE OIL
	CORNMEAL, FOR PANS

CAST-IRON CHALLAH BREAD

YIELD: 2 LOAVES / **ACTIVE TIME:** 30 MINUTES / **TOTAL TIME:** 3 HOURS AND 40 MINUTES

Baked in cast-iron skillets, these loaves are dense, soft, and subtly sweet.

1. In a small bowl, dissolve yeast and 1½ tablespoons sugar in 2 cups warm water (110°F). Cover and set aside for 10 minutes or until bubbles form.

2. In the bowl of a stand mixer fitted with a dough hook, combine flour, remaining sugar, oil, salt, 1 whole egg, and 1 egg white. Mix at a very low speed for 5 minutes.

3. With the mixer running, slowly add the warm water and yeast mixture and continue to knead for 10 minutes.

4. The dough should feel soft and not too sticky. Transfer dough to an oiled bowl, cover with a towel, and allow to rest in a warm place for 1 hour, or until it has doubled in size. Punch down the dough, cover it, and let it rise again in a warm place for 30 minutes.

5. Coat two 8" cast-iron skillets with nonstick cooking spray.

6. Turn the dough out onto a lightly floured surface and divide into 8 equal balls. Roll each ball into a strand about 12" long. Weave 2 horizontal and 2 vertical strands to form a hashtag. Braid strands, moving right to left, always taking the strand underneath and crossing it over the next strand until a circle has formed. Repeat to form a second challah.

7. Tuck remaining ends under, and place each challah in one of the prepared cast-iron pans.

8. In a small bowl, beat together the remaining egg yolk and 1 teaspoon water; brush the top of each challah with egg wash.

9. Set pans in a warm place; allow dough to rise, uncovered, for 1 hour or until doubled in size.

10. Preheat the oven to 350°F.

11. Bake for 35 to 40 minutes, until golden brown. Let cool before serving.

INGREDIENTS:

3	TABLESPOONS ACTIVE DRY YEAST
¾	CUP SUGAR, PLUS 1½ TABLESPOONS
10	CUPS ALL-PURPOSE FLOUR, PLUS MORE FOR DUSTING
¾	CUP VEGETABLE OIL
1	TABLESPOON SALT
2	EGGS (1 WHOLE, 1 SEPARATED)
	NONSTICK COOKING SPRAY

CHALLAH FRENCH TOAST

YIELD: 6 SERVINGS / **ACTIVE TIME:** 10 MINUTES / **TOTAL TIME:** 30 MINUTES

Do people make French toast from anything else? Once you taste how day-old challah makes this classic breakfast treat something magical, you'll never use any other bread for this quick and easy recipe.

1. In a large bowl, combine the eggs, milk, sugar, vanilla bean seeds, and salt and whisk well.

2. Place the challah slices in a shallow baking dish and pour the egg mixture over the bread. Flip the bread over to absorb the egg mixture into both sides and let soak for 5 minutes. Refrigerate for 20 minutes before cooking; this will create a crispy texture and a light custard creamy texture on the inside.

3. Add 2 tablespoons butter to a cast-iron skillet over medium-high heat. When the butter is sizzling, add the soaked challah and lower the heat slightly. Cook 2 to 3 minutes on each side until golden brown. Repeat with the remaining bread adding more butter as needed. You can keep the finished slices warm on a sheet tray in the oven while cooking the remaining batches.

4. Serve hot with maple syrup.

INGREDIENTS:

6	LARGE EGGS
2	CUPS WHOLE MILK
¼	CUP SUGAR
1	VANILLA BEAN, SEEDS SCRAPED
1	PINCH SEA SALT
1	LOAF OF CHALLAH (SEE PAGE 129), DRIED OUT OR DAY-OLD, CUT INTO ¾" SLICES
2	TABLESPOONS UNSALTED BUTTER, PLUS MORE AS NEEDED
	MAPLE SYRUP, FOR SERVING

Chocolate Babka, page 560

CHOCOLATE BABKA

YIELD: 4 SERVINGS / **ACTIVE TIME:** 1 HOUR / **TOTAL TIME:** 24 HOURS

This sweet cake is made from a dough that is doubled and twisted, and rises up to fluffy perfection thanks to yeast. Babka is filled with cinnamon and/or chocolate, which makes a marble pattern when sliced. It originates from Eastern Europe and was made known to the world thanks to that one *Seinfeld* episode.

1. Combine the yeast, milk, sugar, and eggs in the bowl of a stand mixer fitted with the dough hook and allow yeast to bloom. On a very low speed mix in flour, and when fully incorporated add the butter. Dough will be very sticky and elastic and will not want to form a ball. Mix until all the butter is dissolved into dough and smooth, about 15 minutes. Cover and refrigerate the dough overnight.

2. The next day, turn the dough out onto a clean work surface and fold it in over itself for 20 minutes, until the dough forms a ball. Use a bench scraper to assist in the folding process. The dough will be very sticky and you should avoid putting any extra flour on at this point. You want the dough to form a ball by creating gluten through the slap folding process. Slap the dough on the work surface and stretch it until elongated and fold it in on itself. Eventually, enough gluten will be created and the dough will become less sticky and actually form a smooth ball. Use a bench scraper to help form the ball.

3. Using a little oil on your hands turn the dough into a bowl and refrigerate it for 4 hours.

4. To make the filling, add all of the ingredients, setting aside ¼ cup chopped chocolate, to a small saucepan over medium heat and cook until well combined. Allow the chocolate to cool to room temperature before using or the dough will become sticky and unmanageable.

5. On a lightly floured surface, roll out dough to ¼" thick. Don't worry about the square shape.

6. Leaving about a ½" rim around the dough spread the chocolate filling evenly and then sprinkle with the reserved chopped chocolate and pistachios. Make sure to work quickly as it's easier to spread the chocolate filling on chilled dough.

7. Roll the log very tightly. Using a bench scraper, cut the log in half lengthwise and turn the chocolate filling facing up.

INGREDIENTS:

DOUGH

½	OZ. DRIED YEAST
1	CUP FULL-FAT MILK
½	CUP SUGAR
2	EGGS
4	CUPS ALL-PURPOSE WHITE FLOUR (13.2% PROTEIN)
½	CUP UNSALTED BUTTER, CUBED AND SOFTENED

CHOCOLATE FILLING

2	CUPS ROUGHLY CHOPPED 70% COCOA CHOCOLATE
¾	CUP UNSALTED BUTTER
½	CUP SUGAR
2	TABLESPOONS COCOA POWDER
½	CUP CHOPPED PISTACHIOS (RESERVED FOR SPRINKLING)

SUGAR SYRUP GLAZE

1¼	CUPS SUGAR
¼	CUP WATER

8. Braid the two strips with the chocolate filling still facing up.

9. Cut the braid in half so you now have 2 loaves.

10. Put each loaf in a greased parchment-lined bread pan and allow to rise for 4 hours, or overnight in the refrigerator, until the dough has doubled in size.

11. Preheat the oven to 375°F.

12. Bake until golden brown and delicious, about 40 minutes.

13. While baking the dough, combine sugar and water in a small saucepan and bring to boil. Cook for 5 minutes and allow to cool completely to room temperature before brushing on finished Babka.

CHOCOLATE CRANBERRY
CHALLAH ROLLS WITH CITRUS SUGAR

YIELD: 1 LARGE LOAF / **ACTIVE TIME:** 40 MINUTES / **TOTAL TIME:** 5 HOURS

Cake for breakfast is meshuggeneh, but challah . . . eh, live a little. Chocolate and cranberry braided throughout and sprinkled with a citrusy sugar make it a sweet treat perfect for starting the day, nibbling with coffee, or ending a meal.

1. In a small bowl, combine the yeast, 1 teaspoon sugar, and luke-warm water. Allow to stand for about 10 minutes, until it becomes foamy on top.

2. In the bowl of a stand mixer fitted with the whisk attachment, add 1½ cups flour, salt, the remaining sugar, vanilla, cinnamon, and nutmeg. After the water and yeast mixture has become foamy, add to the flour mixture along with the oil and whisk thoroughly.

3. Add another cup flour and the eggs and mix until smooth. Switch to the dough hook attachment if you are using a stand mixer.

4. Add another 1½ cups flour, mixing thoroughly and then remove from the bowl and place on a floured surface. Knead remaining ½ cup flour into dough, continuing to knead for about 5 minutes. Try not to add too much flour—the less flour you add, the lighter the challah.

5. Place dough in a greased bowl and cover with a damp towel. Allow to rise 3 to 4 hours, punching down at least once if possible.

6. Preheat the oven to 350°F.

7. In a small bowl, combine sanding sugar and orange zest, mix well, and set aside.

8. Braid challah into desired shape (1 large loaf, 2 smaller loaves, or rolls). Allow challah to rise another 45 minutes to 1 hour, or until you can see the size has grown and the challah seems light.

9. In a small bowl, beat the egg yolks with 1 teaspoon water.

10. Brush egg wash liberally over challah and then sprinkle citrus sugar on top.

11. If making one large challah, bake for about 30 minutes; if making two smaller loaves bake for 24 minutes; if making rolls, bake for 22 minutes, or until golden on top.

INGREDIENTS:

CHALLAH

1½	TABLESPOON DRY YEAST
½	CUP SUGAR, PLUS 1 TEASPOON, DIVIDED
1¼	CUPS LUKEWARM WATER
4½-5	CUPS ALL-PURPOSE UNBLEACHED FLOUR
½	TABLESPOON SALT
1	TEASPOON VANILLA
1	TEASPOON CINNAMON
¼	TEASPOON NUTMEG
¼	CUP VEGETABLE OIL
2	EGGS
½	CUP DARK OR SEMI-SWEET CHOCOLATE CHIPS
½	CUP DRIED CRANBERRIES

TOPPING

½	CUP SANDING SUGAR
½	TABLESPOON ORANGE ZEST
2	EGG YOLKS
1	TEASPOON WATER

EGGY CHALLAH TOAST

YIELD: 2 SERVINGS / **ACTIVE TIME:** 20 MINUTES / **TOTAL TIME:** 30 MINUTES

This combination of sweet coconut milk and herbs creates a surprising and savory twist on a classic.

1. In a bowl, combine the eggs, coconut milk, brown sugar, soy sauce, fish sauce, garlic, turmeric, salt, cilantro, scallions, and black pepper and whisk well.

2. Place the slices of challah in the coconut batter and pierce each piece with a fork a few times to help promote soakage. Let sit for 10 minutes, flipping over several times throughout.

3. Add 1 tablespoon coconut oil to a cast-iron skillet over medium heat. Carefully transfer 2 of the soaked slices to the skillet and lower the heat to medium-low. Cook undisturbed for 2 minutes per side. Repeat with the remaining slices.

4. Enjoy hot with a drizzle of coconut milk and honey.

INGREDIENTS:

2	EGGS
⅓	CUP COCONUT MILK
2	TABLESPOONS BROWN SUGAR
2	TEASPOONS SOY SAUCE
2	TEASPOONS FISH SAUCE
2	GARLIC CLOVES, GRATED
¼	TEASPOON TURMERIC
½	TEASPOON KOSHER SALT
1	TABLESPOON FINELY CHOPPED CILANTRO, FINELY CHOPPED
1	SCALLION, GREEN TIPS ONLY, FINELY CHOPPED
½	TEASPOON BLACK PEPPER
4	SLICES OF DAY-OLD CHALLAH, ½" CUT ON DIAGONAL
¼	TEASPOON CHILI OIL
1	TABLESPOON COCONUT OIL
	COCONUT MILK, FOR SERVING
	HONEY, FOR SERVING

Honey Brioche, page 566

HONEY BRIOCHE

YIELD: 2 BATCHES / **ACTIVE TIME:** 35 MINUTES / **TOTAL TIME:** 7 HOURS

Top-quality honey makes all the difference here, as it both enriches the flavor of this brioche and helps keep it moist. The brioche is best eaten the day it is baked, although it can be tightly wrapped and stored for a day or two or frozen for up to 1 month; thaw, still wrapped, at room temperature. Make it as a whole loaf or turn it into rolls. Any way you bake it, it's a winner.

1. Prepare the sponge in the bowl of the heavy-duty mixer by combining the milk, yeast, and honey and stir to blend.

2. Let stand until foamy, about 5 minutes. Add the egg and half the flour and stir to blend. The sponge will be soft and sticky. Sprinkle with the remaining flour to cover the sponge dough, but don't mix it in.

3. Set aside to rest, uncovered, for 30 minutes. The sponge should erupt slightly, cracking the layer of flour. This indicates that the yeast is alive and doing its job.

4. Add the honey, salt, eggs, and flour to the sponge. Mix at low speed just until the ingredients come together, about 1 minute. Increase the mixer speed to medium and beat for 5 minutes.

5. Before adding the butter, it should be the same consistency as the dough. To prepare the butter, place it on a flat work surface, and with the pastry scraper, smear it bit by bit across the surface. (If you do not have a pastry scraper, use the back of a large metal spoon.) When it is ready, the butter should be smooth, soft, but still cool—not warm, oily, or greasy.

6. With the mixer on medium-low speed, add the butter a few tablespoons at a time. When all the butter has been added, increase the mixer speed to medium-high for 1 minute, then reduce the speed to medium and continue to beat for 5 minutes more. The dough will be soft and pliable but shouldn't stick to your hands.

7. Cover the bowl tightly with plastic wrap. Let the dough rise at room temperature until doubled in size, about 2 hours.

8. Punch down the dough. Cover the bowl tightly with plastic wrap and refrigerate the dough overnight, or for at least 4 hours, during which time it should double in size again.

INGREDIENTS:

SPONGE

- ⅓ CUP WHOLE MILK, LUKEWARM
- 1 PACKAGE (ABOUT 2 TEASPOONS) ACTIVE DRY YEAST OR INSTANT YEAST
- 1 TABLESPOON MILD, FRAGRANT HONEY, SUCH AS LAVENDER
- 1 LARGE EGG, LIGHTLY BEATEN
- 2 CUPS UNBLEACHED ALL-PURPOSE FLOUR

DOUGH

- ⅓ CUP MILD, FRAGRANT HONEY, SUCH AS LAVENDER
- 1 TEASPOON FINE SEA SALT
- 4 LARGE EGGS, LIGHTLY BEATEN
- 1½ CUPS UNBLEACHED ALL-PURPOSE FLOUR
- ¾ CUP UNSALTED BUTTER

EGG WASH

- 1 LARGE EGG, LIGHTLY BEATEN

9. Divide the dough into 12 equal pieces, each weighing about 2½ oz. Roll each piece of dough tightly into a ball and place 6 pieces in a bread pan, staggering them in two rows of 3; there will be some space left at either end of the loaf but it will fill up when the dough rises again. Cover the pans with a clean cloth and let the dough rise at room temperature until doubled in size, 1 to 1½ hours.

10. Center a rack in the oven. Preheat the oven to 375°F

11. Lightly brush the dough with the beaten egg. Working quickly, using the tip of a pair of sharp scissors, snip a cross on the top of each dough ball; this will help the brioche rise evenly as it bakes. Bake until the loaves are puffed and deeply golden, 30 to 35 minutes. Place the pans on a baking rack to cool. Turn the loaves out after they have cooled.

TIP: When using instant yeast, there is no need to let the yeast proof in warm milk; it can be added directly to the flour. Don't omit the milk, however, as this will change the balance of liquid to dry ingredients in the recipe. Instant yeast and active dry yeast can be used interchangeably in the same quantities.

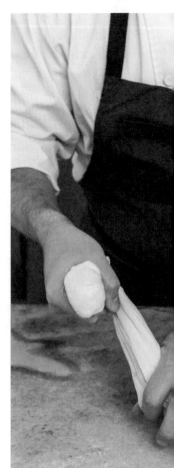

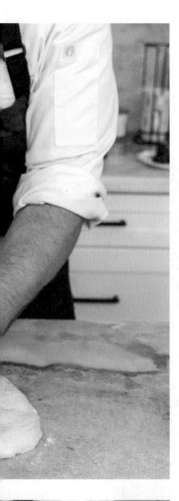

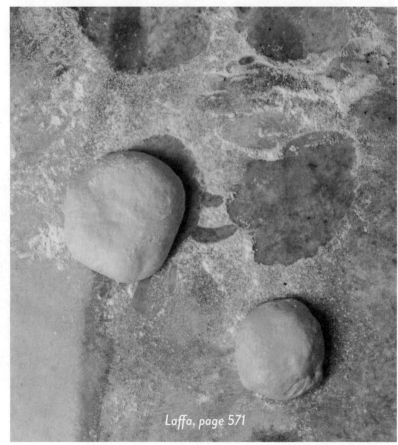

Laffa, page 571

LAFFA

YIELD: 8 BREADS / **ACTIVE TIME:** 30 MINUTES / **TOTAL TIME:** 1 HOUR AND 30 MINUTES

This flatbread is common across the Middle East and is thicker and chewier than pita. Often served with kebabs and shawarma, it also goes very well with all manner of dips.

1. In a bowl, combine the water, yeast, and sugar and let stand until foamy, about 5 to 10 minutes.

2. Combine the all-purpose flour, bread flour, and salt in the bowl of a stand mixer fitted with a dough hook. Mix on low until fully blended.

3. Add yeast mixture, another ½ cup water, and oil and mix on low until a ball forms and pulls away from the sides of the mixer. If after a minute or so a ball is not forming add some more water by the tablespoon to bring it together. The moment the dough ball is pulling away from the bottom and sides of the mixing bowl cleanly, immediately add another ½ cup water and continue to mix until fully incorporated and hydrated. The dough should feel tacky when slapped with a clean hand but it should not be sticky. If it sticks, add a touch more flour, a tablespoon at a time.

4. Cover the dough with plastic wrap and let rise at room temperature until doubled in size, about an hour. Or let it rise in the refrigerator overnight.

5. Set a baking stone or an inverted sheet pan on an oven rack in the upper third of the oven and preheat it to 500°F degrees.

6. Roll the dough into 8 balls the size of baseballs. Cover with a cloth and let rise until they are the size of softballs.

7. Roll each dough ball as thin as possible—less than ⅛" is ideal—on a floured surface using a floured rolling pin.

8. When the dough is rolled out and the hot baking stone is ready, carefully drape one laffa over your hand and stretch, quickly lay the stretched laffa onto the baking stone, quickly pulling any wrinkles flat.

9. Bake laffa until puffy and cooked through, about 1 minute. Serve immediately.

INGREDIENTS:

1½	CUPS WARM WATER (ABOUT 80°F), DIVIDED
2½	TEASPOONS ACTIVE DRY YEAST
2	TEASPOONS SUGAR
2	CUPS ALL-PURPOSE FLOUR
2	CUPS BREAD FLOUR
1	TEASPOON SEA SALT
2	TABLESPOONS OLIVE OIL

RYE BREAD

YIELD: 1 LOAF / **ACTIVE TIME:** 55 MINUTES / **TOTAL TIME:** 3 HOURS

Some techniques have changed over the ages, but one thing is for sure: rye is a staple on many a table and is, more often than not, begging to be piled high with corned beef. Before the mid-19th century, all breads were made with sour starters. For Jewish rye bread, the sour rye starter was called roshtshine. To add color, moistness, and a deeper flavor, bakers used an altus or alte brot, old bread.

1. In a large bowl, or the mixing bowl of a stand mixer fitted with the dough hook, combine the yeast and water. Let sit until foamy, 5 to 10 minutes. If the yeast doesn't react, discard the mixture and start again with fresh yeast.

2. In another large bowl, whisk together the flours and salt.

3. Add the brown sugar, molasses, oil, and caraway seeds to the yeast mixture. Add 2 cups of the flour mixture, and stir with a wooden spoon or mix on low speed for 1 to 2 minutes, until well blended. Then add the remaining flour.

4. Add the remaining flour, stir the dough well with a wooden spoon, then turn it out onto a lightly floured surface and knead for 5 to 10 minutes, until the dough is smooth, elastic, and slightly tacky. Or mix it with the dough hook for 1 minute on low speed, then 3 to 5 minutes on medium speed, until the dough pulls into a ball and is smooth and slightly tacky but not sticky. Remove the dough hook.

5. If kneading by hand, spread a little oil in the bowl (you don't need to clean it first), and place the dough ball back in the bowl. Cover with a tea towel or plastic wrap and set aside to rise until doubled in size, about 1 hour.

6. Punch down the dough, place on a lightly floured surface, and knead a few times. Shape the dough into a roundish oval, smoothing the top with your hands as you work. Place on a parchment-lined baking pan, cover, and set aside to rise, 45 minutes to 1 hour.

7. Preheat the oven to 350°F.

8. Use a sharp knife to make three or four shallow, diagonal slashes in the top of the loaf. Bake until the loaf is firm, golden on the bottom, and sounds hollow when tapped, about 30 to 35 minutes. Transfer to a rack to cool.

INGREDIENTS:

- 1 PACKET ACTIVE DRY YEAST, ABOUT 2¼ TEASPOONS
- 1¼ CUPS WARM WATER
- 2 CUPS ALL-PURPOSE FLOUR
- 1 CUP WHITE WHOLE-WHEAT FLOUR
- 1 CUP RYE FLOUR
- ½ TEASPOON SEA SALT
- 2 TABLESPOONS BROWN SUGAR
- 2 TABLESPOONS MOLASSES
- 2 TABLESPOONS CANOLA OR GRAPESEED OIL
- 1 TABLESPOON CARAWAY SEEDS

DESSERTS & BEVERAGES

We're not just talking milk and honey... discover the recipes to quench your thirst and finish meals with just the perfect amount of sweetness.

ALL-BUTTER PASTRY DOUGH

YIELD: 1 PIE CRUST / **ACTIVE TIME:** 20 MINUTES / **TOTAL TIME:** 1 HOUR AND 20 MINUTES

Use this for any and all pies.

1. In a bowl, combine the flour, sugar, and salt, whisk well, and then blend in butter with your fingertips or a pastry blender (or pulse in a food processor) just until most of the mixture resembles coarse meal with small (roughly pea-size) butter lumps.

2. Drizzle 9 tablespoons ice water evenly over the mixture and gently stir with a fork (or pulse in the food processor) until incorporated.

3. Squeeze a small handful. If it doesn't hold together, add more ice water 1 tablespoon at a time, stirring (or pulsing) until just incorporated, then test again. Do not overwork the mixture, or pastry will be tough.

4. Turn out mixture onto a lightly floured surface and divide into 8 portions. With the heel of your hand, smear each portion once or twice in a forward motion to help distribute fat. Gather dough together with a bench scraper and press into a ball, then flatten into a 6" disk. Refrigerate dough, wrapped in plastic wrap, until firm, at least 1 hour.

INGREDIENTS:

2½ CUPS ALL-PURPOSE FLOUR (NOT UNBLEACHED)

2 TEASPOONS SUGAR

¾ TEASPOON SEA SALT

2 STICKS OF COLD UNSALTED BUTTER, CUT INTO ½" PIECES

9-12 TABLESPOONS ICE WATER

CALVADOS APPLESAUCE

YIELD: 6 SERVINGS / **ACTIVE TIME:** 25 MINUTES / **TOTAL TIME:** 45 MINUTES

I f you like applesauce, and you like Calvados, you'll love this, which works as both a dessert and a sweet side dish.

1. Peel and core apples, then cut into 1" pieces.

2. Add apples, water, sugar, zest, and cinnamon to a saucepan over medium-high heat and bring to a boil, stirring occasionally, then reduce heat and simmer, covered, for 15 minutes.

3. Remove the lid and simmer until most of the liquid is evaporated, 5 to 10 minutes. Add Calvados and simmer, stirring occasionally, 1 minute. Mash apples with a potato masher or a fork to a coarse sauce, then remove from heat and let cool.

INGREDIENTS:

1	LB. GALA APPLES
½	CUP WATER
½	CUP SUGAR
½	TEASPOON LEMON ZEST
⅛	TEASPOON CINNAMON
2	TABLESPOONS CALVADOS

Apple & Calvados Tart, page 582

APPLE & CALVADOS TART

YIELD: 8 SERVINGS / **ACTIVE TIME:** 2 HOURS AND 30 MINUTES / **TOTAL TIME:** 3 HOURS AND 45 MINUTES

Sweet, spicy, and caramelized flavors all rolled up into one, this easy Rosh Hashanah apple dessert is the perfect excuse to practice your French (and break out the Calvados).

INGREDIENTS:

	ALL-BUTTER PASTRY DOUGH (SEE PAGE 578)
1¾	LBS. GALA APPLES
2	TEASPOONS FRESH LEMON JUICE
⅓	CUP PLUS ½ TABLESPOON GRANULATED SUGAR
	CALVADOS APPLESAUCE (SEE RECIPE)
3	TABLESPOONS UNSALTED BUTTER, CUT INTO ½" PIECES
1½	TABLESPOONS APPLE JELLY
1	CUP CHILLED HEAVY CREAM
1	TABLESPOON CONFECTIONERS' SUGAR
1½	TABLESPOONS CALVADOS

1. Using a floured rolling pin, roll out pastry on a lightly floured surface into a rough 16" round (⅛" thick), then transfer carefully to a large parchment-lined baking sheet. Loosely fold in the edge of pastry where necessary to fit on the baking sheet; cover loosely with plastic wrap then refrigerate for 30 minutes.

2. Preheat the oven to 425°F.

3. While pastry is chilling, peel and core apples, then cut into ⅛"-thick slices. Toss slices with lemon juice and ⅓ cup sugar.

4. Put the baking sheet with pastry on a work surface and unfold any edges so pastry is flat. Spread applesauce over pastry, leaving a 2" border, and top sauce with sliced apples, mounding slightly.

5. Fold edges of dough over filling, partially covering apples (center will not be covered) and pleating dough as necessary. Dot apples with butter, then brush pastry edges lightly with water and sprinkle with remaining sugar. Bake in the middle of the oven until the pastry is golden and apples are tender, 40 to 45 minutes.

6. While the tart is baking, melt apple jelly in a small saucepan over moderately low heat, stirring.

7. Once baked, slide the tart on parchment onto a rack, then brush with melted jelly and let cool until warm or room temperature.

8. In a bowl, combine the cream and confectioners' sugar and beat with an electric mixer until cream just holds soft peaks, then beat in Calvados.

9. Serve tart topped with dollops of Calvados cream.

APPLE BRIOCHE TART

YIELD: 12" TART / **ACTIVE TIME:** 1 HOUR / **TOTAL TIME:** 14 HOURS

This fluffy golden-brown brioche tart with apple slices inside is a nice balance of lightly sweet and gently decadent.

1. In the bowl of a stand mixer fitted with the dough hook, combine the flour, sugar, and salt and mix on low to combine. Add the yeast and mix to combine, 10 to 15 seconds more. Add the eggs and milk and mix for 4 minutes. The dough should form a sticky, shaggy ball around the hook.

2. Increase the speed to medium and slowly add the butter 1 tablespoon at a time, being careful to incorporate each addition before adding the next. Scrape the bowl down once or twice to make sure everything is homogeneous. Then knead the dough until it is smooth and uniform, 1 minute more.

3. Grease a large bowl with nonstick spray. Transfer the dough to the bowl, cover the bowl with plastic wrap, and refrigerate for at least 12 hours.

4. Use the butter to generously grease an 18" x 13" baking sheet, including the rim.

5. On a lightly floured surface, roll out the dough to a ½" thick rectangle a little larger than the pan, so that the dough comes up the sides of the pan.

6. Roll up the dough around the rolling pin and transfer the dough to the prepared baking sheet.

7. Use a pastry wheel to trim the edges so they are flush with the edges of the pan. Cover the baking sheet with greased plastic wrap and let the dough rise in a warm place for 30 to 35 minutes.

8. Preheat the oven to 350°F with a rack in the middle.

9. Meanwhile, peel, quarter, and core the apples, then slice crosswise ⅛" to ¼" thick.

10. In a small bowl, combine the brown sugar and cinnamon and whisk well. Uncover the dough and sprinkle it evenly with half the cinnamon sugar. Arrange the apple slices across the dough. Sprinkle the remaining cinnamon sugar evenly over the apples. Finish with the salt.

11. Bake the tart until the edges of the crust are golden brown, the apples are tender when pierced with the tip of a paring knife, and the sugar has caramelized, 32 to 36 minutes. Cool the tart for at least 15 minutes before slicing and serving, warm or at room temperature. This tart is best the same day it's made.

INGREDIENTS:

5 CUPS PLUS 3 TABLESPOONS BREAD FLOUR

½ CUP GRANULATED SUGAR

1 TABLESPOON FINE SEA SALT

1 TABLESPOON INSTANT YEAST

5 LARGE COLD EGGS, LIGHTLY WHISKED

1 CUP WHOLE MILK

14 OZ. UNSALTED BUTTER, AT ROOM TEMPERATURE

5 APPLES

½ CUP BROWN SUGAR

2 TABLESPOONS CINNAMON

1 TEASPOON SEA SALT

APPLE CAKE

YIELD: 9 SERVINGS / **ACTIVE TIME:** 10 MINUTES / **TOTAL TIME:** 1 HOUR AND 10 MINUTES

L'shanah tovah! If you want your new year—and Rosh Hashanah celebration—to be truly sweet, you're going to need a lot of apples. This apple cake recipe is the kind you keep in your back pocket for celebrations, no matter the time of year

1. Preheat the oven to 350°F.

2. In a large bowl, cream ¼ cup butter and 1 cup sugar. Beat in egg and vanilla.

3. In a separate bowl, combine flour, baking soda, cinnamon, salt and nutmeg, mix well, and gradually add to the creamed mixture. Stir in apples and walnuts.

4. Pour the batter into a greased 8" square baking dish. Bake for 40 to 45 minutes, or until a toothpick inserted in the center comes out clean.

5. Meanwhile, add the remaining butter to a saucepan over medium heat. Once the butter is melted, stir in the remaining sugar, brown sugar, and cream and bring to a boil, stirring constantly. Reduce heat and simmer, uncovered, for 15 minutes, stirring occasionally. Serve over warm cake.

INGREDIENTS:

¾ CUP UNSALTED BUTTER, SOFTENED AND DIVIDED

1½ CUPS SUGAR, DIVIDED

1 EGG

1 TEASPOON VANILLA EXTRACT

1 CUP ALL-PURPOSE FLOUR

1 TEASPOON BAKING SODA

½ TEASPOON CINNAMON

¼ TEASPOON SALT

¼ TEASPOON NUTMEG

2 MEDIUM TART APPLES, PEELED AND GRATED

½ CUP CHOPPED WALNUTS

BUTTER SAUCE

½ CUP BUTTER

½ CUP SUGAR

½ CUP PACKED BROWN SUGAR

½ CUP HALF-AND-HALF CREAM

APPLE WALNUT BUNDT CAKE

YIELD: 12 SERVINGS / **ACTIVE TIME:** 20 MINUTES / **TOTAL TIME:** 3 HOURS

This fragrant olive oil cake stays moist and flavorful for over a week, so feel free to make it a few days before serving. The caramel glaze is optional, but highly recommended.

1. Thirty minutes to 1 hour ahead, set the eggs on the counter at room temperature.

2. Twenty minutes or longer before toasting the walnuts, set an oven rack in the lower third of the oven and preheat to 350°F.

3. Spread the walnuts evenly on a cookie sheet and bake for 5 minutes. Turn the walnuts onto a clean dish town and roll and rub them around to loosen the skins. Discard any loose skins and let the nuts cool completely. Chop medium coarse.

4. In a medium bowl, combine the flour, baking soda, salt, and cinnamon and whisk well.

5. Peel, core, and cut the apples into ⅛" to ¼" dice.

6. Add the eggs to the bowl of a stand mixer, followed by the oil, sugars, and the vanilla. Attach the flat beater and beat on medium for 1 minute, until blended.

7. Add the flour mixture and beat on low for 20 seconds, just until incorporated. Scrape down the sides of the bowl.

8. Detach the bowl from the stand and with a large spoon stir in the apples and walnuts. Spoon the batter into the prepared pan.

9. Bake for 50 minutes to 1 hour, or until a wire cake tester inserted near the center comes out clean and the cake springs back when pressed lightly in the center.

10. Let the cake cool in the pan on a wire rack for 30 minutes. If using a straight sided pan, run a metal spatula between the sides of the pan and the cake. Invert the cake onto a wire rack that has been lightly coated with nonstick cooking spray and cool completely for about 1½ hours.

11. Drizzle Caramel Sauce and Glaze over the cake after unmolding, if desired.

TIP: The pan must be a minimum 12 cup capacity with 10 to 15 cup capacity, or a 12-cup Bundt pan, coated with baking spray with flour; or a 16-cup two-piece angel food pan, bottom lined with parchment, then coated with baking spray with flour.

Continued . . .

INGREDIENTS:

3	LARGE EGGS
1	CUP WALNUT HALVES
2½	CUPS BLEACHED ALL-PURPOSE FLOUR
1	TEASPOON BAKING SODA
1	TEASPOON FINE SEA SALT
2	TEASPOONS CINNAMON
4	LARGE TART APPLES
1¼	CUPS CANOLA OIL
1	CUP GRANULATED SUGAR
¾	CUP LIGHT BROWN SUGAR
2	TEASPOONS PURE VANILLA EXTRACT
	CARAMEL SAUCE AND GLAZE (OPTIONAL; SEE RECIPE)

CARAMEL SAUCE AND GLAZE

2	TABLESPOONS UNSALTED BUTTER
¼	CUP PLUS 2 TABLESPOONS HEAVY CREAM
1	CUP SUGAR, PREFERABLY SUPERFINE
2	TABLESPOONS CORN SYRUP
⅜	TEASPOON CREAM OF TARTAR (OPTIONAL)
¼	CUP WATER
2	TEASPOONS PURE VANILLA EXTRACT

CARAMEL SAUCE AND GLAZE

1. About 30 minutes ahead, cut the butter into a few pieces and set it on the counter at room temperature.

2. Pour the cream into a measuring cup with a spout and heat in the microwave until hot, then cover it.

3. Have ready near the cooktop a 2-cup measuring glass with a spout, lightly coated with nonstick cooking spray.

4. Add the sugar, corn syrup, cream of tartar (if using), and water to a nonstick saucepan and stir until all of the sugar is moistened.

5. Heat, stirring constantly with a silicone spatula, until the sugar dissolves and the syrup is bubbling. Stop stirring and let it boil undisturbed until it turns a deep amber and the temperature reaches 370°F, or a few degrees below, as the temperature will continue to rise. Remove it from heat as soon as it reaches temperature.

6. Slowly and carefully pour the hot cream into the caramel; it will bubble up furiously.

7. Use a silicone spatula or wooden spoon to stir the mixture gently, scraping the thicker part that settles on the bottom. Return it to a very low heat, continuing to stir gently for 1 minute, until the mixture is uniform in color and the caramel is fully dissolved.

8. Remove the caramel from heat and gently stir in the butter until incorporated. The mixture will be a little streaky but will become uniform once cooled and stirred.

9. Pour the caramel into the prepared measuring glass and let it cool for 3 minutes. Gently stir in the vanilla and let it cool until room temperature and thickened, stirring it gently once or twice.

APPLE-CRANBERRY CRISP
WITH OATMEAL-COOKIE CRUMBLE

YIELD: 12 SERVINGS / **ACTIVE TIME:** 1 HOUR / **TOTAL TIME:** 3 HOURS

Tangy cranberries and sweet orange zest add a floral tartness to this apple crisp. Topped with an oatmeal cookie crumble studded with almonds, the mixture of textures enhances the combination of flavors.

1. In a large bowl, combine flour, granulated sugar, oats, brown sugar, vanilla, baking powder, cinnamon, salt, and nutmeg and mix well. Add butter and mix with your hands until mixture feels like damp sand and clumps form. Add almonds and mix with a wooden spoon until evenly distributed and large, walnut-sized clumps form. Freeze for 30 minutes.

2. In a separate large bowl, combine apples, cranberries, granulated sugar, flour, orange zest and juice, cinnamon, salt, and nutmeg, toss well, and let stand 10 minutes.

3. Meanwhile, preheat the oven to 350°F. Place the baking dish on a foil-lined rimmed baking sheet (if using a Dutch oven, you don't need the baking sheet).

4. Toss the apple mixture again, then transfer to a baking dish, leaving some juices behind. Break crumble into smaller pieces, leaving some larger clumps. Top apples with crumble, mounding slightly if needed.

5. Bake apple crisp until crumble is golden brown and filling is bubbling through in the center, about 1 hour. Transfer the baking dish to a wire rack and let cool for 10 minutes.

6. Serve warm with whipped cream or ice cream topped with almonds.

TIP: You will need a 4-quart baking dish, braising pan, or Dutch oven (at least 12" in diameter and 2½" deep) Crumble can be made 1 week ahead; cover and freeze. Crisp can be assembled 1 day ahead; cover and chill.

INGREDIENTS:

1	CUP ALL-PURPOSE FLOUR
1	CUP GRANULATED SUGAR
1	CUP OLD-FASHIONED OATS
½	CUP LIGHT BROWN SUGAR
1	TEASPOON VANILLA EXTRACT
¾	TEASPOON BAKING POWDER
¾	TEASPOON GROUND CINNAMON
½	TEASPOON KOSHER SALT
¼	TEASPOON FRESHLY GRATED NUTMEG
¾	CUP UNSALTED BUTTER, CUT INTO PIECES, ROOM TEMPERATURE
½	CUP SLICED ALMONDS

APPLE-CRANBERRY FILLING

7½	LBS. BAKING APPLES, PEELED, CORED, CUT INTO 1/8" SLICES
1¼	CUPS FRESH OR FROZEN CRANBERRIES, THAWED IF FROZEN
1	CUP GRANULATED SUGAR
½	CUP ALL-PURPOSE FLOUR
½	TEASPOON FINELY GRATED ORANGE ZEST
2	TABLESPOONS FRESH ORANGE JUICE
1	TEASPOON GROUND CINNAMON
¾	TEASPOON KOSHER SALT
½	TEASPOON FRESHLY GRATED NUTMEG
	WHIPPED CREAM OR VANILLA ICE CREAM
	TOASTED ALMONDS

BLACK & WHITE COOKIES

YIELD: 24 COOKIES / **ACTIVE TIME:** 40 MINUTES / **TOTAL TIME:** 1 HOUR

A New York City icon in and of itself, these can be found in bodegas, bakeries, and bagel shops in all five boroughs, but when you don't feel like schlepping out of the house, make your own batch of these cake-like cookies.

1. Preheat the oven to 375°F.

2. Spray 2 baking sheets with nonstick spray, or line with parchment paper.

3. In a large mixing bowl, combine sugar and butter. Mix by machine or hand until fluffy. Add eggs, milk, and vanilla and lemon extracts, and mix until smooth.

4. In a medium bowl, combine cake flour, all-purpose flour, baking powder and salt. Stir until mixed. Add dry mixture to the wet in batches, stirring well after each addition. Using a soup spoon, place heaping spoonfuls of the dough 2" apart on the baking sheets. Bake until edges begin to brown, 18 to 20 minutes. Cool completely.

5. Place confectioners' sugar in a large mixing bowl. Gradually stir in enough boiling water to the sugar to make a thick, spreadable mixture.

6. Put half the frosting in the top half of a double-boiler. Add the chocolate and corn syrup, and set over simmering water. Warm the mixture, stirring, until chocolate is melted and frosting is smooth. Turn off the heat, but leave chocolate frosting over hot water to keep it spreadable. With a brush, coat half of the top of each cookie with chocolate frosting, and the other half with white frosting. Let dry, and store in an airtight container.

INGREDIENTS:

1¾ CUPS GRANULATED SUGAR

1 CUP UNSALTED BUTTER, AT ROOM TEMPERATURE

4 LARGE EGGS

1½ CUPS MILK

½ TEASPOON VANILLA EXTRACT

¼ TEASPOON LEMON EXTRACT

2½ CUPS CAKE FLOUR

2½ CUPS ALL-PURPOSE FLOUR

½ TEASPOON BAKING POWDER

½ TEASPOON SALT

4 CUPS CONFECTIONERS' SUGAR

⅓-½ CUP BOILING WATER

1 OZ. BITTERSWEET CHOCOLATE

1 TEASPOON LIGHT CORN SYRUP

BLACK & WHITE HALVAH

YIELD: 16 SERVINGS / **ACTIVE TIME:** 35 MINUTES / **TOTAL TIME:** 3 HOURS AND 40 MINUTES

A simple sesame-based delicacy, yet swirling black and white tahini together for a marble effect makes for an impressive presentation, trust us.

1. Lightly coat an 8½" x 4½" loaf pan with nonstick spray and line with parchment paper, leaving a 2" overhang on long sides. Place a sheet of parchment paper on the work surface and lightly coat with nonstick spray. Beat white tahini and ½ teaspoon salt in the bowl of a stand mixer fitted with the paddle attachment on low speed just until smooth.

2. Meanwhile, place ⅔ cup sugar in a small saucepan and remaining ⅔ cup sugar in another small saucepan. Add ¼ cup water to each saucepan and set both saucepans over low heat. Cook, stirring with a rubber spatula to dissolve, about 4 minutes. Keep 1 saucepan over low and increase heat to medium-high for the other saucepan and fit with a thermometer. Cook syrup, brushing down sides of saucepan with a wet pastry brush to dissolve any crystals, until the thermometer registers 248°F, 7 to 10 minutes.

3. Immediately remove the saucepan with boiling syrup from heat. Increase mixer speed to medium and gradually stream syrup into white tahini, aiming for the space between the sides of the bowl and the paddle. Beat just until halvah comes together in a smooth mass, less than a minute. (Do not overmix or it will be crumbly.) Working quickly, scrape onto prepared parchment and flatten with spatula until ¾" thick. Invert a medium bowl over halvah to keep warm.

4. Rinse any hardened sugar off the thermometer; clip to the second saucepan. Increase heat to medium-high and cook syrup, brushing down sides of saucepan with wet pastry brush, until the thermometer registers 248°F, about 4 minutes.

5. While the syrup is cooking, briefly beat black tahini and remaining ½ teaspoon salt in the same bowl of stand mixer (no need to clean it out unless you have lots of hardened sugar stuck around sides) until smooth. Stream in syrup and mix just until halvah comes together in a smooth mass.

INGREDIENTS:

- NONSTICK VEGETABLE OIL SPRAY
- ¾ CUP WHITE TAHINI
- 1 TEASPOON KOSHER SALT, DIVIDED
- 1⅓ CUPS SUGAR, DIVIDED
- ¾ CUP BLACK TAHINI

6. Uncover white halvah (it should still be warm) and scrape black halvah on top; flatten to about the same shape as the white halvah. Using the sides of the parchment to lift edges, fold stacked halvah in half and flatten slightly. Repeat folding and flattening motions 4 to 5 times, rotating halvah as you work, to create a marbled effect (be careful not to work it too much or mixture will be crumbly). Press into the prepared pan. Fold sides of parchment paper over top of halvah and let cool, at least 3 hours.

7. Lift halvah out of the pan using parchment overhang. Peel away parchment; cut halvah crosswise into ½" thick slices.

8. Halvah can be made 3 days ahead. Leave in the pan. Store tightly wrapped at room temperature.

TIP: This recipe requires a candy thermometer to correctly gauge tahini temperature.

CARAMELIZED-HONEY NUT & SEED TART

YIELD: 8 SERVINGS / **ACTIVE TIME:** 35 MINUTES / **TOTAL TIME:** 1 HOUR AND 30 MINUTES

Ascrumptious combination of textures, this sweet tart has an undeniable crunch. The richness of the nuts and seeds balances the sweet honey.

1. Pulse flour, powdered sugar, and salt in a food processor to combine. Add butter and pulse to work in just until mixture is the texture of coarse meal with a few pea-size pieces of butter remaining.

2. Beat egg yolks with 1 tablespoon water in a small bowl just to combine. With the motor running, gradually pour into the food processor. Process until dough starts to come together in large pieces.

3. Using lightly floured fingers, press dough about 1" up sides and then evenly into the bottom of the springform pan, making sides slightly thicker than bottom. Use a floured flat, straight-sided measuring cup or glass to compact and smooth dough; freeze until solid, 15 to 20 minutes.

4. Preheat the oven to 350°F. Prick bottom of dough in a few places with a fork and bake until golden all over, 20 to 25 minutes. Transfer pan to a wire rack. (Leave the oven on if you're not making the crust ahead and are making the filling next.)

5. Crust can be baked 1 day ahead. Let cool; store tightly wrapped at room temperature.

6. Bring honey and 1 tablespoon water to a simmer in a small saucepan over low heat, swirling pan often, until mixture is darkened in color and nutty smelling, about 2 minutes. Add granulated sugar, heavy cream, butter, corn syrup, salt, and vanilla and carefully stir until mixture is smooth. Increase heat to medium; bring to a boil. Cook, swirling pan, until caramel is slightly darkened in color and thick enough to coat a spoon, 5 to 8 minutes. Remove from heat, add nuts and seeds to caramel, and stir to coat.

7. Scrape filling into warm or room-temperature crust, pushing to the edges to evenly fill. Bake until the filling is deep golden brown and caramel is bubbling, 25 to 30 minutes. Let cool.

INGREDIENTS:

CRUST

1½	CUPS ALL-PURPOSE FLOUR
¼	CUP POWDERED SUGAR
½	TEASPOON KOSHER SALT
½	CUP (1 STICK) CHILLED UNSALTED BUTTER, CUT INTO PIECES
2	LARGE EGG YOLKS

FILLING & ASSEMBLY

¼	CUP HONEY
¼	CUP GRANULATED SUGAR
⅓	CUP HEAVY CREAM
4	TABLESPOONS UNSALTED BUTTER
2	TABLESPOONS LIGHT CORN SYRUP
½	TEASPOON KOSHER SALT
½	TEASPOON VANILLA EXTRACT
2	CUPS MIXED UNSALTED, ROASTED NUTS (SUCH AS PECANS, HAZELNUTS, PEANUTS, PISTACHIOS, AND/OR SLICED ALMONDS)
⅓	CUP UNSALTED, ROASTED SEEDS (SUCH AS PUMPKIN AND/OR SUNFLOWER)

CHOCOLATE MACAROONS

YIELD: 14 SERVINGS / **ACTIVE TIME:** 20 MINUTES / **TOTAL TIME:** 35 MINUTES

If you're used to the almost sickly-sweet tinned version of macaroons, prepare to be wowed by these homemade bites.

1. Line two large baking sheets with parchment paper, put each baking sheet on top of another baking sheet (or use two insulated baking sheets) and fit a large pastry bag with a plain ½" or ⅜" tip; set these aside for the moment.

2. Sift almond flour with the confectioner's sugar and cocoa. If you're starting with almonds, place the almonds, sugar and cocoa in the work bowl of a food processor fitted with the metal blade and process until the mixture is as fine as flour, at least 3 minutes. Stop every minute to check your progress and to scrape down the sides of the bowl. This is not a quick on-and-off operation. Although the almonds may look as though they're pulverized after a minute or so, they won't be. The nuts really need 3 to 5 minutes to be ground to a powder or flour. When the mixture is ground, press it through a medium strainer. In all probability, you'll have about 2 tablespoons of solids that won't go through the strainer—discard them.

3. Measure the egg whites by taking a fork and beating them and pouring them into a liquid measure cup. Bring the eggs to room temperature so they can be beaten to their fullest volume. You can leave the whites on the counter until they reach room temperature. To keep the eggs warm, run the mixer bowl under hot water, dry the bowl well, pour the whites into the bowl and fit the mixer with the whisk attachment.

4. Beat the egg whites at low to medium speed until they are white and foamy. Turn the speed up and whip them on high just until they are firm but still glossy and supple—when you lift the whisk the whites should form a peak that droops just a little. Keep the whites in the mixer bowl or transfer them to a large bowl. Working with a rubber spatula, fold the dry ingredients gently into the whites in 3 or 4 additions. There are a lot of dry ingredients to go into a relatively small amount of whites, but keep folding and you'll get everything in. When the dry ingredients are incorporated, the mixture will look like a cake batter; if you lift a little with your finger, it should form a gentle, quickly falling peak.

Continued . . .

INGREDIENTS:

- 5 OZ. ALMOND POWDER (FINELY GROUND, OR 5 OZ. BLANCHED ALMONDS, SEE STEP 3)
- 2 CUPS CONFECTIONER'S SUGAR
- ¼ CUP DUTCH COCOA POWDER (UNSWEETENED, PREFERABLY VALRHONA, PLUS MORE FOR DUSTING)
- ½ CUP EGG WHITES (ABOUT 4 LARGE EGG WHITES, SEE STEP 3)
- 2 TABLESPOONS ALMOND FLOUR
- 8 OZ. BITTERSWEET CHOCOLATE (PREFERABLY VALRHONA GUANAJA, FINELY CHOPPED)
- 1 CUP HEAVY CREAM
- 4 TABLESPOONS UNSALTED BUTTER (AT ROOM TEMPERATURE AND CUT INTO 4 PIECES)

5. Spoon the batter into the pastry bag and pipe it out onto the prepared baking sheets. (To keep the paper steady, "glue" it down by piping a bit of batter at each corner of the baking sheet.) Pipe the batter into rounds about 1" in diameter, leaving about an inch between each round. When you've piped out all the macaroons, lift each baking sheet with both hands and then bang it down on the counter. Don't be afraid—you need to get the air of the batter. Set the baking sheets aside at room temperature for 15 minutes while you preheat the oven.

6. Center a rack in the oven and preheat the oven to 425°F. You need to bake these one pan at a time, so dust the tops of the macaroons on one pan with cocoa powder and slide one of the sheets into the oven. As soon as the baking sheet is in the oven, turn the temperature down to 350°F and insert the handle of a wooden spoon between the oven and the door to keep the door slightly ajar. Bake the macaroons for 10 to 12 minutes, or until they are smooth and just firm to the touch. Transfer the baking sheet to a cooling rack (see step 8 for information on removing the macaroons from the parchment), close the oven door, turn the heat back up to 425°F and, when the oven is at the right temperature, repeat with the second sheet of macaroons.

7. To remove the macaroons from the parchment—and they should be removed as soon as they come from the oven—you need to create moisture under the cookies. Carefully loosen the parchment at the four corners and, lifting the paper at one corner, pour a little hot water under the parchment paper onto the baking sheet. The water may bubble and steam, so make sure your face and hands are away from the sheet. Move the parchment around or tilt the baking sheet so that the parchment is evenly dampened. Allow the macaroons to remain on the parchment, soaking up the moisture, for about 15 seconds, then peel the macaroons off the paper and place them on a cooling rack.

8. To finish: For the Bittersweet Cream and Butter Ganache, heat cream and butter until melted, pour over chocolate and mix until smooth. Let the ganache cool, keeping a spreadable consistency.

9. When the macaroons are cool, sandwich them with either ganache or ice cream.

10. For the ganache: Pipe a dollop of ganache about ½" across on the flat side of one cookie and use the flat side of another to complete the sandwich and to spread the ganache so that it runs to the edge. Transfer the filled macaroons to a covered container and place them in the refrigerator to soften overnight before serving.

CHOCOLATE-CINNAMON "BABKALLAH"

YIELD: 12 SERVINGS / **ACTIVE TIME:** 40 MINUTES / **TOTAL TIME:** 30 HOURS

Fun to say, even more fun to bake. A decadent babka and challah mash-up, this non-traditional dish is as delicious as it looks. It's similar to a traditional babka but the crumb and texture is more like challah. Makes a great French toast!

1. Heat milk in a small saucepan until warm. Transfer to a large bowl and whisk in yeast; let sit until foamy, 5 to 10 minutes.

2. Whisk in egg yolks, vanilla, and ½ cup butter. Add sugar, salt, and 3 cups flour; mix until a shaggy dough forms.

3. Knead dough on a lightly floured surface until supple, smooth, and no longer shiny, 5 to 10 minutes.

4. Transfer to a large buttered bowl. Cover and let sit in a warm place until doubled in size, 1½ to 2½ hours.

5. Turn out dough onto a lightly floured surface; divide into three portions. Shape each into a 12" long rope. Roll out each rope to a 12" x 6" rectangle about ⅛" thick. Brush with butter and top with chocolate mixture, pressing gently. Roll up to form a log; pinch seam to seal.

6. Place logs, seam side down, side by side on a parchment-lined baking sheet. Pinch logs together at one end; braid, then pinch ends together and tuck under. Cover loosely and let sit in a warm place until 1½ times larger, 1 to 2 hours.

7. Preheat the oven to 350°F.

8. Beat egg yolk with 1 tablespoon water in a small bowl. Brush dough with egg wash; sprinkle with granulated sugar. Bake until the top is golden brown and "Babkallah" sounds hollow when the bottom is tapped, 35 to 45 minutes. Let cool on a wire rack.

INGREDIENTS:

DOUGH

½	CUP WHOLE MILK
¼	OZ. ENVELOPE ACTIVE DRY YEAST
4	LARGE EGG YOLKS
1	TEASPOON VANILLA EXTRACT
½	CUP UNSALTED BUTTER, MELTED, COOLED, PLUS MORE
⅓	CUP GRANULATED SUGAR
1	TEASPOON KOSHER SALT
3	CUPS ALL-PURPOSE FLOUR, PLUS MORE

FILLING AND ASSEMBLY

6	OZ. BITTERSWEET CHOCOLATE, FINELY CHOPPED
⅓	CUP LIGHT BROWN SUGAR
1½	TEASPOONS GROUND CINNAMON
	ALL-PURPOSE FLOUR (FOR SURFACE)
¼	CUP UNSALTED BUTTER, AT ROOM TEMPERATURE
1	LARGE EGG YOLK
	GRANULATED SUGAR (FOR SPRINKLING)

COCONUT MACAROONS

YIELD: 10 SERVINGS / **ACTIVE TIME:** 10 MINUTES / **TOTAL TIME:** 45 MINUTES

A Passover staple because they have no flour or leavening, macaroons were originally made with an almond base before the coconut version became an American tradition. You don't have to wait for the holidays to enjoy these now-classic treats.

1. Put the oven rack in the middle position and preheat the oven to 300°F. Butter a baking sheet, then line with foil and lightly butter and flour foil, knocking off excess flour.

2. Stir together egg white, sugar, vanilla, almond extract, and a pinch of salt until combined, then stir in coconut. Divide coconut mixture into fourths, then drop in 4 mounds (about 2" apart) onto the baking sheet.

3. Bake until the tops are pale golden in spots, 15 to 20 minutes, then carefully lift foil with cookies from baking sheet and transfer to a rack to cool completely, about 15 minutes. Peel macaroons from foil.

INGREDIENTS:

	BUTTER AND FLOUR FOR PREPARING BAKING SHEET AND FOIL
1	PINCH ALMOND FLOUR, FOR DUSTING
1	LARGE EGG WHITE
1	TABLESPOON SUGAR
¼	TEASPOON VANILLA
⅛	TEASPOON ALMOND EXTRACT
¾	CUP SWEETENED FLAKED COCONUT

FLOURLESS CHOCOLATE CAKE

YIELD: 16 SERVINGS / **ACTIVE TIME:** 50 MINUTES / **TOTAL TIME:** 1 HOUR AND 25 MINUTES

Even on Passover, when flour is forbidden, chocolate cake is not. This is a staple recipe to always have at the ready.

1. Let egg whites stand at room temperature for 30 minutes. In a heavy saucepan, melt butter, ¼ cup sugar and chocolates over low heat, stirring constantly. Cool until the mixture is lukewarm.

2. In a large bowl, beat egg yolks until thick and lemon-colored, about 3 minutes. Beat in vanilla. Gradually beat in pecans and chocolate mixture.

3. In a small bowl and with clean beaters, beat egg whites on medium speed until soft peaks form. Gradually add remaining sugar, 1 tablespoon at a time, beating on high speed until stiff peaks form. Stir a small amount of whites into the chocolate mixture. Fold in remaining whites.

4. Pour into a greased 9" springform pan. Place on a baking sheet and bake at 350°F for 40 to 50 minutes or until a toothpick inserted in the center comes out with a few moist crumbs. Cool on a wire rack for 20 minutes.

5. Carefully run a knife around the edge of the pan to loosen; remove sides of pan and cool completely. Frost with Chocolate Ganache if desired. Garnish with strawberries and mint if desired.

INGREDIENTS:

4	LARGE EGGS, SEPARATED
10	TABLESPOONS BUTTER, CUBED
½	CUP SUGAR, DIVIDED
6	OZ. SEMISWEET CHOCOLATE, CHOPPED
3	OZ. UNSWEETENED CHOCOLATE, CHOPPED
2	TEASPOONS VANILLA EXTRACT
¼	CUP FINELY GROUND PECANS, TOASTED
	CHOCOLATE GANACHE, OPTIONAL (SEE PAGE 602)
	SLICED STRAWBERRIES AND FRESH MINT, FOR GARNISH (OPTIONAL)

CHOCOLATE GANACHE

YIELD: 1⅔ CUPS / **ACTIVE TIME:** 50 MINUTES /**TOTAL TIME:** 50 MINUTES

If you ever want to make a dessert even more decadent, whip up this chocolate goodness.

1. Place chocolate chips in a small bowl. In a small saucepan, bring cream just to a boil. Pour over chocolate; whisk until smooth.

2. For a pourable ganache, cool, stirring occasionally, until mixture reaches 85°F to 90°F and is slightly thickened, about 40 minutes. Pour over cake, allowing some to drape down the sides. Spread ganache with a spatula if necessary to evenly coat, working quickly before it thickens. Let stand until set.

3. For spreadable ganache, chill, stirring occasionally, until mixture reaches a spreading consistency. Spread over cake.

INGREDIENTS:

- 1 CUP SEMISWEET CHOCOLATE CHIPS
- ⅔ CUP HEAVY WHIPPING CREAM

GOLDEN BROWN COOKIES WITH APPLE FILLING

YIELD: 24 COOKIES / **ACTIVE TIME:** 20 MINUTES / **TOTAL TIME:** 30 MINUTES

Why should apple cakes have all the fun? These cookies are a delicious alternative for a Rosh Hashanah treat.

1. Preheat the oven to 375°F. Cream butter until smooth, add brown sugar and cream further.

2. Add egg, vanilla, salt, cinnamon, and cloves and mix until light and creamy.

3. Sift together flour, baking soda, and baking powder. Add flour mixture in one step to creamed mixture and mix until just combined, do not over mix.

4. Mix into cookie batter along with craisins and walnuts.

5. Scoop dough using a medium size ice cream scoop and set aside.

6. In a bowl, combine the sugar, cinnamon, nutmeg, and ginger and mix well.

7. Roll each ball in the sugar/cinnamon mixture.

8. Place on the parchment-covered baking sheet about 2" apart and slightly flatten.

9. Bake at 350°F for 12 minutes. Do not over bake; they will be a little soft when they are removed from the oven but they will harden.

INGREDIENTS:

10	TABLESPOONS UNSALTED BUTTER, SOFT
1	CUP DARK BROWN SUGAR
1	LARGE EGG, ROOM TEMPERATURE
1	TEASPOON VANILLA EXTRACT
½	TEASPOON SEA SALT
2	CUPS ALL-PURPOSE FLOUR
½	TEASPOON BAKING SODA
½	TEASPOON BAKING POWDER
1	SMALL GRANNY SMITH APPLE, PEELED AND DICED
1	CUP CRAISINS
1	CUP WALNUTS PIECES

CINNAMON-SUGAR MIXTURE

3	TABLESPOON GRANULATED WHITE SUGAR
¼	TEASPOON GINGER
2	TEASPOONS CINNAMON
¼	TEASPOON GROUND CLOVES
½	TEASPOON NUTMEG

HALVAH

YIELD: 14 SERVINGS / **ACTIVE TIME:** 20 MINUTES / **TOTAL TIME:** 20 MINUTES

Halvah is a confection enjoyed in many different regions and countries, but is perhaps most closely associated with the Middle East. There are many varieties, but are originally based on fried semolina. The sesame or pistachio variations are perhaps better known now, at least in North America and Europe.

1. Heat honey on medium heat until your candy or instant-read thermometer reads 240°F, or indicates the "softball" stage of candy making. To confirm that you are at the "softball" stage, drop a bit of the honey into a cup of cold water. It should form a sticky and soft ball that flattens when removed from the water.

2. Have the tahini ready to heat in a separate small pot, and once the honey is at the appropriate temperature, set the honey aside and heat tahini to 120°F.

3. Add the warmed tahini to the honey and mix with a wooden spoon to combine. At first it will look separated but after a few minutes, the mixture will come together smoothly.

4. Add the nuts and continue to mix until the mixture starts to stiffen, about 6 to 8 minutes.

5. Pour mixture into a well-greased loaf pan, or into a greased cake pan with a removable bottom.

6. Let cool to room temperature and wrap tightly with plastic wrap. Leave in the refrigerator for up to 36 hours. This will allow the sugar crystals to form, which will give the halvah its distinctive texture.

7. Invert to remove from the pan and cut into pieces with a sharp knife.

INGREDIENTS:

2   CUPS HONEY

1½   CUPS TAHINI, WELL
     STIRRED TO COMBINE

     UP TO 2 CUPS TOASTED
     SLICED ALMONDS OR
     OTHER NUTS

HALVAH FIVE WAYS

YIELD: 1 POUND / **ACTIVE TIME:** 20 MINUTES / **TOTAL TIME:** 20 MINUTES

It's surprisingly easy to make this confection, and family fun to customize the flavors.

PLAIN HALVAH

1. Line an 8" x 8" baking pan or a 9" x 4" loaf pan with parchment paper, leaving a 2" overhang on 2 sides. Using a wooden spoon, mix tahini, salt, and vanilla in a medium heatproof bowl.

2. Pour ¼ cup water into a small saucepan, then stir in sugar. Attach a candy thermometer to the side of the pan.

3. Bring sugar to a boil over medium-high heat and cook, stirring occasionally to help sugar dissolve, until the thermometer registers 250°F. Immediately remove syrup from heat. Gradually stream syrup into tahini mixture, mixing tahini constantly with a wooden spoon. Continue to stir just until halvah comes together in a smooth mass and starts to pull away from the sides of the bowl (less than a minute). Be careful not to overmix or halvah will be crumbly.

4. Working quickly, scrape halvah into prepared pan, pushing toward edges; smooth top. Let cool to room temperature, then cover tightly with plastic and chill at least 2 hours. Remove from the pan using parchment overhang. Slice as desired to serve.

PISTACHIO-ROSE HALVAH

1. Place a rack in the middle of the oven; preheat to 300°F. Spread 1 cup unsalted shelled pistachios on a rimmed baking sheet. Toast until fragrant and lightly golden, about 10 minutes. Transfer nuts to a plate. Let cool, then coarsely chop.

2. Prepare halvah, adding half of the chopped pistachios and ¼ teaspoon rosewater to the tahini, salt, and vanilla mixture.

3. Stir sugar syrup into the tahini mixture and form halvah as directed. Sprinkle remaining nuts over, pressing gently to adhere. Cover and chill as directed.

INGREDIENTS:

- 1½ CUPS WELL-STIRRED TAHINI, ROOM TEMPERATURE
- ¼ TEASPOON KOSHER SALT
- ½ TEASPOON VANILLA EXTRACT
- 1¼ CUPS SUGAR

PISTACHIO-ROSE HALVAH
- 1 CUP UNSALTED, SHELLED PISTACHIOS, TOASTED
- ¼ TEASPOON ROSEWATER

CARDAMOM-CHOCOLATE HALVAH
- ½ TEASPOON GROUND CARDAMOM
- ¾ COARSELY CHOPPED DARK CHOCOLATE

LEMON-POPPY SEED HALVAH
- 1 TABLESPOON POPPY SEEDS
- 1 TABLESPOON FINELY GRATED LEMON ZEST

CHOCOLATE-ZA'ATAR HALVAH
- ½ TEASPOON ZA'ATAR (SEE PAGE 545)
- ¾ COARSELY CHOPPED DARK CHOCOLATE

CARDAMOM-CHOCOLATE HALVAH

1. Prepare halvah, adding ½ teaspoon ground cardamom to the tahini, salt, and vanilla mixture.

2. Stir sugar syrup into the tahini mixture, then quickly stir in ½ cup coarsely chopped dark chocolate just to combine (you want to see streaks of chocolate). Form halvah as directed. Sprinkle ¼ cup coarsely chopped dark chocolate over, pressing gently to adhere. Cover and chill as directed.

LEMON–POPPY SEED HALVAH

1. Prepare halvah adding 1 tablespoon poppy seeds to the tahini, salt, and vanilla mixture.

2. Add 1 tablespoon finely grated lemon zest to water in a saucepan before making the sugar syrup, then prepare syrup as directed.

3. Form halvah as directed. Sprinkle 1 tablespoon poppy seeds over, pressing very gently just to adhere. Cover and chill as directed.

CHOCOLATE-ZA'ATAR HALVAH

1. Prepare halvah, adding ½ teaspoon za'atar to the tahini, salt, and vanilla mixture.

2. Stir sugar syrup into tahini mixture as directed, then quickly stir in ½ cup coarsely chopped dark chocolate just to combine (you want to see streaks of chocolate). Form halvah as directed. Sprinkle ¼ cup coarsely chopped dark chocolate over, pressing gently to adhere. Cover and chill as directed.

HALVAH MILLE-FEUILLES

YIELD: 4 SERVINGS / **ACTIVE TIME:** 35 MINUTES / **TOTAL TIME:** 1 HOUR

Mille Feuilles is French for 1,000 layers. The texture created by the phyllo and halvah is phenomenal when you crunch into the 1,000 layers creating a delicious mouth feel. Though this recipe calls for a raspberry garnish, feel free to swap in caramelized apples or toasted pistachios. When working with phyllo dough, make sure to keep the unused phyllo sheets covered as much as possible, as they tend to dry out quickly.

1. Preheat the oven to 350°F. Line 2 baking sheets with parchment paper. Stack the 8 sheets of phyllo and cut in half crosswise.

2. Brush 1 half sheet of phyllo with oil and sprinkle with sugar. Layer another half sheet on top of the first and repeat with oil and sugar to form a stack of 4 half sheets, finishing the top layer with oil and sugar.

3. Repeat with remaining half sheets to form 3 more stacks. Cut each of the stacks into 4 equal pieces to make 16 stacks.

4. Transfer stacks to baking sheets and bake until golden brown, 8 to 12 minutes.

5. Let cool to room temperature, about 15 minutes.

6. Meanwhile, in a small bowl, stir together the honey or date syrup with the tahini. If using non-dairy whipped topping, place in a large bowl and gently fold in the honey-tahini mixture. If using cream, beat until soft peaks form.

7. Gently incorporate the honey-tahini mixture and whip to stiff peaks. Refrigerate until ready to use.

8. Place one phyllo stack on a dessert plate. Spread with a scant ¼ cup halvah cream.

9. Repeat with 3 more phyllo stacks and 2 more layers of halvah cream. Repeat this process to form 3 more servings.

10. Drizzle each stack with honey or date syrup, sprinkle with halvah crumbles, and garnish with raspberries.

INGREDIENTS:

- 8   SHEETS PHYLLO DOUGH, DEFROSTED IF NECESSARY

-    CANOLA OR OLIVE OIL, FOR BRUSHING

-    GRANULATED SUGAR, FOR SPRINKLING

- ⅓   CUP HONEY OR SILAN (DATE SYRUP, AVAILABLE AT MIDDLE EASTERN MARKETS OR ONLINE)

- ⅓   CUP PURE TAHINI PASTE

- 2   CUPS NON-DAIRY WHIPPED TOPPING (DEFROSTED IF NECESSARY) OR 1 CUP HEAVY CREAM

- ½   CUP CRUMBLED HALVAH (SEE PAGE 605)

-    HONEY OR DATE SYRUP, FOR SERVING

-    FRESH RASPBERRIES, FOR SERVING

HONEY CAKE

YIELD: 1 (10") CAKE / **ACTIVE TIME**: 1 HOUR / **TOTAL TIME**: 4 HOURS

With its velvety chocolate glaze and snowy flakes of sea salt, this dressed-up honey cake is perfect for Rosh Hashanah.

CAKE

1. Heat oven to 350°F with rack in middle. Generously spray pan, including center tube, with baking spray.

2. Whisk together flour, baking powder and soda, salt, and spices in a large bowl.

3. Whisk eggs well in another large bowl and whisk in sugar, oil, honey, coffee, and zest until well combined.

4. Make a well in the center of the flour mixture and add the honey mixture, then stir with the whisk until the batter is smooth.

5. Pour batter into pan and bake in the oven until springy to the touch and a cake tester comes out clean, 45 to 50 minutes.

6. Let the cake cool in the pan on a rack for 20 minutes.

7. Loosen the cake from the pan with a thin rubber spatula, then invert cake onto the rack and cool completely.

CHOCOLATE GLAZE

1. Bring coconut milk and corn syrup to a simmer in a small heavy pan, stirring until combined.

2. Remove pan from heat and add chocolate. Let chocolate stand 1 minute, then stir until chocolate is melted and glaze is smooth.

3. Let glaze stand, stirring occasionally, until thickened slightly, but still pourable.

4. Transfer cake to a cake plate and slowly pour the chocolate glaze over the top of the cake, letting it drip down the sides. If desired, let the cake stand at room temperature until glaze is set.

5. Just before serving, sprinkle glaze lightly with flaky sea salt, if using.

INGREDIENTS:

CAKE

- BAKING SPRAY
- 2½ CUPS ALL-PURPOSE FLOUR
- 2 TEASPOONS BAKING POWDER
- ½ TEASPOON BAKING SODA
- ½ TEASPOON SALT
- 2 TEASPOONS CINNAMON
- ¼ TEASPOON GROUND GINGER
- ¼ TEASPOON GROUND CLOVE
- 3 LARGE EGGS
- 1 CUP SUGAR
- 1¼ CUPS AVOCADO OIL
- 1 CUP PURE HONEY
- ¾ CUP LUKEWARM COFFEE (BREWED, OR INSTANT DISSOLVED IN WATER)
- 1½ TEASPOONS PACKED GRATED ORANGE ZEST

CHOCOLATE GLAZE

- ¼ CUP PLUS 2 TABLESPOONS WELL-STIRRED CANNED UNSWEETENED COCONUT MILK (NOT LIGHT)
- 2 TEASPOONS LIGHT CORN SYRUP
- 4 OZ. BITTERSWEET (60% CACAO) CHOCOLATE, FINELY CHOPPED

GARNISH

- FLAKY SEA SALT, SUCH AS MALDON (OPTIONAL)

Continued . . .

TIP: Measuring oil and honey: Both should be measured in a liquid measuring cup. The oil is listed first, because if you measure the honey in it afterward, without washing the cup, the honey will slide out easily, with barely any help needed from a rubber spatula.

INVERTING THE CAKE ONTO A RACK: The best way to do this is to place a rack over the top of the pan, then, holding the rack and pan together, flip the cake pan and rack over so that the cake can slide safely out of the pan onto the rack.

CHOPPING CHOCOLATE: The easiest way to chop chocolate is with a long serrated bread knife. Or you can break the chocolate into squares (if you are using a bar) and pulse it in a food processor.

HONEY POMEGRANATE CAKE

YIELD: 4 SERVINGS / **ACTIVE TIME:** 10 MINUTES / **TOTAL TIME:** 1 HOUR

May dry honey cakes be forever banished from your Rosh Hashanah table! This version with the oh-so important addition of pomegranate is sure to be a favorite.

1. Using a hand mixer or a stand mixer to beat eggs and sugar until smooth. Add oil, brewed tea, and honey and mix well.

2. In a separate bowl, combine dry ingredients and slowly add to liquid ingredients. Pour into a 10" ungreased angel food cake pan, not a bundt pan.

3. Preheat the oven to 350°F. Bake for 15 minutes then reduce heat to 300°F and bake for an additional 45 minutes.

4. When the cake is done invert and allow to cool completely before removing.

5. For the glaze, combine pomegranate juice, sugar, and lemon juice in a small pot over medium heat. Bring to a boil then let simmer uncovered for 15 minutes, stirring frequently. It will become syrup and reduce to about half. Remove from heat, let cool slightly, and whisk in powdered sugar until smooth.

6. Stir in pomegranate seeds and pour over the cake.

INGREDIENTS:

CAKE

4	EGGS
1	CUP SUGAR
1	CUP CANOLA OIL
1	CUP COLD BREWED POMEGRANATE TEA (BREWED FOR 30 MINUTES)
1½	CUPS HONEY
3	CUPS FLOUR
3	TEASPOONS BAKING POWDER
½	TEASPOON BAKING SODA

GLAZE

½	CUP POMEGRANATE JUICE
¼	CUP SUGAR
	JUICE OF ½ LEMON
4	TABLESPOONS POWDERED SUGAR
¼	CUP POMEGRANATE SEEDS

HAMANTASCHEN

YIELD: 50 COOKIES / **ACTIVE TIME**: 1 HOUR AND 30 MINUTES / **TOTAL TIME**: 4 HOURS AND 30 MINUTES

Along with the Jewish holiday Purim comes a delicious cookie filled with a jelly center. The triangular shape symbolizes a hat that belonged to Haman, the villain at the center of the Purim story.

1. Place the yeast, sugar, vanilla extract (if using), and water into a large mixing bowl. Mix the ingredients well with a wooden spoon. Add 2 tablespoons of flour and stir until combined. Cover with plastic wrap and set the bowl aside for 10 minutes or until the mixture is foamy.

2. Add the salt and 2 more tablespoons of flour into the yeast, sugar, flour and water mixture. Mix well until combined. Cover the bowl with plastic wrap and set it aside for 30 minutes in a warm place to rise by about one-quarter.

3. Add the avocado oil and gradually add about 5 cups of flour into the mixture. Continue stirring the mixture with a wooden spoon until it forms into a dough. Knead the dough by hand and add more flour (1 tablespoon at a time) until the dough stops sticking to your hands. If needed. Transfer the dough to a lightly floured surface and roll it into a large ball. Rub about ½ teaspoon of oil all over the dough and transfer the dough into a clean and large mixing bowl. Cover with plastic wrap and a towel. Set the dough aside in a warm place for one hour or until it doubles in size.

4. Meanwhile, place the poppyseeds into a heatproof bowl and cover with enough boiling water to completely submerge the poppy seeds. Cover the bowl with a lid or plastic wrap and set it aside for 1 hour.

5. Drain the poppy seeds through a cheesecloth lined colander or a sieve. Transfer the wet poppy seeds into a spice grinder or food processor. Add the sugar and lemon zest and grind the mixture well until it is finely processed into a paste. Transfer the filing into a bowl.

6. Once the dough has proofed, transfer it onto a lightly floured surface and divide it into 2 equal pieces. Roll each piece of dough out into a ¼" thick circle.

7. Use a 3" cookie cutter or glass cup to cut 3" circles into the dough. Pull the dough scraps off of the dough and set aside. Place about ½ tablespoon of the filling into the center of each circle of dough. Brush the edges of the circles with a bit of water. Roll up 3

INGREDIENTS:

DOUGH
2¼ TEASPOONS DRY YEAST

6 TABLESPOONS SUGAR

1 TEASPOON VANILLA EXTRACT (OPTIONAL)

2½ CUPS LUKEWARM WATER

6-7 CUPS ALL-PURPOSE FLOUR, DIVIDED, PLUS MORE FOR ROLLING OUT

½ TEASPOON KOSHER SALT

½ CUP PLUS ½ TEASPOON AVOCADO OIL

FILLING
3 CUPS DRIED POPPY SEEDS

¾ CUP SUGAR

2 TABLESPOONS LEMON ZEST

EGG WASH
3 EGG YOLKS

½ TEASPOON HONEY

edges of the circle to form a triangular shape and pinch the edges together to seal the cookies. Roll the dough scraps into a ball of dough, roll it out to a ¼" thick circle and repeat to make more cookies. Transfer the cookies onto a few parchment lined baking sheets, leaving about 1½" between each cookie. Gently cover with a towel and let the cookies rise for about 20 minutes.

8. Preheat the oven to 375°F.

9. Place the egg yolks into a small bowl and whisk well with the honey. Brush the tops of the cookies with egg wash.

10. Transfer the cookies into the oven and bake for 20 to 25 minutes or until the cookies are baked and golden brown.

11. Let the cookies cool until they are at room temperature and serve.

HUNGARIAN GOLDEN PULL-APART CAKE
WITH WALNUTS & APRICOT JAM

YIELD: 8 SERVINGS / **ACTIVE TIME:** 20 MINUTES / **TOTAL TIME:** 1 HOUR AND 20 MINUTES

Aranygaluska, also called golden dumpling cake, butter puffs, and monkey bread, has been extolled by Jewish immigrants from Hungary for years. There are sweet and savory variations. For example, Jews who separated meat from dairy in their diet would serve it with a fish or non-meat soup.

1. Dissolve the yeast in the warm milk in the bowl of a standing mixer equipped with a paddle attachment. Add ¼ cup sugar, the eggs, orange zest, vanilla, and 1 stick of butter. Gradually add the flour and salt, beating until mixed. Cover the bowl and leave for an hour, or until the dough has about doubled in size.

2. Preheat the oven to 350°F and butter a 10" round pan with some of the second stick of butter.

3. Melt what is left of the second stick of butter plus the remaining half stick and put it in a small bowl. In a separate bowl, mix the walnuts, brown sugar, remaining white sugar, cinnamon, and the cake or cookie crumbs.

4. Roll the dough into a ½" thick circle. Using a 1" cookie or biscuit cutter, cut circles of dough. Dip the circles first in the butter, then in the nut mixture and set in the pan, almost touching each other. After a layer is completed, spoon on dollops of jam. Make a second layer, filling in the holes with dough, then jam, continuing and rerolling until the dough is used up, ending with the walnut topping but not the jam. Bake in the oven for 35 to 40 minutes, or until golden brown and set. Leave in the pan for a few minutes, then turn onto a plate and serve warm. You can either cut the cake or pull the sections apart. Serve for a sweet breakfast treat, or as a dessert, served with good vanilla or rum raisin ice cream.

TIP: Substitute ¼ cup good-quality unsweetened cocoa and ¾ cup sugar for the nut topping. Then, after dipping the rounds in butter, dip them in the chocolate-sugar mixture and proceed as above. Substitute the jam with Nutella or another chocolate spread.

INGREDIENTS:

1	TABLESPOON ACTIVE DRY YEAST
1	CUP WARM MILK
½	CUP SUGAR, PLUS 2 TABLESPOONS
4	LARGE EGGS
	ZEST OF 1 ORANGE
1	TEASPOON VANILLA
1	CUP PLUS 4 TABLESPOONS UNSALTED BUTTER, AT ROOM TEMPERATURE, DIVIDED
4½	CUPS UNBLEACHED ALL-PURPOSE FLOUR (ABOUT)
1	TEASPOON SALT
1½	CUPS GROUND WALNUTS
6	TABLESPOONS BROWN SUGAR
¾	TEASPOON CINNAMON
3	TABLESPOONS CAKE OR BUTTER COOKIE CRUMBS
¾	CUP APRICOT OR PLUM JAM

KNAFEH CHEESECAKE

YIELD: 8 SERVINGS / **ACTIVE TIME:** 20 MINUTES / **TOTAL TIME:** 1 HOUR

Kunafa is a famous Middle Eastern pastry and Middle Eastern dessert dish. Typical kunafa is orange-colored string pastry with layered cheese, soaked in a sugary syrup and sometimes garnished with smashed pistachios. In Israel, kunafa is a popular dessert, especially Palestinian knafeh nabulseyeh that comes with white cheese called nabulsi. At the end of the day, all you need to know is that there's cheese and sugar.

1. Preheat the oven to 350°F.

2. In a heavy-bottomed saucepan, place sugar, water, and lemon juice. Bring to a boil and then simmer on low heat for approximately 10 minutes or until the liquid has become a syrup. Remove from heat and leave to cool.

3. When the syrup has cooled, add the rosewater and set aside to be used later.

4. Use a little of the butter to grease an 11" springform pan.

5. In a large bowl, break apart the kataifi pastry until all the shreds are loose. Mix the rest of the melted butter in, using your hands, so the pastry is well coated.

6. Beat together the mascarpone cheese, cream cheese, egg yolks and sugar until smooth.

7. Sprinkle blanched almonds over the bottom of the pan. Take half of the kataifi dough and place over the almonds, pressing it down.

8. Spread the cheese mixture over the kataifi, using a palette knife so you have an even layer. Take the other half of the kataifi dough and press over the top.

9. Bake for approximately 30 minutes until golden.

10. Remove from the oven and sprinkle ground pistachios on the top. Pour the rosewater syrup evenly over the cake. Leave to cool and remove from the pan.

INGREDIENTS:

1½	CUPS SUGAR
8	OZ. WATER
2	TABLESPOONS FRESH LEMON JUICE
¼	TEASPOON ROSEWATER
7	OZ. UNSALTED BUTTER, MELTED
12	OZ. KATAIFI PASTRY
9	OZ. MASCARPONE CHEESE
9	OZ. CREAM CHEESE
2	LARGE EGG YOLKS
¼	CUP SUGAR
1	CUP BLANCHED ALMONDS

MALABI

YIELD: 6 SERVINGS / **ACTIVE TIME:** 20 MINUTES / **TOTAL TIME:** 20 MINUTES

This is the Israeli version of a milk pudding that has legendary origins dating to Sassanid Persia, and today is popular in Turkey, Israel, and other Mediterranean countries.

1. In a medium bowl mix 1 cup milk with cornstarch and rose water. Mix until smooth.

2. To a medium size pot pour 3 cups milk and heavy cream. Add sugar and bring to a simmer, stirring constantly. Once the milk boils, turn the heat to low and add the cornstarch mixture. Cook over low heat for 3 to 4 minutes, stirring constantly until the mixture begins to thicken.

3. Pour into serving dishes. Cover immediately with plastic wrap and cool to room temperature, then refrigerate for at least 4 hours or overnight.

4. Make the syrup: in a pan over medium-high heat bring to a boil water, sugar and rose water. When boiling add food coloring. Let boil for 2 more minutes and turn off the heat. Let cool completely.

5. When the malabi is chilled pour 1 to 2 tablespoons of the syrup on the malabi, add crushed peanuts or pistachios and shredded coconut.

INGREDIENTS:

PUDDING

4	CUPS MILK
1	CUP HEAVY CREAM
⅔	CUP CORNSTARCH
½	CUP SUGAR
1	TEASPOON ROSE WATER

SYRUP

½	CUP WATER
½	CUP SUGAR
1	TEASPOON ROSE WATER
	FEW DROPS OF RED FOOD COLORING

TOPPING

½	CUP PEANUTS OR PISTACHIOS
	SHREDDED COCONUT

MANDEL BREAD

YIELD: 36 COOKIES / **ACTIVE TIME:** 20 MINUTES / **TOTAL TIME:** 3 HOURS

This twice-baked "almond bread" is a sweet, crunchy snack that is similar to Italian biscotti, but uses no butter.

1. In a bowl, combine eggs, sugar, and oil and beat well.

2. Add remaining ingredients and mix well.

3. Refrigerate dough for several hours or overnight.

4. Preheat the oven to 350°F

5. On a heavily floured surface, shape into 3 narrow loaves.

6. Bake on a floured sheet pan for 20 to 25 minutes.

7. Slice diagonally while hot.

8. Place slices on a greased and floured sheet and toast for 2 minutes per side at 450°F.

INGREDIENTS:

2	EGGS
½	CUP SUGAR
½	CUP AVOCADO OIL
2	CUPS SIFTED ALL-PURPOSE FLOUR
1	TEASPOON BAKING POWDER
½	TEASPOON BAKING SODA
1	TEASPOON VANILLA
1	TEASPOON ALMOND FLAVORING
½	CUP CHOPPED WALNUTS, ALMONDS, OR PECANS
1	TEASPOON LEMON ZEST

NEW YEAR'S HONEY CAKE

YIELD: 8 SERVINGS / **ACTIVE TIME:** 15 MINUTES / **TOTAL TIME:** 1 HOUR

Let the adults enjoy this one. This irresistible cake is lightly spiced and scented with coffee, fresh orange juice, and rye whiskey.

1. Preheat the oven to 350°F. Lightly grease the pan(s). For tube and angel food pans, line the bottom with lightly greased parchment paper.

2. In a large bowl, whisk together the flour, baking powder, baking soda, salt, and spices. Make a well in the center and add the oil, honey, sugars, eggs, vanilla, coffee, orange juice, and rye or whisky.

3. Using a strong wire whisk or an electric mixer on slow speed, combine the ingredients well to make a thick batter, making sure that no ingredients are stuck to the bottom of the bowl.

4. Spoon the batter into the prepared pan(s) and sprinkle the top of the cake(s) evenly with the almonds. Place the cake pan(s) on 2 baking sheets stacked together and bake until the cake springs back when you touch it gently in the center. For angel and tube cake pans, bake for 1 hour to 1 hour and 10 minutes; loaf cakes, 45 to 55 minutes. For sheet-style cakes, the baking time is 40 to 45 minutes. This is a liquidy batter and, depending on your oven, it may need extra time.

5. Let the cake stand for 15 minutes before removing it from the pan. Then invert it onto a wire rack to cool completely.

INGREDIENTS:

- 3½ CUPS ALL-PURPOSE FLOUR
- 1 TABLESPOON BAKING POWDER
- 1 TEASPOON BAKING SODA
- ½ TEASPOON SALT
- 4 TEASPOONS GROUND CINNAMON
- ½ TEASPOON GROUND CLOVES
- ½ TEASPOON GROUND ALLSPICE
- 1 CUP VEGETABLE OIL
- 1 CUP HONEY
- 1½ CUPS GRANULATED SUGAR
- ½ CUP BROWN SUGAR
- 3 EGGS
- 1 TEASPOON VANILLA EXTRACT
- 1 CUP WARM COFFEE OR STRONG TEA
- ½ CUP FRESH ORANGE JUICE
- ¼ CUP RYE OR WHISKY
- ½ CUP SLIVERED OR SLICED ALMONDS (OPTIONAL)

MELKTERT

YIELD: 8 SERVINGS / **ACTIVE TIME:** 3 MINUTES / **TOTAL TIME:** 2 HOURS

The creamy, custard-like filling enhanced with spices in this South African milk tart makes for the perfect sweet treat at the end of a meal, or an ideal nosh to accompany your afternoon coffee or tea.

1. Blend together flour, butter, and salt in a bowl with your fingertips or a pastry blender (or pulse in a food processor) just until the mixture resembles coarse meal with some small (roughly pea-size) butter lumps. Drizzle 3 tablespoons ice water evenly over mixture and gently stir with a fork (or pulse) until incorporated.

2. Squeeze a small handful of dough: If it doesn't hold together, add more ice water, ½ tablespoon at a time, stirring (or pulsing) until incorporated. Do not overwork dough, or pastry will be tough.

3. Turn out dough onto a work surface. Divide dough into 4 portions. With the heel of your hand, smear each portion once or twice in a forward motion to help distribute fat. Gather all dough together with a pastry scraper. Press into a ball, then flatten into a 5" disk.

4. Wrap dough in plastic wrap and chill until firm, at least 1 hour.

5. Set the oven at 400°F. Lightly grease a 10" shallow enamel plate or quiche tin. Roll out the pastry and line the baking plate or tin. Press in a piece of oiled foil and bake for 10 minutes. Remove foil and bake the crust for about 5 minutes more until crisp and golden.

6. Allow to cool.

7. Measure three quarters of the milk into a saucepan, add the cinnamon and heat to just below boiling point. Set aside to infuse for about 15 minutes.

INGREDIENTS:

CRUST

1¼	CUPS ALL-PURPOSE FLOUR
1	STICK (½ CUP) UNSALTED BUTTER
¼	TEASPOON SALT
3-5	TABLESPOONS ICE WATER

FILLING

2	CUPS FULL-CREAM MILK (WHOLE MILK)
1	STICK CINNAMON
3	EGGS, SEPARATED
⅓	CUP CAKE FLOUR
1	TABLESPOON CORNFLOUR (CORNSTARCH)
⅓	CUP SUGAR
½	TEASPOON BAKING POWDER
2	TABLESPOONS BUTTER
1	TABLESPOON VANILLA EXTRACT
1	PINCH GROUND CINNAMON

8. Mix together the remaining milk, egg yolks, flour, cornstarch, sugar and baking powder. Strain the cinnamon-flavoured milk, pour into a clean saucepan and cook, stirring, until the custard thickens. Remove from the heat, and whisk in the butter and vanilla extract. Cool to room temperature. Reduce oven temperature to 350°F.

9. Whisk the egg white stiffly and fold into the custard. Pour into the pastry shell and bake for 10 minutes. Reduce oven temperature to 325°F and bake for about 30 minutes more, until the filling is set. Slide the hot tart onto a plate, sprinkle with ground cinnamon and serve warm.

OLIVE OIL APPLE CAKE WITH SPICED SUGAR

YIELD: 1 CAKE / **ACTIVE TIME:** 30 MINUTES / **TOTAL TIME:** 1 HOUR AND 30 MINUTES

This dairy-free cake hits all the right autumnal notes: it's fruity and tender thanks to the olive oil, and pleasantly warm with spices.

1. Preheat the oven to 350°F.

2. Add 1 tablespoon oil to a 9" x 5" loaf pan and coat bottom and sides with fingertips. Sprinkle granulated sugar onto the sides and bottom of the pan to lightly coat.

3. Grate apples, peel and all, on the large holes of a box grater. Gather apples in a clean kitchen towel and wring out excess liquid. Be aggressive! You want them as dry as possible when they go into the batter.

4. Whisk cinnamon, pepper, cardamom, and ginger in a medium bowl. Transfer ¼ teaspoon spice mixture to a small bowl; set aside. Add flour and baking powder to the remaining spice mixture and whisk to combine.

5. Whisk together eggs, egg yolks, brown sugar, vanilla, salt, and ½ cup granulated sugar in a large bowl. Continue whisking vigorously until lightened in color and thickened. Whisking with one hand and pouring with the other, slowly stream 1 cup oil into egg mixture until combined. Gently fold flour mixture into whipped eggs with a flexible rubber spatula just until combined, taking care not to overmix.

6. Fluff up grated apples and scatter over batter. Gently fold to incorporate.

7. Transfer batter to prepared pan; smooth top. Add 2 teaspoon granulated sugar to reserved spice mixture and mix to combine. Sprinkle spiced sugar evenly over top of batter.

8. Bake cake until deep golden brown and a tester inserted into the center comes out clean, 1 hour to 1 hour and 10 minutes. Let the cake cool in the pan. Run a butter knife or offset spatula along the edge of cake to loosen and invert onto a platter.

INGREDIENTS:

1	CUP MILD EXTRA VIRGIN OLIVE OIL, PLUS MORE FOR PAN
½	CUP PLUS 2 TEASPOONS GRANULATED SUGAR, PLUS MORE FOR PAN
2	SWEET APPLES, SUCH AS GOLDEN DELICIOUS OR GALA
1	TEASPOON CINNAMON
½	TEASPOON FRESHLY GROUND BLACK PEPPER
½	TEASPOON CARDAMOM
½	TEASPOON GROUND GINGER
1½	CUPS ALL-PURPOSE FLOUR
2	TEASPOONS BAKING POWDER
2	LARGE EGGS
2	EGG YOLKS
½	CUP BROWN SUGAR
1	TEASPOON VANILLA EXTRACT
½	TEASPOON KOSHER SALT

ORANGE-SPICED RYE HONEY CAKE

YIELD: 12 SERVINGS / **ACTIVE TIME:** 15 MINUTES / **TOTAL TIME:** 1 HOUR AND 35 MINUTES

Honey cake emerges from its hibernation around the High Holidays in the fall, when honey and other sweet foods are eaten to usher in a sweet new year. Make it once and you might find that it's the cake you want to bake all season long.

1. Preheat the oven to 350°F. Generously grease a 9" x 5" inch loaf pan with oil.

2. In a large bowl, whisk together the 1½ cups of oil, the eggs, sugar, honey, coffee, and orange zest. In a separate large bowl, whisk together the flours, baking powder, baking soda, salt, cinnamon, ginger, and cloves.

3. Make a well in the center of the flour mixture and pour in the egg mixture, then stir with a fork or a whisk until the batter is smooth and free of lumps.

4. Pour the batter into the prepared pan and bake for 50 to 55 minutes, until set in the middle—the cake should hold firm when lightly pressed on top. Be careful not to leave it in the oven for too long or it will dry out.

5. Let the cake cool in the pan for at least 30 minutes—1 hour for a Bundt cake (see note)—before very carefully inverting it and removing the pan. Slice and serve with fresh fruit and tea.

INGREDIENTS:

1½ CUPS VEGETABLE OIL, PLUS MORE FOR GREASING THE PAN

3 LARGE EGGS

1 CUP SUGAR

1 CUP PURE HONEY

¾ CUP LUKEWARM COFFEE

1 TEASPOON PACKED ORANGE ZEST

1½ CUPS ALL-PURPOSE FLOUR

1 CUP RYE FLOUR

2 TEASPOONS BAKING POWDER

½ TEASPOON BAKING SODA

½ TEASPOON KOSHER SALT

2 TEASPOONS GROUND CINNAMON

¼ TEASPOON GROUND GINGER

¼ TEASPOON GROUND CLOVES

PECAN-ORANGE BAKLAVA PIE

YIELD: 16 SERVINGS / **ACTIVE TIME:** 1 HOUR / **TOTAL TIME:** 1 HOUR AND 45 MINUTES

Bourbon-honey syrup and fragrant orange zest add rich flavor to this showstopper of a dessert. Why choose between baklava and pie when you can have both?

1. Preheat the oven to 350°F. Bring honey, cinnamon sticks, 1 cup sugar, and 1 cup water to a boil in a medium heavy saucepan over medium-high heat, stirring until sugar dissolves. Reduce heat to medium and continue to boil until syrup is reduced to about 1½ cups, 15 to 18 minutes. Transfer to a medium bowl, stir in bourbon, and let cool.

2. Meanwhile, spread pecans on a large rimmed baking sheet and toast until golden brown, 13 to 15 minutes. Let cool. Transfer nuts to a food processor. Add ground cinnamon, 1 teaspoon orange zest, and remaining ½ cup sugar and pulse until coarsely chopped.

3. Place a stack of phyllo sheets on a work surface. Keep any phyllo you're not currently working with covered under a layer of plastic wrap topped with a slightly damp kitchen towel. Using the base of the springform pan as a guide, and starting at the edge of phyllo, carefully cut out 20 (9") circles, leaving as much phyllo remaining as possible. Cover phyllo circles. Using the base of the pan as a guide, cut remaining phyllo into 20 (4½") half-circles.

4. Insert base into pan and secure the latch. Brush base with butter. Place 1 phyllo circle in the pan and brush generously with butter. Top with 2 half-circles to create a full circle, brush with butter. Top with full circle, brush again. Top with 2 more half-circles at a 90° angle from the first half-circle layer, brush with butter. Top with a full circle, and brush again. You should have 5 layers of pastry (full circle-half-circles-full circle-half circles-full circle), with butter spread between each layer. Spread one-fifth of nut mixture over phyllo. Repeat layering 4 more times. Top with the 5 remaining phyllo circles; brush top with butter.

5. Using a sharp knife, score the top layer (do not cut through to the bottom of the pan) to divide into 4 quadrants. Working with 1 quadrant at a time, make 1 straight cut to divide the quadrant into 2 even wedges. Make 4 more straight cuts (2 each on either side of, and parallel to, the quadrant division line), spacing evenly apart. Now working within each wedge, make 2 evenly-spaced cuts parallel to the outside edge of the quadrant, connecting at points

INGREDIENTS:

- ⅔ CUP HONEY
- 2 (3") CINNAMON STICKS
- 1½ CUPS SUGAR, DIVIDED
- 3 TABLESPOONS BOURBON
- 3 CUPS RAW PECANS
- ½ TEASPOON GROUND CINNAMON
- 1 TEASPOON FINELY GRATED ORANGE ZEST, PLUS 1 TEASPOON ORANGE CURLS
- 20 (17" X 12") SHEETS FRESH PHYLLO PASTRY OR FROZEN, THAWED
- 1 CUP (2 STICK) UNSALTED BUTTER, MELTED

with the previous cuts to form a diamond pattern. Repeat with the remaining quadrants to create a starburst pattern. Transfer pan to a rimmed baking sheet and bake until phyllo is golden brown, about 45 minutes.

6. Spoon cooled syrup over hot baklava in 4 additions. Place orange curls on top. Let cool completely in the pan. Remove the springform ring and cut baklava along the scored lines.

POMEGRANATE TRUFFLES

YIELD: 10 SERVINGS / **ACTIVE TIME:** 1 HOUR / **TOTAL TIME:** 6 HOURS AND 30 MINUTES

Dark chocolate truffles pair well with bright, acidic fruits like raspberry or cherry—but the ever-important, symbolic pomegranate makes these treats perfect for a holiday.

POMEGRANATE MOLASSES

1. Heat pomegranate juice over medium heat in a small saucepan until just simmering.

2. Stir in sugar and lemon juice until completely dissolved.

3. Continue to simmer for about an hour, stirring every 10 minutes, until it leaves a thin coat on the spoon.

4. It should reduce down to about ¾ cup molasses.

5. Remove from heat and store in the refrigerator.

TRUFFLE

1. Toast the pistachios and chop finely

2. Finely chop the chocolate.

3. Add 6 oz. of bittersweet chocolate and the heavy cream to a small mixing bowl.

4. Using the double boiler method, in a small saucepan bring water to a gentle simmer.

5. Place the mixing bowl on top of the saucepan and stir gently until the chocolate has melted.

6. Take it off the heat and mix in 1 tablespoon of pomegranate molasses.

7. Let it cool in the fridge for 2 hours.

8. Line a baking sheet with parchment paper.

9. Set aside. After 2 hours, scoop out the chocolate mixture using a teaspoon and gently roll it in balls.

10. Lay them out on the parchment lined baking sheet.

11. Cool them in the fridge for another 2 hours.

12. While the truffles are cooling in the fridge, make the pomegranate sugar for coating.

INGREDIENTS:

POMEGRANATE MOLASSES

2	CUPS 100% POMEGRANATE JUICE
⅓	CUP GRANULATED WHITE SUGAR WHITE SUGAR
2½	TABLESPOONS FRESH LEMON JUICE

TRUFFLE

11	OZ. BITTERSWEET CHOCOLATE
½	CUP HEAVY CREAM
½	CUP GRANULATED WHITE SUGAR
2	TABLESPOONS UNSALTED BUTTER, SOFTENED
¼	TEASPOON CAYENNE
¼	CUP POMEGRANATE LIQUEUR
1	CUP PISTACHIOS, ROASTED AND CHOPPED VERY FINELY

13. Mix ½ cup of sugar with 1 teaspoon of the molasses thoroughly.

14. Spread out the pomegranate sugar on a plate.

15. Spread out the roasted and chopped pistachios on a plate.

16. When the truffles have hardened up in the fridge, start making the final coating of chocolate.

17. Using the double boiler method, melt 6 oz. of the bittersweet chocolate.

18. Let cool for 1 minute

19. Take the truffles out of the fridge.

20. Roll the truffle in the melted chocolate, and remove with a slotted spoon.

21. Roll the truffle around the chopped pistachio plate.

22. Lay it on the parchment covered baking sheet.

23. Chill the truffles again for 2 hours in the fridge.

24. Serve at room temperature.

PUMPKIN CRANBERRY CUPCAKES

YIELD: 12 CUPCAKES / **ACTIVE TIME:** 15 MINUTES / **TOTAL TIME:** 35 MINUTES

Right on time for autumn baking, these cupcakes are a fun addition to your Rosh Hashanah celebration. Pumpkins and squash are symbolic New Year's staples, and one can pray that their good deeds "call out their merit" before consuming them.

1. Preheat the oven to 350°F and line a cupcake pan with paper or silicone liners. In a bowl, whisk together the flour, baking soda and powder, and spices; set aside. In a separate bowl, cream the sugars and butter together until fluffy. Add the eggs, vanilla, and pumpkin puree, stirring until fully combined. Fold in the cranberries.

2. Slowly add the dry ingredients to the wet, stirring until just combined. Pour batter into prepared cupcake tins, filling each tin approximately ¾ full. Bake for 20 to 25 minutes until a tester comes out clean. Allow to fully cool, then frost as desired or sprinkle with confectioners sugar.

INGREDIENTS:

1	(15 OZ.) CAN OF PUMPKIN PUREE
1	EGG
1	TEASPOON VANILLA
½	CUP UNSALTED BUTTER, SOFTENED
½	CUP GRANULATED SUGAR
1½	TEASPOONS GROUND CINNAMON
1	PINCH NUTMEG
½	CUP PACKED LIGHT BROWN SUGAR
1	TEASPOON GINGER
1	TEASPOON BAKING SODA
1½	TEASPOONS BAKING POWDER
½	CUP DRIED CRANBERRIES
2	CUPS ALL-PURPOSE FLOUR

PURIM ROSES

YIELD: 12 COOKIES / **ACTIVE TIME:** 20 MINUTES / **TOTAL TIME:** 1 HOUR

Also known as Debla, Purim Roses are a festive Libyan dessert. The delicate addition of orange blossom water makes this fried treat light enough to consume after a big meal, or the perfect bite to have post-fast.

1. In a bowl, beat the eggs.

2. Add the baking soda and 2½ cups of flour, mixing well to form the dough.

3. Separate the dough into 5 pieces and roll out each piece in paper-thin strips.

4. Heat the oil in a deep frying pan to 325°F.

5. Cut the large strips into strips 2" wide and about 12" long, and prick the dough with a fork.

6. Wrap the strip around the prong of a wide fork while frying it.

7. Keep coiling it around itself as it fries and fry until lightly browned.

8. Remove from the oil and drain in a paper lined colander.

9. Repeat the process with the remaining dough.

10. To make the syrup, combine the sugar, lemon juice, orange blossom and rose flower water, and vanilla with 1½ cups water in a pan. Cover and simmer over low heat for 45 minutes to thicken the syrup.

11. Stir and remove from the heat, set aside.

12. Dip the roses into the heated syrup, soaking it well, and drain in a colander.

13. Place the roses on a platter and serve.

INGREDIENTS:

5	LARGE EGGS
1	TEASPOON BAKING SODA
3	CUPS ALL-PURPOSE FLOUR, DIVIDED
2	CUPS AVOCADO OIL, FOR FRYING
2	CUPS WHITE GRANULATED SUGAR
⅛	TEASPOON FRESH LEMON JUICE
⅛	TEASPOON ORANGE BLOSSOM FLOWER WATER
⅛	TEASPOON ROSE WATER
⅛ T	EASPOON VANILLA EXTRACT

RUGELACH

YIELD: 48 COOKIES / **ACTIVE TIME:** 1 HOUR / **TOTAL TIME:** 2 HOURS

Croissant-shaped but packing a crunchy bite, rugelach is a beloved treat for American and European Jews. The filling can vary from baker to baker, but traditionally, rugelach comes bursting with chocolate, cinnamon, nuts, or dried fruit.

1. In a large bowl, beat butter and cream cheese until smooth. Combine flour and salt; gradually add to cream cheese mixture and mix well. Divide dough into fourths. Wrap each portion in plastic wrap; refrigerate for 1 hour or until easy to handle.

2. Roll out each portion between two sheets of waxed paper into a 12" circle. Remove the top sheet of waxed paper. Combine sugar and cinnamon. Brush each circle with 1 tablespoon melted butter. Sprinkle each with 3 tablespoons cinnamon-sugar and 2 tablespoons pecans. Cut each into 12 wedges.

3. Roll up wedges from the wide end; place pointed side down 2 in. apart on ungreased baking sheets. Curve ends to form a crescent shape.

4. Bake at 350°F for 24 to 26 minutes or until golden brown. Remove to wire racks. Brush warm cookies with remaining butter; sprinkle with remaining cinnamon-sugar.

INGREDIENTS:

DOUGH

1   CUP BUTTER, SOFTENED

1   PACKAGE (8 OZ.) CREAM CHEESE, SOFTENED

2   CUPS ALL-PURPOSE FLOUR

½   TEASPOON SALT

FILLING

1   CUP SUGAR

2   TABLESPOONS GROUND CINNAMON

½   CUP BUTTER, MELTED, DIVIDED

½   CUP FINELY CHOPPED PECANS

Rugelach, page 641

RAINBOW COOKIES

YIELD: 8 DOZEN / **ACTIVE TIME:** 1 HOUR / **TOTAL TIME:** 13 HOURS

These classic New York treats are traditionally served in synagogues and at Jewish celebrations but actually have Italian roots. To make, you'll bake three thin cakes, spread jam between them and coat with smooth melted chocolate.

1. Grease the bottoms of 3 matching 13" x 9" baking pans (or reuse 1 pan). Line the pans with waxed paper; grease the paper.

2. Place almond paste in a large bowl; break up with a fork. Cream with butter, sugar and egg yolks until light and fluffy, 5 to 7 minutes. Stir in flour. In another bowl, beat egg whites until soft peaks form. Fold into dough, mixing until thoroughly blended.

3. Divide dough into 3 portions (about 1⅓ cups each). Color 1 portion with red food coloring and 1 with green; leave the remaining portion uncolored. Spread each portion into the prepared pans. Bake at 350°F until the edges are light golden brown, 10 to 12 minutes.

4. Invert onto wire racks; remove waxed paper. Place another wire rack on top and turn over. Cool completely.

5. Place the green layer on a large piece of plastic wrap. Spread evenly with raspberry jam. Top with an uncolored layer and spread with apricot jam. Top with pink layer. Bring plastic wrap over layers. Slide onto a baking sheet and set a cutting board or a heavy, flat pan on top to compress layers. Refrigerate overnight.

6. The next day, melt chocolate in a microwave; stir until smooth. Spread over the top layer; allow to harden. With a sharp knife, trim edges. Cut into ½" strips across the width; then cut each strip into 4 to 5 pieces. Store in airtight containers.

INGREDIENTS:

1	(8 OZ.) CAN OF ALMOND PASTE
1	CUP UNSALTED BUTTER, SOFTENED
1	CUP SUGAR
4	LARGE EGGS, SEPARATED, ROOM TEMPERATURE
2	CUPS ALL-PURPOSE FLOUR
6-8	DROPS RED FOOD COLORING
6-8	DROPS GREEN FOOD COLORING
¼	CUP SEEDLESS RED RASPBERRY JAM
¼	CUP APRICOT PRESERVES
1	CUP SEMISWEET CHOCOLATE CHIPS

SFENJ DONUTS

YIELD: 15 SERVINGS / **ACTIVE TIME:** 40 MINUTES / **TOTAL TIME:** 3 HOURS

A hot, crunchy, deep- fried gift with Moroccan origins. It's not particularly sweet on its own, but pairs perfectly with tea or coffee and acts as a satisfying bite to be had at the start of the day or end of the evening.

1. In a large bowl, mix the flour, yeast, salt, and sugar. Add the egg yolks and slowly drizzle in the water while mixing by hand.

2. Knead until a sticky, smooth, soft dough has formed.

3. Spray the dough with oil spray and cover the bowl with plastic wrap or a plastic bag. Let the dough rise for about 1 to 2 hours.

4. Grease a large cookie sheet with some vegetable oil. Set aside.

5. Divide the dough into 15 parts, roll each piece into a ball, and place it on the greased cookie sheet. Cover the dough balls with a slightly damp kitchen towel for a second rise, about 30 minutes to 1 hour.

6. Pour the vegetable oil into a wide, deep pan, about one-third to halfway full. Heat the oil to 340°F to 400°F.

7. Using your forefinger and thumb, create a hole in the center of each dough ball and place it gently into the hot oil. Fry for about 3 minutes on each side. The sfenj are ready when lightly golden.

8. Sprinkle the sfenj with powdered sugar or drizzle with honey and serve immediately.

INGREDIENTS:

4   CUPS ALL-PURPOSE FLOUR

2   TEASPOONS DRIED YEAST

1   TEASPOON SALT

1   TABLESPOON SUGAR

2   LARGE EGG YOLKS

1½   CUPS LUKEWARM WATER

      AVOCADO OIL

      POWDERED SUGAR OR
      HONEY, FOR SERVING

SFRATTI

YIELD: 6 SERVINGS / **ACTIVE TIME:** 30 MINUTES / **TOTAL TIME:** 3 HOURS

Not only do we have Jewish-Italian grandmothers to thank for sfratti, but also the original Sephardic population that settled in Italy while fleeing the Spanish Inquisition. Originating in Pitigliano, a medieval Tuscan village that was considered by its Jewish inhabitants to be a Little Jerusalem, "sfratti" means eviction—which all Pitigliano Jews faced before settling there. These rod-shaped cookies are now eaten on Rosh Hashanah to ward off further evictions.

1. Combine flour, sugar, and salt in a medium bowl. Cut in the butter until it resembles coarse crumbs. Add the wine a little at a time, mixing with a fork to moisten the dough. Continue adding wine until the dough just holds together. Divide dough in half and press into balls. Flatten balls into discs, then wrap and refrigerate for at least an hour.

2. Dough can be made up to 3 days ahead. When ready to use, allow dough to stand at room temperature until malleable but not soft.

3. In a medium saucepan over medium heat, bring the honey for the filling to a boil and cook for 5 minutes. If it starts to foam over, lower heat slightly. Add remaining ingredients and cook, stirring constantly for another 3 to 5 minutes, then remove from heat. If the mixture begins to turn dark, it is starting to burn—remove from the heat immediately and keep stirring!

4. Let the mixture stand, stirring occasionally, until it is cool enough to handle. Pour mixture onto a floured surface, divide into 6 equal portions, and shape the portions into 14" long sticks.

5. Preheat the oven to 350°F. Line a large baking sheet with parchment paper.

6. On a piece of waxed paper or plastic wrap or on a lightly floured surface, roll each disc of dough into a 14" x 12" rectangle, then cut each rectangle lengthwise into three long rectangles. Place one of the strips of filling near a long side of each rectangle, then roll the dough around the filling.

7. You will have six long sticks of dough with filling in each. Cut these into 2" sticks. Place seam side down on the prepared baking sheet, leaving 1" between the cookies. Brush with the egg wash.

8. Bake cookies until golden, about 20 minutes. Transfer to a rack and let cool.

INGREDIENTS:

1	LARGE EGG BEATEN WITH 1 TABLESPOON OF WATER
¼	TEASPOON FRESHLY GRATED BLACK PEPPER
	DASH OF NUTMEG
¼	TEASPOON GROUND GINGER
¾	TEASPOON GROUND CINNAMON
2	TEASPOONS GRATED ORANGE ZEST
2	CUPS CHOPPED WALNUTS
1	CUP HONEY
⅔	CUP CHILLED DRY WHITE WINE
⅓	CUP COLD, UNSALTED BUTTER (OR ⅓ CUP VEGETABLE OIL)
1	PINCH SALT
1	CUP SUGAR
3	CUPS UNBLEACHED, ALL-PURPOSE FLOUR

SPICED HONEY CAKE
WITH CREAM CHEESE FROSTING

YIELD: 8 SERVINGS / **ACTIVE TIME:** 20 MINUTES / **TOTAL TIME:** 1 HOUR AND 20 MINUTES

This cake is divine. You won't be able to eat just a bissel.

1. Preheat the oven to 350°F. Coat a 9" cake pan with nonstick spray and line the bottom with a parchment paper round. Whisk flour, baking powder, baking soda, salt, cinnamon, ginger, and nutmeg in a large bowl to combine.

2. Combine granulated sugar, brown sugar, oil, honey, egg, and egg yolk in another large bowl. Scrape in seeds from vanilla bean; discard pod. Using an electric mixer on medium speed, beat mixture until pale and thickened, about 4 minutes. Reduce speed to medium-low and gradually pour in orange juice and whey. Beat until frothy, about 2 minutes. Reduce speed to low and gradually add dry ingredients; beat just until smooth and homogenous (it will be thin, like pancake batter).

3. Pour into the prepared pan and bake until the cake is golden brown and the center springs back when gently pressed (a cake tester will not come out clean), 45 to 55 minutes. Transfer to a wire rack and let cool in the pan, 20 minutes. Run a knife around the edges of the cake to loosen and invert onto the rack; let cool completely.

4. Make the frosting, using an electric mixer on medium-high speed, beat cream cheese and butter in a medium bowl until smooth. Add powdered sugar, lemon zest, and salt and scrape in seeds from vanilla bean; discard pod. Beat on low speed until mixture is very light and thickened, about 2 minutes; scrape down sides of bowl. With motor running, add coconut cream by the tablespoonful and beat until very soft peaks form (save coconut milk for another use).

5. Pile frosting on top of cake and spread to edges (it's okay if it cascades over the sides).

INGREDIENTS:

CAKE

	NONSTICK VEGETABLE OIL SPRAY
2	CUPS GLUTEN-FREE ALL-PURPOSE BAKING FLOUR
1½	TEASPOONS BAKING POWDER
½	TEASPOON BAKING SODA
½	TEASPOON SEA SALT
1½	TEASPOONS CINNAMON
½	TEASPOON GROUND GINGER
⅛	TEASPOON FRESHLY GRATED NUTMEG
⅔	CUP GRANULATED SUGAR
¼	CUP (PACKED) LIGHT BROWN SUGAR
½	CUP AVOCADO OIL
½	CUP HONEY
1	LARGE EGG
1	LARGE EGG YOLK
½	VANILLA BEAN, SPLIT LENGTHWISE
½	CUP FRESH ORANGE JUICE
½	CUP BUTTERMILK

FROSTING

3	OZ. CREAM CHEESE, ROOM TEMPERATURE
3	TABLESPOONS UNSALTED BUTTER, ROOM TEMPERATURE
1	CUP POWDERED SUGAR
1	TEASPOON LEMON ZEST
1	PINCH SEA SALT
½	VANILLA BEAN, SPLIT LENGTHWISE
1	(13½ OZ.) CAN OF UNSWEETENED COCONUT MILK, CREAM SEPARATED FROM MILK, ROOM TEMPERATURE

STRUDEL WITH TROPICAL FRUITS, CHIPOTLE CHOCOLATE & WHIPPED CREAM

YIELD: 12 / **ACTIVE TIME:** 30 MINUTES / **TOTAL TIME:** 1 HOUR AND 30 MINUTES

Made with tropical fruits, chipotle chocolate, and whipped cream, this strudel combines delicious Central and South American flavors with an Eastern European pastry.

1. Preheat the oven to 375°F and line a baking sheet with parchment paper. Set aside.

2. In a bowl, mix mango, banana, apricots, lime zest, and pears with orange juice.

3. Stir in cinnamon, nutmeg, cornstarch, sugars, chipotle, and chocolate. Set aside.

4. Lay a sheet of phyllo dough on a clean surface. Brush with melted butter and cover with another sheet of phyllo. Repeat with remaining sheets.

5. Leaving a 1" border at the sides, place the mixture on one half of the dough lengthwise.

6. Starting on the side with the filling, gently roll the pastry together, with the seam on the bottom.

7. Pinch together the open sides, then tuck them under the strudel.

8. Whisk a room temperature egg with 1 tablespoon water of water to make an egg wash.

9. Brush strudel with egg wash, sprinkle with almond flakes and bake for 30 minutes, until golden brown.

10. Remove from the oven and let cool for at least 20 minutes.

11. Dust with powdered sugar and whip cream.

INGREDIENTS:

½ CUP CHOPPED MANGO

½ BANANA, CHOPPED

¼ CUP DICED DRIED APRICOTS

1 PEAR, PEELED AND CHOPPED

1 TABLESPOON ORANGE JUICE

½ TEASPOON LIME ZEST

1 TEASPOON CINNAMON

¼ TEASPOON GROUND NUTMEG

2½ TABLESPOONS CORNSTARCH

2 TABLESPOONS LIGHT BROWN SUGAR

3½ OZ. DARK CHOCOLATE, ROUGHLY CHOPPED

½ TEASPOON CHIPOTLE CHILI POWDER

6 SHEETS OF PHYLLO DOUGH

1 STICK OF UNSALTED BUTTER, MELTED

¼ CUP ALMOND FLAKES

1 EGG

1 TABLESPOON WATER

2 TABLESPOONS POWDERED SUGAR

1 OZ. WHIPPED CREAM

SUMAC, SPELT & APPLE CAKE

YIELD: 4 SERVINGS / **ACTIVE TIME:** 20 MINUTES / **TOTAL TIME:** 1 HOUR AND 20 MINUTES

There's a lot to love about this apple cake, which gets its citrusy fragrance from sumac, as well as a rustic look and nutty flavor from spelt flour. It happens to be vegan, too, for your meshuge grandkids.

1. Make the applesauce by adding the apple pieces to a saucepan with the lemon juice and water. Let them simmer for 10 to 12 minutes, or until they have completely softened. Remove from the heat and mash the apples with a fork until smooth. You will need roughly 1½ cups for this recipe.

2. Preheat the oven to 350°F. Grease a 1-pound loaf pan and line with parchment paper.

3. Mix together the flour, almonds, sumac, baking powder and baking soda in a large bowl and set aside. In a medium bowl, combine the oil, sugar and applesauce.

4. Add the wet ingredients into the dry ingredients and stir gently, ensuring there are no lumps of flour. The batter will be fairly thick. Mix in the chopped apples and pour the batter into the prepared loaf pan. Bake for 45 to 50 minutes, or until a toothpick inserted comes out clean. Leave to cool completely in the pan before turning it out.

5. To make the drizzle, mix the sugar and lemon juice in a medium bowl until it's thick enough to coat the back of a spoon. If it's too thin, add some more sugar or loosen it up by adding more lemon juice. Once the cake is completely cool, use a teaspoon to drizzle the icing and sprinkle on a little more sumac.

INGREDIENTS:

APPLESAUCE
- 2   LARGE GRANNY SMITH APPLES, PEELED, CORED AND ROUGHLY CHOPPED
- 1   TABLESPOON LEMON JUICE
- ½   CUP WATER

LOAF
- 1⅔   CUPS WHOLEMEAL SPELT FLOUR
- ½   CUP GROUND ALMONDS
- 1   TABLESPOON SUMAC
- 1   TEASPOON BAKING POWDER
- 1   TEASPOON BAKING SODA
- ¼   CUP AVOCADO OIL
- ½   CUP PLUS 2 TABLESPOON SUGAR
- 1½   CUPS APPLESAUCE
- 3   GOLDEN APPLES, PEELED, CORED AND DICED INTO SMALL CHUNKS

DRIZZLE
- ½   CUP CONFECTIONERS' SUGAR
- 1   TABLESPOON LEMON JUICE
-      SUMAC, TO DUST

VANILLA CAKE RUSKS

YIELD: 18 SERVINGS / **ACTIVE TIME:** 15 MINUTES / **TOTAL TIME:** 1 HOUR

Mandelbrodt (almond bread) in Yiddish, rusks in South Africa, biscotti in Italy. No matter what you call it, it's always the perfect accompaniment to a cup of coffee.

1. Preheat the oven to 350°F and prepare an 8" x 10" baking pan by lining it with parchment paper.

2. Sift the flour with baking powder and salt in a bowl. Set aside.

3. In a mixing bowl, using a hand mixer, beat the butter and sugar until fluffy and pale in color.

4. Add the yellow food color and mix well. Add the eggs one at a time, beating well after each addition.

5. Now add in the flour and mix until just combined. Lastly, add the vanilla extract and fold it in gently.

6. Pour the cake rusk batter into the prepared baking pan and bake for about 15 to 20 minutes or until a toothpick inserted comes out clean.

7. Remove the cake from the oven and let cool. Then remove the cake from the baking pan, and let it completely cool. Reduce the oven temperature to 300 F.

8. Once the cake has cooled, use a sharp knife to cut the cake into 1" strips.

9. Transfer the cake slices to a baking sheet and bake for 15 minutes. Remove the baking tray from the oven, turn the cake rusk sides and bake for another 15 minutes, until golden brown and crisp.

10. Remove from the oven and cool on a wire rack.

INGREDIENTS:

1	CUP ALL-PURPOSE FLOUR
1	TEASPOON BAKING POWDER
1	PINCH SEA SALT
½	CUP UNSALTED BUTTER, AT ROOM TEMPERATURE
3	EGGS, AT ROOM TEMPERATURE
¾	CUP WHITE GRANULATED SUGAR
1	TEASPOON VANILLA EXTRACT
2-3	DROPS OF YELLOW FOOD COLOR

VANILLA NUTMEG BABKA

YIELD: 2 LOAVES / **ACTIVE TIME:** 2 HOURS / **TOTAL TIME:** 17 HOURS

Texture and sweetness are added to this babka thanks to the streusel topping.

1. Sprinkle the yeast over the milk in a liquid measuring cup. Add a pinch of sugar, stir and set aside until bubbly, about 7 minutes.

2. Add the flour, the remaining ⅓ cup of sugar, eggs, vanilla extract, salt, cinnamon, nutmeg, lemon zest, and the milk and yeast mixture into a large bowl or into the bowl of a stand mixer fitted with the dough hook attachment. Knead the mixture until a dough comes together, about 5 minutes. If using a stand mixer, mix the dough on medium speed until the dough comes together, about 3 to 5 minutes.

3. Knead the butter, by hand or with the stand mixer on medium speed, into the dough in three additions, mixing each addition completely before adding more butter. (The dough will initially start to tear and lose elasticity when the butter is added; dust the dough with a bit of flour if it's too sticky.)

4. Transfer the dough to a large bowl; cover with plastic wrap and let rise at room temperature until doubled in size, about 1½ hours. Punch down the dough, re-cover with plastic wrap, and let it rise in the fridge overnight.

5. To make the filling, place the bittersweet chocolate chips, butter, and vanilla in a medium heat-proof bowl.

6. Heat the heavy cream, sugar, and salt in a small nonstick saucepan over high heat, mixing often, until it just starts to boil, about 5 minutes.

7. Pour the cream mixture over the chocolate chips and butter and whisk until the chocolate mixture is smooth and shiny. Let cool to room temperature.

INGREDIENTS:

DOUGH

¼	OZ. ACTIVE DRY YEAST
½	CUP WHOLE MILK, AT ROOM TEMPERATURE
4½	CUPS ALL-PURPOSE FLOUR, PLUS MORE FOR DUSTING
⅓	CUP SUGAR, PLUS A PINCH
5	LARGE EGGS
1	TEASPOON PURE VANILLA EXTRACT
1½	TEASPOONS KOSHER SALT
½	TEASPOON GROUND CINNAMON
¼	TEASPOON GROUND NUTMEG
1	TEASPOON FRESHLY GRATED LEMON ZEST
10	TABLESPOONS UNSALTED BUTTER, CUT INTO SMALL CUBES, AT ROOM TEMPERATURE

FILLING

1	CUP BITTERSWEET CHOCOLATE CHIPS
8	TABLESPOONS UNSALTED BUTTER, CUT INTO PIECES, AT ROOM TEMPERATURE
2	TEASPOONS PURE VANILLA EXTRACT
¾	CUP HEAVY CREAM
½	CUP SUGAR
1	PINCH KOSHER SALT

Continued . . .

8. To make the topping, whisk the flour, sugar, cocoa powder, and salt in a small bowl. Smash and work the butter in with your fingers until the mixture is sandy and chunky. Mix in the chocolate chips and set aside in a cool place.

9. Coat two 9" x 5" loaf pans with cooking spray and line with parchment paper, then spray the parchment with cooking spray. Set aside.

10. Turn out the risen dough onto a lightly floured surface. Cut the dough in half with a bench scraper or chef's knife. Using a rolling pin, roll each half into a 12" x 16" rectangle on a lightly floured surface. Using an offset spatula, spread half of the chocolate filling over each dough rectangle, all the way to the edges.

11. Starting from a long side of the dough, tightly roll each rectangle into a log. Wrap each log in plastic wrap and refrigerate for 15 minutes.

12. Unwrap the logs and gently cut each in half lengthwise with a bench scraper or chef's knife. Twist the halves together a few times, starting from the middle. Place each dough twist snugly into each prepared pan, tucking the ends under as needed. Cover with plastic wrap and let rise 1½ hours at room temperature.

13. Preheat the oven to 350°F. Brush each loaf with melted butter and sprinkle with the streusel topping. Bake until puffed and browned, about 45 minutes.

14. Meanwhile, make the simple syrup: Combine the sugar and water in a small saucepan. Bring to a boil over high heat, stirring until the sugar dissolves, about 5 minutes. Let cool completely.

15. Remove the loaves from the oven and immediately pour ½ cup of simple syrup evenly over each loaf.

16. Let the loaves sit for 10 minutes, then remove the babka from the pans, remove the parchment, and let the loaves cool completely on a wire rack.

17. Serve the babka at room temperature.

TOPPING

⅛	CUP ALL-PURPOSE FLOUR
¼	CUP SUGAR
¼	CUP COCOA POWDER
⅛	TEASPOON SEA SALT
½	CUP UNSALTED BUTTER
¼	CUP MINI CHOCOLATE CHIPS

LOAVES

	NON-STICK COOKING SPRAY
4	TABLESPOONS UNSALTED BUTTER, MELTED
¾	CUP SUGAR

YEASTED APPLE COFFEE CAKE

YIELD: 12 SERVINGS / **ACTIVE TIME:** 30 MINUTES / **TOTAL TIME:** 3 HOURS

Another apple dessert essential for Rosh Hashanah. Jump right into fall baking with this flavorful, bready cake topped with tart apple slices and an irresistible cinnamon-oat streusel.

1. Butter a 13" x 9" shallow baking dish. Mix yeast, 2 tablespoons brown sugar, and ¼ cup warm water in the bowl of a stand mixer; let sit until it foams, about 5 minutes. Whisk in egg and remaining brown sugar, then stir in 1 cup flour and mix with a wooden spoon to incorporate. Sprinkle the remaining 2 cups flour over top but do not mix in. Cover with plastic wrap and let sit in a warm, draft-free spot until mixture is visibly puffed and flour has cracks in places, 1 hour to 1 hour and 30 minutes.

2. Add sour cream, orange zest, orange juice, baking powder, and salt to the mixture and mix on medium speed with a dough hook until smooth, elastic, and just sticking to the sides of the bowl, about 4 minutes. Add 6 tablespoons butter in 2 additions, beating well between additions; beat until a soft, slightly glossy, sticky dough-batter hybrid forms, about 4 minutes.

3. Using buttered fingers, pat dough into a prepared pan in an even layer, spreading to edges. Cover and let sit in a warm, draft-free spot until puffed and nearly doubled in size, 1 hour to 1 hour and 10 minutes.

4. Just before the dough is finished rising, preheat the oven to 350°F. Pulse flour, oats, brown sugar, granulated sugar, cinnamon, and a pinch of salt in a food processor a few times to combine. Add butter and process in long pulses until streusel is the consistency of moist crumbs.

5. Working with several slices at a time, fan out the apples slightly and arrange over dough, shingling rows in different directions; sprinkle streusel over top. Bake until apples are tender and a tester inserted into the center comes out clean, 35 to 45 minutes. Transfer to a wire rack and let cool

6. Whisk powdered sugar, orange juice, and a pinch of salt in a medium bowl, adding more orange juice by the teaspoonful as needed, until the icing is very thick and smooth and falls back onto itself in a slowly dissolving ribbon. Drizzle over coffee cake.

INGREDIENTS:

CAKE
6	TABLESPOONS UNSALTED BUTTER, MELTED, SLIGHTLY COOLED, PLUS MORE
1¼	OZ. ENVELOPE ACTIVE DRY YEAST (ABOUT 2¼ TEASPOONS)
⅔	CUP (PACKED) LIGHT BROWN SUGAR, DIVIDED
1	LARGE EGG, ROOM TEMPERATURE
3	CUPS ALL-PURPOSE FLOUR, DIVIDED
½	CUP SOUR CREAM, ROOM TEMPERATURE
2	TEASPOONS FINELY GRATED ORANGE ZEST
⅓	CUP FRESH ORANGE JUICE
2	TEASPOONS BAKING POWDER
1	TEASPOON SEA SALT

STREUSEL
½	CUP ALL-PURPOSE FLOUR
½	CUP OLD-FASHIONED OATS
⅓	CUP (PACKED) LIGHT BROWN SUGAR
2	TABLESPOONS GRANULATED SUGAR
1	TEASPOON GROUND CINNAMON
	SEA SALT, TO TASTE
6	TABLESPOONS UNSALTED BUTTER, MELTED, SLIGHTLY COOLED
2	LBS. FIRM BAKING APPLES, HALVED, CORED, VERY THINLY SLICED
1½	CUPS POWDERED SUGAR
2	TABLESPOONS FRESH ORANGE JUICE

BEVERAGES

HAWAIJ HOT COCOA
WITH CINNAMON WHIPPED CREAM

YIELD: 2 SERVINGS / **ACTIVE TIME:** 15 MINUTES / **TOTAL TIME:** 15 MINUTES

A rich, warm, comforting treat to be sipped or slurped with those you consider mishpocheh. The mix of chocolate and cinnamon is a favorite flavor of Mexico.

1. Add milk, sugar, and chocolate to a heavy saucepan over medium-high heat and whisk until chocolate begins to melt.

2. Add cocoa powder, Hawaij Spice Blend, to taste, and salt. Continue to whisk until all chocolate is melted, spices are incorporated, and milk just begins to simmer.

3. Remove from heat and divide the cocoa between 4 mugs. Top with whipped cream and garnish with cinnamon sticks, if desired.

HAWAIJ SPICE BLEND: In a small bowl, combine 1½ tablespoons ground ginger, 1 tablespoon ground cinnamon, ½ tablespoon ground cardamom, ½ teaspoon ground clove, and 1 pinch nutmeg, mix well, and store in an airtight container.

CINNAMON WHIPPED CREAM: Combine 2 cups heavy cream, 2 tablespoons sugar, 1 teaspoon vanilla, and ½ teaspoon cinnamon in a stand mixer fitted with whisk attachment. Place mixer on low setting for 1 minute, then increase to high for 2 to 3 minutes until whipped cream begins to form stiff peaks.

INGREDIENTS:

- 2 CUPS MILK
- 2 TABLESPOON SUGARS
- 1 OZ. DARK OR SEMI-SWEET CHOCOLATE CHIPS OR CHUNKS OR LEFTOVER HANUKKAH GELT
- 1 SCANT TABLESPOON COCOA POWDER
- 1-2 TEASPOONS HAWAIJ SPICE BLEND
- 1 PINCH SALT
- CINNAMON WHIPPED CREAM
- CINNAMON STICKS FOR GARNISH (OPTIONAL)

EGG CREAM

YIELD: 1 SERVING / **ACTIVE TIME:** 5 MINUTES / **TOTAL TIME:** 5 MINUTES

Don't let the name fool you, there aren't eggs in this frothy chocolate drink. We'll never know for certain, but the most commonly accepted story about its creation is that Louis Auster made one by accident at the soda fountain of his Brooklyn candy shop, and the rest is rich and creamy history. Be sure to pour one out for Gem Spa in New York City's East Village.

1. Pour chocolate syrup and milk (or half-and-half) into a pint glass.

2. While beating vigorously with a fork, slowly add club soda until the glass is almost full.

3. Add a straw and serve very cold.

INGREDIENTS:

- 3 TABLESPOONS FOX'S U-BET CHOCOLATE FLAVOR SYRUP
- ¼ CUP COLD WHOLE MILK OR HALF-AND-HALF
- 13 OZ. ICE-COLD CLUB SODA OR SELTZER WATER

LIMONANA

YIELD: 4 SERVINGS / **ACTIVE TIME:** 5 MINUTES / **TOTAL TIME:** 5 MINUTES

Israel's classic summer beverage, limonana (a combination of the Hebrew words for lemon and mint) is a refreshing mix of icy lemonade and crushed mint leaves. Ubiquitous in cafés and restaurants throughout the country, this is a summer favorite that is sure to cool you down.

1. In a blender, combine the lemon juice, mint, sugar, and ½ cup water and blend until fully liquified.

2. Strain through a fine-mesh sieve, reserving the liquid and discarding the solids.

3. In a pitcher, stir together the mint mixture and the remaining 3 ½ cups water. Serve over ice.

INGREDIENTS:

1½ CUPS FRESHLY SQUEEZED LEMON JUICE

3 CUPS LOOSELY PACKED MINT LEAVES

1 CUP GRANULATED SUGAR

4 CUPS WATER

ICE CUBES

POMEGRANATE PROSECCO PUNCH

YIELD: 8 SERVINGS / **ACTIVE TIME:** 5 MINUTES / **TOTAL TIME:** 5 MINUTES

Sure, you could just pour a glass of sparkling Prosecco and call it a day, but turning it into a celebratory punch rich with fruity, tart pomegranate juice and citrus takes things in an even livelier direction.

1. Stir together juices and sugar in a large punch bowl until sugar has dissolved. Stir in Prosecco and serve garnished with fruit.

TIP: Punch, without Prosecco, can be made 1 day ahead and chilled; add Prosecco when ready to serve.

INGREDIENTS:

1   QUART CHILLED POMEGRANATE JUICE

2   TABLESPOONS FRESH LIME JUICE

¼   CUP SUPERFINE GRANULATED SUGAR

2   (750ML) BOTTLES CHILLED PROSECCO

2   CLEMENTINES, THINLY SLICED CROSSWISE, FOR GARNISH

1   LIME, THINLY SLICED CROSSWISE, FOR GARNISH

SACHLAV

YIELD: 8 SERVINGS / **ACTIVE TIME:** 15 MINUTES / **TOTAL TIME:** 15 MINUTES

With roots in Turkey where it was traditionally made using ground orchid bulbs, in Israel this thick and creamy milk-based drink is served hot and topped with pistachios, grated coconut, and raisins. It's perfect to keep you warm during winter months, and we've been told it's also quite the aphrodisiac . . . we're already schvitzing.

1. In a bowl, whisk together ¼ cup milk with the cornstarch to form a slurry.

2. Heat a pot over medium-low heat and add the remaining milk, vanilla, sugar or honey, and salt. Once the milk is hot but is not quite simmering, whisk in the slurry. Continue to whisk or stir the milk with a spoon, until the sweetener completely dissolves into the liquid, and the sachlav thickens enough to coat a spoon, about 3 to 5 minutes. If whisking, your milk will become frothy like a cappuccino, if using a spoon it will thicken more like a custard; either way, make sure the liquid never reaches a boil.

3. Once thickened, remove the sachlav from the heat and add the rose water or orange blossom water. Taste, and add more if desired. If the mixture becomes too thick for your liking, dilute it with a little more milk.

4. Serve the sachlav alongside your desired garnishes.

INGREDIENTS:

4	CUPS WHOLE MILK OR COCONUT MILK
¼	CUP CORNSTARCH
2	TEASPOONS VANILLA EXTRACT OR 1 VANILLA BEAN, SPLIT AND SEEDS SCRAPED OUT OF THE POD
3	TABLESPOONS SUGAR OR HONEY, OR TO TASTE
1	PINCH SALT
½	TEASPOON ROSE OR ORANGE BLOSSOM WATER, OR TO TASTE
	FINELY CHOPPED PISTACHIOS, FOR SERVING
	SHREDDED COCONUT, FOR SERVING
	GROUND CINNAMON OR CARDAMOM, FOR SERVING

SEPHARDIC-INSPIRED SANGRIA – TWO WAYS

YIELD: 6 SERVINGS / **ACTIVE TIME:** 10 MINUTES / **TOTAL TIME:** 4 HOURS

Wine, spices, and fruity flavors combined into a refreshing drink. What's not to love?

WHITE PEACH SANGRIA WITH ORANGE BLOSSOM WATER

1. Add 1 peach worth of slices to a blender or food processor with a splash of water and pulse until smooth.

2. In a tall pitcher, add peach puree, sliced peach, rum, simple syrup, orange blossom water, and wine. Mix well and refrigerate for at least 4 hours.

3. When ready to serve, pour into glasses and top with either sparkling wine or sparkling water

STRAWBERRY ROSÉ SANGRIA

1. Add the frozen strawberries to a blender or food processor with a splash of water and pulse until smooth.

2. In a tall pitcher, add strawberry puree, simple syrup, fresh strawberries, plum, rum, rose water, and wine. Mix well and refrigerate for at least 4 hours.

3. When ready to serve, pour into glasses and top with either sparkling water or sparkling wine.

INGREDIENTS:

WHITE PEACH SANGRIA WITH ORANGE BLOSSOM WATER

2   LARGE PEACHES, PITTED AND SLICED

2   TABLESPOONS LIGHT RUM

¼   CUP SIMPLE SYRUP

2   TEASPOONS ORANGE BLOSSOM WATER

1   (750ML) BOTTLE WHITE WINE (WE RECOMMEND PINOT GRIGIO)

    SPARKLING WATER OR SPARKLING WINE, FOR SERVING

STRAWBERRY ROSÉ SANGRIA

1   CUP FROZEN STRAWBERRIES

1   CUP FRESH STRAWBERRIES, LEFT WHOLE OR CUT IN HALF

1   RED PLUM, PITTED AND SLICED

2   TABLESPOONS LIGHT RUM

½   CUP SUGAR

2   TEASPOONS ROSE WATER

1   (750ML) BOTTLE ROSÉ WINE

    SPARKLING WATER OR SPARKLING WINE, FOR SERVING

SALEP

YIELD: 2 SERVINGS / **ACTIVE TIME:** 5 MINUTES / **TOTAL TIME:** 15 MINUTES

This warming drink dates back to the Ottoman Empire.

1. Add rice flour and milk to a small saucepan over medium heat and bring to a simmer, whisking constantly to avoid clumping.

2. When the mixture has thickened, about 2 minutes longer, add sugar and rose water and stir until sugar dissolves completely.

3. Divide salep between two mugs and garnish with cinnamon and pistachios.

INGREDIENTS:

2	TABLESPOONS GLUTINOUS RICE FLOUR
2	CUPS WHOLE MILK
4	TEASPOONS SUGAR
¼	TEASPOON ROSE WATER
	GROUND CINNAMON, FOR GARNISH
	FINELY CHOPPED PISTACHIOS, FOR GARNISH

INDUSTRY INSIDER

*I*sraeli-American chef Avi Shemtov opened The Chubby Chickpea as a quick-serve Israeli street-food concept in 2010 in the suburbs of Boston, Massachusetts. Credited with being part of the global movement to popularize Israeli cuisine, Shemtov launched The Chubby Chickpea Food Truck less than two years later to critical acclaim. The Chubby Chickpea continues to operate multiple food trucks and catering outlets in the Boston area. Today, Shemtov serves as Executive Chef of Simcha, located in Sharon, Massachusetts. Focused on a New England-influenced modern Israeli menu, Simcha was named one of Boston's 15 Best New Restaurants by both *Boston Magazine* and *The Boston Globe*.

Roasted & Stuffed Sardines, page 678

ROASTED & STUFFED SARDINES

YIELD: 2 SERVINGS / **ACTIVE TIME:** 20 MINUTES / **TOTAL TIME:** 40 MINUTES

This is an ideal way to use up leftover bread, which absorbs so much flavor in this preparation. Keep in mind that the sardines' bones are edible.

1. Clean the sardines by making an incision in their belly from head to tail. Remove the guts and, carefully, snap their spine at the neck and tail. This will leave the sardine intact enough to hold shape when roasted. Rinse and set aside.

2. Add 2 tablespoons olive oil to a medium-sized frying pan over medium-high heat. When the oil begins to shimmer add the onion, celery, salt, paprika, cumin, and garlic. Allow the onions to sweat for 4 to 5 minutes, or until they become translucent.

3. Add water and simmer for 3 or 4 minutes. Add the parsley and bread. Stir often, allowing the bread to absorb the liquids and brown a bit. After 5 minutes remove from heat.

4. Preheat oven to 450°F.

5. Place sardines in a cast-iron skillet, keeping them nestled into each other as much as possible so they help each other hold shape. Stuff the sardines' bellies with the stuffing. Sprinkle them with the remainder of the olive oil and roast for 15 to 20 minutes, or until they reach an internal temperature of 145°F.

6. Serve hot with tahini.

INGREDIENTS:

5	WHOLE FRESH SARDINES
3	TABLESPOONS EXTRA VIRGIN OLIVE OIL, DIVIDED
½	WHITE ONION, CHOPPED
¼	CUP CHOPPED CELERY
1	TEASPOON KOSHER SALT
1	TABLESPOON PAPRIKA
1	PINCH CUMIN
2	GARLIC CLOVES, MINCED
2	TABLESPOONS WATER
¼	CUP CHOPPED PARSLEY
1	CUP CUBED DAY-OLD BREAD
	TAHINI, TO SERVE

OLIVE OIL-POACHED FLUKE

YIELD: 2 SERVINGS / **ACTIVE TIME:** 15 MINUTES / **TOTAL TIME:** 2 HOURS

Similar to crudo, this dish highlights the beauty of stellar ingredients.

1. Using an immersion circulator submerged in a container filled with water, set temperature to 145°F.

2. In a zip lock bag, place the fluke and 1 cup extra-virgin olive oil. Place into the water, making sure to remove all air from the bag and leave the top of the bag outside of the water—no water in the bag; I find the best method is to leave the bag open and slowly submerge it, allowing the water to create a vacuum seal, then chip clip the bag to the side of your container. Sous vide for 1 hour.

3. Leaving the top of the bag open, refrigerate the fish for at least 1 hour.

4. Slice the fish into 1" thick pieces and plate chilled. Season with salt and pepper, pool the remainder of the olive oil around the fish, garnish with parsley, and squeeze lemon over the top.

INGREDIENTS:

8	OZ. FLUKE FILLET
1¼	CUP EXTRA VIRGIN OLIVE OIL, DIVIDED
1	TEASPOON KOSHER SALT
½	LEMON
1	PINCH BLACK PEPPER
1	PINCH PARSLEY, FOR GARNISH

Olive Oil-Poached Fluke, page 679

Ensalada de Pulpo, page 684

ENSALADA DE PULPO

YIELD: 8 SERVINGS / **ACTIVE TIME:** 30 MINUTES / **TOTAL TIME:** 2 HOURS AND 30 MINUTES

Super tender tentacles are the trick to this dish, and you get there by simply breaking down the protein. This version uses our herb-filled verde sauce paired with astringent quick pickles for texture contrast.

1. Fill a pot, large enough to fully submerge the octopus under water, with water and bring it to a hard boil. Once the water is boiling, add the frozen octopus and cover the pot. Boil for 1 hour and 40 minutes (if the water reduces too much add water as needed). By the time you remove the octopus from the water, it should be tender enough to fall apart when grabbed by tongs. Separate the tentacles and put them aside to cool.

2. While the octopus is boiling, cut ⅛" thick radish slices, salt them, and cover them with half the vinegar in a bowl. In a separate bowl place ¼" thick pear slices, skin on, and also salt and submerge those in the remainder of the vinegar.

3. When you are ready to plate, heat a frying pan or grill and sear each octopus tentacle; if using a pan, add a few drops of extra-virgin olive oil so the octopus doesn't stick to the pan.

4. To serve, spoon 1 tablespoon of Verde Sauce onto the plate and place a full tentacle alongside it. Put the greens in a small pile on the plate and add radish and pear slices.

VERDE SAUCE

1. Add all of the ingredients to a medium saucepan over high heat, bring to a boil, then reduce to medium-high heat amd simmer for 40 minutes.

2. Allow to cool for 15 to 20 minutes, then process in a blender or food processor. Use a course strainer to remove any large pulp or food particles. Keeps in refrigerator for up to 2 weeks.

INGREDIENTS:

1	WHOLE OCTOPUS, FROZEN
3	RADISHES
2	TEASPOONS KOSHER SALT
1	CUP WHITE VINEGAR, DIVIDED
1	PEAR
½	CUP VERDE SAUCE (SEE RECIPE)
2	CUPS MESCLUN GREENS

VERDE SAUCE

4	MEDIUM JALAPEÑOS, CHOPPED
1	WHITE ONION, CHOPPED
1	TABLESPOON CUMIN
1	TEASPOON WHITE PEPPER
1	TABLESPOON KOSHER SALT
1	TABLESPOON CHOPPED CILANTRO
1	TABLESPOON CHOPPED PARSLEY
2	CUPS WHITES VINEGAR
1	CUP WATER

CRISPY SALMON RICE

YIELD: 2 SERVINGS / **ACTIVE TIME:** 15 MINUTES / **TOTAL TIME:** 30 MINUTES

When cutting sides of salmon into portions, or making lox, I always remove the belly. This makes for more evenly cooked salmon, but it also lets me keep the most precious part of the fish to incorporate in other dishes in smaller amounts. I feel strongly about this philosophy as it ties into my grandmother's kitchen and the way that my father has always cooked: rich ingredients go a long way in hearty peasant dishes. This rice is a beautiful side or a weekday main.

1. Add the oil to a large frying pan over high heat; use the largest pan available as the surface area is critical for this recipe. When the oil begins to shimmer add the onion, scallions, parsley, and salt. Stirring often, cook until the onions are translucent.

2. Add the rice and stir frequently, until the rice gets crispy, about 3 to 5 minutes. Add the salmon, turn down the heat to medium-high and allow to warm through, about 3 minutes.

3. In a small bowl, whisk the molasses and vinegar together. Before removing the rice from heat add this mixture to the rice and stir. Remove from heat and serve hot.

INGREDIENTS:

- 2 TABLESPOONS CANOLA OIL
- ½ WHITE ONION, MINCED
- ¼ CUP SLICED SCALLIONS
- ¼ CUP CHOPPED PARSLEY
- 2 TEASPOONS KOSHER SALT
- 2 CUPS COOKED WHITE RICE, COLD
- 6 OZ. SALMON BELLY
- 1 TABLESPOON POMEGRANATE MOLASSES
- 1 TABLESPOON APPLE CIDER VINEGAR

Crispy Salmon Rice,
page 685

Turkish Eggplant Salad,
page 690

TURKISH EGGPLANT SALAD

YIELD: 4 SERVINGS / **ACTIVE TIME:** 30 MINUTES / **TOTAL TIME:** 1 HOUR AND 30 MINUTES

At its core, our food is Turkish in one form or another. My grandmother was Turkish through and through, and my father's food bears the same fingerprints. Our eggplant salad is more than likely the purest show of our Turkish heritage: unmistakably garlic heavy, smoky, earthy.

1. In either a 450°F oven or on a grill set to high, char eggplants until they are fully softened and somewhat shriveled; this not an exact science, but longer is better, 40 minutes to 1 hour. Allow to cool.

2. Add the oil to a large frying pan over high heat. When the oil begins to shimmer add the tomatoes and onions, followed by the remainder of the ingredients, except the parsley. Cook for approximately 20 minutes, stirring occasionally. Remove from heat.

3. Split open the eggplants and scoop out the soft flesh and fold it i into the tomato mixture, adding the parsley as you go. Serve at room temperature.

INGREDIENTS:

2	LARGE EGGPLANTS
2	TABLESPOONS OLIVE OIL
3	MEDIUM TOMATOES, LARGE DICE
1	WHITE ONION, JULIENNED
4	GARLIC CLOVES
1	TABLESPOON PAPRIKA
1	TEASPOON KOSHER SALT
1	TEASPOON CUMIN
1	TEASPOON CAYENNE
½	CUP CHOPPED PARSLEY

SHAVED SNAP PEA SALAD

YIELD: 2 SERVINGS / **ACTIVE TIME:** 30 MINUTES / **TOTAL TIME:** 1 HOUR

This salad depends on the thin slicing of the snap peas and the quality of the honey to fully blossom into the beautiful salad it is meant to be. At its best, this is a vibrant mix of sweet and acidic, herby and crunchy.

1. Using a sharp knife, stack 4 snap peas at a time and cut thin slices on the bias. Once all of the snap peas are cut, put them into a medium-sized bowl.

2. By hand, mix all of the other ingredients into the peas, making sure to thoroughly incorporate them all.

3. Allow the salad to stand for at least 30 minutes, and up to an hour, before serving.

INGREDIENTS:

1	LB. SNAP PEAS
1	TABLESPOON CHOPPED DILL
1	TABLESPOON CHOPPED BASIL
1	TABLESPOON CHOPPED MINT
2	TEASPOONS HONEY
¼	CUP WHITE VINEGAR
1	TEASPOON KOSHER SALT
1	TABLESPOON CRUSHED TOASTED WALNUTS

Shaved Snap Pea Salad, page 691

Sumac & Apple-Roasted Cauliflower,
page 696

SUMAC & APPLE-ROASTED CAULIFLOWER

YIELD: 4 SERVINGS / **ACTIVE TIME:** 20 MINUTES / **TOTAL TIME:** 1 HOUR AND 15 MIN

Whole roasted cauliflower is a staple of the modern Israeli kitchen. By roasting the cauliflower covered it gets very soft while also absorbing the onion, apple, and sumac flavors. This soft but crispy version is sweet and creamy.

1. Preheat the oven to 400°F.

2. Combine the apple, onion, sumac, salt, sugar, and water in a food processor and pulse.

3. Using a sharp knife, remove any leaves from the cauliflower and square off the stem. Place the cauliflower head in a roasting pan and coat with the apple and onion mixture. Wrap with foil and roast for 45 minutes, until the cauliflower is soft enough to cut into with a fork. Set the oven to 450°F and finish the cauliflower for 10 more minutes uncovered.

4. To serve, set the cauliflower on a rimmed plate and drizzle with honey and tahini.

INGREDIENTS:

1	APPLE, PEELED AND QUARTERED
1	ONION, QUARTERED
1	TABLESPOON SUMAC
1	TABLESPOON KOSHER SALT
1	TABLESPOON SUGAR
½	CUP WATER
1	WHOLE CAULIFLOWER
2	TABLESPOONS HONEY
2	TABLESPOONS TAHINI

PITA BREAD

YIELD: 8 SERVINGS / **ACTIVE TIME:** 1 HOUR / **TOTAL TIME:** 3 HOURS

At its heart, Simcha is a restaurant built around this bread. We installed our centerpiece wood-fired oven specifically to produce fresh hot pita. It isn't as easy at home with your oven, but it is doable and the result is remarkable.

1. In a large bowl combine the water, yeast, and sugar. Let sit for 15 minutes or so, until the water is foamy and bubbling. Add the flours and salt, mixing until the flour and water form a dough. Sprinkle with flour when necessary to work the dough. Knead the dough for 1 minute or so, just until the ball is smooth and uniform; it does not need to be kneaded otherwise. Set aside, covered by a towel or plastic wrap, for 2 hours.

2. Preheat the oven to 500°F and place a cast-iron pan or upside-down baking sheet in the oven.

3. Separate the dough into 8 even pieces and ball them up. One at a time, on a floured surface, press the ball down and then, using a rolling pin, roll into a flat surface about ¼" thick.

4. Bake the pitas, 1 at a time. It will take approximately 3 minutes to puff up and 5 minutes or so to brown slightly and be done baking. Serve hot or keep at room temperature.

INGREDIENTS:

1	CUP LUKEWARM WATER
3	TEASPOONS DRY ACTIVE YEAST
3	TEASPOONS WHITE SUGAR
1¾	CUPS ALL-PURPOSE WHITE FLOUR
1	CUP WHEAT FLOUR
1	TABLESPOON KOSHER SALT

Pita Bread, page 697

RED ZHOUG

YIELD: 20 OZ. / **ACTIVE TIME**: 10 MINUTES / **TOTAL TIME**: 10 MINUTES

My dad calls zhoug "Israeli ketchup" because he puts it on everything. To me, it's more like our Sriracha. It varies drastically, not only by the region, but even by the household.

1. Cut the chilis into 5 pieces each. Place the chilis, parsley, onion, garlic, and lemon juice in a food processor and pulse until all of the ingredients are combined and rough chopped.

2. Add the salt, cayenne, cumin, paprika, and, while on high, slowly pour in the olive oil. If the mixture doesn't blend smoothly, add the water to help it along. The finished product should be smooth and a little pasty and will keep in the refrigerator for up to 2 weeks.

INGREDIENTS:

4	FRESNO CHILES, STEMS REMOVED
2	CUPS PARSLEY
1	ONION, ROUGH CHOPPED
5	GARLIC CLOVES
	JUICE OF 1 LEMON
1	TABLESPOON KOSHER SALT
1	TEASPOON CAYENNE
1	TABLESPOON CUMIN
2	TABLESPOONS PAPRIKA
¾	CUP EXTRA VIRGIN OLIVE OIL
¼	CUP WATER, AS NEEDED

GREEN ZHOUG

YIELD: 20 OZ. / **ACTIVE TIME:** 10 MINUTES / **TOTAL TIME:** 10 MINUTES

Not only does this work as a stand-alone condiment, it makes for an outstanding marinade.

1. Cut the jalapeños into 5 pieces each. Place the peppers, parsley, cilantro, mint, onion, garlic and lemon juice into a food processor and pulse until all ingredients are combined and rough chopped.

2. Add the salt and, while on high, slowly pour in the olive oil. If the mixture doesn't blend smoothly, add the water to help it along. The finished product should be the texture of a chimichurri and it will keep in the refrigerator for up to 1 week.

INGREDIENTS:

4	JALAPEÑOS, STEMS REMOVED
2	CUPS PARSLEY
¼	CUP CILANTRO
6	MINT LEAVES
1	ONION, ROUGH CHOPPED
5	GARLIC CLOVES
	JUICE OF 1 LEMON
1	TABLESPOON KOSHER SALT
½	CUP EXTRA VIRGIN OLIVE OIL
¼	CUP WATER

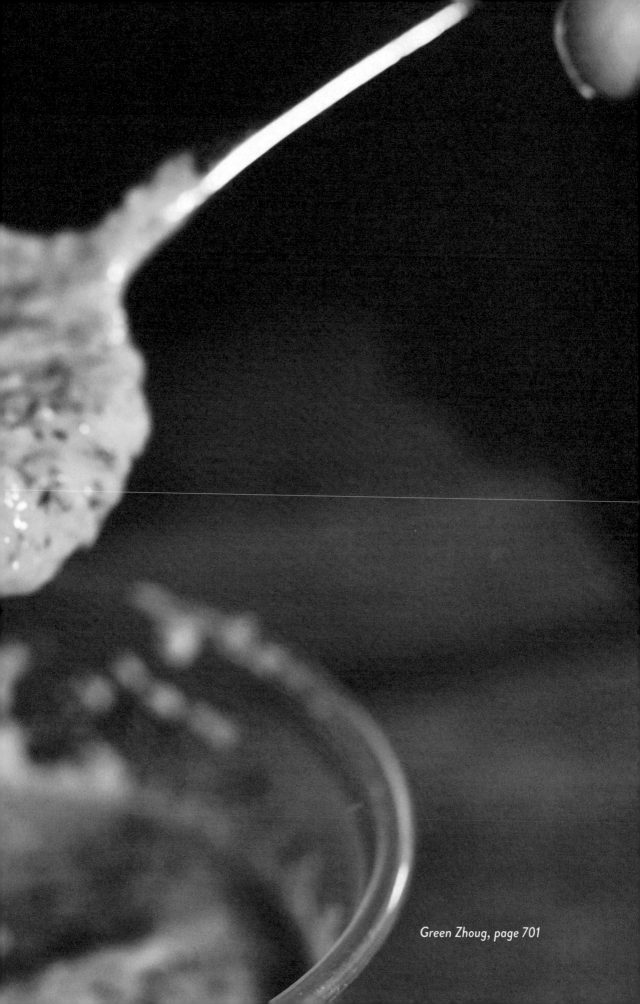

Green Zhoug, page 701

Couscous Arancini, page 706

COUSCOUS ARANCINI

YIELD: 2 SERVINGS / **ACTIVE TIME:** 30 MINUTES / **TOTAL TIME:** 1 HOUR AND 25 MINUTES

One of the many things we believe in as a team, hand-in-hand with supporting local farmers and butchers, is limiting food waste. Our couscous arancini comes from us needing a way to repurpose leftover couscous. I love them because like a lot of our menu items, they are familiar and yet completely different.

1. Bring the water to a boil.

2. In a medium-sized bowl, combine the couscous and the seasonings and mix well. Add the boiling water to the couscous and cover the bowl with plastic wrap. After 10 minutes use a fork to fluff the couscous. Add ½ cup feta to the couscous and mix well.

3. In a deep pot heat at least 4 inches of canola oil to 350°F.

4. Using your hands, ball up about 1 oz. couscous and, by pressing into the ball with your thumb, make a divot and fill it with feta and close the ball around it.

5. Once all of the couscous balls are formed and filled, fry them, 4 at a time, for approximately 4 minutes until they're golden brown. Serve hot.

INGREDIENTS:

2½	CUPS WATER
2	CUPS COUSCOUS
1	TABLESPOON PAPRIKA
1	TABLESPOON GRANULATED GARLIC
2	TEASPOONS KOSHER SALT
1	TEASPOON CUMIN
1	CUP CRUMBLED FETA CHEESE
	CANOLA OIL, FOR FRYING

TUNA KIBBEH NAYEH

YIELD: 2 SERVINGSS / **ACTIVE TIME:** 20 MINUTES / **TOTAL TIME:** 45 MINUTES

During summer months our New England customers lean toward the ocean a bit and I found it was important to highlight high-quality local fish with ceviches and crudos. This dish was inspired by my love of herbaceous tuna ceviche and spicy tuna rolls.

1. Add the bulger wheat a small saucepan, cover with water, and cook for 15 to 20 minutes, or until tender. Strain and run under cold water until cool.

2. Slice the tuna and then dice it into ¼" chunks.

3. In a bowl, combine the herbs, citrus juices, salt, and black pepper and mix well. Stir in the tuna. Allow to sit for 5 minutes, then add the bulgur wheat, red onion, and the aioli.

4. Cut the avocado into ¼" chunks, then gently fold these into the mixture, breaking them up as little as possible.

5. The mixture can be served over lettuce wraps, on its own with chips, or in a bowl as a snack. At Simcha, we pan-fry shredded phyllo dough until it is golden brown, and serve the Kibbe spooned over the buttery pastry. To do this, warm a nonstick frying pan and melt the butter. Place 1 cup of the phyllo into the melted butter and use a spatula to flatten it into a pancake. Brown on both sides, approximately 1 minute per side. Repeat with the remainder of the phyllo. Serve warm with the cold Kibbe.

SMOKED EGG AIOLI

1. Place the yolks in a metal bowl. Place the bowl in a deep baking pan. In a cast-iron skillet over high heat, get the wood chips hot and light them. Place the cast iron on a sheet pan also, next to the bowl, and cover the pan with foil. Allow the smoke to flavor the yolks for 20 minutes.

2. In a small bowl, combine the yolks and vinegar and gently break the yolks and allow them to sit for 5 minutes.

3. Add the salt and slowly drizzle the oil into the yolks as you beat them, using an electric hand mixer or immersion blender. The mixture will thicken. If it remains too thin, slowly add a little more oil. Refrigerate for up to 6 days.

INGREDIENTS:

1	CUP BULGUR WHEAT
8	OZ. SUSHI-GRADE TUNA
2	BASIL LEAVES, CHIFFONADE
2	MINT LEAVES, CHIFFONADE
	JUICE OF 1 LIME
	JUICE OF 1 LEMON
1	TEASPOON KOSHER SALT
1	PINCH BLACK PEPPER
¼	CUP RED ONION, FINE DICE
2	TABLESPOONS SMOKED EGG AIOLI (SEE RECIPE)
1	RIPE AVOCADO
2	CUPS SHREDDED PHYLLO DOUGH (OPTIONAL)
2	TABLESPOONS UNSALTED BUTTER (OPTIONAL)

SMOKED EGG AIOLI

2	EGG YOLKS
½	CUP WOOD CHIPS, FOR SMOKING
1	TABLESPOON WHITE VINEGAR
1	TEASPOON KOSHER SALT
1	CUP CANOLA OIL

Tuna Kibbeh Nayeh, page 707

MARINATED LAMB HEART

YIELD: 2 SERVINGS S / **ACTIVE TIME:** 20 MINUTES / **TOTAL TIME:** 4 HOURS

The first animal that we started butchering in-house was lamb, and it was a real transition for me in the way I viewed animals and food waste. Feeling the weight of the still warm lamb when I left the slaughterhouse, I felt more committed than ever to use as much of the animal as possible. When Joe, our butcher, finished breaking the meat down I got a pan hot and seared the heart. We all shared the tender meat; it was a very communal end to a process that had begun much earlier. Aside from the desire not to waste food, lamb heart is tasty and tender—it eats very much like filet. This interesting and delicious meat is a beautiful complement to a creamy starch.

1. Add all of the ingredients, except the lamb heart, to a bowl and mix well.

2. Place the lamb heart on a cutting board and use a sharp knife to remove the connective tissue—white with honeycomb-like texture—from the outside of the lamb heart. Place the heart in the marinade and refrigerate for 2 to 4 hours.

3. On a hot grill or in a very hot skillet, place the lamb heart topside down. For medium-rare, after approximately 2 minutes turn over the lamb heart. After another 2 minutes, remove the lamb from the heat and allow to rest for a few minutes. For more well-done meat add a few minutes of cooking time for each side.

4. Slice the lamb heart into ½" slices and serve hot.

INGREDIENTS:

½	CUP WHITE VINEGAR
2	TABLESPOONS EXTRA VIRGIN OLIVE OIL
¼	CUP CHOPPED PARSLEY
1	TEASPOON CORIANDER
½	WHITE ONION, MINCED
3	MINT LEAVES, CHOPPED
3	BASIL LEAVES, CHOPPED
2	GARLIC CLOVES, MINCED
2	TEASPOONS KOSHER SALT
1	(6-8 OZ.) LAMB HEART

Sumac & Lime Mahi-Mahi with Pickled Apple Couscous, page 714

SUMAC & LIME MAHI-MAHI
WITH PICKLED APPLE COUSCOUS

YIELD: 2 SERVINGSS / **ACTIVE TIME:** 20 MINUTES / **TOTAL TIME:** 45 MINUTES

Mahi-mahi is such a tender, gently flavored fish and it takes marinades very well. This preparation is bright and warm, pairing beautifully with the subtle flavors in the couscous.

1. In a small bowl, whisk together the lime juice, sumac, honey, 1 teaspoon salt, and garlic. Add the mahi-mahi and refrigerate for at least 2 hours.

2. Add 1 tablespoon of olive oil to a frying pan over medium heat, and when warm add onion and the remainder of the salt. Stir in the parsley, mint, cilantro, and basil and remove from heat.

3. In a medium-sized bowl thoroughly mix these ingredients with the couscous. Pour in the boiling water and cover the bowl with plastic wrap. After 10 minutes remove the plastic wrap and, using a fork, fluff the couscous. Set aside.

4. Add the remainder of the olive oil to a small frying pan over medium heat. When the oil begins to shimmer, add the mahi-mahi, bottom-side down. Let the fish cook on that side for 4 to 5 minutes, and then turn it over, allowing the second side to also cook for 4 to 5 minutes. Once the fish easily flakes apart (or is 145°F) it is done.

5. Serve on top of the couscous.

INGREDIENTS:

	JUICE OF 2 LIMES
1	TABLESPOON SUMAC
1	TEASPOON HONEY
2	TEASPOONS KOSHER SALT, DIVIDED
1	GARLIC CLOVE, MINCED
2	(6 OZ.) MAHI-MAHI FILLETS
2	TABLESPOONS EXTRA VIRGIN OLIVE OIL, DIVIDED
½	WHITE ONION, DICED
¼	CUP CHOPPED PARSLEY
1	TABLESPOON CHOPPED MINT
1	TABLESPOON CHOPPED CILANTRO
1	TABLESPOON CHOPPED BASIL
1	CUP COUSCOUS
1	CUP BOILING WATER

WHOLE BRANZINO

YIELD: 2 SERVINGSS / **ACTIVE TIME:** 20 MINUTES / **TOTAL TIME:** 40 MINUTES

Pan-roasted whole fish is completely about technique and patience, rather than about ingredients. Fresh fish is no doubt the major component, but after that, it is a show of cooking expertise rather than a simple mixing of ingredients. Similarly, ordering and eating whole fish requires its own sort of expertise. The fat content of branzino, often called "fatty bass," provides a lot of leeway when cooking. I much prefer this fish crisped up in a pan rather than grilled, as doing it this way steams the meat perfectly.

1. Preheat the oven to 425°F.

2. After the fish has been cleaned and scaled, pat dry using paper towels. Rub the fish with basil leaves and evenly distribute the salt and pepper on both sides.

3. Add the olive oil to a large cast-iron pan over high heat. When the oil begins to shimmer swirl it around in the pan. Set the fish in the coated pan and allow to brown on one side, approximately 4 to 5 minutes, and then turn and repeat for another 4 to 5 minutes. Place the pan in the oven and roast the fish for about 10 minutes, or until it registers an internal temperatures of 145°F.

4. Once the fish is out of the oven, use a spatula to place it onto a plate. Squeeze the lemon over the top and serve hot.

INGREDIENTS:

1	(1-2 LB.) WHOLE BRANZINO
1	TABLESPOON KOSHER SALT
1	TABLESPOON FRESH CRACKED BLACK PEPPER
2	FRESH BASIL LEAVES
2	TABLESPOONS EXTRA VIRGIN OLIVE OIL
½	LEMON

Whole Branzino, page 715

APPENDIX

BASIC RECIPES

STOCKS

Depending on dietary needs, ingredients on hand, and personal preference, it is always good to have solid stock recipes close by.

TIPS:

1. Stocks can stay in a freezer for up to six months.

2. This is a large recipe, which can easily be reduced to half or one-quarter the amount. However, as the same amount of time is required, it is always best to make a larger quantity and save some for the future.

VEAL, BEEF, OR LAMB STOCK

YIELD: 6 QUARTS / **ACTIVE TIME:** 30 MINUTES / **TOTAL TIME:** 6 TO 7 HOURS

Veal bones make a smoother, lighter stock than pure beef bones. However, beef bones are a more readily available (and cheaper) option. If you are making a lamb stock, try to use half beef or veal bones and half lamb bones, as lamb bones provide a pungent, often overpowering flavor.

1. Preheat oven to 350°F.

2. Lay the bones on a flat baking tray, place in the oven, and cook for 30 to 45 minutes, until they are golden brown. Remove and set aside.

3. Meanwhile, in a large stockpot, add the oil and warm over low heat. Add the vegetables and cook until any additional moisture has evaporated. This allows the flavor of the vegetables to become concentrated.

4. Add the water to the stockpot. Add the bones, aromatics, peppercorns, salt, and tomato paste to the stockpot, raise heat to high, and bring to a boil.

5. Reduce heat so that the stock simmers and cook for a minimum of 2 hours. Skim fat and impurities from the top as the stock cooks. Cook until the desired flavor is achieved, around 4 to 5 hours.

6. When the stock is finished cooking, strain through a fine strainer or cheesecloth. Place the stock in the refrigerator to chill.

7. Once cool, skim the fat layer from the top and discard. Use immediately, refrigerate, or freeze.

INGREDIENTS:

10	LBS. VEAL, BEEF, OR LAMB BONES
½	CUP VEGETABLE OIL
1	LEEK, TRIMMED AND CAREFULLY WASHED, CUT INTO 1-INCH PIECES
1	LARGE YELLOW ONION, UNPEELED, ROOT CLEANED, CUT INTO 1-INCH PIECES
2	LARGE CARROTS, PEELED AND CUT INTO 1-INCH PIECES
1	CELERY STALK WITH LEAVES, CUT INTO 1-INCH PIECES
10	QUARTS WATER
8	FRESH SPRIGS PARSLEY
5	FRESH SPRIGS THYME
2	BAY LEAVES
1	TEASPOON PEPPERCORNS
1	TEASPOON SALT
1	CUP TOMATO PASTE

CHICKEN STOCK

YIELD: 6 QUARTS / **ACTIVE TIME:** 20 MINUTES / **TOTAL TIME:** 6 TO 7 HOURS

A good homemade chicken stock should be good enough to eat on its own. As with most stocks, the longer they cook, the more flavorful they become, so feel free to increase the cooking time. This recipe will work with most poultry.

1. Preheat the oven to 350°F.

2. Lay the bones on a flat baking tray, place in the oven, and cook for 30 to 45 minutes, until they are golden brown. Remove and set aside.

3. Meanwhile, in a large stockpot, add the oil and warm over low heat. Add the vegetables and cook until any additional moisture has evaporated. This allows the flavor of the vegetables to become concentrated.

4. Add the water to the stockpot. Add the chicken carcasses and/or stewing pieces, the aromatics, the peppercorns, and the salt to the stockpot, raise heat to high, and bring to a boil.

5. Reduce heat so that the stock simmers and cook for a minimum of 2 hours. Skim fat and impurities from the top as the stock cooks. Cook until the desired flavor is achieved, around 4 to 5 hours.

6. When the stock is finished cooking, strain through a fine strainer or cheesecloth. Place stock in the refrigerator to chill.

7. Once cool, skim the fat layer from the top and discard. Use immediately, refrigerate, or freeze.

INGREDIENTS:

10	LBS. CHICKEN CARCASSES AND/OR STEWING CHICKEN PIECES
½	CUP VEGETABLE OIL
1	LEEK, TRIMMED AND CAREFULLY WASHED, CUT INTO 1-INCH PIECES
1	LARGE YELLOW ONION, UNPEELED, ROOT CLEANED, CUT INTO 1-INCH PIECES
2	LARGE CARROTS, CUT INTO 1-INCH PIECES
1	CELERY STALK WITH LEAVES, CUT INTO 1-INCH PIECES
10	QUARTS WATER
8	FRESH SPRIGS PARSLEY
5	FRESH SPRIGS THYME
2	BAY LEAVES
1	TEASPOON PEPPERCORNS
1	TEASPOON SALT

DASHI STOCK

YIELD: 6 CUPS / **ACTIVE TIME:** 10 MINUTES / **TOTAL TIME:** 40 MINUTES

Kombu is an edible dried kelp, while bonito flakes come from dried and fermented fish. Unlike the other stocks provided here, this stock tends to become bitter if cooked at too high a temperature, making it a quick and easy stock to make. While it can be frozen for later, with such a short cooking time it's well worth the effort to make it fresh.

1. In a medium saucepan, add the water and the kombu. Soak for 20 minutes, remove the kombu, and score gently with a knife.

2. Return the kombu to the saucepan and bring to a boil.

3. Remove the kombu as soon as the water boils, so that the stock doesn't become bitter.

4. Add the bonito flakes and return to a boil. Turn off heat and let stand.

5. Strain through a fine sieve and chill in the refrigerator.

INGREDIENTS:

8	CUPS COLD WATER
2	OZ. KOMBU
1	CUP BONITO FLAKES

FISH STOCK

YIELD: 6 QUARTS / **ACTIVE TIME:** 20 MINUTES / **TOTAL TIME:** 3 HOURS AND 30 MINUTES

White fish works best for this recipe, as other types of fish tend to add extra oil to the stock and overpower the delicate balance of flavors. However, if you're making a thickened or creamed soup, you can stray from that recommendation, as salmon stock is divine in those types of dishes.

1. In a large stockpot, add the oil and warm over low heat. Add the vegetables and cook until any additional moisture has evaporated. This will allow the flavor of the vegetables to become concentrated.

2. Add the whitefish bodies, the aromatics, the peppercorns, the salt, and the water to the pot.

3. Raise heat to high and bring to a boil. Reduce heat so that the stock simmers and cook for a minimum of 2 hours. Skim fat and impurities from the top as the stock cooks. As for when to stop cooking the stock, let the flavor be the judge, typcally 2 to 3 hours total.

4. When the stock is finished cooking, strain through a fine strainer or cheesecloth. Place the stock in the refrigerator to chill.

5. Once cool, skim the fat layer from the top and discard. Use immediately, refrigerate, or freeze.

INGREDIENTS:

½	CUP VEGETABLE OIL
1	LEEK, TRIMMED AND CAREFULLY WASHED, CUT INTO 1-INCH PIECES
1	LARGE YELLOW ONION, UNPEELED, ROOT CLEANED, CUT INTO 1-INCH PIECES
2	LARGE CARROTS, CUT INTO 1-INCH PIECES
1	CELERY STALK WITH LEAVES, CUT INTO 1-INCH PIECES
10	LBS. WHITEFISH BODIES
8	FRESH SPRIGS PARSLEY
5	FRESH SPRIGS THYME
2	BAY LEAVES
1	TEASPOON PEPPERCORNS
1	TEASPOON SALT
10	QUARTS WATER

VEGETABLE STOCK

YIELD: 6 CUPS / **ACTIVE TIME:** 20 MINUTES / **TOTAL TIME:** 3 HOURS

This stock is an excellent way to use up leftover vegetable trimmings you're loath to throw away. However, it's best to avoid starches like potatoes and colorful vegetables like beets, as these will make the stock cloudy or add an unwanted tint. This stock is an ideal replacement for any of the meat stocks in this book.

1. In a large stockpot, add the oil and the vegetables and cook over low heat until any additional moisture has evaporated. This will allow the flavor of the vegetables to become concentrated.

2. Add the aromatics, water, peppercorns, and salt. Raise heat to high and bring to a boil. Reduce heat so that the soup simmers and cook for 2 hours. Skim fat and impurities from the top as the stock cooks.

3. When the stock is finished cooking, strain through a fine strainer or cheesecloth. Place the stock in the refrigerator to chill.

4. Once cool, skim the fat layer from the top and discard. Use immediately, refrigerate, or freeze.

INGREDIENTS:

2   TABLESPOONS VEGETABLE OIL

2   LARGE LEEKS, TRIMMED AND CAREFULLY WASHED

2   LARGE CARROTS, PEELED AND SLICED

2   CELERY STALKS, SLICED

2   LARGE ONIONS, SLICED

3   GARLIC CLOVES, UNPEELED AND SMASHED

2   FRESH SPRIGS PARSLEY

2   FRESH SPRIGS THYME

1   BAY LEAF

8   CUPS WATER

½   TEASPOON BLACK PEPPERCORNS

   SALT, TO TASTE

MUSHROOM STOCK

YIELD: 6 CUPS / **ACTIVE TIME:** 20 MINUTES / **TOTAL TIME:** 3 TO 4 HOURS

You can use any mushroom you have on hand in this stock, so feel free to tailor your choice to the dish you have in mind. The trick to a great mushroom stock is to cook down the mushrooms beforehand to reduce their liquid. This cuts down on cooking time and helps concentrate the flavors.

1. In a large stockpot, add the oil and mushrooms and cook over low heat for 30 to 40 minutes. The longer you cook the mushrooms, the better.

2. Add the onion, garlic, bay leaves, peppercorns, and thyme and cook for 5 minutes.

3. Add the wine, cook for 5 minutes, and then add the water.

4. Bring to a boil, reduce heat so that the stock simmers, and cook for 2 to 3 hours, until you are pleased with the taste.

INGREDIENTS:

2   TABLESPOONS VEGETABLE OIL

3   LBS. MUSHROOMS

1   ONION, CHOPPED

1   GARLIC, MINCED

2   BAY LEAVES

1   TABLESPOON BLACK PEPPERCORNS

2   FRESH SPRIGS THYME

1   CUP WHITE WINE

8   CUPS WATER

CLASSIC CANNED TOMATO SAUCE

YIELD: 10 SERVINGS / **ACTIVE TIME:** 25 MINUTES / **TOTAL TIME:** 1 HOUR

Everyone should have a basic tomato sauce in their repertoire that can be made with pantry basics, as it is the foundation of so many great dishes. The simplicity of this recipe belies a robust, complex flavor.

1. Warm a Dutch oven over low heat for 2 to 3 minutes. Add the oil and raise heat to medium. When it begins to shimmer, add the onion and a couple pinches of salt and stir to combine. Once the onion begins to sizzle, reduce heat to low and stir. Cover and cook, stirring occasionally, until the onion becomes very soft, about 20 minutes.

2. While the onion cooks, use a food processor or blender to puree the tomatoes, working with one can at a time.

3. Pour the tomato puree into the pot and add a few more pinches of salt and the sugar. Raise heat to medium-high and bring to a boil. Reduce heat to medium-low and simmer until the sauce has thickened, about 30 minutes, stirring every 10 minutes or so.

4. If using, place the basil leaves on the surface of the sauce and cover the pot for 5 minutes. Remove the basil before using. Use immediately or let cool, transfer to an airtight container, and refrigerate for up to 3 days or freeze for up to 2 months.

INGREDIENTS:

3   TABLESPOONS OLIVE OIL

1   WHITE OR VIDALIA ONION, GRATED

    SALT, TO TASTE

2   (28 OZ.) CANS WHOLE PEELED PLUM TOMATOES (PREFERABLY SAN MARZANO)

1   TEASPOON SUGAR

    HANDFUL FRESH BASIL LEAVES (OPTIONAL)

FERMENTED HOT SAUCE

YIELD: 2 CUPS / **ACTIVE TIME:** 10 MINUTES / **TOTAL TIME:** 30 DAYS TO 6 MONTHS

If you're addicted to hot sauce, fermented hot sauce will take that addiction to the next level.

1. Remove the tops of the peppers and split them down the middle.

2. Place the split peppers and the garlic, onion, and salt in a mason jar and cover with the water. Cover the jar and shake well.

3. Place the jar away from direct sunlight and let stand for at least 30 days and up to 6 months. Occasionally unscrew the lid to release some of the gases that build up. Based on my own experience, a longer fermenting time is very much worth it.

4. Once you are ready to make the sauce, reserve most of the brine, transfer the mixture to a blender, and puree to desired thickness. If you want your sauce to be on the thin side, keep adding brine until you have the consistency you want. Season with salt, transfer to a container, cover, and store in the refrigerator for up to 3 months.

INGREDIENTS:

2   LBS. CAYENNE PEPPERS

1   LB. JALAPEÑO PEPPERS

5   GARLIC CLOVES

1   RED ONION, QUARTERED

3   TABLESPOONS SALT, PLUS MORE TO TASTE

    FILTERED WATER, AS NEEDED

TORTILLAS

YIELD: ABOUT 12 LARGE TORTILLAS / **ACTIVE TIME:** 25 MINUTES / **TOTAL TIME:** 35 MINUTES

Tortillas are great for more than just tacos. They can be used to make homemade wraps or as a side to larger dishes to help mop up all the extra flavors left behind.

1. Put the flour in a large bowl. Mix in the salt and baking powder.

2. Add the shortening or butter, and, using your fingers, blend it into the flour mix until you have a crumbly dough. Add 1 cup of the water and work it in, then gradually add the remaining ½ cup, working it in with your hands, so that you create a dough that's not too sticky.

3. Lightly flour a work surface and turn out the dough. Knead it for about 10 minutes, until it is soft and elastic. Divide it into 12 equal pieces.

4. Using a lightly floured rolling pin, roll each piece out to almost the size of the bottom of the skillet.

5. Heat the skillet over high heat. Add a tortilla. Cook for just 15 seconds a side. Keep the cooked tortillas warm by putting them on a plate covered with a damp kitchen towel. Serve warm.

INGREDIENTS:

3   CUPS FLOUR, PLUS MORE FOR DUSTING

1   TEASPOON SALT

2   TEASPOONS BAKING POWDER

3   TABLESPOONS VEGETABLE SHORTENING OR 4 TABLESPOONS UNSALTED BUTTER, CHILLED

1½   CUPS WATER, AT ROOM TEMPERATURE

PARATHA

YIELD: 8 SERVINGS / **ACTIVE TIME:** 25 MINUTES / **TOTAL TIME:** 30 MINUTES

There is something joyful in making flatbreads, don't you think? It harkens back to childhood. The soft dough. Gently rolling it into shape. It's like playing, but the results are edible, which is where the real joy comes in. We should all revel in a chance to play with our food.

1. Place the flours and salt in the bowl of a stand mixer. Turn on low and slowly add the warm water. Mix until incorporated and then slowly add the vegetable oil. When the oil has been incorporated, place the dough on a lightly floured work surface and knead until it is quite smooth, about 8 minutes.

2. Divide the dough into 8 small balls and dust them with flour.

3. Use your hands to roll out each ball into a long rope. Spiral each rope into a large disk.

4. Use a rolling pin to flatten the spiraled disks until they are no more than ¼-inch thick. Lightly brush each disk with a small amount of vegetable oil.

5. Place a cast-iron *tava*, cast-iron skillet, or griddle over very high heat for about 4 minutes. Brush the surface with some of the ghee or melted butter and place a disk of the dough on the surface. Cook until it is blistered and brown, about 1 minute. Turn over and cook the other side. Transfer the cooked paratha to a plate and repeat with the remaining disks. Serve warm or at room temperature.

NOTE: If you want to freeze any extras, make sure to place parchment paper between them to prevent them from melding together.

INGREDIENTS:

2   CUPS PASTRY FLOUR, PLUS MORE FOR DUSTING

1   CUP WHOLE WHEAT FLOUR

¼   TEASPOON SALT

1   CUP WARM WATER (110°F)

5   TABLESPOONS VEGETABLE OIL, PLUS MORE AS NEEDED

5   TABLESPOONS GHEE OR MELTED UNSALTED BUTTER

NAAN

YIELD: 8 PIECES / **ACTIVE TIME:** 1 HOUR / **TOTAL TIME:** 3 TO 4 HOURS

This is the bread that is traditionally served with Indian cuisine. It's usually cooked in a tandoor (clay oven) in India, but the cast-iron skillet works just fine.

1. Proof the yeast by mixing it with the sugar and ½ cup of the warm water. Let sit for 10 minutes until foamy.

2. In a bowl, add the remaining water, flour, salt, baking powder, and yeast mix. Stir to combine. Add the yogurt and 2 tablespoons of the butter and stir to form a soft dough.

3. Transfer to a lightly floured surface and knead the dough until it is springy and elastic, about 10 minutes.

4. Coat the bottom and sides of a large mixing bowl (ceramic is best) with butter. Place the ball of dough in the bowl, cover loosely with plastic wrap, put it in a naturally warm, draft-free location, and let it rise until doubled in size, about 1 to 2 hours.

5. Punch down the dough. Lightly flour a work surface again, take out the dough and, using a rolling pin, make a circle of it. Cut it into 8 slices (like a pie).

6. Heat the skillet over high heat until it is very hot, about 5 minutes. Working with individual pieces of dough, roll them out to soften the sharp edges and make the pieces look more like teardrops. Brush both sides with olive oil and, working one at a time, place the pieces in the skillet.

7. Cook for 1 minute, turn the dough with tongs, cover the skillet, and cook the other side for about a minute (no longer). Transfer cooked naan to a plate and cover with foil to keep warm while making the additional pieces. Serve warm.

TIP: You can add herbs or spices to the dough or the pan to make naan with different flavors, like adding ¼ cup chopped fresh parsley to the dough, or sprinkling the skillet lightly with cumin, coriander, or turmeric (or a combination) before cooking the pieces of naan. You can also use a seasoned olive oil to brush the pieces before cooking—one that has been infused with hot pepper flakes or roasted garlic.

INGREDIENTS:

- 1½ TEASPOONS ACTIVE DRY YEAST
- ½ TABLESPOON SUGAR
- 1 CUP WARM WATER (110 TO 115°F)
- 3 CUPS ALL-PURPOSE FLOUR OR 1½ CUPS ALL-PURPOSE AND 1½ CUPS WHOLE WHEAT PASTRY FLOUR, PLUS MORE FOR DUSTING
- ¼ TEASPOON SALT
- 1 TEASPOON BAKING POWDER
- ½ CUP PLAIN YOGURT
- 4 TABLESPOONS UNSALTED BUTTER, MELTED, PLUS MORE FOR GREASING THE BOWL
- ¼ CUP OLIVE OIL

TECHNIQUES

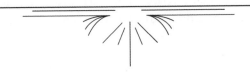

REMOVING THE OUTER LEAVES AND EXPOSING THE MEAT OF AN ARTICHOKE

The tough leaves of the artichoke protect its edible heart. It looks like a lot of work to remove them, but with this method it's not so bad. First, cut the stem and pull off the outer leaves. When you get to the tender yellow leaves, grab the top of the leaves in the center and pull them off, revealing the heart. Dig out the heart with a spoon, and use a small paring knife to remove the bottom leaves and anything clinging to the stem.

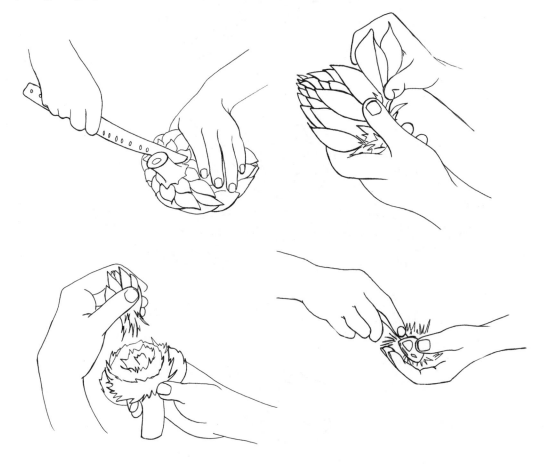

TOMATO CONCASSE

Boil enough water for a tomato to be submerged and add a pinch of salt. While it is heating, prepare an ice bath and score the top of the tomato with a paring knife, taking care not to cut into the meat of the tomato. Place the tomato in the boiling water for 30 seconds, or until the skin begins to blister. Carefully remove it from the boiling water and place it in the ice bath. Once the tomato is cool, remove it from the ice bath and use a paring knife to peel the skin off, starting at the scored top. Cut the tomato into quarters, remove the seeds, and cut according to recipe instructions.

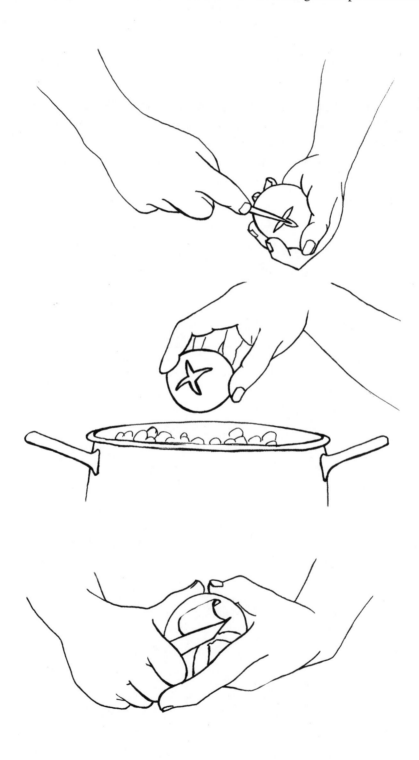

SACHET D'ÉPICES

Cut a 4-inch square of cheesecloth and a 12-inch piece of butcher twine. Place 3 parsley stems, ¼ teaspoon thyme leaves, ½ bay leaf, ¼ teaspoon cracked peppercorns, and ½ garlic clove, minced, in the middle of the cheesecloth and lift each corner to create a purse. Tie one side of the twine around the corners and make a knot. Tie the other side of the twine to the handle of your pot and then toss the sachet d'épices in.

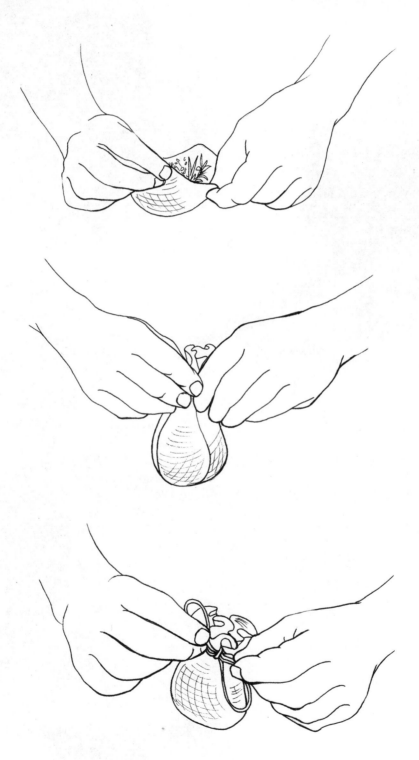

CANNING 101

Proper canning allows you to preserve the best aspects of each season. This time-honored tradition is simple, but it is important to follow each and every step. Once you get the hang of it, you will be canning everything in sight.

---

1. Bring a pot of water to a boil. Place the mason jars in the water for 15 to 20 minutes to sterilize them. Do not boil the mason jar lids, as this may prevent them from creating a proper seal when the time comes.

2. Bring water to a boil in the large canning pot.

3. Fill the sterilized mason jars with whatever you are canning. Place the lids on the jars and secure the bands tightly. Place the jars in the boiling water for 40 minutes.

4. Use the tongs to remove the jars from the boiling water and let them cool. As they are cooling, you should hear the classic "ping and pop" sound of the lids creating a seal.

5. After 4 to 6 hours, check the lids. There should be no give in them and they should be suctioned onto the jars. Discard any lids and food that did not seal properly.

INGREDIENTS:

MASON JARS WITH LIDS AND BANDS

1   LARGE CANNING POT

1   PAIR OF CANNING TONGS

CONVERSION TABLE

WEIGHTS

1 oz. = 28 grams

2 oz. = 57 grams

4 oz. (¼ lb.) = 113 grams

8 oz. (½ lb.) = 227 grams

16 oz. (1 lb.) = 454 grams

VOLUME MEASURES

⅛ teaspoon = 0.6 ml

¼ teaspoon = 1.23 ml

½ teaspoon = 2.5 ml

1 teaspoon = 5 ml

1 tablespoon (3 teaspoons) = ½ fluid oz. = 15 ml

2 tablespoons = 1 fluid oz. = 29.5 ml

¼ cup (4 tablespoons) = 2 fluid oz. = 59 ml

⅓ cup (5 ⅓ tablespoons) = 2.7 fluid oz. = 80 ml

½ cup (8 tablespoons) = 4 fluid oz. = 120 ml

⅔ cup (10 ⅔ tablespoons) = 5.4 fluid oz. = 160 ml

¾ cup (12 tablespoons) = 6 fluid oz. = 180 ml

1 cup (16 tablespoons) = 8 fluid oz. = 240 ml

TEMPERATURE EQUIVALENTS

°F	°C	Gas Mark
225	110	¼
250	130	½
275	140	1
300	150	2
325	170	3
350	180	4
375	190	5
400	200	6
425	220	7
450	230	8
475	240	9
500	250	10

LENGTH MEASURES

¹⁄₁₆ inch = 1.6 mm

⅛ inch = 3 mm

¼ inch = 1.35 mm

½ inch = 1.25 cm

¾ inch = 2 cm

1 inch = 2.5 cm

ACKNOWLEDGMENTS

Special thanks to my longtime friend and brilliant photographer Chef Jim Sullivan; friends and co-authors Scott Gilden, Kimberly Zerkel, and April Downey for all of their professionalism, commitment, and hard work to help me dish these recipes into words. Thank you to my supportive and loving children Sophia, Isabella, and Evan, who inspire me to be a better human every day and to Ashley, Meridith, Tasha, and Ella who have shown me how to live and breathe outside the culinary world: you are all loved. Thank you Mom for sharing all the heritage and knowledge that is Jewish culture and tradition; I will always cherish our talks.

Special thanks to the Jewish community of San Diego, specifically our friends at Milton's Jewish Deli who contributed to this book.

Thank you to our culinary staff, colleagues, chefs, and all of our culinary community for continuing to pioneer and innovate daily. You are all loved and respected!

Thank you to Buzz Poole, John Whalen, and the team at Cider Mill Press for the opportunity to be part of something special and for the faith and trust to create beautiful Jewish food.

Joshua Korn

I have to start by saying I am proud to be Jewish and come from such a rich culinary culture. Growing up in New York surrounded by so many different cultures has been an inspiration to my culinary career.

Many people have contributed toward the creation of this book

Thanks to:

My mother for always cooking and making the kitchen a happy place, filled with great smells and always a spoon to taste your amazing food.

Josh and Jim for bringing me on this fun adventure.

My brothers for always encouraging me.

Asher and Kaiya, you bring so much joy to me every day; can't wait to cook some of these recipes with you.

To Auntie Beth, Grandma Honey, Tina Kuritzy (Nana), Nana Tillie, and Grandma Fannie may your recipes bring joy to everyone as you have brought joy to your family.

Scott Gilden

ABOUT THE AUTHORS

Chef Scott Gilden attended the Culinary Institute of America in Hyde Park, New York. His experience includes more than 20 years of comprehensive large-scale management and hospitality experience in Fortune 500 companies and innumerable start-ups. His diverse experience ranges from corporate dining, family dining, catering, and healthcare food service operations.

He guides his operations to enhance the brand with emphasis on fresh quality ingredients, sustainability, and the highest customer experience. Gilden was highlighted in Forbes Fortune 500 list in 2008 and 2010 for culinary innovation for his work at Qualcomm Inc.

Growing up in New York his early career began as the assistant manager at Gallagher's Steak House, followed by a leadership position at the Columbia University Faculty House, and hospitality management roles with various restaurants around New York City. Catering has been a large part of his career, ranging from large events to private locations for executives. Gilden's took him to Southern California where he was pivotal in working with Qualcomm Inc. and brought their food service program to national acclaim. Scott's career has continued in corporate food service and consulting working with clients such as Universal Pictures, Quicken Loans, and Owens Corning. His creativity and service execution deliver exceptional hospitality experiences that exceed expectations.

Gilden is also a former Hospitality Instructor at Gibbs College of New York City and the Art Institute of San Diego. He is a member of Confrérie De La Chaîne Des Rôtisseurs Society and the National Restaurant Association.

Chef Joshua Korn is a graduate of the Culinary Institute of America and gained his experience working in the family of restaurant kitchens at B. R. Guest, Inc., Myriad Restaurant Group, and Starwood Capital Group in New York City. A former Chef Instructor at the Art Institute of San Diego, he provided culinary and baccalaureate education to students of the San Diego community for over 11 years.

His critically acclaimed American Regional Food has been honored in the pages of *Food and Wine Magazine, The New York Times, The NY Post, Art Culinaire, Food Arts Magazine, Gourmet Magazine, The North County Times, Ranch Coast Magazine and the San Diego Union Tribune*. Korn was highlighted in Forbes Fortune 500 list in 2008 and 2010 as top culinary innovator for his work at Qualcomm Inc. He has appeared on the Bravo Network, Food Network, and Inside Edition television shows in New York City, Orange County, and KUSI Television Network in San Diego.

Korn has cooked for multiple celebrities, such as Robert DeNiro, Cindy Crawford, Nicole Kidman, Senator Hillary Clinton, and many other noteworthy personalities at Miramax film studios in Tribeca, New York. He is an active member of several industry organizations, including the American Institute of Food and Wine, the International Association of Culinary Professionals and Confrerie De La Chaine Des Rotisseurs Society. Korn serves as a member on several Board of Directors for international and domestic firms, providing insight, thought leadership, and advisory.

Korn has broadened his education in the hospitality industry both in business and finance by earning his bachelor's degree in accounting from Stony Brook University and continued his education with an MBA in corporate finance from Argosy University. He is the owner of Culimetrics, LLC, SIE Culinary Management Group, LLC, and Bambucha Kombucha, LLC in Southern California.

Jim Sullivan is a graduate of the culinary program from the Art Institute of California and is a former cook. He is a self-taught photographer, focusing on the culinary arts, portraiture, and lifestyle. His client list includes Michelin, Art Culinaire, Food and Wine Magazine,Imbibe Magazine, and Leica Camera, as well as some of the most prominent chefs in the United States. He is the founder and director of Soigne Films, a production company that focuses on storytelling in the cocktail and restaurant industries.

Sullivan is based in Southern California with his beautiful wife, daughter, and their newly acquired French Bulldog, Mochi.

Kimberly Zerkel is a freelance writer. After a decade of living and teaching in Paris, she returned to the United States to live in San Francisco, California. She has regularly contributed to the *San Francisco Chronicle* and *Represent Collaborative*, amongst other publications. Kimberly currently resides in Joplin, Missouri.

PHOTO CREDITS

INDEX

acorn squash
  Sheet-Pan Roasted
    Squash & Feta Salad,
    490
adobo sauce
  Chicken with Tamarind,
    263
Albondigas with Pine
    Nuts & Currants, 30
Aliciotti con Individa, 224
All-Butter Pastry Dough
  Apple & Calvados Tart,
    582
  recipe, 578
Almodrote, 225
almond paste
  Rainbow Cookies, 645
almonds
  Apple-Cranberry Crisp
    with Oatmeal-Cookie
    Crumble, 588
  Autumn Kale Salad, 423
  Broccolini Salad, 37
  Chicken Salad, 42
  Couscous with Seven
    Vegetables, 431
  Date Coconut Rolls,
    170
  Dukkah, 524
  Halvah, 605

Knafeh Cheesecake, 617
New Year's Honey Cake,
    625
Slow-Roasted Lamb
    Shoulder with
    Brussels Sprouts &
    Crispy Kale, 389
Strudel with Tropical
    Fruits, Chipotle
    Chocolate &
    Whipped Cream, 652
Sumac, Spelt & Apple
    Cake, 653
Vegetable Tanzia, 409
anchovies
  Aliciotti con Individa,
    224
  Eyerlekh mit Tzvible,
    289
  Salsa Verde, 540
appetizers
  Albondigas with Pine
    Nuts & Currants, 30
  Baba Ghanoush, 161
  Blintzes with Berry
    Compote, 33
  Chopped Liver, 46
  Chushki Burek, 47
  Crushed Avocado, 54
  Falafel, 59

Fava Beans with
    Pomegranates, 62
Fried Eggplant with
    Garlic & Cumin, 66
Fried Eggplant with
    Mint Vinaigrette, 67
Ful Medames, 70
Jewish-Style Fried
    Artichokes, 77–78
Latkes, 196
Liverwurst, 94
Modern Hummus, 160
Pomegranate Glazed
    Figs & Cheese, 99
Red Gefilte Fish
    Veragruzana, 101–102
Roasted Beet & Leek
    Risotto, 103
Roasted Beets with
    Cilantro-Basil Pesto,
    104
Roasted Corn & Black
    Bean Salad, 107
apples
  Apple & Calvados Tart,
    582
  Apple Brioche Tart, 583
  Apple Cake, 584
  Apple Walnut Bundt
    Cake, 585–586

Apple-Cranberry Crisp
with Oatmeal-Cookie
Crumble, 588
Balsamic Apple Date
Challah, 550–551
Calvados Applesauce,
579
Charoset, 176, 514
Crunchy Pomegranate
Salad, 51
Golden Brown Cookies
with Apple Filling,
603
Khoresh Sib, 309
Olive Oil Apple Cake
with Spiced Sugar,
630
Salted Honey Apple
Upside-Down Cake,
219
Stuffed Matzo Ball
Soup with Chicken &
Apples, 498
Sumac, Spelt & Apple
Cake, 653
Sumac & Apple-Roasted
Cauliflower, 696
Sumac & Lime Mahi-
Mahi with Pickled
Apple Couscous, 714
Yeasted Apple Coffee
Cake, 657
apricot jam/preserves
Hungarian Golden
Pull-Apart Cake with
Walnuts & Apricot
Jam, 616
Rainbow Cookies, 645

apricots, dried
Chicken with Tamarind,
263
Khoresh Sib, 309
Roasted Apricot
Chicken with Mint
& Sage Butternut
Squash, 358
Sephardic Jeweled Rosh
Hashanah Rice, 169
Strudel with Tropical
Fruits, Chipotle
Chocolate &
Whipped Cream, 652
Tzimmes Chicken with
Apricots, Prunes &
Carrots, 186
Vegetable Tanzia, 409
artichoke hearts
Msoki de Pesaj, 331
artichokes
Boulettes with Chicken
& Vegetable Soup &
Couscous, 234–235
Jewish-Style Fried
Artichokes, 77–78
removing out leaves
from, 743
arugula
Arugula Salad with
Pickled Beets &
Preserved-Lemon
Vinaigrette, 165
Celery Slaw with Seeds
& Dates, 428
Ash Roasted Beets, 420
Ashkenazim, 11–13
Autumn Kale Salad, 423

Avikas, 228
avocado leaves
Beef Mixiote, 229
avocados
Crushed Avocado, 54
Ghormeh Sabzi, 294
Tuna Kibbeh Nayeh,
707

Baba Ghanoush, 161
Bagels, 145
Baharat
Red Wine-Braised
Oxtail, 356
Balsamic Apple Date
Challah, 550–551
Balsamic Vinaigrette
Strawberry Fields Salad,
113
bamboo shoots
Spayty, 396
banana
Strudel with Tropical
Fruits, Chipotle
Chocolate &
Whipped Cream, 652
banana leaves
Beef Mixiote, 229
barberries/berberis
Dolmeh Beh, 282
Rice with Barberries,
471
Sumac Chicken & Rice,
401
barley
Cholent, 209
Mushroom Barley Soup,
91

basil
Chimichurri Sauce, 521
Concia, 50
Grilled Serrano Salsa
Verde, 269
Roasted Beets with
Cilantro-Basil Pesto,
104
Shaved Carrot & Radish
Salad with Herbs &
Toasted Pumpkin
Seeds, 483
Tomato Jam, 542
beans
Avikas, 228
Black-Eyed Peas
with Turmeric &
Pomegranate, 427
Cholent, 209
Egyptian Lentils & Rice,
439
Fava Beans with
Pomegranates, 62
Ful Medames, 70
Ghormeh Sabzi, 294
Messer Wot, 323
Msoki de Pesaj, 331
Mujadara, 463
Roasted Corn & Black
Bean Salad, 107
Romano Beans with
Mustard Vinaigrette
& Walnuts, 179
See also chickpeas; peas
beef
Albondigas with Pine
Nuts & Currants, 30
Avikas, 228

Beef, Beet & Cabbage
Borscht, 34
Beef Brisket, 232
Beef Mixiote, 229
Boulettes with Chicken
& Vegetable Soup &
Couscous, 234–235
Brisket with
Pomegranate-Walnut
Sauce & Pistachio
Gremolata, 238
Chef's Special Sweet &
Sour Meatballs, 253
Chicken with Mehshi
Sfeeha, 248
Cholent, 209
Corned Beef with
Barbeque Sauce,
270
Crockpot Carne con
Papas, 278
Crockpot Sweet & Sour
Brisket, 271
Dafina, 279
Dolmeh Beh, 282
Egyptian Short Rib &
Okra Stew, 287
Ghormeh Sabzi, 294
Kiftahs, 293
Latkes with Short Ribs,
313
Mama Kramer's Brisket,
305
Onion Mahshi, 332
Pastrami, 340
Porcini-Rubbed Beef
Rib Roast, 354
Pot Roast, 199

Red Wine-Braised
Oxtail, 356
Ropa Vieja, 364
Seitan Brisket, 371
Slow-Cooked Short Ribs
with Gremolata, 386
Tomatoes Reinados,
403
Turkish Coffee-Rubbed
Brisket, 406
Turkish Eggplant
Dolma, 407
Zucchini Mahshi,
509
beef liver
Liverwurst, 94
Beef Stock
Beef, Beet & Cabbage
Borscht, 34
Crockpot Carne con
Papas, 278
Crockpot Sweet & Sour
Brisket, 271
Hand-Rolled Couscous,
298
Leg of Lamb with Garlic
& Rosemary, 316
Moroccan Lamb Shanks
with Pomegranate
Sauce, 330
Mushroom Barley Soup,
91
Pot Roast, 199
recipe, 721
Red Wine-Braised
Oxtail, 356
Stuffed Saddle of Lamb,
400

Wine-Braised Brisket
    with Butternut
    Squash, 413
beets
    Arugula Salad with
        Pickled Beets &
        Preserved-Lemon
        Vinaigrette, 165
    Ash Roasted Beets, 420
    Beef, Beet & Cabbage
        Borscht, 34
    Beet Chips with Spicy
        Honey Mayonnaise,
        426
    Crunchy Salty Lemony
        Salad, 443
    Grandpa's Gravlox, 146
    Grandson's Beet &
        Vodka Gravlox, 149
    Heart-Beet Salad, 71
    Kemia de Remolachas,
        86
    Red Cabbage, Date &
        Beet Salad, 153
    Roasted Beet & Leek
        Risotto, 103
    Roasted Beets with
        Cilantro-Basil Pesto,
        104
    Seared Radicchio &
        Roasted Beets, 481
    Shaved Radish Salad
        with Walnuts & Mint,
        482
Berbere Spice Mix
    Chermoula Sauce,
        517
    Chicken Curry, 259

Chicken with Turmeric,
    Tahini, Chickpeas &
    Onions, 266
Lamb Stew, 299
Leg of Lamb with Garlic
    & Rosemary, 316
Messer Wot, 323
    recipe, 323
Red Wine-Braised
    Oxtail, 356
Split Peas with Berbere,
    494
beverages
    Egg Cream, 660
    Hawaij Hot Cocoa with
        Cinnamon Whipped
        Cream, 659
    Limonana, 663
    Pomegranate Prosecco
        Punch, 664
    Sachlav, 665
    Salep, 669
    Sephardic-Inspired
        Sangria—Two Ways,
        668
    Strawberry Rosé Sangria,
        668
    White Peach Sangria
        with Orange Blossom
        Water, 668
Bialy, 554
Black & White Cookies,
    589
Black & White Halvah,
    590–591
Black Bean Salad, Roasted
    Corn &, 107
blackberries

Blintzes with Berry
    Compote, 33
black-eyed peas
    Black-Eyed Peas
        with Turmeric &
        Pomegranate, 427
    Ghormeh Sabzi, 294
Blintzes with Berry
    Compote, 33
blueberries
    Blintzes with Berry
        Compote, 33
    Broccolini Salad, 37
Bone Marrow Matzo Ball
    Soup, 36
Boulettes with Chicken
    & Vegetable Soup &
    Couscous, 234–235
Bourekas
    Eggplant & Chorizo
        Boureka, 284
    recipe, 203
Branzino, Whole, 715
bread(s)
    Bagels, 145
    Balsamic Apple Date
        Challah, 550–551
    Bialy, 554
    Cast-Iron Challah
        Bread, 555
    Challah, 129–130
    Challah French Toast,
        556
    Chocolate Babka,
        560–561
    Chocolate Cranberry
        Challah Rolls with
        Citrus Sugar, 562

Eggy Challah Toast, 563

Everything Spiced
    Malaway with Fried
    Egg, 288

Honey Brioche, 566–
    567

Khachapuri, 306

Laffa, 571

Mandel Bread, 621

Naan, 741

Paratha, 738

Pirozhki, 344–345

Pita Bread, 697

Rye Bread, 572

Tomatoes Reinados, 403

Tori, 737

brisket
    Beef Brisket, 232
    Brisket with
        Pomegranate-Walnut
        Sauce & Pistachio
        Gremolata, 238
    Crockpot Sweet & Sour
        Brisket, 271
    Mama Kramer's Brisket,
        305
    Pastrami, 340
    Pomegranate Brisket
        with Cranberry
        Succotash, 353
    Seitan Brisket, 371
    Turkish Coffee-Rubbed
        Brisket, 406
    Wine-Braised Brisket
        with Butternut
        Squash, 413

broccoli
    Chicken Curry, 259

Broccolini Salad, 37

Brussels sprouts
    Roasted Brussels
        Sprouts, 476
    Roasted Brussels Sprouts
        with Warm Honey
        Glaze, 135, 475
    Slow-Roasted Lamb
        Shoulder with
        Brussels Sprouts &
        Crispy Kale, 389

Bulgarian cheese
    Chushki Burek, 47

bulgur
    Bulgur with Fried
        Onions, 239
    Tuna Kibbeh Nayeh,
        707

butternut squash
    Boulettes with Chicken
        & Vegetable Soup &
        Couscous, 234–235
    Couscous with Seven
        Vegetables, 431
    Roasted Apricot
        Chicken with Mint
        & Sage Butternut
        Squash, 358
    Tunisian Spiced
        Butternut Squash
        Soup, 119
    Vegetable Tanzia, 409
    Vegetarian Yemenite
        Soup Recipe, 121
    Wine-Braised Brisket
        with Butternut
        Squash, 413

cabbage
    Beef, Beet & Cabbage
        Borscht, 34
    Coleslaw, 434
    Red Cabbage, Date &
        Beet Salad, 153

cakes
    Apple Cake, 584
    Apple Walnut Bundt
        Cake, 585–586
    Cheesecake, 190
    Flourless Chocolate
        Cake, 600
    Honey Cake, 609–610
    Honey Pomegranate
        Cake, 611
    Knafeh Cheesecake, 617
    New Year's Honey Cake,
        625
    Olive Oil Apple Cake
        with Spiced Sugar,
        630
    Orange-Spiced Rye
        Honey Cake, 633
    Salted Honey Apple
        Upside-Down Cake,
        219
    Spiced Honey Cake
        with Cream Cheese
        Frosting, 649
    Sumac, Spelt & Apple
        Cake, 653
    Vanilla Cake Rusks, 654
    Yeasted Apple Coffee
        Cake, 657

Calvados
    Apple & Calvados Tart,
        582

Calvados Applesauce,
579
capers
Red Gefilte Fish
Veragruzana, 101–102
Salsa Verde, 540
Tomato Salad, 116
Caramel Sauce and Glaze
Apple Walnut Bundt
Cake, 585–586
recipe, 585–586
caramelized onions
Taco de Gribenes, 402
Caramelized-Honey Nut
& Seed Tart, 592
Cardamom-Chocolate
Halvah, 606–607
carrots
Beef, Beet & Cabbage
Borscht, 34
Boulettes with Chicken
& Vegetable Soup &
Couscous, 234–235
Cast-Iron Roast
Chicken with Fennel
& Carrots, 243
Chef's Special Matzo
Ball Soup, 41
Chicken Curry, 259
Chicken Stock, 722
Coleslaw, 434
Couscous with Seven
Vegetables, 431
Crockpot Sweet & Sour
Brisket, 271
Fish Stock, 726
Gefilte Fish,
180

Ginger Carrot
Vinaigrette, 523
Harissa-Carrot Halwa,
448
Honey Glazed Carrots
with Carrot Top
Gremolata, 140
Honey-Roasted Carrots
with Tahini Yogurt, 450
Honey-Roasted
Vegetable Salad, 451
Israeli Spicy Chickpea
Soup with Crème
Fraîche, 74
Kemia de Zanahorias,
85
Kishka, 79
Macaroni Salad, 461
Mama Kramer's Brisket,
305
Matjes Herring in Red
Wine Sauce or Cream
Sauce, 150
Msoki de Pesaj, 331
Mushroom Barley Soup,
91
Poblano Matzo Ball
Soup, 100
Pot Roast, 199
Quick Pickled Carrots,
537
Red Gefilte Fish
Veragruzana, 101–102
Red Wine-Braised
Oxtail, 356
Roasted Shabbat
Chicken with Spring
Vegetables, 212

Rosemary Rack of Lamb
with Roasted Potatoes
& Carrots, 368
Rustic Matzo Ball Soup,
185
Seitan Brisket, 371
Shaved Carrot & Radish
Salad with Herbs &
Toasted Pumpkin
Seeds, 483
Sheet Pan Tzimmes-
Roasted Chicken
Thighs, 381
Slow-Roasted Chicken
with Honey-Glazed
Carrots & Ginger,
388
Split Pea Soup, 110
Stuffed Lamb, 398–399
Turkish Coffee-Rubbed
Brisket, 406
Tzimmes Chicken with
Apricots, Prunes &
Carrots, 186
Veal, Beef, or Lamb
Stock, 721
Vegetable Soup, 120
Vegetable Stock, 729
Vegetarian Yemenite
Soup Recipe, 121
Cast-Iron Challah Bread,
555
Cast-Iron Roast Chicken
with Fennel &
Carrots, 243
cauliflower
Honey-Roasted
Vegetable Salad, 451

Roasted Cauliflower,
213
Sumac & Apple-Roasted
Cauliflower, 696
Cedar-Plank Salmon, 246
celery
Albondigas with Pine
Nuts & Currants, 30
Beef, Beet & Cabbage
Borscht, 34
Celery Slaw with Seeds
& Dates, 428
Chef's Special Matzo
Ball Soup, 41
Chicken Salad, 42
Chicken Stock, 722
Crockpot Sweet & Sour
Brisket, 271
Fish Stock, 726
Gefilte Fish, 180
Israeli Spicy Chickpea
Soup with Crème
Fraîche, 74
Macaroni Salad,
461
Mama Kramer's Brisket,
305
Mushroom Barley Soup,
91
Poblano Matzo Ball
Soup, 100
Pot Roast, 199
Potato Salad, 470
Red Gefilte Fish
Veragruzana, 101–102
Red Wine-Braised
Oxtail, 356
Relish Tray, 537

Rustic Matzo Ball Soup,
185
Saffron Tomato Fennel
Broth, 539
Split Pea Soup, 110
Stuffed Lamb, 398–399
Veal, Beef, or Lamb
Stock, 721
Vegetable Soup, 120
Vegetable Stock, 729
celery root
Matjes Herring in Red
Wine Sauce or Cream
Sauce, 150
Vegetarian Yemenite
Soup Recipe, 121
Challah
Balsamic Apple Date
Challah, 550–551
Cast-Iron Challah
Bread, 555
Challah French Toast,
556
Challah Stuffing, 429
Chocolate Cranberry
Challah Rolls with
Citrus Sugar, 562
Eggy Challah Toast, 563
recipe, 129–130
Champagne Vinaigrette
Broccolini Salad, 37
recipe, 516
Charoset, 176, 514
Charred Chicken with
Sweet Potatoes &
Oranges, 249
Charred Sweet Potatoes
with Toum, 430

cheese. See individual
cheese types
Cheesecake, 190
Chef's Special Matzo Ball
Soup, 41
Chef's Special Sweet &
Sour Meatballs, 253
Chermoula Sauce, 517
Chermoula Sea Bass, 254
cherries, dried
Chicken Salad, 42
Noodle Kugel, 464
Sephardic Jeweled Rosh
Hashanah Rice, 169
Sumac Chicken & Rice,
401
Cherry Sauce, Chicken
Schnitzel &, 262
chicken
Boulettes with Chicken
& Vegetable Soup &
Couscous, 234–235
Cast-Iron Roast
Chicken with Fennel
& Carrots, 243
Charred Chicken with
Sweet Potatoes &
Oranges, 249
Chef's Special Matzo
Ball Soup, 41
Chef's Special Sweet &
Sour Meatballs, 253
Chicken & Tomato
Stew with
Caramelized Lemon,
258
Chicken Curry, 259
Chicken Salad, 42

Chicken Schnitzel &
    Cherry Sauce, 262
Chicken Stew with
    Potatoes & Radishes,
    242
Chicken Stock, 722
Chicken with Mehshi
    Sfeeha, 248
Chicken with Tamarind,
    263
Chicken with Turmeric,
    Tahini, Chickpeas &
    Onions, 266
Cholent, 209
Crispy Roast Chicken,
    274–275
Dafina, 279
Fesenjan, 132
Jerusalem Mixed Grill,
    304
Kreplach, 88–89
Mahasha, 320
Moroccan Cornish
    Hens with Pine Nut
    Couscous, 329
Poblano Matzo Ball
    Soup, 100
Pomegranate & Honey
    Glazed Chicken, 348
Rack-Roasted Chicken,
    355
Roast Chicken with
    Harissa & Schmaltz,
    359–361
Roasted Apricot
    Chicken with Mint
    & Sage Butternut
    Squash, 358

Roasted Shabbat
    Chicken with Spring
    Vegetables, 212
Rustic Matzo Ball Soup,
    185
Sheet Pan Tzimmes-
    Roasted Chicken
    Thighs, 381
Sheika, 382
Skewers of Chicken &
    Lamb Fat, 385
Skillet Roast Chicken
    with Fennel, Parsnips
    & Scallions, 383
Slow-Roasted Chicken
    with All the Garlic,
    387
Slow-Roasted Chicken
    with Honey-Glazed
    Carrots & Ginger, 388
Spayty, 396
Stuffed Matzo Ball
    Soup with Chicken &
    Apples, 498
Sumac Chicken & Rice,
    401
Taco de Gribenes, 402
Tahini Chicken Salad,
    114–115
Tsyplyonok Tabaka,
    404–405
Turmeric Chicken with
    Toum, 408
Tzimmes Chicken with
    Apricots, Prunes &
    Carrots, 186
Za'atar Chicken with
    Garlicky Yogurt, 414

chicken hearts
    Jerusalem Mixed Grill,
    304
chicken livers
    Chopped Liver, 46
    Jerusalem Mixed Grill,
    304
    Kreplach, 88–89
chicken skin
    Gribenes & Schmaltz,
    528
    Taco de Gribenes, 402
Chicken Stock
    Albondigas with Pine
    Nuts & Currants, 30
    Chef's Special Matzo
    Ball Soup, 41
    Chicken & Tomato
    Stew with
    Caramelized Lemon,
    258
    Chicken Curry, 259
    Chicken Stew with
    Potatoes & Radishes,
    242
    Crockpot Sweet & Sour
    Brisket, 271
    Dolmeh Beh, 282
    Green Beans with
    Za'atar & Lemon, 445
    Hand-Rolled Couscous,
    298
    Leeks Braised in White
    Wine, 457
    Mama Kramer's Brisket,
    305
    Mushroom Barley Soup,
    91

Poblano Matzo Ball
   Soup, 100
Pomegranate & Honey
   Glazed Chicken, 348
Pomegranate Brisket
   with Cranberry
   Succotash, 353
recipe, 722
Roasted Apricot
   Chicken with Mint
   & Sage Butternut
   Squash, 358
Roasted Beet & Leek
   Risotto, 103
Ropa Vieja, 364
Sephardic Jeweled Rosh
   Hashanah Rice, 169
Spaetzle, 495
Spinach Rissoles with
   Lemon Sauce, 397
Stuffed Matzo Ball
   Soup with Chicken &
   Apples, 498
Sumac Chicken & Rice,
   401
Tunisian Spiced
   Butternut Squash
   Soup, 119
White Wine Braised
   Leeks, 216
Wine-Braised Brisket
   with Butternut
   Squash, 413
chickpeas
   Boulettes with Chicken
   & Vegetable Soup &
   Couscous, 234–235
   Bulgur with Fried

Onions, 239
Charred Chicken with
   Sweet Potatoes &
   Oranges, 249
Chicken with Turmeric,
   Tahini, Chickpeas &
   Onions, 266
Couscous with Seven
   Vegetables, 431
Cucumber Tomato
   Mango Relish, 57
Dafina, 279
Egyptian Lentils & Rice,
   439
Falafel, 59
Israeli Spicy Chickpea
   Soup with Crème
   Fraîche, 74
Mahshi Laban, 317
Modern Hummus, 160
See also beans
Chimichurri
   Chimichurri Sauce, 521
   Cilantro-Lime
   Vinaigrette, 522
   Fried Eggplant with
   Garlic & Cumin, 66
Chipotle Chocolate &
   Whipped Cream,
   Strudel with Tropical
   Fruits, 652
chives
   Chermoula Sauce, 517
   Ginger Carrot
   Vinaigrette, 523
   Roasted Corn Sauce,
   533
   Shaved Carrot & Radish

Salad with Herbs &
   Toasted Pumpkin
   Seeds, 483
chocolate
   Black & White Cookies,
   589
   Chocolate Babka,
   560–561
   Chocolate Cranberry
   Challah Rolls with
   Citrus Sugar, 562
   Chocolate Ganache, 602
   Chocolate Glaze,
   609–610
   Chocolate Macaroons,
   593–595
   Chocolate-Cinnamon
   "Babkallah," 596
   Egg Cream, 660
   Flourless Chocolate
   Cake, 600
   Halvah Five Ways,
   606–607
   Hawaij Hot Cocoa with
   Cinnamon Whipped
   Cream, 659
   Pomegranate Truffles,
   636–637
   Rainbow Cookies, 645
   Strudel with Tropical
   Fruits, Chipotle
   Chocolate &
   Whipped Cream, 652
   Vanilla Nutmeg Babka,
   655–656
Chocolate Ganache
   Flourless Chocolate
   Cake, 600

recipe, 602

Chocolate Glaze

Honey Cake, 609–610

recipe, 609–610

Cholent, 209

Chopped Liver, 46

Chorizo Boureka,

Eggplant &, 284

Chushki Burek, 47

cilantro

Boulettes with Chicken

& Vegetable Soup &

Couscous, 234–235

Chermoula Sauce, 517

Chicken with Turmeric,

Tahini, Chickpeas &

Onions, 266

Chimichurri Sauce, 521

Cilantro-Lime

Vinaigrette, 522

Crushed Avocado, 54

Dolmeh Beh, 282

Ghormeh Sabzi, 294

Ginger Carrot

Vinaigrette, 523

Grain Salad with Olives

& Whole-Lemon

Vinaigrette, 444

Grandson's Beet &

Vodka Gravlox, 149

Green Zhoug, 701

Grilled Serrano Salsa

Verde, 269

Honey-Roasted Carrots

with Tahini Yogurt,

450

Kuku Sabzi, 312

Mahasha, 320

Mezze'd Up Salad, 95

Modern Hummus, 160

Moroccan Fish &

Crispy Rice Cake

with Saffron Crust,

327–328

Msoki de Pesaj, 331

Oshi Bakhsh, 337

Poached Fish in Pepper

Sauce, 341

Poblano Matzo Ball

Soup, 100

Pomegranate Brisket

with Cranberry

Succotash, 353

Red Cabbage, Date &

Beet Salad, 153

Roasted Beets with

Cilantro-Basil Pesto,

104

Roasted Corn Sauce,

533

Roasted Pepper Salad,

480

Shaved Carrot & Radish

Salad with Herbs &

Toasted Pumpkin

Seeds, 483

Stuffed Lamb, 398–399

Stuffed Saddle of Lamb,

400

Swiss Chard & Herb

Fritters, 502

Taco de Gribenes, 402

Tomato Jam, 542

Cinnamon Whipped

Cream, Hawaij Hot

Cocoa with, 659

Citrus Salad, 49

Classic Canned Tomato

Sauce, 733

cocoa powder

Chocolate Babka,

560–561

Chocolate Macaroons,

593–595

Hawaij Hot Cocoa with

Cinnamon Whipped

Cream, 659

See also chocolate

coconut

Chocolate Glaze,

609–610

Citrus Salad, 49

Coconut Macaroons,

597

Date Coconut Rolls,

170

Malabi, 620

coconut milk/cream

Eggy Challah Toast, 563

Sachlav, 665

Spayty, 396

Spiced Honey Cake

with Cream Cheese

Frosting, 649

cod

Fried Fish with

Agristada Sauce, 292

Gefilte Fish, 180

coffee

Honey Cake, 609–610

New Year's Honey Cake,

625

Orange-Spiced Rye

Honey Cake, 633

Turkish Coffee-Rubbed
Brisket, 406
Cojada Potato Casserole,
267
Cold Roast Salmon with
Smashed Green Bean
Salad, 268–269
Coleslaw, 434
Concia, 50
cookies
Black & White Cookies,
589
Chocolate Macaroons,
593–595
Coconut Macaroons,
597
Golden Brown Cookies
with Apple Filling,
603
Rainbow Cookies, 645
Coriander & Rosemary,
Slow-Cooked Cherry
Tomatoes with, 491
corn
Pomegranate Brisket
with Cranberry
Succotash, 353
Roasted Corn & Black
Bean Salad, 107
Roasted Corn Sauce,
533
Corn Stock
Israeli Spicy Chickpea
Soup with Crème
Fraîche, 74
Modern Hummus, 160
Corned Beef with
Barbeque Sauce, 270

cottage cheese
Noodle Kugel, 464
couscous
Boulettes with Chicken
& Vegetable Soup &
Couscous, 234–235
Couscous Arancini, 706
Couscous with Seven
Vegetables, 431
Moroccan Cornish
Hens with Pine Nut
Couscous, 329
Sumac & Lime Mahi-
Mahi with Pickled
Apple Couscous, 714
cranberries, dried
Apple-Cranberry Crisp
with Oatmeal-Cookie
Crumble, 588
Broccolini Salad, 37
Chocolate Cranberry
Challah Rolls with
Citrus Sugar, 562
Crockpot Sweet & Sour
Brisket, 271
Dolmeh Beh, 282
Noodle Kugel, 464
Pomegranate Brisket
with Cranberry
Succotash, 353
Pumpkin Cranberry
Cupcakes, 638
Sumac Chicken & Rice,
401
cream cheese
Cheesecake, 190
Knafeh Cheesecake, 617
Mina de Espinaca, 324

Rugelach, 641
Spiced Honey Cake
with Cream Cheese
Frosting, 649
Cream Sauce, Majtes
Herring in Red Wine
Sauce or, 150
Creamy Potato & Leek
Gratin, 437
Crispy Baby Yukon Gold
Potatoes, 438
Crispy Roast Chicken,
274–275
Crispy Salmon Rice,
685
Crockpot Carne con
Papas, 278
Crockpot Sweet & Sour
Brisket, 271
Crunchy Pomegranate
Salad, 51
Crunchy Salty Lemony
Salad, 443
Crushed Avocado, 54
Cucumber Tomato
Mango Relish
Mezze'd Up Salad, 95
cucumbers
Celery Slaw with Seeds &
Dates, 428
Crunchy Salty Lemony
Salad, 443
Cucumber, Mint &
Sumac Salad, 58
Cucumber Tomato
Mango Relish, 57
Israeli Salad, 73
Mezze'd Up Salad, 95

Pickled Cucumber Salad, 154

Yogurt Sauce, 59

Cumin, Fried Eggplant with Garlic &, 66

Currants, Albondigas with Pine Nuts &, 30

Dafina, 279

Dashi Stock, 725

dates
Balsamic Apple Date Challah, 550–551
Celery Slaw with Seeds & Dates, 428
Dafina, 279
Date Coconut Rolls, 170
Red Cabbage, Date & Beet Salad, 153
Roasted Cauliflower, 213

delicata squash
Autumn Kale Salad, 423
Delicata Squash Pasta with Brown Butter & Sage, 281

desserts and sweets
All-Butter Pastry Dough, 578
Apple & Calvados Tart, 582
Apple Brioche Tart, 583
Apple Cake, 584
Apple Walnut Bundt Cake, 585–586
Apple-Cranberry Crisp with Oatmeal-Cookie Crumble, 588

Black & White Cookies, 589

Black & White Halvah, 590–591

Calvados Applesauce, 579

Caramelized-Honey Nut & Seed Tart, 592

Charoset, 176

Cheesecake, 190

Chocolate Ganache, 602

Chocolate Macaroons, 593–595

Chocolate-Cinnamon "Babkallah," 596

Coconut Macaroons, 597

Date Coconut Rolls, 170

Flourless Chocolate Cake, 600

Golden Brown Cookies with Apple Filling, 603

Halvah, 605

Halvah Five Ways, 606–607

Halvah Mille-Feuilles, 608

Hamantaschen, 614–615

Honey Cake, 609–610

Honey Pomegranate Cake, 611

Hungarian Golden Pull-Apart Cake with Walnuts & Apricot Jam, 616

Knafeh Cheesecake, 617

Malabi, 620

Mandel Bread, 621

Melktert, 626–627

New Year's Honey Cake, 625

Olive Oil Apple Cake with Spiced Sugar, 630

Orange-Spiced Rye Honey Cake, 633

Pecan-Orange Baklava Pie, 634–635

Pomegranate Truffles, 636–637

Pumpkin Cranberry Cupcakes, 638

Purim Roses, 640

Rainbow Cookies, 645

Rugelach, 641

Salted Honey Apple Upside-Down Cake, 219

Sfenj Donuts, 646

Sfratti, 648

Spiced Honey Cake with Cream Cheese Frosting, 649

Strudel with Tropical Fruits, Chipotle Chocolate & Whipped Cream, 652

Sufganiyot, 204

Sumac, Spelt & Apple Cake, 653

Vanilla Cake Rusks, 654

Vanilla Nutmeg Babka, 655–656

Yeasted Apple Coffee
Cake, 657
dill
Fava Beans with
Pomegranates, 62
Grandpa's Gravlox, 146
Grandson's Beet &
Vodka Gravlox, 149
Kuku Sabzi, 312
Oven-Poached Salmon,
336
Pirozhki, 344–345
Shaved Carrot & Radish
Salad with Herbs &
Toasted Pumpkin
Seeds, 483
Swiss Chard & Herb
Fritters, 502
Walnut-Garlic Sauce,
543
Dolmeh Beh, 282
duck eggs
Taco de Gribenes, 402
Dukkah
recipe, 115, 524
Tahini Chicken Salad,
114–115

Egg Cream, 660
eggplant
Almodrote, 225
Baba Ghanoush, 161
Chicken with Mehshi
Sfeeha, 248
Eggplant & Chorizo
Boureka, 284
Fried Eggplant with
Garlic & Cumin, 66

Fried Eggplant with
Mint Vinaigrette, 67
Handrajo, 301
Romanian Eggplant
Salad, 108
Sabich, 365
Turkish Eggplant
Dolma, 407
Turkish Eggplant Salad,
690
eggs
Challah French Toast,
556
Chopped Liver, 46
Everything Spiced
Malaway with Fried
Egg, 288
Eyerlekh mit Tzvible,
289
Khachapuri, 306
Kuku Sabzi, 312
Noodle Kugel, 464
Pirozhki, 344–345
Sabich, 365
Shakshuka, 376
Spinach Rissoles with
Lemon Sauce, 397
Swiss Chard & Herb
Fritters, 502
Turkish Eggplant
Dolma, 407
White Shakshuka, 412
Eggy Challah Toast, 563
Egyptian Lentils & Rice,
439
Egyptian Short Rib &
Okra Stew, 287
Ensalada de Pulpo, 684

escarole
Aliciotti con Individa,
224
Sheet-Pan Roasted
Squash & Feta Salad,
490
Everything Spiced Malaway
with Fried Egg, 288
Eyerlekh mit Tzvible, 289

Falafel, 59
farmers cheese
Blintzes with Berry
Compote, 33
Chushki Burek, 47
farro
Grain Salad with Olives
& Whole-Lemon
Vinaigrette, 444
fava beans
Fava Beans with
Pomegranates, 62
Ful Medames, 70
Msoki de Pesaj, 331
Roasted Corn & Black
Bean Salad, 107
fennel
Cast-Iron Roast
Chicken with Fennel
& Carrots, 243
Gefilte Fish, 180
Msoki de Pesaj, 331
Saffron Tomato Fennel
Broth, 539
Shaved Fennel Salad, 486
Skillet Roast Chicken
with Fennel, Parsnips
& Scallions, 383

Strawberry Fields Salad, 113

Turkish Coffee-Rubbed Brisket, 406

Fermented Hot Sauce, 734

Fesenjan, 132

feta cheese

Broccolini Salad, 37

Charred Chicken with Sweet Potatoes & Oranges, 249

Couscous Arancini, 706

Sheet-Pan Roasted Squash & Feta Salad, 490

Swiss Chard & Herb Fritters, 502

figs

Pomegranate Glazed Figs & Cheese, 99

Sephardic Jeweled Rosh Hashanah Rice, 169

Vegetable Tanzia, 409

fish

Aliciotti con Individa, 224

Cedar-Plank Salmon, 246

Chermoula Sea Bass, 254

Cold Roast Salmon with Smashed Green Bean Salad, 268–269

Crispy Salmon Rice, 685

Eyerlekh mit Tzvible, 289

Fish Stock, 726

Fried Fish with Agristada Sauce, 292

Gefilte Fish, 180

Grandpa's Gravlox, 146

Grandson's Beet & Vodka Gravlox, 149

Italian Sweet & Sour Fish, 166

Matjes Herring in Red Wine Sauce or Cream Sauce, 150

Moroccan Fish & Crispy Rice Cake with Saffron Crust, 327–328

Olive Oil-Poached Fluke, 679

Oven-Poached Salmon, 336

Poached Fish in Pepper Sauce, 341

Red Gefilte Fish Veragruzana, 101–102

Roasted & Stuffed Sardines, 678

Spaghetti al Tonno, 392

Spinach Pesto Stuffed Salmon, 393

Sumac & Lime Mahi-Mahi with Pickled Apple Couscous, 714

Tuna Kibbeh Nayeh, 707

Whole Branzino, 715

fish sauce

Cilantro-Lime Vinaigrette, 522

Eggy Challah Toast, 563

Fish Stock, 726

Flourless Chocolate Cake, 600

Fresh Herb Blend

Heart-Beet Salad, 71

Israeli Spicy Chickpea Soup with Crème Fraîche, 74

Roasted Brussels Sprouts, 476

Roasted Cauliflower, 213

Roasted Corn & Black Bean Salad, 107

Strawberry Fields Salad, 113

Fried Eggplant with Garlic & Cumin, 66

Fried Eggplant with Mint Vinaigrette, 67

Fried Fish with Agristada Sauce, 292

Ful Medames, 70

garlic

Albondigas with Pine Nuts & Currants, 30

Aliciotti con Individa, 224

Autumn Kale Salad, 423

Baba Ghanoush, 161

Beef Mixiote, 229

Brisket with Pomegranate-Walnut Sauce & Pistachio Gremolata, 238

Broccolini Salad, 37

Charred Chicken with Sweet Potatoes & Oranges, 249

Charred Sweet Potatoes with Toum, 430

Chef's Special Matzo Ball Soup, 41

Chermoula Sea Bass, 254

Chicken & Tomato Stew with Caramelized Lemon, 258

Chicken Stew with Potatoes & Radishes, 242

Chicken with Mehshi Sfeeha, 248

Chimichurri Sauce, 521

Cholent, 209

Concia, 50

Corned Beef with Barbeque Sauce, 270

Crockpot Carne con Papas, 278

Crockpot Sweet & Sour Brisket, 271

Dafina, 279

Dukkah, 115

Egyptian Short Rib & Okra Stew, 287

Falafel, 59

Fermented Hot Sauce, 734

Fried Eggplant with Garlic & Cumin, 66

Ful Medames, 70

Green Zhoug, 701

Israeli Spicy Chickpea Soup with Crème Fraîche, 74

Kemia de Zanahorias, 85

Khoresh Sib, 309

Lamb Stew, 299

Leg of Lamb with Garlic & Rosemary, 316

Mahasha, 320

Mama Kramer's Brisket, 305

Marinated Olives, 462

Messer Wot, 323

Moroccan Cornish Hens with Pine Nut Couscous, 329

Moroccan Fish & Crispy Rice Cake with Saffron Crust, 327–328

Moroccan Lamb Shanks with Pomegranate Sauce, 330

Mushroom Barley Soup, 91

Pomegranate & Honey Glazed Chicken, 348

Pot Roast, 199

Red Gefilte Fish Veragruzana, 101–102

Red Wine-Braised Oxtail, 356

Red Zhoug, 700

Roast Chicken with Harissa & Schmaltz, 359–361

Roasted Apricot

Chicken with Mint & Sage Butternut Squash, 358

Roasted Garlic Potato Knish, 136

Roasted Shabbat Chicken with Spring Vegetables, 212

Ropa Vieja, 364

Saffron Tomato Coulis, 538

Saffron Tomato Fennel Broth, 539

Shakshuka, 376

Shakshuka with Spinach & Lamb Meatballs, 372

Shashlik, 380

Shawarma-Spiced Braised Leg of Lamb, 377

Sheet Pan Tzimmes-Roasted Chicken Thighs, 381

Slow-Cooked Cherry Tomatoes with Coriander & Rosemary, 491

Slow-Roasted Chicken with All the Garlic, 387

Slow-Roasted Chicken with Honey-Glazed Carrots & Ginger, 388

Spaghetti al Tonno, 392

Split Peas with Berbere, 494

Stuffed Lamb, 398–399

Tsyplyonok Tabaka, 404–405

Tunisian Spiced Butternut Squash Soup, 119

Turkish Coffee-Rubbed Brisket, 406

Turkish Eggplant Salad, 690

Tzimmes Chicken with Apricots, Prunes & Carrots, 186

Vegetable Soup, 120

Vegetable Stock, 729

Vegetarian Yemenite Soup Recipe, 121

Walnut-Garlic Sauce, 543

White Shakshuka, 412

Za'atar Chicken with Garlicky Yogurt, 414

Gefilte Fish
  recipe, 180
  Red Gefilte Fish Veragruzana, 101–102

Ghormeh Sabzi, 294

Gilden, Scott, 9–10

Gilden, Shari Kuritsky, 10

ginger
  Chicken Schnitzel & Cherry Sauce, 262
  Ginger Carrot Vinaigrette, 523
  Kachori, 80
  Messer Wot, 323
  Slow-Roasted Chicken with Honey-Glazed

Carrots & Ginger, 388

Spayty, 396

goat cheese
  Broccolini Salad, 37
  Strawberry Fields Salad, 113
  Golden Brown Cookies with Apple Filling, 603
  Grain Salad with Olives & Whole-Lemon Vinaigrette, 444

Grandpa's Gravlox, 146

Grandson's Beet & Vodka Gravlox, 149

grapes
  Broccolini Salad, 37
  Chicken Salad, 42
  Mezze'd Up Salad, 95

gravlox
  Grandpa's Gravlox, 146
  Grandson's Beet & Vodka Gravlox, 149

green beans
  Cold Roast Salmon with Smashed Green Bean Salad, 268–269
  Green Beans with Za'atar & Lemon, 445
  Romano Beans with Mustard Vinaigrette & Walnuts, 179

Green Zhoug, 701

Gribenes
  Chopped Liver, 46
  Gribenes & Schmaltz, 528

Potato & Schmaltz Kugel, 453

Grilled Serrano Salsa Verde
  recipe, 269

Halvah
  Halvah Five Ways, 606–607
  Halvah Mille-Feuilles, 608
  recipe, 605

Hamantaschen, 614–615

Handrajo, 301

Hand-Rolled Couscous, 298

Hanukkah
  about, 22–23
  menus for, 192–205

harissa
  Harissa-Carrot Halwa, 448
  Kemia de Zanahorias, 85
  Msoki de Pesaj, 331
  Roast Chicken with Harissa & Schmaltz, 359–361
  Swiss Chard & Herb Fritters, 502
  Tunisian Spiced Butternut Squash Soup, 119

Harissa-Carrot Halwa, 448

Hawaij Hot Cocoa with Cinnamon Whipped Cream, 659

Hawaij Spice Blend, 659
hazelnuts
    Autumn Kale Salad, 423
Heart-Beet Salad, 71
Herring in Red Wine
        Sauce or Cream
        Sauce, Matjes, 150
honey
    Beet Chips with Spicy
        Honey Mayonnaise,
        426
    Caramelized-Honey Nut
        & Seed Tart, 592
    Challah, 129–130
    Champagne Vinaigrette,
        516
    Charred Sweet Potatoes
        with Toum, 430
    Cilantro-Lime
        Vinaigrette, 522
    Halvah, 605
    Halvah Mille-Feuilles,
        608
    Honey Brioche, 566–
        567
    Honey Cake, 609–610
    Honey Glazed Carrots
        with Carrot Top
        Gremolata, 140
    Honey Pomegranate
        Cake, 611
    Honey-Roasted Carrots
        with Tahini Yogurt,
        450
    Honey-Roasted
        Vegetable Salad, 451
    New Year's Honey Cake,
        625

Orange & Pomegranate
    Salad with Honey, 96
Orange-Spiced Rye
    Honey Cake, 633
Pecan-Orange Baklava
    Pie, 634–635
Pomegranate & Honey
    Glazed Chicken, 348
Pomegranate
    Vinaigrette, 532
Roasted Brussels Sprouts
    with Warm Honey
    Glaze, 135, 475
Salted Honey Apple
    Upside-Down Cake,
    219
Sfratti, 648
Sheet Pan Tzimmes-
    Roasted Chicken
    Thighs, 381
Slow-Roasted Chicken
    with Honey-Glazed
    Carrots & Ginger,
    388
Spiced Honey Cake
    with Cream Cheese
    Frosting, 649
Sumac & Apple-Roasted
    Cauliflower, 696
Tzimmes Chicken with
    Apricots, Prunes &
    Carrots, 186
horseradish
    Grandpa's Gravlox, 146
    Grandson's Beet &
        Vodka Gravlox, 149
    Horseradish-Yogurt
        Sauce, 438

Maror, 529
Slow-Cooked Short Ribs
    with Gremolata, 386
Horseradish-Yogurt Sauce
    Crispy Baby Yukon
        Gold Potatoes, 438
    Porcini-Rubbed Beef
        Rib Roast, 354
    recipe, 354, 438
hummus, 160
Hungarian Golden Pull-
    Apart Cake with
    Walnuts & Apricot
    Jam, 616

Israeli Salad, 73
Israeli Spicy Chickpea
    Soup with Crème
    Fraîche, 74
Israeli Yogurt Sauce, 529
Italian Sweet & Sour Fish,
    166

Jerusalem Mixed Grill,
    304
Jewish cuisine
    holidays and, 17–23
    introduction to, 9–10
    origins of, 11–16
Jewish-Style Fried
    Artichokes, 77–78

Kachori, 80
kale
    Autumn Kale Salad,
        423
    Heart-Beet Salad, 71
    Khachapuri, 306

Mezze'd Up Salad, 95

Msoki de Pesaj, 331

Slow-Roasted Lamb
Shoulder with
Brussels Sprouts &
Crispy Kale, 389

Strawberry Fields Salad,
113

Kartoffel Kugel, 139

Kasha Varnishkes, 456

kashkaval cheese
Almodrote, 225
Bourekas, 203
Chushki Burek, 47

kataifi pastry
Knafeh Cheesecake, 617

Keftes de Espinaca, 200

Kemia de Remolachas, 85

Kemia de Zanahorias, 85

Khachapuri, 306

Khoresh Sib, 309

kidney beans
Avikas, 228
Cholent, 209

Kiftahs, 293

Kishka/Kishke
Cholent, 209
recipe, 79

Knafeh Cheesecake, 617

kombu
Dashi Stock, 725

Korn, Joshua, 10

Koshary
Egyptian Lentils & Rice,
439

Kreplach, 88

Kuku Sabzi, 312

Labneh
Fava Beans with
Pomegranates, 62
recipe, 530
White Shakshuka, 412

Laffa
recipe, 571
Sabich, 365

lamb
Cholent, 209
Dolmeh Beh, 282
Khoresh Sib, 309
Lamb Stew, 299
Lamb Stock, 721
Leg of Lamb with Garlic
& Rosemary, 316
Marinated Lamb Heart,
711
Moroccan Lamb Shanks
with Pomegranate
Sauce, 330
Msoki de Pesaj, 331
Oshi Bakhsh, 337
Rosemary Rack of Lamb
with Roasted Potatoes
& Carrots, 368
Shakshuka with Spinach
& Lamb Meatballs,
372
Shashlik, 380
Shawarma-Spiced Braised
Leg of Lamb, 377
Skewers of Chicken &
Lamb Fat, 385
Slow-Roasted Lamb
Shoulder with
Brussels Sprouts &
Crispy Kale, 389

Stuffed Lamb, 398–399

Stuffed Saddle of Lamb,
400

Latkes, 196

Latkes with Short Ribs,
313

leeks
Beef, Beet & Cabbage
Borscht, 34
Chicken Stock, 722
Creamy Potato & Leek
Gratin, 437
Fish Stock, 726
Ghormeh Sabzi, 294
Leeks Braised in White
Wine, 457
Leeks with Thyme &
Pomegranate, 458
Msoki de Pesaj, 331
Pot Roast, 199
Roasted Beet & Leek
Risotto, 103
Veal, Beef, or Lamb
Stock, 721
Vegetable Soup, 120
Vegetable Stock
White Wine Braised
Leeks, 216

Leg of Lamb with Garlic
& Rosemary, 316

Lemon-Poppy Seed
Halvah, 606–607

lemons, preserved
Arugula Salad with
Pickled Beets &
Preserved-Lemon
Vinaigrette, 165
Moroccan Fish &

Crispy Rice Cake
with Saffron Crust,
327–328
lemons/lemon juice
Chicken & Tomato
Stew with
Caramelized Lemon,
258
Fried Fish with
Agristada Sauce, 292
Grain Salad with Olives
& Whole-Lemon
Vinaigrette, 444
Green Beans with
Za'atar & Lemon, 445
Israeli Yogurt Sauce, 529
Jewish-Style Fried
Artichokes, 77–78
Lemony Yogurt Sauce,
269
Limonana, 663
Oven-Poached Salmon,
336
Red Gefilte Fish
Veragruzana, 101–102
Roasted Cauliflower,
213
Sheet Pan Tzimmes-
Roasted Chicken
Thighs, 381
Slow-Cooked Short Ribs
with Gremolata, 386
Spinach Rissoles with
Lemon Sauce, 397
Tomato Jam, 542
Tzimmes Chicken with
Apricots, Prunes &
Carrots, 186

Za'atar Okra & Lemons,
506
Lemony Yogurt Sauce
Cold Roast Salmon with
Smashed Green Bean
Salad, 268–269
recipe, 269
lentils
Egyptian Lentils & Rice,
439
Messer Wot, 323
Mujadara, 463
See also beans
limes/lime juice
Cilantro-Lime
Vinaigrette, 522
Ghormeh Sabzi, 294
Slow-Roasted Chicken
with Honey-Glazed
Carrots & Ginger,
388
Sumac & Lime Mahi-
Mahi with Pickled
Apple Couscous, 714
Tomato Jam, 542
Limonana, 663
Liverwurst, 94

Macaroni Salad, 461
Mahasha, 320
Mahi-Mahi with Pickled
Apple Couscous,
Sumac & Lime, 714
Mahshi Laban, 317
Malabi, 620
Mama Kramer's Brisket,
305
Mandel Bread, 621

mango
Cucumber Tomato
Mango Relish, 57
Strudel with Tropical
Fruits, Chipotle
Chocolate &
Whipped Cream, 652
Marinated Lamb Heart,
711
Marinated Olives, 462
Maror, 529
marrow bones
Cholent, 209
mascarpone cheese
Knafeh Cheesecake, 617
Pomegranate Glazed
Figs & Cheese, 99
Matjes Herring in Red
Wine Sauce or Cream
Sauce, 150
matzo ball soup
Bone Marrow Matzo
Ball Soup, 36
Chef's Special Matzo
Ball Soup, 41
Stuffed Matzo Ball
Soup with Chicken &
Apples, 498
Matzo Brei, 175
Matzo Balls
recipe, 185
meatballs
Albondigas with Pine
Nuts & Currants, 30
Chef's Special Sweet &
Sour Meatballs, 253
Kiftahs, 293

Shakshuka with Spinach & Lamb Meatballs, 372

Melktert, 626–627

Messer Wot, 323

Mezze'd Up Salad, 95

Mina de Espinaca, 324

mint
Brisket with Pomegranate-Walnut Sauce & Pistachio Gremolata, 238
Chicken & Tomato Stew with Caramelized Lemon, 258
Chimichurri Sauce, 521
Cucumber, Mint & Sumac Salad, 58
Egyptian Short Rib & Okra Stew, 287
Fava Beans with Pomegranates, 62
Fried Eggplant with Mint Vinaigrette, 67
Ghormeh Sabzi, 294
Grain Salad with Olives & Whole-Lemon Vinaigrette, 444
Honey-Roasted Vegetable Salad, 451
Limonana, 663
Msoki de Pesaj, 331
Olive Salad, 183
Oshi Bakhsh, 337
Red Cabbage, Date & Beet Salad, 153

Roasted Apricot Chicken with Mint & Sage Butternut Squash, 358
Salsa Verde, 540
Shaved Carrot & Radish Salad with Herbs & Toasted Pumpkin Seeds, 483
Shaved Fennel Salad, 486
Shaved Radish Salad with Walnuts & Mint, 482
Tomato Jam, 542

mirin/aji-mirin
Ginger Carrot Vinaigrette, 523
Israeli Spicy Chickpea Soup with Crème Fraîche, 74
Roasted Corn Sauce, 533
Tomato Jam, 542

Mizrahim, 15–16

Modern Hummus, 160

Moroccan Cornish Hens with Pine Nut Couscous, 329

Moroccan Fish & Crispy Rice Cake with Saffron Crust, 327–328

Moroccan Lamb Shanks with Pomegranate Sauce, 330

Msoki de Pesaj, 331

muenster cheese
Khachapuri, 306

Mujadara, 463

mushrooms
Challah Stuffing, 429
Mushroom Barley Soup, 91
Mushroom Stock, 730
Porcini-Rubbed Beef Rib Roast, 354
Roasted Corn & Black Bean Salad, 107
Vegetarian Yemenite Soup Recipe, 121

Naan, 741

New Year's Honey Cake, 625

Noodle Kugel, 464

nuts, mixed
Caramelized-Honey Nut & Seed Tart, 592
See also individual nut types

oats
Apple-Cranberry Crisp with Oatmeal-Cookie Crumble, 588
Yeasted Apple Coffee Cake, 657

octopus
Ensalada de Pulpo, 684
Okra Stew, Egyptian Short Rib &, 287
Olive Oil Apple Cake with Spiced Sugar, 630
Olive Oil-Poached Fluke, 679

olives
Charred Chicken with Sweet Potatoes & Oranges, 249
Grain Salad with Olives & Whole-Lemon Vinaigrette, 444
Marinated Olives, 462
Olive Salad, 183
Red Gefilte Fish Veragruzana, 101–102
Relish Tray, 537
Strawberry Fields Salad, 113
Stuffed Lamb, 398–399

onions
Beef, Beet & Cabbage Borscht, 34
Beef Brisket, 232
Bialy, 554
Boulettes with Chicken & Vegetable Soup & Couscous, 234–235
Bulgur with Fried Onions, 239
Challah Stuffing, 429
Chef's Special Matzo Ball Soup, 41
Chicken Stock, 722
Chicken with Turmeric, Tahini, Chickpeas & Onions, 266
Cholent, 209
Chopped Liver, 46
Classic Canned Tomato Sauce, 733
Cojada Potato Casserole, 267

Corned Beef with Barbeque Sauce, 270
Couscous with Seven Vegetables, 431
Crispy Roast Chicken, 274–275
Crockpot Carne con Papas, 278
Crockpot Sweet & Sour Brisket, 271
Cucumber Tomato Mango Relish, 57
Dolmeh Beh, 282
Eggplant & Chorizo Boureka, 284
Egyptian Lentils & Rice, 439
Eyerlekh mit Tzvible, 289
Fish Stock, 726
Gefilte Fish, 180
Ghormeh Sabzi, 294
Handrajo, 301
Jerusalem Mixed Grill, 304
Kasha Varnishkes, 456
Khoresh Sib, 309
Kishka, 79
Kreplach, 88–89
Lamb Stew, 299
Latkes, 196
Latkes with Short Ribs, 313
Mahasha, 320
Mama Kramer's Brisket, 305

Matjes Herring in Red Wine Sauce or Cream Sauce, 150
Messer Wot, 323
Moroccan Cornish Hens with Pine Nut Couscous, 329
Moroccan Lamb Shanks with Pomegranate Sauce, 330
Msoki de Pesaj, 331
Mujadara, 463
Mushroom Stock, 730
Onion Mahshi, 332
Pickled Cucumber Salad, 154
Poached Fish in Pepper Sauce, 341
Pomegranate Brisket with Cranberry Succotash, 353
Potato & Schmaltz Kugel, 453
Potato Kugel, 469
Red Gefilte Fish Veragruzana, 101–102
Red Wine-Braised Oxtail, 356
Red Zhoug, 700
Roasted Corn & Black Bean Salad, 107
Roasted Corn Sauce, 533
Roasted Shabbat Chicken with Spring Vegetables, 212
Romanian Eggplant Salad, 108

Ropa Vieja, 364

Rustic Matzo Ball Soup, 185

Saffron Tomato Fennel Broth, 539

Seitan Brisket, 371

Sephardic Jeweled Rosh Hashanah Rice, 169

Shashlik, 380

Shawarma-Spiced Braised Leg of Lamb, 377

Sheet Pan Tzimmes-Roasted Chicken Thighs, 381

Sheika, 382

Spayty, 396

Split Pea Soup, 110

Split Peas with Berbere, 494

Stuffed Lamb, 398–399

Stuffed Saddle of Lamb, 400

Sumac Chicken & Rice, 401

Swiss Chard & Herb Fritters, 502

Taco de Gribenes, 402

Tsyplyonok Tabaka, 404–405

Turkish Coffee-Rubbed Brisket, 406

Tzimmes Chicken with Apricots, Prunes & Carrots, 186

Veal, Beef, or Lamb Stock, 721

Vegetable Soup, 120

Vegetable Stock, 729

Vegetable Tanzia, 409

White Shakshuka, 412

Wine-Braised Brisket with Butternut Squash, 413

Za'atar Chicken with Garlicky Yogurt, 414

orange blossom water

Msoki de Pesaj, 331

Purim Roses, 640

Sachlav, 665

Turmeric Chicken with Toum, 408

White Peach Sangria with Orange Blossom Water, 668

oranges/orange juice

Charred Chicken with Sweet Potatoes & Oranges, 249

Citrus Salad, 49

Crockpot Carne con Papas, 278

Heart-Beet Salad, 71

Honey Glazed Carrots with Carrot Top Gremolata, 140

New Year's Honey Cake, 625

Orange & Pomegranate Salad with Honey, 96

Orange-Spiced Rye Honey Cake, 633

Pecan-Orange Baklava Pie, 634–635

Red Gefilte Fish Veragruzana, 101–102

Spiced Honey Cake with Cream Cheese Frosting, 649

Yeasted Apple Coffee Cake, 657

oregano

Chimichurri Sauce, 521

Tomato Jam, 542

Oshi Bakhsh, 337

Oven-Poached Salmon, 336

Oxtail, Red Wine-Braised, 356

Paprika Oil

Moroccan Fish & Crispy Rice Cake with Saffron Crust, 327–328

recipe, 328

Paratha, 738

Parmesan cheese

Autumn Kale Salad, 423

Chushki Burek, 47

Crunchy Salty Lemony Salad, 443

Delicata Squash Pasta with Brown Butter & Sage, 281

Mina de Espinaca, 324

Roasted Beets with Cilantro-Basil Pesto, 104

Shaved Fennel Salad, 486

Shaved Radish Salad with Walnuts & Mint, 482

Spaetzle, 495

parsley

Boulettes with Chicken
& Vegetable Soup &
Couscous, 234–235

Chermoula Sauce, 517

Chermoula Sea Bass,
254

Chimichurri Sauce, 521

Coleslaw, 434

Crispy Salmon Rice,
685

Crockpot Sweet & Sour
Brisket, 271

Eggplant & Chorizo
Boureka, 284

Falafel, 59

Fava Beans with
Pomegranates, 62

Ful Medames, 70

Ghormeh Sabzi, 294

Ginger Carrot
Vinaigrette, 523

Grain Salad with Olives
& Whole-Lemon
Vinaigrette, 444

Green Zhoug, 701

Grilled Serrano Salsa
Verde, 269

Kuku Sabzi, 312

Marinated Lamb Heart,
711

Msoki de Pesaj, 331

Mushroom Barley Soup,
91

Red Gefilte Fish
Veragruzana, 101–102

Red Zhoug, 700

Roasted & Stuffed
Sardines, 678

Roasted Corn Sauce,
533

Roasted Shabbat
Chicken with Spring
Vegetables, 212

Romanian Eggplant
Salad, 108

Romano Beans with
Mustard Vinaigrette
& Walnuts, 179

Rustic Matzo Ball Soup,
185

Salsa Verde, 540

Shaved Carrot & Radish
Salad with Herbs &
Toasted Pumpkin
Seeds, 483

Sheet Pan Tzimmes-
Roasted Chicken
Thighs, 381

Slow-Cooked Short Ribs
with Gremolata, 386

Sumac & Lime Mahi-
Mahi with Pickled
Apple Couscous, 714

Swiss Chard & Herb
Fritters, 502

Tomato Jam, 542

Turkish Eggplant Salad,
690

Vegetable Soup, 120

Walnut-Garlic Sauce,
543

parsnips

Chef's Special Matzo
Ball Soup, 41

Rustic Matzo Ball Soup,
185

Saffron Tomato Fennel
Broth, 539

Skillet Roast Chicken
with Fennel, Parsnips
& Scallions, 383

Tunisian Spiced
Butternut Squash
Soup, 119

Vegetable Soup, 120

Vegetarian Yemenite
Soup Recipe, 121

Passover

about, 20, 22

menus for, 172–191

pasta and noodles

Bulgur with Fried
Onions, 239

Delicata Squash Pasta
with Brown Butter &
Sage, 281

Egyptian Lentils & Rice,
439

Kasha Varnishkes, 456

Macaroni Salad, 461

Noodle Kugel, 464

Spaghetti al Tonno,
392

Pastrami, 340

Pâte Fermentée

Challah, 129–130

recipe, 131

Peach Sangria with
Orange Blossom
Water, White, 668

peanuts

Malabi, 620

pears
  Ensalada de Pulpo, 684
  Strudel with Tropical
    Fruits, Chipotle
    Chocolate &
    Whipped Cream, 652
peas
  Chicken Curry, 259
  Kachori, 80
  Shaved Snap Pea Salad,
    691
  Split Pea Soup, 110
  Split Peas with Berbere,
    494
  See also beans
pecans
  Chicken Salad, 42
  Crunchy Pomegranate
    Salad, 51
  Flourless Chocolate
    Cake, 600
  Pecan-Orange Baklava
    Pie, 634–635
  Rugelach, 641
peppers, bell
  Chushki Burek, 47
  Crockpot Carne con
    Papas, 278
  Israeli Salad, 73
  Israeli Spicy Chickpea
    Soup with Crème
    Fraîche, 74
  Lamb Stew, 299
  Macaroni Salad, 461
  Moroccan Fish &
    Crispy Rice Cake
    with Saffron Crust,
    327–328

Poached Fish in Pepper
  Sauce, 341
Potato Salad, 470
Roasted Corn & Black
  Bean Salad, 107
Roasted Corn Sauce,
  533
Roasted Pepper Salad,
  480
Romanian Eggplant
  Salad, 108
Ropa Vieja, 364
Salata Mechouia, 109
Split Peas with Berbere,
  494
Tomato Salad, 116
peppers, hot
  Beef Mixiote, 229
  Chimichurri Sauce, 521
  Dolmeh Beh, 282
  Egyptian Short Rib &
    Okra Stew, 287
  Ensalada de Pulpo, 684
  Fermented Hot Sauce,
    734
  Green Zhoug, 701
  Grilled Serrano Salsa
    Verde, 269
  Kachori, 80
  Moroccan Fish &
    Crispy Rice Cake
    with Saffron Crust,
    327–328
  Poblano Matzo Ball
    Soup, 100
  Red Zhoug, 700
  Roasted Corn & Black
    Bean Salad, 107

Roasted Corn Sauce,
  533
Salata Mechouia, 109
Shakshuka, 376
Stuffed Lamb, 398–399
Stuffed Saddle of Lamb,
  400
Three-Chile Harissa,
  359–361
Tomato Jam, 542
Verde Sauce, 684
pesto
  Roasted Beets with
    Cilantro-Basil Pesto,
    104
  Spinach Pesto Stuffed
    Salmon, 393
phyllo dough
  Halvah Mille-Feuilles,
    608
  Pecan-Orange Baklava
    Pie, 634–635
  Strudel with Tropical
    Fruits, Chipotle
    Chocolate &
    Whipped Cream, 652
  Tuna Kibbeh Nayeh,
    707
Pickled Cucumber Salad,
  154
Pickled Green Tomatoes,
  157
pike
  Gefilte Fish, 180
pine nuts
  Albondigas with Pine
    Nuts & Currants,
    30

Italian Sweet & Sour
Fish, 166
Moroccan Cornish
Hens with Pine Nut
Couscous, 329
Roasted Beets with
Cilantro-Basil Pesto,
104
Roasted Brussels
Sprouts, 476
Spinach Pesto Stuffed
Salmon, 393
Sumac Chicken & Rice,
401
pineapple
Chef's Special Sweet &
Sour Meatballs, 253
Chimichurri Sauce, 521
Citrus Salad, 49
Tomato Jam, 542
Pirozhki, 344–345
pistachios
Arugula Salad with
Pickled Beets &
Preserved-Lemon
Vinaigrette, 165
Chocolate Babka,
560–561
Cold Roast Salmon with
Smashed Green Bean
Salad, 268–269
Dolmeh Beh, 282
Dukkah, 115, 524
Halvah Five Ways,
606–607
Malabi, 620
Pomegranate Truffles,
636–637

Sachlav, 665
Sephardic Jeweled Rosh
Hashanah Rice, 169
Pita
Sabich, 365
Pita Bread, 697
plums
Roasted Plums with
Tahini Dressing, 477
Strawberry Rosé Sangria,
668
Poached Fish in Pepper
Sauce, 341
Poblano Matzo Ball Soup,
100
Polenta Medallions, 348
Pomegranate Confiture
Fesenjan, 132
recipe, 132
pomegranate juice
Brisket with
Pomegranate-Walnut
Sauce & Pistachio
Gremolata, 238
Honey Pomegranate
Cake, 611
Leeks with Thyme &
Pomegranate, 458
Moroccan Lamb Shanks
with Pomegranate
Sauce, 330
Pomegranate Brisket
with Cranberry
Succotash, 353
Pomegranate Glazed
Figs & Cheese, 99
Pomegranate Molasses,
636

Pomegranate Prosecco
Punch, 664
Pomegranate Truffles,
636–637
Pomegranate
Vinaigrette, 532
Seared Radicchio &
Roasted Beets, 481
Sephardic Jeweled Rosh
Hashanah Rice, 169
pomegranate molasses
Crispy Salmon Rice,
685
Fava Beans with
Pomegranates, 62
Onion Mahshi, 332
Pomegranate & Honey
Glazed Chicken, 348
Pomegranate Truffles,
636–637
Shashlik, 380
Stuffed Saddle of Lamb,
400
Zucchini Mahshi, 509
pomegranate seeds/arils
Baba Ghanoush, 161
Black-Eyed Peas
with Turmeric &
Pomegranate, 427
Crunchy Pomegranate
Salad, 51
Fava Beans with
Pomegranates, 62
Leeks with Thyme &
Pomegranate, 458
Olive Salad, 183
Orange & Pomegranate
Salad with Honey, 96

Oshi Bakhsh, 337

Pomegranate & Honey
Glazed Chicken,
348

Pomegranate Confiture,
132

Seared Radicchio &
Roasted Beets, 481

Sephardic Jeweled Rosh
Hashanah Rice, 169

Stuffed Saddle of Lamb,
400

pomegranate syrup
Black-Eyed Peas
with Turmeric &
Pomegranate, 427

pomegranate tea
Honey Pomegranate
Cake, 611

Pomegranate Vinaigrette
Heart-Beet Salad, 71
recipe, 532

Porcini-Rubbed Beef Rib
Roast, 354

Pot Roast, 199

potatoes
Beef, Beet & Cabbage
Borscht, 34

Boulettes with Chicken
& Vegetable Soup &
Couscous, 234–235

Bourekas, 203

Chicken Stew with
Potatoes & Radishes,
242

Cholent, 209

Cojada Potato Casserole,
267

Creamy Potato & Leek
Gratin, 437

Crispy Baby Yukon
Gold Potatoes, 438

Crispy Roast Chicken,
274–275

Crockpot Carne con
Papas, 278

Dafina, 279

Eyerlekh mit Tzvible,
289

Kartoffel Kugel, 139

Keftes de Espinaca, 200

Latkes, 196

Latkes with Short Ribs,
313

Mina de Espinaca, 324

Pirozhki, 344–345

Pot Roast, 199

Potato & Schmaltz
Kugel, 453

Potato Kugel, 469

Potato Salad, 470

Potato Tahdig, 468

Rack-Roasted Chicken,
355

Rice with Barberries,
471

Roasted Garlic Potato
Knish, 136

Rosemary Rack of Lamb
with Roasted Potatoes
& Carrots, 368

Sheet Pan Tzimmes-
Roasted Chicken
Thighs, 381

Spayty, 396

Stuffed Lamb, 398–399

Turkish Coffee-Rubbed
Brisket, 406

Vegetarian Yemenite
Soup Recipe, 121

Prosecco Punch,
Pomegranate, 664

prunes/prune juice
Kiftahs, 293

Sheet Pan Tzimmes-
Roasted Chicken
Thighs, 381

Tzimmes Chicken with
Apricots, Prunes &
Carrots, 186

Vegetable Tanzia, 409

puff pastry sheets
Bourekas, 203

Handrajo, 301

pumpkin
Honey-Roasted
Vegetable Salad,
451

Pumpkin Cranberry
Cupcakes, 638

pumpkin seeds
Caramelized-Honey Nut
& Seed Tart, 592

Shaved Carrot & Radish
Salad with Herbs &
Toasted Pumpkin
Seeds, 483

Purim Roses, 640

Quick Pickled Carrots,
537

quinces
Dolmeh Beh, 282

Khoresh Sib, 309

Stuffed Saddle of Lamb, 400

quinoa
Mezze'd Up Salad, 95

Rack-Roasted Chicken, 355

radicchio
Seared Radicchio & Roasted Beets, 481
Sheet-Pan Roasted Squash & Feta Salad, 490

radishes
Chicken Stew with Potatoes & Radishes, 242
Cold Roast Salmon with Smashed Green Bean Salad, 268–269
Crunchy Salty Lemony Salad, 443
Ensalada de Pulpo, 684
Shaved Carrot & Radish Salad with Herbs & Toasted Pumpkin Seeds, 483
Shaved Radish Salad with Walnuts & Mint, 482

Rainbow Cookies, 645

raisins
Autumn Kale Salad, 423
Golden Brown Cookies with Apple Filling, 603
Italian Sweet & Sour Fish, 166

Roasted Apricot Chicken with Mint & Sage Butternut Squash, 358

Ras el Hanout
Chermoula Sauce, 517
Chicken with Mehshi Sfeeha, 248
Cojada Potato Casserole, 267
Couscous with Seven Vegetables, 431
Ful Medames, 70
Leg of Lamb with Garlic & Rosemary, 316

Red Cabbage, Date & Beet Salad, 153

Red Gefilte Fish Veragruzana, 101–102

red mullet
Fried Fish with Agristada Sauce, 292

Red Wine-Braised Oxtail, 356

Red Zhoug, 700

Relish Tray, 537

rice
Chicken with Mehshi Sfeeha, 248
Chicken with Tamarind, 263
Crispy Salmon Rice, 685
Crockpot Carne con Papas, 278
Egyptian Lentils & Rice, 439
Egyptian Short Rib & Okra Stew, 287

Kiftahs, 293
Mahasha, 320
Mahshi Laban, 317
Moroccan Fish & Crispy Rice Cake with Saffron Crust, 327–328
Mujadara, 463
Onion Mahshi, 332
Oshi Bakhsh, 337
Poblano Matzo Ball Soup, 100
Potato Tahdig, 468
Rice with Barberries, 471
Roasted Beet & Leek Risotto, 103
Ropa Vieja, 364
Sephardic Jeweled Rosh Hashanah Rice, 169
Stuffed Lamb, 398–399
Sumac Chicken & Rice, 401
Tahdig, 503
Zucchini Mahshi, 509

Rich Brown Chicken Stock
Bone Marrow Matzo Ball Soup, 36

ricotta cheese
Bourekas, 203
Chushki Burek, 47
Khachapuri, 306
Pomegranate Glazed Figs & Cheese, 99
Roast Chicken with Harissa & Schmaltz, 359–361

Roasted & Stuffed
     Sardines, 678
Roasted Apricot Chicken
     with Mint & Sage
     Butternut Squash,
     358
Roasted Beet & Leek
     Risotto, 103
Roasted Beets with
     Cilantro-Basil Pesto,
     104
Roasted Brussels Sprouts,
     476
Roasted Brussels Sprouts
     with Warm Honey
     Glaze, 135, 475
Roasted Cauliflower,
     213
Roasted Corn & Black
     Bean Salad, 107
Roasted Corn Sauce, 533
Roasted Garlic Potato
     Knish, 136
Roasted Pepper Salad, 480
Roasted Plums with
     Tahini Dressing, 477
Roasted Shabbat
     Chicken with Spring
     Vegetables, 212
Romanian Eggplant Salad,
     108
Romano Beans with
     Mustard Vinaigrette
     & Walnuts, 179
Ropa Vieja, 364
rose water
     Knafeh Cheesecake, 617
     Malabi, 620

Purim Roses, 640
Sachlav, 665
Salep, 669
Sephardic-Inspired
     Sangria–Two Ways,
     668
rosemary
     Leg of Lamb with Garlic
          & Rosemary, 316
     Rosemary Rack of Lamb
          with Roasted Potatoes
          & Carrots, 368
     Slow-Cooked Cherry
          Tomatoes with
          Coriander &
          Rosemary, 491
Rosh Hashanah
     about, 19
     menus for, 158–171
Rugelach, 641
rum
     Strawberry Rosé Sangria,
          668
     White Peach Sangria
          with Orange Blossom
          Water, 668
Rustic Matzo Ball Soup,
     185
rutabaga
     Beef, Beet & Cabbage
          Borscht, 34
     Chef's Special Matzo
          Ball Soup, 41
Rye Bread, 572
rye whisky
     New Year's Honey Cake,
          625

Sabich, 365
Sachet d'Épices, 745
Sachlav, 665
Saffron Tomato Coulis,
     538
Saffron Tomato Fennel
     Broth, 539
Saffron Water
     Moroccan Fish &
          Crispy Rice Cake
          with Saffron Crust,
          327–328
     recipe, 328
sage
     Delicata Squash Pasta
          with Brown Butter &
          Sage, 281
     Roasted Apricot
          Chicken with Mint
          & Sage Butternut
          Squash, 358
salads
     Arugula Salad with
          Pickled Beets &
          Preserved-Lemon
          Vinaigrette, 165
     Broccolini Salad, 37
     Celery Slaw with Seeds
          & Dates, 428
     Chicken Salad, 42
     Citrus Salad, 49
     Cold Roast Salmon with
          Smashed Green Bean
          Salad, 268–269
     Coleslaw, 434
     Concia, 50
     Crunchy Pomegranate
          Salad, 51

Crunchy Salty Lemony
Salad, 443
Cucumber, Mint &
Sumac Salad, 58
Ensalada de Pulpo, 684
Grain Salad with Olives
& Whole-Lemon
Vinaigrette, 444
Heart-Beet Salad, 71
Honey-Roasted
Vegetable Salad, 451
Israeli Salad, 73
Kemia de Remolachas,
85
Kemia de Zanahorias,
85
Macaroni Salad, 461
Mezze'd Up Salad, 95
Olive Salad, 183
Orange & Pomegranate
Salad with Honey, 96
Oven-Poached Salmon,
336
Pickled Cucumber
Salad, 154
Potato Salad, 470
Red Cabbage, Date &
Beet Salad, 153
Roasted Pepper Salad,
480
Romanian Eggplant
Salad, 108
Romano Beans with
Mustard Vinaigrette
& Walnuts, 179
Salata Mechouia, 109
Shaved Carrot & Radish
Salad with Herbs &

Toasted Pumpkin
Seeds, 483
Shaved Fennel Salad,
486
Shaved Snap Pea Salad,
691
Sheet-Pan Roasted
Squash & Feta Salad,
490
Strawberry Fields Salad,
113
Tahini Chicken Salad,
114–115
Tomato Salad, 116
Turkish Eggplant Salad,
690
Salata Mechouia, 109
Salep, 669
salmon
Cedar-Plank Salmon,
246
Crispy Salmon Rice,
685
Grandpa's Gravlox, 146
Grandson's Beet &
Vodka Gravlox, 149
Spinach Pesto Stuffed
Salmon, 393
Salsa Verde
recipe, 540
Taco de Gribenes,
402
Salted Honey Apple
Upside-Down Cake,
219
sangria
Strawberry Rosé Sangria,
668

White Peach Sangria
with Orange Blossom
Water, 668
Sardines, Roasted &
Stuffed, 678
scallions
Crispy Salmon Rice,
685
Eyerlekh mit Tzvible,
289
Israeli Salad, 73
Kuku Sabzi, 312
Latkes with Short Ribs,
313
Pirozhki, 344–345
Potato Salad, 470
Red Cabbage, Date &
Beet Salad, 153
Roasted Brussels Sprouts
with Warm Honey
Glaze, 135, 475
Roasted Garlic Potato
Knish, 136
Skillet Roast Chicken
with Fennel, Parsnips
& Scallions, 383
Tahini Chicken Salad,
114–115
Tomato Salad, 116
Schmaltz
Chef's Special Matzo
Ball Soup, 41
Chopped Liver, 46
Kartoffel Kugel, 139
Kasha Varnishkes, 456
Kishka, 79
Kreplach, 88–89
Liverwurst, 94

Mama Kramer's Brisket,
305
Poblano Matzo Ball
Soup, 100
Potato & Schmaltz
Kugel, 453
Potato Kugel, 469
Roast Chicken with
Harissa & Schmaltz,
359–361
Roasted Garlic Potato
Knish, 136
Rustic Matzo Ball Soup,
185
Sheika, 382
Stuffed Matzo Ball
Soup with Chicken &
Apples, 498
Sea Bass, Chermoula, 254
seafood. *See* fish; octopus
Seared Radicchio &
Roasted Beets, 481
Seitan Brisket, 371
Sephardic Jeweled Rosh
Hashanah Rice, 169
Sephardic-Inspired
Sangria–Two Ways,
668
Sephardim, 13–14
Serrano Salsa Verde
Cold Roast Salmon with
Smashed Green Bean
Salad, 268–269
sesame seeds
Dukkah, 115, 524
Za'atar, 545
Sfenj Donuts, 646
Sfratti, 648

Shabbat
about, 17
menus for, 206–219
Shakshuka, 376
Shakshuka with Spinach
& Lamb Meatballs,
372
shallots
Black-Eyed Peas
with Turmeric &
Pomegranate, 427
Celery Slaw with Seeds
& Dates, 428
Dukkah, 115
Grain Salad with Olives
& Whole-Lemon
Vinaigrette, 444
Lamb Stew, 299
Leeks Braised in White
Wine, 457
Rack-Roasted Chicken,
355
Red Gefilte Fish
Veragruzana, 101–102
Slow-Roasted Chicken
with Honey-Glazed
Carrots & Ginger,
388
Tunisian Spiced
Butternut Squash
Soup, 119
White Wine Braised
Leeks, 216
Shashlik, 380
Shaved Carrot & Radish
Salad with Herbs &
Toasted Pumpkin
Seeds, 483

Shaved Fennel Salad, 486
Shaved Radish Salad with
Walnuts & Mint, 482
Shaved Snap Pea Salad,
691
Shawarma-Spiced Braised
Leg of Lamb, 377
Sheet Pan Tzimmes-
Roasted Chicken
Thighs, 381
Sheet-Pan Roasted Squash
& Feta Salad, 490
Sheika, 382
short ribs
Egyptian Short Rib &
Okra Stew, 287
Latkes with Short Ribs,
313
Slow-Cooked Short Ribs
with Gremolata, 386
silan
Halvah Mille-Feuilles,
608
Skewers of Chicken &
Lamb Fat, 385
Skillet Roast Chicken
with Fennel, Parsnips
& Scallions, 383
Slow-Cooked Cherry
Tomatoes with
Coriander &
Rosemary, 491
Slow-Cooked Short Ribs
with Gremolata, 386
Slow-Roasted Chicken
with All the Garlic,
387
Slow-Roasted Chicken

with Honey-Glazed
Carrots & Ginger,
388

Slow-Roasted Lamb
Shoulder with
Brussels Sprouts &
Crispy Kale, 389

Smoked Egg Aioli
Tuna Kibbeh Nayeh,
707

soups and stews
Beef, Beet & Cabbage
Borscht, 34
Bone Marrow Matzo
Ball Soup, 36
Boulettes with Chicken
& Vegetable Soup &
Couscous, 234–235
Chef's Special Matzo
Ball Soup, 41
Chicken & Tomato
Stew with
Caramelized Lemon,
258
Chicken Stew with
Potatoes & Radishes,
242
Chicken Stock, 722
Egyptian Short Rib &
Okra Stew, 287
Fesenjan, 132
Israeli Spicy Chickpea
Soup with Crème
Fraîche, 74
Kreplach, 88–89
Lamb Stew, 299
Mushroom Barley Soup,
91

Poblano Matzo Ball
Soup, 100
Rustic Matzo Ball Soup,
185
Split Pea Soup, 110
Stuffed Matzo Ball
Soup with Chicken &
Apples, 498
Tunisian Spiced
Butternut Squash
Soup, 119
Vegetable Soup, 120
Vegetarian Yemenite
Soup Recipe, 121
Yeasted Apple Coffee
Cake, 657

sour cream
Noodle Kugel, 464
Salted Honey Apple
Upside-Down Cake,
219
Spaetzle, 495
Spaghetti al Tonno, 392
Spayty, 396

spelt
Grain Salad with Olives
& Whole-Lemon
Vinaigrette, 444
Spiced Honey Cake
with Cream Cheese
Frosting, 649

spinach
Honey-Roasted
Vegetable Salad, 451
Keftes de Espinaca, 200
Mina de Espinaca, 324
Msoki de Pesaj, 331
Shakshuka with Spinach

& Lamb Meatballs,
372
Spinach Pesto Stuffed
Salmon, 393
Spinach Rissoles with
Lemon Sauce, 397

Split Pea Soup, 110
Split Peas with Berbere,
494

squash, winter
Autumn Kale Salad, 423
Boulettes with Chicken
& Vegetable Soup &
Couscous, 234–235
Couscous with Seven
Vegetables, 431
Delicata Squash Pasta
with Brown Butter &
Sage, 281
Roasted Apricot
Chicken with Mint
& Sage Butternut
Squash, 358
Sheet-Pan Roasted
Squash & Feta Salad,
490
Tunisian Spiced
Butternut Squash
Soup, 119
Vegetable Tanzia, 409
Vegetarian Yemenite
Soup Recipe, 121
Wine-Braised Brisket
with Butternut
Squash, 413

stocks
about, 720
Beef Stock, 721

Dashi Stock, 725

Fish Stock, 726

Lamb Stock, 721

Mushroom Stock, 730

Veal Stock, 721

Vegetable Stock, 729

strawberries

Blintzes with Berry
Compote, 33

Mezze'd Up Salad, 95

Strawberry Fields Salad,
113

Strawberry Rosé Sangria,
668

Strudel with Tropical
Fruits, Chipotle
Chocolate &
Whipped Cream, 652

Stuffed Lamb, 398–399

Stuffed Matzo Ball Soup
with Chicken &
Apples, 498

Stuffed Saddle of Lamb,
400

Sufganiyot, 204

sumac

Cucumber, Mint &
Sumac Salad, 58

Cucumber Tomato
Mango Relish, 57

Sumac, Spelt & Apple
Cake, 653

Sumac & Apple-Roasted
Cauliflower, 696

Sumac & Lime Mahi-
Mahi with Pickled
Apple Couscous,
714

Sumac Chicken & Rice,
401

sunflower seeds

Caramelized-Honey Nut
& Seed Tart, 592

sweet potatoes

Charred Chicken with
Sweet Potatoes &
Oranges, 249

Charred Sweet Potatoes
with Toum, 430

Sheet Pan Tzimmes-
Roasted Chicken
Thighs, 381

Sweet Potato & Tahini
Dip with Za'atar, 499

Vegetable Tanzia, 409

Swiss Chard & Herb
Fritters, 502

Taco de Gribenes, 402

Tahdig, 503

tahini

Baba Ghanoush, 161

Black & White Halvah,
590–591

Chicken with Turmeric,
Tahini, Chickpeas &
Onions, 266

Falafel, 59

Halvah, 605

Halvah Five Ways,
606–607

Halvah Mille-Feuilles,
608

Honey-Roasted Carrots
with Tahini Yogurt,
450

Modern Hummus, 160

Roasted Plums with
Tahini Dressing, 477

Shakshuka with Spinach
& Lamb Meatballs,
372

Sumac & Apple-Roasted
Cauliflower, 696

Sweet Potato & Tahini
Dip with Za'atar, 499

Tahini Chicken Salad,
114–115

Tahini Mayonnaise,
114–115

Tahini-Yogurt Sauce,
450

tamarind concentrate

Chicken with Tamarind,
263

Stuffed Lamb, 398–399

Turkish Eggplant
Dolma, 407

tangerines

Citrus Salad, 49

tarragon

Chermoula Sauce, 517

Ginger Carrot
Vinaigrette, 523

Roasted Corn Sauce, 533

Shaved Carrot & Radish
Salad with Herbs &
Toasted Pumpkin
Seeds, 483

tehina

Red Cabbage, Date &
Beet Salad, 153

Three-Chilie Harissa
recipe, 359–361

Roast Chicken with
Harissa & Schmaltz,
359–361
Thyme & Pomegranate,
Leeks with, 458
tilapia
Moroccan Fish &
Crispy Rice Cake
with Saffron Crust,
327–328
tomatillos
Tomato Jam, 542
tomatoes
Beef, Beet & Cabbage
Borscht, 34
Chicken & Tomato
Stew with
Caramelized Lemon,
258
Chicken Stew with
Potatoes & Radishes,
242
Classic Canned Tomato
Sauce, 733
Couscous with Seven
Vegetables, 431
Crockpot Carne con
Papas, 278
Cucumber Tomato
Mango Relish, 57
Egyptian Lentils & Rice,
439
Egyptian Short Rib &
Okra Stew, 287
Ful Medames, 70
Handrajo, 301
Israeli Salad, 73
Israeli Spicy Chickpea

Soup with Crème
Fraîche, 74
Khoresh Sib, 309
Kiftahs, 293
Lamb Stew, 299
Mahasha, 320
Moroccan Cornish
Hens with Pine Nut
Couscous, 329
Pickled Green Tomatoes,
157
Red Gefilte Fish
Veragruzana, 101–102
Roasted Apricot
Chicken with Mint
& Sage Butternut
Squash, 358
Romanian Eggplant
Salad, 108
Saffron Tomato Coulis,
538
Saffron Tomato Fennel
Broth, 539
Salata Mechouia, 109
Shakshuka, 376
Shakshuka with Spinach
& Lamb Meatballs,
372
Shawarma-Spiced Braised
Leg of Lamb, 377
Slow-Cooked Cherry
Tomatoes with
Coriander &
Rosemary, 491
Spaghetti al Tonno, 392
Stuffed Lamb, 398–399
tomato concasse
technique, 744

Tomato Jam, 542
Tomato Salad, 116
Tomatoes Reinados,
403
Turkish Eggplant Salad,
690
Wine-Braised Brisket
with Butternut
Squash, 413
Tortillas
recipe, 737
Taco de Gribenes, 402
Toum
Charred Sweet Potatoes
with Toum, 430
Turmeric Chicken with
Toum, 408
Tsyplyonok Tabaka,
404–405
tuna
Spaghetti al Tonno, 392
Tuna Kibbeh Nayeh,
707
Tunisian Spiced Butternut
Squash Soup, 119
Turkish Coffee-Rubbed
Brisket, 406
Turkish Eggplant Dolma,
407
Turkish Eggplant Salad,
690
turmeric
Black-Eyed Peas
with Turmeric &
Pomegranate, 427
Turmeric Chicken with
Toum, 408
turnips

Boulettes with Chicken & Vegetable Soup & Couscous, 234–235

Chef's Special Matzo Ball Soup, 41

Couscous with Seven Vegetables, 431

Msoki de Pesaj, 331

Roasted Shabbat Chicken with Spring Vegetables, 212

Vegetable Tanzia, 409

Tzimmes Chicken with Apricots, Prunes & Carrots, 186

Vanilla Cake Rusks, 654

Vanilla Nutmeg Babka, 655–656

veal

Albondigas with Pine Nuts & Currants, 30

Veal Stock, 721

Vegetable Soup, 120

Vegetable Stock

Couscous with Seven Vegetables, 431

Israeli Spicy Chickpea Soup with Crème Fraîche, 74

Modern Hummus, 160

Polenta Medallions, 348

Pomegranate & Honey Glazed Chicken, 348

recipe, 729

Roasted Beet & Leek Risotto, 103

Split Pea Soup, 110

Vegetable Soup, 120

Vegetarian Yemenite Soup Recipe, 121

Wine-Braised Brisket with Butternut Squash, 413

Vegetable Tanzia, 409

Vegetarian Yemenite Soup Recipe, 121

Veracruzana Sauce recipe, 101–102

Red Gefilte Fish Veragruzana, 101–102

Verde Sauce

Ensalada de Pulpo, 684

Vodka Gravlox, Grandson's Beet &, 149

walnuts

Apple Cake, 584

Apple Walnut Bundt Cake, 585–586

Brisket with Pomegranate-Walnut Sauce & Pistachio Gremolata, 238

Charoset, 176, 514

Chicken Salad, 42

Fesenjan, 132

Golden Brown Cookies with Apple Filling, 603

Hungarian Golden Pull-Apart Cake with Walnuts & Apricot Jam, 616

Mandel Bread, 621

Romano Beans with Mustard Vinaigrette & Walnuts, 179

Sfratti, 648

Shaved Fennel Salad, 486

Shaved Radish Salad with Walnuts & Mint, 482

Shaved Snap Pea Salad, 691

Vegetable Tanzia, 409

Walnut-Garlic Sauce, 543

whisky

New Year's Honey Cake, 625

White Peach Sangria with Orange Blossom Water, 668

White Shakshuka, 412

White Wine Braised Leeks, 216

Whole Branzino, 715

wine, red

Balsamic Apple Date Challah, 550–551

Beef, Beet & Cabbage Borscht, 34

Chicken Schnitzel & Cherry Sauce, 262

Crockpot Sweet & Sour Brisket, 271

Lamb Stew, 299

Leg of Lamb with Garlic & Rosemary, 316

Maror, 529

Moroccan Lamb Shanks with Pomegranate

Sauce, 330
Pomegranate Brisket
    with Cranberry
    Succotash, 353
Pot Roast, 199
Red Gefilte Fish
    Veragruzana, 101–102
Red Wine-Braised
    Oxtail, 356
Seitan Brisket, 371
Shashlik, 380
wine, rosé
    Strawberry Rosé Sangria,
    668
wine, white
    Gefilte Fish, 180
    Leeks Braised in White
        Wine, 457
    Maror, 529
    Mushroom Stock, 730
    Red Gefilte Fish
        Veragruzana, 101–102
    Roasted Beet & Leek
        Risotto, 103
    Ropa Vieja, 364
    Saffron Tomato Coulis,
        538
    Saffron Tomato Fennel
        Broth, 539
    Sfratti, 648
    Tzimmes Chicken with
        Apricots, Prunes &
        Carrots, 186
    White Peach Sangria
        with Orange Blossom
        Water, 668
    White Wine Braised
        Leeks, 216

Wine-Braised Brisket
    with Butternut
    Squash, 413

Yeasted Apple Coffee
    Cake, 657
yogurt
    Honey-Roasted Carrots
        with Tahini Yogurt,
        450
    Honey-Roasted
        Vegetable Salad, 451
    Horseradish-Yogurt
        Sauce, 354, 438
    Israeli Yogurt Sauce, 529
    Labneh, 530
    Lemony Yogurt Sauce,
        269
    Naan, 741
    Tahini-Yogurt Sauce,
        450
    Turmeric Chicken with
        Toum, 408
    Za'atar Chicken with
        Garlicky Yogurt, 414
Yogurt Sauce
    Falafel, 59
    recipe, 59
Yom Kippur
    about, 20
    menus for, 126–157

Za'atar
    Chermoula Sauce, 517
    Crushed Avocado, 54
    Cucumber Tomato
        Mango Relish, 57
    Falafel, 59

Fava Beans with
    Pomegranates, 62
Green Beans with
    Za'atar & Lemon, 445
Halvah Five Ways,
    606–607
Israeli Yogurt Sauce, 529
Labneh, 530
Modern Hummus, 160
Pomegranate
    Vinaigrette, 532
recipe, 545
Roasted Cauliflower,
    213
Sweet Potato & Tahini
    Dip with Za'atar, 499
Za'atar Chicken with
    Garlicky Yogurt, 414
Za'atar Okra & Lemons,
    506
zucchini
    Almodrote, 225
    Boulettes with Chicken
        & Vegetable Soup &
        Couscous, 234–235
    Concia, 50
    Couscous with Seven
        Vegetables, 431
    Mahshi Laban, 317
    Msoki de Pesaj, 331
    Roasted Shabbat
        Chicken with Spring
        Vegetables, 212
    Zucchini Mahshi, 509

ABOUT CIDER MILL PRESS BOOK PUBLISHERS

Good ideas ripen with time. From seed to harvest, Cider Mill Press brings fine reading, information, and entertainment together between the covers of its creatively crafted books. Our Cider Mill bears fruit twice a year, publishing a new crop of titles each spring and fall.

"Where Good Books Are Ready for Press"

Visit us online at

cidermillpress.com

or write to us at

PO Box 454
12 Spring St.
Kennebunkport, Maine 04046

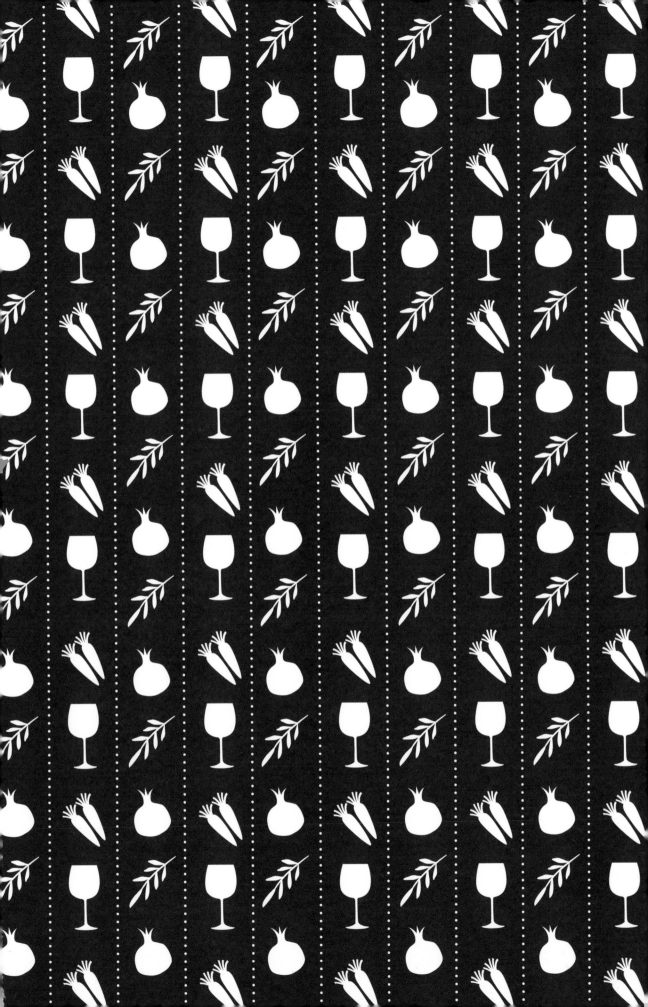